THE REMINISCENCES OF
Admiral Noel A. M. Gayler
U.S. Navy (Retired)

INTERVIEWED BY
Paul Stillwell

U.S. Naval Institute • Annapolis, Maryland

Copyright © 2012

Preface

In the early days of World War II, Lieutenant Noel Gayler was among the first Navy fighter pilots to get into action against the Japanese; he was also one of the early aces with five aerial victories and received three Navy Crosses. As it happened, though, his combat career was relatively short because the carrier from which he was flying, the *Lexington* (CV-3), was sunk during the Battle of the Coral Sea in May 1942. For much of the rest of the war he was a test pilot who flew many of the newest American aircraft, as well as captured enemy planes. That tour of duty presaged a number of others during his career in which he was involved in the development and testing of new aircraft, particularly fighters. He headed the fighter design branch in the Bureau of Aeronautics, commanded Air Development Squadron Three (VX-3), and helped develop the requirements for the F-4 Phantom II, which became the Navy's principal fighter during the Vietnam War.

During his overall career, which included more than 40 years of commissioned service, he preferred command billets over staff positions. During our interviews, he had particular zest in describing his commands: Fighter Squadron 12 (VF-12); the air development squadron, VX-3; the former tender *Greenwich Bay* (AVP-41), which served as Middle East Force flagship; the USS *Ranger* (CVA-61), when she was one of the Navy's early big-deck super carriers; Carrier Division 20; the National Security Agency; and the entire joint-service U.S. Pacific Command when the Vietnam War ended. He also had a notable tour as aide to Secretary of the Navy Thomas S. Gates; while in that billet he worked with future Chief of Naval Operations Elmo R. Zumwalt in developing equitable promotion policies for naval officers commissioned during World War II.

Among the most striking portions of the oral history is Admiral Gayler's discussion of nuclear weapons. As a professional military man, part of his service was involved in developing tactics for the delivery of nuclear bombs; in a later tour, as a flag officer, he was part of the organization that managed the U.S. targeting strategy for missiles and bombs. As a senior admiral, he might have been in the chain of command that ordered their use if the President authorized. Despite those experiences—or perhaps because of them—Admiral Gayler came to abhor the use of such destructive devices.

When I interviewed him, he worked at the American Committee on East-West Accord. He wrote papers and gave congressional testimony against the use of such weapons, even though his views were counter to those of many other retired flag officers.

I remember Admiral Gayler as a friendly, vigorous person, seemingly younger than his chronological age, an individual with a commanding presence and a quick mind. In reviewing the transcript, it was interesting to see how many times he challenged premises that I put forth in my questions. He put on the record his observations on many individuals, starting with his father, a naval officer whom he admired greatly. He was candid in his assessments of the national strategy concerning the Vietnam War.

Some years after the interviews, I had one meeting with Admiral Gayler. During the interval, he had been divorced and remarried. One thing I recall from that later visit was his remark that memory loss had by then become a problem for him. I am thus grateful that I was able to interview him when I did.

For a variety of reasons, the release of this memoir has taken much longer than expected. Admiral Gayler had expressed the hope of doing an additional interview to supplement those in this volume. Unfortunately, that never came to pass. I have included inputs the admiral made in responding to the original transcript, and I have done some slight editing and added footnotes to provide background information. In the wake of Admiral Gayler's death in 2011, his first wife Caroline and widow Jeanne provided information that is included in the biographical summary at the beginning of the volume. Ms. Janis Jorgensen of the Naval Institute staff has coordinated the printing and binding of the finished product.

In completing this volume, the Naval Institute expresses its gratitude to the Tawani Foundation and the Pritzker Military Library of Chicago for their generous financial support of the oral history program that produced this memoir.

Paul Stillwell
U.S. Naval Institute
February 2012

ADMIRAL NOEL ARTHUR MEREDYTH GAYLER
UNITED STATES NAVY (RETIRED)

Noel Gayler, son of Navy Captain Ernest R. Gayler and Anne Yates (Roberts) Gayler of Seattle, Washington, was born on 25 December 1914. As the son of a career naval officer, Gayler spent much of his childhood at naval stations in the United States and abroad. He did settle in Bremerton, Washington, long enough to complete most of his secondary education. He attended Bremerton High School from 1927 until 1930, when his father was transferred to Hawaii. He briefly attended McKinley High School in Honolulu in the autumn of 1930 before entering the West Point Prep School at Schofield Barracks, where he received his high school diploma.

Gayler sought and won an appointment to the Naval Academy, Annapolis, Maryland, entering in 1931 and graduating in 1935 at the age of 20. His first assignment as a new ensign in June 1935 was on board the battleship *Maryland* (BB-46), as a gunnery and engineering officer. Promoted to lieutenant (junior grade) in June 1938, he was reassigned to the destroyer *Maury* (DD-401) as the assistant engineer officer. This was followed by an assignment as gunnery officer on board the destroyer *Craven* (DD-382) from June 1939 to March 1940.

While serving on a weekend watch on board the *Craven* in San Diego Harbor, he watched patrol planes practicing touch-and-go landings. He liked what he saw and applied for flight school. He was accepted and began training at the Naval Air Station, Pensacola, Florida, in March 1940. Upon completion of his training in November, he was assigned to patrol plane duty.

With the United States on the brink of World War II, Lieutenant Gayler talked one of his former flight school classmates into swapping orders. As a result, he was assigned to Fighting Squadron Three (VF-3) on board the aircraft carrier *Saratoga* (CV-3). Following the Japanese attack on Pearl Harbor on 7 December 1941, the squadron was transferred to the carrier *Lexington* (CV-2), which soon sailed for the South Pacific. During this period with Fighting Squadron Three his skills as a fighter pilot achieved for him the honor of receiving three Navy Cross Awards.

It began on 20 February 1942, when the *Lexington* first engaged Japanese aircraft, and ended some three months later after the Battle of the Coral Sea. Lieutenant Gayler came out of this conflict as one of the *Lexington*'s aces with five verified Japanese planes shot down and playing a major role in the destruction of three others. When the first wave of nine Japanese twin-engine bombers struck the *Lexington* on 20 February, *Lexington* pilots shot down eight of them. Lieutenant Gayler was credited with shooting down one of them and assisting in the destruction of two others. When the second wave struck that same day, the enemy met with no better success. Again the *Lexington* fighters scored on eight of the nine Japanese bombers. The ace of the second wave was Lieutenant Gayler's teammate, Lieutenant Edward H. "Butch" O'Hare, who accounted for five of the Japanese bombers.

The first gold star in lieu of a second Navy Cross came as a result of his action in New Guinea ports on 10 March 1942. He attacked a concentration of Japanese ships. While flying in a squadron protecting a wave of torpedo planes, he mixed with a Japanese seaplane fighter and shot it down. Not content with that, he loaded his fighter with bombs and attacked two Japanese destroyers, causing heavy damage.

The second gold star, in lieu of the third Navy Cross, was awarded for his action in the Battle of the Coral Sea on 7 and 8 May 1942. He piloted one of four fighters escorting torpedo planes in a strike against a Japanese aircraft carrier, which was left a burning wreck. While on station, the four fighters encountered a fleet of Japanese Zero fighters. Three of the American fighters failed to return, although each apparently shot down a Zero. Lieutenant Gayler shot down two of the Japanese planes, damaged to others, and returned safely to the *Lexington*.

With the loss of the *Lexington* during the Battle of the Coral Sea, Lieutenant Gayler was reassigned in June 1942 to the Washington, D.C., area as a fighter test pilot at the naval air stations at Anacostia and Patuxent River. In June 1944, by now a commander, Gayler became commanding officer of Fighter Squadron 12 (VF-12) and subsequently was on the staff of Vice Admiral John S. McCain, Commander Second Carrier Task Force, from May to September of 1945. From the decks of the aircraft carriers *Enterprise* (CV-6), *Saratoga*, and *Randolph* (CV-15), he saw action during the knockout strikes against Japan that brought about the end of World War II. For service in this capacity he was awarded the Bronze Star with combat "V."

From October 1945 to January 1946 he served temporary duty on the staff of Carrier Group 61 with the Atlantic Fleet. In January 1946 he was assigned as deputy director, Special Devices Center, Office of Research and Inventions, at Sand Point, Fort Washington, New York. For development work in this area, he received the Sperry Award from the Institute of Aeronautical Sciences in 1948. From April 1948 to September 1949 he served as operations officer of the aircraft carrier *Bairoko* (CVE-115). From there, in October 1949, he was ordered to the Bureau of Aeronautics as head of the fighter design branch.

In June 1951, Commander Gayler was appointed commanding officer of Air Development Squadron Three (VX-3), based in Atlantic City, New Jersey. During this assignment he was selected for captain in November 1953 and was assigned to the Office of the Chief of Naval Operations in January 1954. As part of his work in the Air Warfare Division's Military Requirements Branch, he was involved in drawing up the requirements specifications that led to the development of the F-4 Phantom jet fighter.

In January 1956, Captain Gayler was given his first ship command, the USS *Greenwich Bay* (AVP-41). He served as skipper of this Middle East Force flagship until February 1957, when he was assigned as operations officer for Commander in Chief Pacific Fleet. This assignment was short-lived, however, when he was selected by the Secretary of the Navy, Thomas S. Gates Jr., to be his aide. He served in this capacity from June 1957 until April 1959.

The attack aircraft carrier *Ranger* (CVA-61) became Captain Gayler's second ship command. While serving as her commanding officer from May 1959 to June 1960, he was selected for flag rank. In August 1960, Rear Admiral Gayler was appointed U.S. naval attaché to the American ambassador in London, where he served until August 1962. From August 1962 to August 1963, Rear Admiral Gayler was assigned as Commander Carrier Division 20 in the U.S. Atlantic Fleet. In August 1963, he reported for duty in the Office of the Chief of Naval Operations as Director, Development Programs. In March 1965, he became Assistant Deputy Chief of Naval Operations (Development). He was awarded the Legion of Merit for exceptionally meritorious service during this period.

In September 1967, he was selected for the rank of vice admiral and assumed duty as Deputy Director of the Joint Strategic Target Planning Staff at Offutt Air Force Base, Nebraska. included in his duties were the decision of which components of the U.S. strategic deterrent force (Polaris/Poseidon submarines, Minutemen missiles, Strategic Air Command bombers, and Navy aircraft carriers) were assigned to which potential targets on any given day. For outstanding service in this command, he was awarded a gold star in lieu of a second Legion of Merit medal.

In July 1969, Vice Admiral Gayler assumed duty as Director, National Security Agency, Fort George G. Meade, Maryland, where he served until the end of August 1972. Upon his departure, he was awarded the Distinguished Service Medal by Secretary of the Navy John Warner. On 1 September 1972, he was appointed to the rank of admiral and became the ninth naval officer to serve as Commander in Chief Pacific. He held that billet until 30 August 1976. He retired from active duty on 1 September of that year.

Admiral Gayler died 14 July 2011 in Alexandria, Virginia.

Family and Personal Data:

Wives:	Caroline Groves, married 3 November 1941; divorced 23 September 1986 Jeanne Malette Thompson, married 26 October 1986
Children:	Caroline Gayler Maness – 6 April 1943 Anne Gayler – 26 January 1945 Deborah Gayler Poisot – 24 November 1946 Alexander Gayler – 20 October 1948 Christopher Noel Gayler – 20 January 1951

Dates of Rank:

6 June 1935	Ensign
6 June 1938	Lieutenant (Junior Grade)
1 September 1941	Lieutenant

1 May 1943	Lieutenant Commander
1 March 1944	Commander
1 November 1953	Captain
1 July 1961	Rear Admiral
28 September 1967	Vice Admiral
1 September 1972	Admiral

Chronological Record of Service:

Jun 1935-Jun 1938	USS *Maryland* (BB-46), gunnery and engineering
Jun 1938-Jun 1939	USS *Maury* (DD-401), assistant engineer officer
Jun 1939-Mar 1940	USS *Craven* (DD-382) gunnery officer
Mar 1940-Nov 1940	Naval Air Station, Pensacola, Florida, student
Nov 1940-Jun 1942	Fighting Squadron Two (VF-2) and Fighting Squadron Three (VF-3), flight officer
Jun 1942-May 1944	Naval Air Stations Anacostia and Patuxent River, fighter test pilot and project officer
Jun 1944-Feb 1945	Fighter Squadron 12 (VF-12) commanding officer
Feb 1945-May 1945	Air Force Pacific Fleet, staff
May 1945-Sep 1945	Second Carrier Task Force, staff operations officer
Oct 1945-Jan 1946	Carrier Group 61, Atlantic Fleet, staff
Jan 1946-Apr 1948	Special Devices Center, Office of Research and Inventions, Sands Point, Fort Washington, New York, deputy director
Apr 1948-Sep 1949	USS *Bairoko* (CVE-115), operations officer
Oct 1949-Jun 1951	Fighter Design Branch, Bureau of Aeronautics, Navy Department, Washington, D.C., branch head
Jun 1951-Jan 1954	Air Development Squadron Three (VX-3), Atlantic City, New Jersey, commanding officer
Jan 1954-Jan 1956	Air Warfare Division, Military Requirements Branch, Office of the Chief of Naval Operations, Washington, D.C.

Jan 1956-Feb 1957	USS *Greenwich Bay* (AVP-41), commanding officer
Feb 1957-Jun 1957	Pacific Fleet staff, operations officer
Jul 1957-Apr 1959	Naval aide to the Secretary of the Navy, Thomas S. Gates Jr.
May 1959-Jun 1960	USS *Ranger* (CVA-61), commanding officer
Aug 1960-Aug 1962	U.S. Naval Attaché, London, England
Aug 1962-Aug 1963	Commander Carrier Division 20
Aug 1963-Aug 1967	Director, Development Programs, OpNav, Washington, D.C. Assistant Deputy Chief of Naval Operations (Development)
Sep 1967-Jul 1969	Deputy Director, Joint Strategic Target Planning Staff, Offutt Air Force Base, Nebraska
Jul 1969-Aug 1972	Director, National Security Agency
Sep 1972-Aug 1976	Commander in Chief Pacific
1 September 1976	Retired from active duty

Authorization

The U.S. Naval Institute is hereby authorized to make available to individuals, libraries, and other repositories of its choosing the transcripts of nine oral history interviews concerning the life and career of the undersigned. The interviews were recorded on 25 October 1983, 4 November 1983, 1 December 1983, 30 January 1984, 7 February 1984, 10 April 1984, 20 April 1984, 7 May 1984, and 6 July 1984 in collaboration with Paul Stillwell for the U.S. Naval Institute.

The undersigned does hereby release and assign to the U.S. Naval Institute all right, title, restrictions, and interest in the interviews. The copyright in both the oral and transcribed versions shall be the sole property of the U.S. Naval Institute. The tape recordings of the interviews are and will remain the property of the U.S. Naval Institute.

Signed and sealed this ___4___ day of ___July___ 1994.

Admiral Noel A. M. Gayler, USN (Ret.)

Interview Number 1 with Admiral Noel A. M. Gayler, U.S. Navy (Retired)

Place: Admiral Gayler's office at the American Committee on East-West Accord, Washington, D.C.

Date: Tuesday, 25 October 1983

Paul Stillwell: Admiral, the typical format in these oral histories is to cover the entire life, going back to the beginning. I note with some interest the coincidence of your first name and your date of birth on Christmas of 1914. Where did your other names come from?

Admiral Gayler: I was named after Arthur Meredyth Roberts, who was my uncle. He was a very early aviator and was killed in Issoudun, France, in World War I while preparing to go into combat.

Paul Stillwell: Was he also a naval aviator?

Admiral Gayler: No, he was Army.*

Paul Stillwell: Since you were a Navy junior, I'm sure your boyhood was spent wandering all over from duty station to duty station. How did you come to be born in Alabama?

Admiral Gayler: My mother was there at the time.

Paul Stillwell: Did she have relatives there?

---

* In 1914 the Aviation Section of the Signal Corps took control of Army aviation. The Army's First Aero Squadron arrived in France in 1917 to take part in World War I.

Admiral Gayler: Yes. [Laughter] Mother comes from an old family in Charleston, South Carolina. In fact, her lineal ancestors were the first and second colonial governors of South Carolina. Naturally, it was a Confederate family, and on her side of the family we have deep roots with the Old South. She married a young naval officer by the name of Ernest Gayler, who came from a family of German immigrants in St. Louis. Two branches of the family had come over one jump ahead of the cops, one during of the European revolutions of the 1860s and one ahead of Bismarck's cops.[*]

Anyway, this daughter of a very old Southern family, a very gifted girl musically and in many other ways, met and married a young second-generation German naval officer in Charleston. In the meantime, my mother's father had gone to Birmingham, Alabama, to make his fortune, and he did indeed. He was one of the two pioneers in coal and iron production in northern Alabama. So it was then her family's home, and that's how she was there when I was born.

Paul Stillwell: Was your father remarkable in an intellectual sense also? Did he have gifts, as your mother did?

Admiral Gayler: Yes, he did. He was extraordinarily interested in anything that you could think of, but particularly in the sciences. I remember his talking to me about nuclear energy when I was a very little boy, and the splitting of the atom had yet, of course, to be demonstrated. But even then he was prescient about it. I remember his showing me a glass of water and saying, "In that, locked up, is enough energy to drive an ocean liner across the ocean." I don't quite know where he got his catholic interest in everything, but he certainly had it.

He spent his lifetime career as a civil engineer officer in the Navy.[†] When he was a young man, a college graduate from Washington University in St. Louis, he got a civilian job with the Navy around the turn of the century. The Navy then sent him out as the engineer to build a coaling station in newly acquired American Samoa. He built that

---

[*] Prince Otto Eduard Leopold von Bismarck-Schoenhausen was first Chancellor of the German Empire, 1877-90.
[†] Captain Ernest R. Gayler, CEC, USN, eventually retired from active duty as a captain on 1 December 1938 and settled in St. Louis, Missouri.

station and lived by himself in Samoa for almost five years. I think then there were five or six other white people in the whole island group. He spoke Samoan to the day of his death—if he could find anybody to talk Samoan to him.

Paul Stillwell: Typically, the Navy did send its smartest officers in that time into engineering, either civil engineering or naval architecture, so it fits the pattern.

Admiral Gayler: I think that's right.

My father was sent to the Republic of Haiti during our occupation, which began during World War I.* When Dad went to there, he was a lieutenant. The times were so different, he was personally brought in and briefed by the Secretary of State, Mr. Lansing, and his orders were signed by Woodrow Wilson.† He told the story that when the Secretary of State finished briefing him, he said, "Lieutenant, if you do well, you'll be okay. If you do anything wrong, we'll snatch you out of there before you know what hit you." That was his parting admonition.

My earliest recollections are of living in Haiti. I went there, I think, when I was a little over two years old and left when I was almost five, but I can still remember some of the scenes.

Paul Stillwell: Could you describe them?

Admiral Gayler: It was an incredibly primitive country. When we occupied Haiti, we gave it the only decent government it had for 100 years. In my judgment, it was the only decent government it has had since. But the Haitians, as you probably know, had thrown out the French 100 years before, when Napoleon's fortunes fell.‡ And they really had not touched their country from that time on.

---

* In 1915 President Woodrow Wilson sent U.S. Marines to restore order in Haiti. Occupation forces remained until 15 August 1934, when the last elements of the First Marine Brigade withdrew and Haiti regained control of its own affairs.
† Robert Lansing was Secretary of State, 1915-20; Woodrow Wilson was President, 1913-21.
‡ Napoleon Bonaparte, also known as Napoleon I, was a military leader who served as Emperor of France from 1804 to 1815.

I remember a section of the main waterline supplying Port-au-Prince, the biggest city. This waterline was originally perhaps eight inches in diameter. But it had been almost completely closed by deposits, so that a tiny little hole was all that was left for water to trickle through. The deposits were so hard that Dad had a section cut out of it and put on a desk. One side was polished, and it was like so much marble.

The roads had not been touched. They weren't really roads; they were paths. Oh, I could talk to you a lot about Haiti. Dad was extraordinarily bold, and he would go on these long expeditions into the wilds. We have pictures showing our little Model T Ford being hauled out of a gully by 20 Haitians. I remember some of it.

Everybody traveled on horseback. I had a donkey that was led by a Haitian, because I was a very small boy. I remember sleeping in the open on the seat of the old Ford. I saw these incredible roads and trails that beat up the cars. I can remember Father and his assistant taking out the steering rod, which was called the wishbone on the Model T. It had been bent by hitting something, and so they pounded it straight with a couple of rocks in the bright Haitian moonlight. Then, after lashing a suitable limb of a tree to it for reinforcement, they put it back in, and off we went.

Paul Stillwell: Was there a sense of adventure to all this, that you were getting the real thing instead of vicariously?

Admiral Gayler: Oh, I was so small I think that, as little children do, I just accepted everything as being the way life was. Of course, the family has talked about that period so much that I have some difficulty sorting out what are really my recollections and what I've been told. But I do have little vignettes and visions.

I can remember, for instance, the night that some insurgents attacked Port-au-Prince and set the city on fire. The water supply, of course, was needed to deal with the fires, and that was Dad's job. So he went tearing down to the city from our house, which was on a hill. You could hear the machinegun fire and occasional rifle fire and musket fire and everything else. Mother had Dad's .45 for protection, and I remember seeing her surrounded in the bright moonlight by 18 terrified Haitians as we looked down at the town burning below us. I saw that, and that's still in my vision. She is a very gutsy person. She's still alive. She's 101 years old now, and she is writing her memoirs, which you'd find more interesting than mine.[*]

Paul Stillwell: For a family with roots in the Old South, was there any reluctance about going to a country so largely black?

Admiral Gayler: Oh, no, no, Mother was great. In fact, she was never mistrustful.

Paul Stillwell: One of the interviews in our oral history collection is with Rear Admiral Kent Melhorn, who was the U.S. Navy medical officer in Haiti during that period.[†] One of the points he made was that the primitive local medical conditions were rooted in voodooism, witchcraft.

Admiral Gayler: Oh, yes. It was primitive, all right. Mother, for the day, was very much up on sanitary precautions. We never drank water that wasn't boiled, drank a lot of tea for that reason. I remember that when I'd been out playing or anything and had some contact with Haitians, she used to wash me down with rum, which was the only alcohol available. So she took very, very good care of us children. Haiti was a very malarial country in those days. The malaria was a very infectious kind and was endemic. So we always slept behind mosquito nettings. We also took precautions about what we ate. To the best of my recollection, nobody ever was seriously ill, but it was a very dangerous country from that standpoint.

Other local diseases were dengue and yaws. I remember seeing Haitians hideously disfigured from yaws. Oh, people had everything you could think of, including parasitic things. Pretty terrible. Another of the major things the U.S. occupation did was to give the Haitians personal safety, as well as medical care. For the first time rural Haitians were not afraid to walk into the city with their produce on their heads. Before that time, they were kidnapped, killed, raped, you name it. We also gave them roads, we

---

[*] Mrs. Gayler eventually died at age 103, still sharp mentally and dictating her memoirs to Admiral Gayler's brother.
[†] Rear Admiral Kent C. Melhorn, Medical Corps, USN (Ret.).

gave them clean water, we gave them a chance. Then we left, and conditions reverted to what they had been before.

Paul Stillwell: You mentioned your siblings.

Admiral Gayler: Yes, I have an older brother whose name is Ernest. He's always been called Pete since he was a little boy. We lived in the Bremerton Navy Yard at the time he got that name.[*] As little boys will, he had friends among the sailors on the tugs and whatnot. One of them said, "What's your name?"

He said, "It's Ernest."

The sailor said, "That's no name for a boy. You ought to have a name like Pete." So he came home and announced from that time on his name was Pete, and it stuck. What's very amusing is that Mother insists on referring to him as Peter, because she thinks that's a little bit more dignified. My oldest daughter's child, whom she named after my brother, is christened Peter. But his name was never Peter; it was always Pete.

Paul Stillwell: You had only one brother?

Admiral Gayler: I had only one brother and one sister, both older than I. My sister married in the Navy and lived as a Navy wife.[†] She lost her husband some years ago, and she lives now in Birmingham, Alabama.

Paul Stillwell: What's her name?

Admiral Gayler: Her name is Anne Gayler Miller. She has two daughters and two grandchildren. I have five children and, at the present count, six grandchildren.

Paul Stillwell: What has become of your brother?

---

[*] Puget Sound Navy Yard, Bremerton, Washington.
[†] Admiral Gayler's sister married Louis Newcomb Miller, who was in the Naval Academy class of 1923. Miller retired as a captain in 1953 and died in 1975.

Admiral Gayler: He's retired, lives in Seattle with Mother. I just visited them and will be going out at the end of this week to spend more time with them.

Paul Stillwell: You mentioned Bremerton. What memories do you have from there?

Admiral Gayler: Oh, those are much better developed. I grew up essentially in the Bremerton Navy Yard. A Navy yard was a wonderful place for a small boy. In those days, Bremerton was the Navy's principal ship-repair facility in the Pacific. All the battleships, the battle line, came in there on a regular schedule.

Of course, that was a marvelous place to know the people in the shops. I used to go around to the print shop and get old type that I could melt up to make bullets for my slingshot. I remember one birthday my dad gave me a gasoline blowtorch, the old-fashioned kind. I wanted that more than anything in the world. I can still remember that. And Mr. Kidd, I think it was, the master printer, was a friend, and he would give me the pied type that I could melt up for various purposes.

It was a sort of rural living in a way, with gardens and places where kids could roam. We had a fine little gang of kids of our own. We were between 8 and 11 years old, I guess, in our crowd. I remember there was a little animal we called a mountain beaver—I don't know what it was really, now that I think about it—but it was a little gray animal with fur. It was well known that the skin was worth 75 cents, six bits, although nobody I knew had ever participated in any such transaction. We spent all of our savings on traps for mountain beavers. We'd go up on the golf course and set the traps in the hopes of getting a mountain beaver and getting the bonanza of 75 cents, which was a considerable amount of money in those days.

Nothing happened, of course, for a long time. Then one day, my God, we caught one of the hapless creatures. It was the kind of trap that killed them instantly. There we were with this animal in the trap. We didn't know quite what to do with it, but we finally decided we would skin it. We didn't have the foggiest notion how to skin anything, and we had nothing but dull pocketknives anyway. But we essayed it, and after a while it got to be messy and bloody and clearly impractical. So we stopped and thought what in the world we would do with this.

Then somebody got the bright idea that we ought to cook it. I had a feeling that maybe Mother wouldn't approve of cooking it in our kitchen, but our next-door neighbor was a very pleasant childless couple by the name of Cake. Commander Cake was a rather slight man, and Mrs. Cake was, as sometimes happens, a big, imposing-looking woman.* So they were known as "Mrs. Cake and Cookie." [Laughter] Anyway, they were a childless couple, middle-aged, and always very kind to us children.

So we thought, "Well, maybe the Cakes wouldn't mind if we cooked in their kitchen." We rattled at the back door, no answer. The Navy yard security was awfully good in those days, and nobody locked their doors. So we went in the kitchen, and we got out a frying pan and some butter and put the animal in the frying pan with the butter, fur and all. We started to cook him, and after a while the stench was such we decided that wasn't a very good idea. We cleaned up as boys will—I'm sure not very well—and left the kitchen with the stench in it.

As I recall, we took the poor thing out and gave it a Christian service and burial with a cross over its grave somewhere in the garden. I've often wondered what Mrs. Cake thought when she got home and found this terrible stench in her kitchen, because we never confessed. I don't know what ever happened to them.

But Bremerton was a marvelous place to grow up.

Paul Stillwell: To this day you don't know whether there really was a bounty on those animals.

Admiral Gayler: No, no. [Laughter]

Paul Stillwell: Bremerton now is sort of a dingy place. Was it that way then?

Admiral Gayler: No. As I say, it was the very center of fleet activities. Duty there was sort of a prize, if you were a civil engineer, as Dad was, because of the tremendous construction of the dry docks and whatnot going on. All the battleships and all the spit and polish of the prewar Navy were there. And we, of course, entertained the admirals

---

* Commander Stuart W. Cake, USN.

and the battleship captains. It was the cutting edge of the Navy. It was the Pacific Fleet battle line's place there.

Another interesting event during that time was my first ride in an airplane, when I was 11 years old. It was in a Navy seaplane operating out of Lake Washington, in Seattle. The pilot was Lieutenant Arthur Radford, who was a great friend of my father's.[*] Dad was the civil engineer officer building the Sand Point Naval Air Station.[†] Raddy was later the commanding officer.[‡] As they were both doers, they got along fine. Raddy, seeing this little boy with his big eyes looking at the airplanes, offered me a ride, which was completely non-reg, I suppose. I remember standing up in the forward part, the gunner's cockpit of this airplane, with the wind whistling through my ears. It must have been making all of 75 knots in taking a turn around Lake Washington, landing in a great flurry of foam.

Paul Stillwell: He apparently enjoyed being a pilot, even in considerably later years when he was CinCPac. He used to take a plane up every once in a while, and one of our interviewees described such a time.[§] Radford had difficulty communicating to the control tower who the pilot was. Finally, he asked the question, "Do you know who is the Commander in Chief of the Pacific Fleet?"

The man on duty said, "Well, yes, of course, it's Admiral Radford."

"That's the pilot." [Laughter]

Admiral Gayler: Okay.

Paul Stillwell: Were there any prominent individuals from that era that you remember being in your home?

---

[*] Lieutenant Arthur W. Radford, USN, flew as a member of Observation Squadron One in the mid-1920s. The observation planes from the Battle Fleet were based at Sand Point during that period. Later, as a four-star admiral, Radford served as Commander in Chief Pacific, 1949-53, and Chairman of the Joint Chiefs of Staff, 1953-57.
[†] Construction of the Sand Point Naval Air Station began in 1923.
[‡] As a commander Radford served as commanding officer of Naval Air Station Seattle (Sand Point) from 1937 to 1940.
[§] This is in the Naval Institute oral history of Commander Albert K. Murray, USNR (Ret.).

Admiral Gayler: Oh, let's see. Names from the old Navy that you would recognize: Pownall, Nimitz.* Nimitz was much younger then. I remember when the news was announced in 1941 that Admiral Nimitz was going to take over the Pacific. I was a jaygee at the time, and for some reason I was home when this was announced. I was sitting at the table with Mother and Dad, and I can remember Mother saying, "Chester Nimitz. Chester Nimitz. Oh, he was that nice young ensign that used to come over and play tennis with us." So that's their generation.

I knew Admiral Sims, if you can believe it, but that was at the Naval War College.† Dad was one of the few staff corps officers to go to the Naval War College. That was a very interesting year at Newport. He had two tours in Bremerton. The first tour I was a very small boy, and the second tour I was an adolescent. In between that were Washington and the Naval War College for a year. I remember meeting Admiral Sims then.

Paul Stillwell: He was sort of the patriarch of the Navy at that point.

Admiral Gayler: He sure was. Also Admiral J. M. Reeves.‡

Paul Stillwell: What do you remember of Newport?

Admiral Gayler: I remember Newport quite well. We lived in Jamestown Island in the harbor. I was still a small boy. I think I was six or seven, but I remember it very well. The ferryboats were still running. They had walking beams with reciprocating engines and paddle wheels. The huge connecting rod, called the walking beam, would go up and down, and motion was translated into the great big stern paddle—very spectacular for a

---

* Lieutenant Commander Charles A. Pownall, USN, later a flag officer and carrier task force commander during World War II. Pownall's oral history is in the Naval Institute collection. Commander Chester W. Nimitz, USN, later Commander in Chief Pacific Fleet, 1941-45.
† Admiral William S. Sims, USN, had been Commander U.S. Naval Forces Operating in European Waters during World War I. He reverted to rear admiral after the war and served as president of the Naval War College from 1919 until he retired in 1922.
‡ Captain Joseph M. Reeves, USN, was on the faculty of the Naval War College in the mid-1920s. Later he did pioneering work with the Navy's first aircraft carrier, the USS *Langley* (CV-1), in fleet operations. In the 1930s he was a four-star admiral and Commander in Chief U.S. Fleet.

small boy to see. I used to love to ride those things back and forth. I can remember my first emancipation when I wanted to go over to Newport from Jamestown by myself. I think I was six. I pestered Mother to let me do it. She finally said, "Are you sure you can find your way over there and come back?"

I said, "Yes." That was my first independent venture. It was a lot of fun.

Paul Stillwell: Were your parents fairly strict disciplinarians, or did they give you your head?

Admiral Gayler: They were remarkable. They gave me my head. They were not unconcerned, and I now see that they were very careful about it, but yes, they gave me a lot. They gave me the feeling of responsibility pretty early.

Paul Stillwell: Was your father one to tell Navy stories?

Admiral Gayler: No, he wasn't a great raconteur. He was more interested in things of the mind. Nowadays he would be called an intellectual, I think. He was not a sea-story teller. Neither am I, for that matter.

Paul Stillwell: What sorts of things would he read, typically?

Admiral Gayler: Oh, we've had *Scientific American* around ever since I can remember. He would read engineering journals of one sort or another. He and Mother were both fluent in French, and they loved to read French literature, Victor Hugo and some of the classics.* Also, interestingly enough, Mother and my brother still read in French to each other every morning. I'm the only one in the family who isn't fluent in French.

Paul Stillwell: Was French the language between parents when they didn't want you to overhear something?

---

* Victor M. Hugo, a 19th century author, led the romantic movement in French literature. Among his best-known works are *The Hunchback of Notre Dame* and *Les Miserables.*

Admiral Gayler: It certainly was. Certainly was. Of course, it didn't work with my sister, because she understood French and so did my brother. You see, among other things, Haiti is a francophone country. They speak a kind of corrupt patois, which is basically French. My parents sometimes shifted to German, which they both understood.

Paul Stillwell: Did all this traveling around rub off on you and help develop an interest in the Navy and making that your career?

Admiral Gayler: I've often thought how much conscious thought there was and how much was just sort of taken for granted. I think the answer is yes, it probably did. I thought the Navy was a pretty good outfit to be associated with. When I got to the age when you think about things like that, late adolescence, I thought of the Navy as the shield of our civilization, which it was then. And that was a pretty good place to be.

Paul Stillwell: Why was your father selected as a civil engineer to go to the war college? You mentioned that was unusual.

Admiral Gayler: I don't know. I think he was a rather distinguished officer in his profession. He had done a lot of original work, but I don't know. This is mere speculation, but I think it was a time when the ferment was live about what might be our role in the Pacific. Even then, those in the Navy could see the war with Japan coming. Possibly they realized that they needed a civil engineer for the bases that they would construct. It was a role that was finally taken by Ben Moreell.[*] Dad was retired at that time, but Ben had been one of his assistants and a good friend. I remember how enthusiastic dad was about the Seabee idea, but he had already retired at the time.[†]

Father went back on active duty, as so many retired people did in World War II. He was appointed a member of the Army-Navy Munition Safety Board. Among other

---

[*] In 1937 Rear Admiral Ben Moreell, CEC, USN, became Chief of the Bureau of Yards and Docks. He held the position until 1945, after World War II had ended, having been promoted to vice admiral in 1944. He was in charge of developing the wartime naval shore establishment, which amounted to some 900 installations around the world.
[†] In late December 1941 Admiral Moreell founded the Naval Construction Battalions (Seabees) of engineers and trained construction crews who would do work in forward areas.

things, he specialized in safe stowage of ammunition and, in fact, developed the igloos that are still in use. He traveled very extensively during World War II and did, I believe, a hell of a job. He got a bunch of commendations for that. He was already out of the island-hopping business for which I suspect he had been groomed.

Paul Stillwell: You said he did original work. What would be some examples of that?

Admiral Gayler: He did some of the first construction of heavy concrete structures underwater. He did original designs in pre-stressed concrete. He was one of the pioneers of that, and developed these ammunition stowage igloos that I mentioned. I'm a little hazy on the details, but he was an original man, and he did original design work.

Paul Stillwell: Were you already thinking at that point about going into aviation?

Admiral Gayler: No, aviation came along later. As a youngster I was still very much imbued with the salt-water Navy. Of course I'd had a boat all my life, for one thing. I didn't go to flight school until I had been five years in the fleet.

Paul Stillwell: What was the process by which you sought an appointment to the Naval Academy? I know there was an Army prep school in there somewhere.

Admiral Gayler: You've done some homework, haven't you?

Paul Stillwell: Yes.

Admiral Gayler: Dad was ordered to Hawaii when I was about 14 years old. It was his second tour. It was my first time to see the islands, and as everybody does, I fell in love with them. Even in my lifetime they've changed beyond all recognition. It was really a lovely society in those days. We lived in the Navy yard, still in that row of old quarters they called Holy Row.

I went briefly to McKinley High School downtown, which was and is multiracial. I recall the deep and abiding respect I had for the brains of Chinese people. Those Chinese boys were smart. The competition was really tough. But it turned out that in Hawaii of the day there was no way to get a technical education and specifically no way to study physics, which was an entrance requirement for the Naval Academy.

So Dad had a bright idea. He found out through friends that the Army ran a West Point Preparatory School at Schofield Barracks. To this day, I don't know whether the arrangement was legal or informal, but anyway, at the age of 15, I was fully grown and strong. I went up there on some kind of reserve enlistment and spent almost a year as a soldier in the Army. I was at the West Point Prep School, living in one of those old barracks with the red dust and mud, with 24 soldiers in a squad room. And you lived and died at the pleasure of the first sergeant. If you were okay with him, you were okay. If you weren't okay with him, life was very hard indeed.

We studied very hard. The commandant of the school was a captain of Army engineers by the name of Merrow Sorley.* He had two assistants, both Army officers, whose names now escape me. We studied like a son-of-a-bitch, and we exercised like hell. I guess somebody in retrospect would say it was pretty tough, but I didn't think so. I enjoyed it.

In the first place, it was heady being there as an adult among adults. We lived in a squad room with 24 soldiers in it, double-deck bunks, apple pie at all times or real trouble. This was in the days of campaign hats and spiral puttees. Damn spiral puttees— my God, the problems I had getting those things to be satisfactory to the first sergeant. As I recall, we turned out at 5:20 and had 20 minutes to get cleaned up, shaved, spit and polish and out on parade for the sergeant and one of the officers to look over. Then it was off to the classroom, classes all day long, and then drill.

I remember the guy in the next bunk. He was what I thought of as an old Pole. He guess he might have been all of 24, with a bullet head and a heavy stubble of blue beard. He would shave it off every morning, pat Aqua Velva on it, and then he would

---

* Captain Merrow E. Sorley, USA, who was in the West Point class of 1924 and eventually retired as a colonel in 1954.

take the same big bottle of Aqua Velva and glug, glug, glug, two or three swigs like that, and off to breakfast.

They took me down to Waihalu Street a couple of times. I don't know whether you know Honolulu. That was where all the girls were, and I never really understood what was going on, let alone participate. Well, you can imagine what an impression all this made on me. It was a real eye-opener for a kid.

Paul Stillwell: That's the sort of thing that James Jones portrayed in *From Here to Eternity.*[*]

Admiral Gayler: Yes, although this was ten years or so before Jones.

Paul Stillwell: Was it comparable to what he depicted?

Admiral Gayler: I don't know of anybody who intrigued with the officer wives or anything like that, but, yes, that was the general atmosphere. I was a very innocent fellow. I'm sure I didn't know or understand half of what was going on.

Paul Stillwell: What was the quality of the instruction?

Admiral Gayler: I thought it was very high. I took the exams to the Naval Academy at the end of that year for practice, in order to familiarize myself so that I could make a good competitive showing. Dad didn't have any political contacts to get a congressional appointment, so the idea was that I would try for one of the President's 15 appointments, which were given competitively. I placed in the 15 when I took the practice run, so I just went at that time. When I reported in, I was just 16 years old.

Paul Stillwell: Had you done considerable reading as a boy and a teenager?

---

[*] This novel, made into a popular movie in the early 1950s, depicted Army garrison life in Hawaii leading up to the period when Pearl Harbor was attacked in 1941.

Admiral Gayler: Oh, yes. I think I was rather notorious, even in a well-read family, for the amount of reading I did. I remember Dad used to chase me out of the house sometimes, because he felt that I ought to spend at least some time outdoors. I read all the time. I read very fast. I don't read as fast anymore.

Paul Stillwell: What sorts of things did you read?

Admiral Gayler: You're not going to believe this. We had a beautiful bound set of the *Encyclopedia Britannica*. I used to love to sit down with that thing and go through it. But I also read a lot of other things too, such as Scott and Stevenson.[*] I don't think they did it overtly, but I think Mother and Dad saw to it the classics were under my nose rather than something else.

Paul Stillwell: You mentioned *Scientific American*.

Admiral Gayler: Oh, yes. I used to lap that up too. And sometimes textbooks appeared, and I read them, if you can believe it, for the fun of it.

Paul Stillwell: Did you also have facility in mathematics?

Admiral Gayler: Oh, average, I would think. My greatest facility both then and later was in English.

Paul Stillwell: How did that come about?

Admiral Gayler: From reading. It's the only way to teach English, I think. To learn how to write well, read Winston Churchill.[†]

---

[*] Sir Walter Scott (1771-1832), author of *Ivanhoe*; Robert Louis Stevenson (1850-1894), author of *Treasure Island* and *Dr. Jekyll and Mr. Hyde*.

[†] Winston L. S. Churchill (1874-1965), who fought in the Boer War, was Great Britain's First Lord of the Admiralty in World War I, Prime Minister during World War II, and again Prime Minister from 1951 to 1955. Afterward he remained as a member of Parliament. He was also a prolific author.

Paul Stillwell: Was speed-reading something you got some special training for or just a gift or what?

Admiral Gayler: I could just read fast; that's all. I always have. I used to chew up a book a day sometimes. I don't read that fast anymore, mostly because my eyes get a little tired.

Paul Stillwell: Well, then you went to the Naval Academy. Was the transition fairly easy because of the Army training?

Admiral Gayler: Yes. In fact, it was a piece of cake. The Army was really much stricter, even in plebe year.[*] It seems a crazy thing to say, but I enjoyed my plebe year.

Paul Stillwell: Why?

Admiral Gayler: It was active, it was fun, it was a new scene. I don't know. Why do you like to live? It was living.

Paul Stillwell: Was this a fulfillment of the expectations you had from years before?

Admiral Gayler: I don't think I knew a great deal about it. It was not that much of a surprise to me. I sort of took it in stride.

Paul Stillwell: The *Lucky Bag* entry for you depicts you as quite a procrastinator.[†] Is that a fair portrait?

Admiral Gayler: It sure is, and I still am. It's been a devil all my life.

---

[*] A midshipman in his or her first year is called a plebe; second year, youngster or third classman; third year, second classman; fourth year, first classman.
[†] *Lucky Bag* is the name of the Naval Academy yearbook. Typically, an individual's biographical sketch is written by his or her roommate.

Paul Stillwell: Why so?

Admiral Gayler: Why do people procrastinate?

Paul Stillwell: Why do you? Why did you?

Admiral Gayler: Well, the other day I heard about a book on procrastination, which is very good. I meant to get it, but I've been putting it off. [Laughter]

Paul Stillwell: The suggestion in the *Lucky Bag* was that you could wait till the last minute and then do something that was quite good.

Admiral Gayler: I'm afraid that's an accurate description of my work habits.

Paul Stillwell: Was it because you were able to do things fairly easily that you were able to put them off?

Admiral Gayler: I don't mean to give the impression that things were all that easy. I worked very hard. I don't know. I really don't. But it is true. You talked about Captain Thompson the other day.[*] I think I did a very good job as a destroyer officer for him, except for one damn thing. He was always after to me to get the log written up on time, and I never did. There was always something else to do. I don't know. But it is true about the procrastination; it's an accurate characterization. Ask Jesse Gay.[†] He's in town here, by the way. I play tennis with him every now and then. He was an unusual combination of a first-class wrestler and a first-class tennis player.

---

[*] Lieutenant Commander Edward M. Thompson, USN, commanded the USS *Maury* (DD-401) when Gayler was serving in the ship as a junior officer in the late 1930s.
[†] Captain Jesse B. Gay Jr., USN (Ret.), was Gayler's roommate when they were midshipmen at the Naval Academy.

Paul Stillwell: He was apparently a first-class scholar too, because he finished very high in the class.*

Admiral Gayler: Yes, he was good. His work habits were very different from mine. He used to worry about me and cluck at me for a while, but after a while he gave up.

Paul Stillwell: Did he think that you were beyond hope, or he just didn't need to?

Admiral Gayler: I think he felt that I wasn't going to change. I can still remember marching in ranks to an examination. I would try to march and take a look at the textbook at the same time, last-minute prepping. I'd get down there and get put on the report.

Paul Stillwell: Did you get any nicknames when you were a midshipman?

Admiral Gayler: No, no.

Paul Stillwell: I think you were exceptional, then, because many people did acquire them there.

Admiral Gayler: When I was a little boy, I was self-conscious about being named Noel. I would have given anything to be named "Chick" or "Hank" or "Chuck" or "Pete" or one of those names. But by the time I got to the Naval Academy, I rather liked the name I had.

Paul Stillwell: Captain Gay told me that you had a disadvantage in coming from the South, sort of, in that you got ribbing about Grant and his exploits against Richmond

---

* Of the 442 graduates in the Naval Academy class of 1935, Gay stood 37th, and Gayler was 44th.

from people in the North.* But when you went to the South, you were viewed as an outsider there too.

Admiral Gayler: Yes, when I was a little kid, I was always having to fight, because I was Yankee or Rebel, depending on where I was.

Paul Stillwell: Were the North-South feelings still fairly strong at that time?

Admiral Gayler: Yes, particularly at the school-kid level.

Paul Stillwell: What about your sports participation at the Naval Academy?

Admiral Gayler: I tried a lot, but I didn't do very well with sports at the Naval Academy. It's easy enough to think of excuses. I was full grown, but I was still only 16, and I was not very well coordinated. I rowed but not varsity, and I played football but not varsity. That was about it. I didn't play tennis in those days. I'm a tennis nut now, but I took it up in my 40s. I used to play golf when I was a youngster.

Paul Stillwell: Did you take French at the academy to keep up with your family?

Admiral Gayler: No, I outsmarted myself on that one very badly. The year that we went there was the first year that they had one section from each battalion that they taught either German or Italian. It happened in the way I'd been brought up in various high schools that I'd never had any language training, and I was acutely aware of the competitive disadvantage that would put me in. So I thought, "Well, it's the first year they're starting Italian. I'll take Italian, so I'll start out at least on a par." But I'd forgotten about all the guys named Gambacorta and all the rest of them, so I had a hell of

---

* General Ulysses S. Grant was in command of the Union Army at the end of the Civil War and accepted General Robert E. Lee's surrender in April 1865. Grant later served as President of the United States from 1869 to 1877.

a time with Italian.* All the Italian kids had taken it for competitive reasons. [Laughter] I really outsmarted myself.

Paul Stillwell: Do you have a facility for memory work? That's useful in language?

Admiral Gayler: No. I have a fair memory, but I certainly don't have a memorizing kind of memory.

Paul Stillwell: Well, that was a real asset in the style of instruction that was used in that day, so did that put you at a disadvantage?

Admiral Gayler: Some places, and some places not. It didn't help you much in math. It didn't help you much in English. My good subjects were always English and engineering. Math I was fair. Italian I was miserable. Seamanship I was all right. I'd had a boat all my life. I was okay on that. I do recall that in mass class I visualized earth satellites long before Sputnik.† The instructor stopped the class to discuss the concept.

Paul Stillwell: Were you helped any in engineering through the background from your father?

Admiral Gayler: Not directly, but I was not uneasy about it. It had sort of a general familiarity to me.

Paul Stillwell: What do you remember about the life in Bancroft Hall and the atmosphere there?‡

---

* Midshipman Francis M. Gambacorta, USN.
† On 4 October 1957, the Soviet Union launched Sputnik I, the first artificial earth satellite. It caused great uproar in the United States, which had expected to be first in space.
‡ Bancroft Hall is the large multi-wing dormitory that houses Naval Academy midshipmen. It also contains the offices of members of the executive department, including the commandant, executive officer, and battalion and company officers.

Admiral Gayler: I think I was on the disciplinary ship only six days after I had been sworn in.[*] In the Army barracks nobody ever bothered to put any clothes on or put a towel around him when he was going to the showers and whatnot. I don't mean to impute anything sexual or homosexual or anything; it was just you were in barracks and you walked around that way. So I did the same thing at the Naval Academy without thinking about it, going from my room down to the heads. The DO came along and put me on the report, and I was sent to the disciplinary ship.[†]

Paul Stillwell: How was life in the *Reina Mercedes*?

Admiral Gayler: It was all right. It was no great problem, except you had a few extra yards to cover every day to go to class, and you slept in a hammock.

Paul Stillwell: What do you remember about the executive leadership, the executive officer, Commander Badger, and commandant?[‡]

Admiral Gayler: I remember Oscar Badger very well. I also remember Tommy Hart very well.[§] He wore collars like Herbert Hoover, with those round bottoms, and affected a very distant and forbidding air.[**] Badger was, I think, well liked. My company officer was Charles P. Cecil, who later on had a ship named after him.[††] I remember the start he gave me once when I had CarDiv 20 and the *Charles P. Cecil* joined up at sea.

Paul Stillwell: What are your recollections of Cecil?

---

[*] USS *Reina Mercedes* (IX-25), captured during the Spanish-American War, served as a station ship at the Naval Academy from 1912 to 1957. Until 1940, midshipmen being punished for various disciplinary infractions slept and took meals on board the ship but continued to go to classes ashore.
[†] DO – duty officer.
[‡] Commander Oscar C. Badger, USN, who later served as a flag officer in World War II.
[§] Rear Admiral Thomas C. Hart, USN, was superintendent of the Naval Academy from May 1931 to June 1934.
[**] Herbert C. Hoover was President of the United States from 1929 to 1933.
[††] Lieutenant Commander Charles P. Cecil, USN. He was awarded two Navy Crosses in World War II, serving as Commander Destroyer Squadron Five and commanding officer of the cruiser *Helena* (CL-50). As a rear admiral, he was killed in an airplane crash in 1944. DD-835 was named for him.

Admiral Gayler: In those days, if you were put on the report for any infraction at all, you reported to the company officer. Since I was always hasty and slightly sloppy, I would sometimes leave my locker door open, which was a one demerit. And the punishment didn't consist of just the one demerit; it consisted of standing in line for half an hour or an hour at a time for your interview with the company officer. He would always ask me, "Why did you leave your locker door open?"

Well, how the hell do you answer a question like that? You didn't leave a locker door open with any motive or any explanation; you just left it open. [Laughter] I'm not doing him justice, I'm sure. This is a very worm's eye view.

Slim Beecher was a company officer, and he was very well liked.[*] He was a musician and a composer and had composed several songs that were very popular, particularly in Hawaii.[†] I wish I could think of the names; they were really very nice. He was known as "Spot One," because he was tall. You see, Spot One being the tallest spotting station on the battleships.

Paul Stillwell: Did you have any musical inclination yourself?

Admiral Gayler: Yes, but only as a listener, not a performer. Mother was a great singer. I have always appreciated music, but I've never made any.

Paul Stillwell: You described Admiral Hart as sort of an aloof figure. How would you compare him with Admiral Sellers?[‡]

Admiral Gayler: I never knew Admiral Sellers at all.

Paul Stillwell: How was the social life at the academy?

---

[*] Lieutenant (junior grade) William G. Beecher, USN.
[†] In World War II he composed an amusing song called "Halsey, Nimitz and Me," implying that the war in the Pacific was being fought by three people, the sailor-singer and two admirals.
[‡] Rear Admiral David F. Sellers, USN, was superintendent of the Naval Academy from June 1934 to February 1938.

Admiral Gayler: Oh, it was fun. I didn't go in for frenching out much, but I did a lot of dragging.* I think I only frenched out two or three times. I never made the mistake of going over the wall by the stadium, where everybody else was picked up. In fact, I had a very pleasant friend who had a canoe, and she would come up along the seawall in the canoe.

Paul Stillwell: An ingenious way.

Admiral Gayler: A very easy way and a very pleasant way to get in and out. [Laughter]

Paul Stillwell: Saves wear and tear.

Admiral Gayler: Yes.

Paul Stillwell: Were you at any disadvantage socially in that you were younger than most of your contemporaries there?

Admiral Gayler: Disadvantage isn't quite the right word. I think I was a little bit out of it.

Paul Stillwell: Typically, where would your dates come from?

Admiral Gayler: Both local girls and the yard engines, as we used to call them.† A couple of times I dragged a sister of a classmate of mine who came from Waycross, Georgia. She was a sweet girl. And lot of blind dates would be arranged, sometimes pleasant, sometimes a bit of a trial. Those were innocent days. They were not like these days—at least they weren't for me.

---

* Frenching out was the practice of leaving the Naval Academy grounds without permission; dragging was the nickname for dating girls.
† "Yard engine" was the term used for a girl who lived on the "yard" or Naval Academy campus, presumably the daughter of a senior officer stationed at the academy.

Paul Stillwell: The repeal of Prohibition came about halfway through your time at the academy.* Did that make any difference?

Admiral Gayler: I don't remember that it did. There were always speakeasies before then, but I never went to them. In the first place, I didn't want to get put on the report for it. In the second place, I really wasn't that interested in drinking anyway. I didn't do much drinking until I was already graduated.

Paul Stillwell: What do you recall of your summer cruises?

Admiral Gayler: Oh, they were great. I remember that on my youngster cruise in 1932 we went to sea on the *Wyoming*, which you may remember was partly demilitarized.† Her after turret was taken off. I slept swinging in a hammock.

The first thing that happened was we got into a considerable storm off Cape Hatteras, and she really rolled the guts out of her, as a result of which about 90% of the people in the ship were seasick. We didn't have anything but cold chow and boiled eggs, I remember. I thought I had enough hard-boiled eggs for the rest of my life before that storm was over. But for some reason I wasn't much affected by the seasickness, so I took a lot of extra watches up on the bridge, standing in awe of the captain, who was none other than the famous Benjamin Dutton.‡

He was a very fine man. He was aloof, as a skipper would be, but he wasn't really aloof. Every now and then he'd pass some comment to me. I liked him enormously. Also, I had a nice feeling that if the ship was going to capsize, it would be

---

* The 18th Amendment to the Constitution was ratified in 1919 and went into effect in 1920, prohibiting the consumption of alcoholic beverages in the United States. The Volstead Act, enacted by Congress in 1919, spelled out the penalties for violations. In December 1933 the ratification of the 21st Amendment to the Constitution repealed the 18th Amendment and thus ended national prohibition.
† USS *Wyoming* (BB-32) was commissioned as a battleship in 1912 and served in that role until being demilitarized as a result of the 1930 London Treaty on the limitation of naval armaments. She was redesignated AG-17 in 1931 and thereafter served into the mid-1940s as a training ship for gunnery and for midshipman cruises.
‡ Captain Benjamin Dutton Jr., USN, commanded the *Wyoming* from 1931 to 1933. He was the author of *Navigation and Piloting*, a standard textbook on the subject. Since taken over by other authors, it is now in its 14th edition.

in the company of the Navy's most famous navigator. Because she did roll. Boy, did she roll.

Paul Stillwell: Was she top-heavy?

Admiral Gayler: Yes, she was. I think that's why they took off that turret. I don't know quite why she was that bad, but she was awash most of the time in that storm, rolling like a bathtub.

We had a sort of a truncated cruise. We didn't go to Europe; we went to ports in the Caribbean. Grungy little sailors' towns, full of liquor and 15-year-old whores and all that stuff. I can't even remember the name of them anymore.

Paul Stillwell: Gonaives, Haiti, was on the list then of undesirable places to visit.

Admiral Gayler: This wasn't Haiti. One of them was Portuguese, actually. Ponta Delgada in the Azores was one of the ports. I forget what the other one was.

I remember that the new third classmen slung their hammocks, while the first class had cots underneath. And my hammock was slung right over the cot of a first classman who was well known as a penine. That term may or may not be obscene; I've never known. Anyway, I remember this fellow's name very well, but I don't believe I'll put it on the tape. He was a bastard. He was a bully. First classman, red face, shouting all the time. And I happened to have the hammock right above him.

One day I was sitting in my hammock, and I took several turns on the footrope. I was taking up on it as tight as I could to make it as flat as I could to sleep in. All of a sudden, the damn thing broke. The head was secured at one end, and the tail fitting broke. I swung down on to the first classman's cot and smashed it into kindling. I wasn't hurt, so I just picked up my bedroll and hammock and went into another part of the ship. I found a vacant place, slung my hammock there, and never went back. I heard he was roaring around the ship for days trying to find out what had happened to his cot and who had done it, but he never did. [Laughter] That's about all I remember of my fourth class cruise.

Paul Stillwell: I understand one advantage of those hammocks was that they would stay steady, and the ship would roll around them.

Admiral Gayler: Oh, yes. Actually, sleeping in a hammock was better than a cot. You know how the rates are.

Paul Stillwell: Did you experience any hazing during your plebe year?

Admiral Gayler: Oh, sure, but not undue. Nobody got after me, no tail beating or anything like that. Just ordinary disciplinary hazing. Memorizing things, sitting on the edge of your chair, getting ready to get the red-eye bottle.[*] You would be sitting at the mess table when everybody went like that, and threw it at you, and you just better catch it.[†] That sort of thing. Maybe memory has softened a little bit, but I don't remember having any trouble with hazing.

Paul Stillwell: Most people remember being on the receiving end far better than they remember being on the delivering end.

Admiral Gayler: Yes. I never did any hazing, and I don't remember receiving any.

Paul Stillwell: What about your first-class cruise? Where was that?

Admiral Gayler: Oh, that was a lot more interesting. We went to Europe. We went to Italy, of course—to Rome. We were received by the Pope in camera.[‡] The great incident of the day involved Hank Muller, who was a classmate of mine and a cheerleader.[§] He was a very ebullient character, and without pre-arrangement or anything, in the presence the Holy Father, he jumped on the table and led us in, Four N's, one Navy, "Pope! Pope!

---

[*] Red-eye – ketchup.
[†] The tape didn't catch the physical gesture that accompanied this story; it was what Admiral Gayler referred to as the classic one-finger "salute."
[‡] Pius XI was Pope from 1922 to 1939.
[§] Midshipman Henry L. Muller, USN.

Pope!" The whole Vatican crowd was astonished. His Holiness seemed to be amused more than anything else. [Laughter]

On the same trip we were received by Mussolini, who reviewed us.[*] He was a tiny little fellow. I remember looking down on the top of his bald head, which had a wart on it. I'm only about 5-11 now; I guess I was about 6 feet then. I was in the second platoon, not very tall, and I remember seeing him right under my eyes, looking right down on him. Then he made a very graceful little speech to us about a naval officer's life. It was in good English. I've never seen it mentioned that he was fluent in English, but that's what he did. It's been my fortune in life to know quite a few dictators. And all of them seemed to go sour in their later life, but in their younger period, when I knew them—I didn't know Mussolini, but I saw him—they were not so bad.

Paul Stillwell: Did you have a chance to use the Italian there that you had taken at the Naval Academy?

Admiral Gayler: Of course I tried. The Italians love for you to try the language. They are very different from the French. The French are insulted if you screw up French. But the Italians like you to stumble over it if you give it a try, and so, yes, I could speak it to a certain extent. I was not a credit to our marvelous head of the department, whose name was Humbert Ziroli.[†] What a dedicated guy he was. He had set up the Italian course, and as far as I could tell, it was his great objective in life. And I was a terrible disappointment to him.

Paul Stillwell: What else was included in the itinerary for the cruise?

Admiral Gayler: We went to London also. That was the first time I ever saw London. We were sent ashore in uniform. I've forgotten how we got from Portsmouth to London. We must have gone on the train. Then all of a sudden you were on your own with your buddies in a big city. The Brits were just charmed to see us, girls and all. [Laughter]

---

[*] Benito Mussolini, a dictator ran Italy from 1922 to 1943, when he was deposed. He was later hanged in 1945.
[†] Lieutenant Commander Humbert W. Ziroli, USN, a 1916 graduate of the Naval Academy.

Paul Stillwell: Was there any sense of your good fortune in getting this education and this worldwide travel in Depression America?*

Admiral Gayler: Oh, yes. Dad talked to me very seriously about that. He said he didn't want me to go to the Naval Academy to save the family money or just because it was the thing to do. He wanted me to be very sure that it was what I wanted to do, and it was my choice. And it was. But I did recognize it.

Paul Stillwell: Well, that sounds like a logical progression from the sort of upbringing you depicted earlier.

Admiral Gayler: The Depression was very much with us in one sense but not with us in another. It didn't affect us personally very much, but it certainly was a daily topic that everyone talked about.

Paul Stillwell: What ship did you make that cruise in?

Admiral Gayler: The *Wyoming* and the *Arkansas* went over together, and for this cruise I was in the *Arkansas*.†

Paul Stillwell: Those two ships were sisters, so obviously very similar.

Admiral Gayler: Yes. I can remember I was plug man on the 12-inch gun. That's the guy that takes 13 and a half turns to get that breech plug open. By that time I'd gotten a lot stronger, and they picked out the stronger fellows to do that. That big rammer would come in there to push in the powder bags. To get out of the way, I'd stand up and cringe

---

* Following the crash of the New York Stock Exchange in late October 1929, the United States was plunged into the Great Depression, from which it did not recover until the nation geared up for World War II at the beginning of the 1940s. The Depression was marked by high unemployment and many business failures.
† USS *Arkansas* (BB-33) was commissioned 17 September 1912. Following modernization in the mid-1930s she had a standard displacement of 26,100 tons, was 562 feet long and 106 feet in the beam. Her top speed was 21 knots. She was armed with 12 12-inch guns and 16 5-inch guns. She was the oldest U.S. battleship in active service during World War II. She was decommissioned in 1946.

up against the after bulkhead, and the whole damn piece of steel would come back at me. I never knew if it was going to stop or not. [Laughter]

Paul Stillwell: Those turrets in the *Arkansas* and *Wyoming* were less sophisticated than the World War II types.

Admiral Gayler: Yes.

Paul Stillwell: Much more manual labor involved.

Admiral Gayler: Yes. Of course, the projectile itself was handled by machinery. A hoist would bring it up from below, then it would flop over into the tray, and the big articulated rammer would shove it home. But the powder bags were handled by manpower.

Paul Stillwell: Well, men did have to handle that tray also.

Admiral Gayler: That's right. It was a polished brass tray that folded down for each round, then got back up out of the way when it was time to shoot.

Paul Stillwell: How did you spend the middle summer, the one between the two cruises?

Admiral Gayler: Oh, that was second-class summer in those days. We had the business of bringing in the plebes for plebe summer, and we were in charge of running them around. It was rather a relaxed, easy time.

Paul Stillwell: Now it's more an orientation visit to the Marine Corps and aviation.

Admiral Gayler: We didn't do anything like that. We stayed at the Naval Academy. We did a lot of seamanship and a lot of sailing. It was fairly relaxed, actually, for the second class.

Paul Stillwell: Was there any aviation indoctrination?

Admiral Gayler: No. Many, many years later I had a little seaplane of my own, and I remember landing on the Severn in the middle of all the boats in second-class summer with my three young daughters, and we all went swimming. [Laughter] It really took me back.

Paul Stillwell: As a first classman you were company commander of seventh company. What did that entail?

Admiral Gayler: The company commander, of course, was the midshipman military officer in charge of the formations and the drill and everything else. I was rather surprised to find myself there for a start. I had not shone—let's put it that way—on the military aspects. I was not the best-polished midshipman, the best-drilled midshipman, or any of those things. I think it came about as a result of the cruise. Picking the company commanders was a very competitive thing.

I remember we had a very enthusiastic guy by the name of Dave Kaigler, who had gone to a military academy in the South.[*] He was all for getting the commanding edge in the company competition by excellence in drill. So I made Dave sort of a drillmaster. I think in those days I was as lazy as I am now. I portioned out all of the various jobs to anybody who was willing to take them, and, of course, Dave did a good job.

Paul Stillwell: I think that's called leadership.

Admiral Gayler: Perhaps. [Laughter]

Paul Stillwell: Did your Army training benefit you in this job?

Admiral Gayler: Yes, it gave me a head start and some familiarity with drill and whatnot. Of course, by that time, after three years at the Naval Academy, I already knew the drill

---

[*] Midshipman David Kaigler, Jr., USN.

manual pretty well. The Army and Marines both gave me something. When I was a kid of 14, Dad arranged for me to go out and spend a couple of weeks at the Marine rifle range outside of Bremerton. I went with a company of Marines doing rifle training out there. I remember an old gunnery sergeant there who taught me how to shoot right along with the rest of the recruits. The difference was that I paid attention and the rest of them didn't. I had very good eyes in those days, so pretty soon I was shooting expert.

When I went to the Naval Academy, I remember they got all the plebes out there banging around, and I shot an expert score. They immediately had me up to see what the hell was going on and wanted me to go out for the rifle team, but I didn't want to do that. I think that's the principal edge I had in military things. I've always been a good shot.

Paul Stillwell: Did you give any thought to taking a Marine Corps commission?

Admiral Gayler: No, I wanted to be a naval officer.

Paul Stillwell: Do you remember your classmate Robert Cushman, who later became Commandant?*

Admiral Gayler: Sure. I remember Bob very well.

Paul Stillwell: What do you recall about him as a midshipman?

Admiral Gayler: Well, you have to have some feel for how isolated and parochial you are within what was then the regiment. He was in another company, and I didn't see much of him, to be truthful. I just know of him as a pleasant friend, and that's about it. I can't help you much.

Paul Stillwell: Were there any other midshipmen whom you were particularly close to?

---

* General Robert E. Cushman, USMC, was Commandant of the Marine Corps, 1972-75.

Admiral Gayler: I was very close to my roommate, Jess Gay. Others were Larry Edge and Roscoe Dillen; they were both killed in the war.* Edes Talman was another.† I could tell you a story about Edes.

Paul Stillwell: Please do.

Admiral Gayler: Edes is a Washingtonian of an old family: tall, very courtly fellow, even as a youngster, and the kindest guy in the world, but he was accident-prone. Something was always happening to him. I remember when the captain of the *Maryland*, Captain L. P. Davis, and his wife gave a reception for all the officers on the ship.‡ Edes showed up, and in making a courtly bow to Mrs. Davis, he knocked over the table, which had all the set-ups for the refreshments. Everything crashed on to the ground.

Later on, he did the same damn thing at the Hillenkoetters, the same Hillenkoetter who was later on the first head of the CIA.§ But the really funny story concerned Edes as the exec and navigator of a four-pipe destroyer during the war. The ship was in the North Atlantic in this damn little bucket, heaved around by the terrible seas and staying at sea, in and out. As you've read about in those days, you know how tough it was. And nary a goddamn contact.

Then finally, by God, they got a contact. They were running in on it, with captain on the bridge and Edes in the pilothouse with the dead reckoning tracer. About the time they were making the final adjustments, the captain hollered in through the port, "Talman! Talman! Talman! What's the course?" Final adjustment on the DRT.

Edes said, "I can't tell you, Captain. I've got my tie caught in the dead reckoning tracer." [Laughter] It was his one submarine contact during the war. Poor old Edes died of heart trouble some years ago, but he was a wonderful guy.

---

* Midshipman Lawrence L. Edge, USN; Midshipman Roscoe F. Dillen Jr., USN.
† Midshipman Benjamin Long Edes Talman, USN.
‡ Captain Louis P. Davis, USN, commanded the battleship *Maryland* (BB-46) from 20 June 1936 to 16 December 1937.
§ Lieutenant Roscoe H. Hillenkoetter, USN, was then serving in the *Maryland*. In 1947, as a rear admiral, he was director when the Central Intelligence Agency was formed.

Roscoe Dillen was killed in the Battle of the Java Sea.[*] He was the turret officer on the *Houston*. He was killed the day before that battle. That was the turret that was knocked out by a Japanese bomb. Those are most of them, I guess. I don't think any of them are left, except Jess. We lost a hell of a lot of my class in World War II.

Paul Stillwell: As your graduation from the Naval Academy approached, had you given thought to what you wanted to do after that, or did you have much choice?

Admiral Gayler: Yes, you had a choice all right. I wanted to go to the fleet. Actually, I wanted battleships, and that's what I got.

Paul Stillwell: Was there a choice of a specific one, or did you just take what was handed out?

Admiral Gayler: Several friends of mine went together to the *Maryland*. That can't have been coincidence. We must have all put in for the same ship and wound up in the *Maryland*. I didn't really care, as long as it was one of the battle line ships.

Altogether I spent three years on the *Maryland*. Gee, it's just incredible to think of the changes in the Navy since then. I suppose the median term of service in the ship was six years. We had sailors who had been in that ship ever since it was commissioned. I joined her in 1935, and she was commissioned in '21, as I remember it.[†] Still on board were some plank owners who had been there ever since she was commissioned.[‡]

I remember the exec called me in and made me coach of the football team as soon as I arrived. I was sort of horrified, because I knew I wasn't much of a football player. I had turned out and got my nose pushed in the mud regularly, but I wasn't awfully good. And I thought, "Jesus Christ, Commander . . ." But it turned out that I had a tackle that had been playing for seven years, I had a quarterback, Cadles Minnick, I'll never forget

---

[*] Naval Academy records indicate that Lieutenant Dillen was killed when the submarine *Shark* (SS-174) was lost in mid-February 1942 while operating in the Far East.

[†] USS *Maryland* (BB-46) was commissioned 21 July 1921. She had a standard displacement of 32,600 tons, was 624 feet long and 98 feet in the beam. Her top speed was 21.2 knots. She was armed with eight 16-inch guns and 12 5-inch broadside guns. She remained in active service until decommissioned on 3 April 1947, following World War II.

[‡] "Plankowner" is a term for an original crew member of a given ship.

him, who had been calling plays for four years. They didn't need a coach; they needed an officer mascot. They let me play with them, and that was my reward. So that was kind of fun.

The stability in that life was unbelievable. We actually had a fleet operating schedule that was printed on a printing press. It's easy to get things printed now, computer offset and whatnot, but this was an annual operating schedule. And you could damn well expect that on June 17 next you would be in Santa Barbara, California, or whatnot. The schedule, in fact, was so reliable that we used to schedule football games against smaller colleges. We didn't play the big football powers like the University of Washington or California, but the number-two rank like Willamette University. I remember we used to play and even had printed tickets. Amazing. We sold tickets to the games, just as if we'd been another college.

I remember the ship's barber. This was before the ship's serviceman rate existed. So the custom was to have certain men, in effect, become ship's servicemen, and they never had any rate of their own; they were always seamen second class.* One barber's name was Fiegels. I thought of him as an old man in those days. He had long white hair slicked back, but his rate was seaman second. We got a new exec aboard, and he decreed that every sailor in the ship would take the training course for the next higher rate—without exceptions. He was that kind of a guy. He wasn't a very popular exec. But anyway . . .

Paul Stillwell: Roland Smoot was in that ship, and he did not remember him fondly either.†

Admiral Gayler: I remember Roland Smoot fondly. Interestingly enough, I just spent last weekend with the elders of the Mormon Church, talking about Roland Smoot.

The point of all of this is that there was a guy who had been in the ship about 15 years. He was an old man with white hair and the ship's barber who ran the barbershop

---

* Seaman second class is equivalent to the current rate of seaman apprentice.
† Lieutenant Roland N. Smoot, USN. Smoot, who retired as a vice admiral, is the subject of an oral history in the Naval Institute collection.

with some assistants. He had to take another course for seaman first. The ship just rocked with laughter on that one.

I used to wonder why the sailors congregated as they did in the barbershop. I mean, I would see a whole lot more guys than were getting haircuts or even in line for it. The discussion was animated, and then when an officer or even a fresh-caught ensign like me would show up, the conversation would sort of die down. It took me a long time to figure out that the barber was also the ship's bookie. [Laughter]

I first went in as assistant communications head in charge of coding and decoding and running the coding board. That was kind of fun. I remember the admiral's suite was empty. We didn't have an admiral on board. He had a lot of safes in there, so I kept the coding books in the safe. I remember going in, locking the door behind me, all by myself, opening the safe with fear and trembling, taking out the master codebooks and familiarizing myself with them, and carefully locking them up, locking the cabin door and all the rest of it.

The coding board did principally ciphering, not coding and decoding. We had these old-fashioned cipher machines and another with strips of paper on a strip cipher. The combat coding board was made up of the paymaster and the assistant paymaster. There were also a couple of other supernumeraries plus this fresh-caught ensign, who was supposed to be the head of it.

We had a competition every year as part of the annual inspection. I remember a lazy old bastard of a supply officer. He was a commander, and he had trained in security and couldn't be bothered with anything except playing acey-deucey in the wardroom.[*] (I got a permanent aversion to acey-deucey aboard ship from that one.) I never had it in the *Ranger*.[†] Everybody learned their lesson and did it well except this old bastard. He lost us our competition.

After about a year in the *Maryland* I went in as JO in the third division, which had the after high turret.[‡] Then something happened to my division officer, and I had the delight of being the acting division officer for almost a year. It was very heady stuff for

---

[*] Acey-deucy is a nautical version of the board game backgammon.
[†] As a captain Gayler was commanding officer of the aircraft carrier *Ranger* (CVA-61), 1959-60.
[‡] JO—junior officer. The ship had four centerline turrets. The first and fourth turrets were at deck level; the second and third were a level higher to be able to shoot over the lower ones.

an ensign. While I had that job, the ship went up to the Bremerton Navy Yard, which, of course, was very familiar to me, old stamping grounds. So I took some leave.

In those days, a division officer signed Title B cards to accept custody for everything in his division. So I was signed up for one 16-inch gun turret, together with two 16-inch guns. I went on leave, and when I came back, my God, my guns were gone. [Laughter] Of course, they had come down with one of those enormous cranes and taken them up to the shop. I never forgot the shock of walking down, coming back aboard, and my damn guns were gone.

Paul Stillwell: Did the yard workmen take those out through the gun ports, or did they have to take the roof of the turret off?

Admiral Gayler: They certainly didn't take the roof of the turret off. No, they must have taken them out forward. They had a huge hammerhead crane designed for just that purpose. As it happened, my dad had built the crane. Now that I remember, they slid them forward out of the sleeves, and then picked them up. I wasn't there when they did it.

Paul Stillwell: What do you recall of the wardroom life, starting out as a junior ensign?

Admiral Gayler: Oh, We had a junior officers' mess, and that was terrific, because there we were, all by ourselves, two classes. In my case, it was the classes of '34 and '35 initially. Later it was my class and class of '36, which was a rather small class, so essentially it was pretty much us '35ers.

We had a marvelous time. We had a mess of our own. We were meticulous about our manners and whatnot, but it was ours. There were no senior officers there to damp the thing. It used to be a marvelous way to date, particularly if you didn't have much money. The sequence was this: you would get your work done on the division and go like hell in order to catch the 4:00 o'clock shore boat. There I learned a facility which I have retained all my life. I can get dressed about as fast as anybody you ever saw, because I've had so much practice with about three minutes to go to get the 4:00 o'clock shore boat. You'd go in to Long Beach and play squash or surf. Squash was a great game in the Navy in those days. Or you might play golf and clean up at the club. Then you'd go collect your date.

I had a half interest in a 12-cylinder Auburn car. Those were the days of the gas wars in Southern Cal. Gas got down to nine cents a gallon. We all had some kind of vehicle like that, a glossy old Cadillac or Auburn or something. So you'd pick up your date and stop at Topsy's, which was very close to the dock, and throw one quick martini into her and yourself, and get on the 6:00 o'clock boat. And, of course, that martini wouldn't even hit bottom until you were all in the JO mess, where we had hilarious dinners. Everybody dragged. It was such an interesting atmosphere. We all knew the same crowd of girls, and we were not as exclusive as they are today. We paired off to a certain extent, but also we were friends of everybody. If your classmate had a girl out for dinner, it was not offensive to ask her in his presence for a date the following night or something like that. It was all taken as a matter of course.

Then, after this wonderful, hilarious dinner, practically everybody who wasn't on duty would go ashore and bring a girl out. It was a marvelous way to entertain. Then we'd go up to the movie on deck, topside, put a blanket around her, and look at the movie, reel by reel, with stops between the reels. We'd sit there under the stars with the tops just barely moving in the harbor there.[*] Then we would rush to catch the 10:00 o'clock boat back ashore and get into these cars and go steaming north to Los Angeles to the Cotton Club and dance all night at the famous Door. Sometimes we would end up with Louie Prima, and I remember a man with a hot violin by the name of Stuffy Smith.

By that time of morning it was always foggy in Southern California. You'd go tearing through the fog, trying to get your date home and catch the last shore boat, which the ship ran for the officers until 4:00 A.M. About half the time you'd catch it, half the time you wouldn't. I'd grumble if I had to put out $2.00 for a water taxi to take me out to the ship. And from the water taxi, you never went up the gangway. You had to come up over the boat booms. So there in the fog you were crawling up over the boat booms, which were always varnished and very slick. Usually it was beginning to be daylight

---

[*] In the battleships of that era, each mast had at the top of it a three-level "top," a structure that contained the fire control equipment for aiming the guns.

about then. You would get back aboard in the cold, gray dawn just in time for reveille and get your division out for muster. Boy, the things you can do when you're 20 years old you just wouldn't believe. [Laughter] That was a fairly typical kind of dating scene. From the social side of it, that JO mess was a lot of fun.

Paul Stillwell: Well, why don't we pick it up from there next time?

Admiral Gayler: Okay. That's great.

Interview Number 2 with Admiral Noel A. M. Gayler, U.S. Navy (Retired)

Place: Admiral Gayler's office at the American Committee on East-West Accord, Washington, D.C.

Date: Friday, 4 November 1983

Paul Stillwell: Admiral, in our last interview you said that you talked to members of the Mormon Church about Roland Smoot, one of your shipmates in the *Maryland*. Maybe you could give me some of the substance of that interview about him.

Admiral Gayler: Well, Roland Smoot was very well liked. He was the first division officer, as I recall. And he, of course, was a Mormon, as are many of the Smoot family in Salt Lake City. He was also a great friend of my sister's. I don't think I had anything much more to say about that, except that I mentioned that I was on my way to Salt Lake City the last time we talked. I did talk to the elders of the Mormon Church, and the Smoot family is very proud of them. I was much impressed—learned and cosmopolitan.

Paul Stillwell: What do you remember about him professionally as a naval officer in the *Maryland*?

Admiral Gayler: I remember him very favorably. He was well liked and well respected. He used to *de facto* take over the job of gunnery officer in battle practice with the 16-inch guns, because the fellow who nominally had the job wasn't that swift. We put the actual gunnery officer on a pair of telephones and sort of kept him out of the way. At least that was an ensign's eye view of it. Smoot was the one who really ran things.

I remember how those 16-inch guns would shake the ship. They shook everything out of it like a housewife shaking a rug. We saw pieces of paint, dust, and crud all over ship after those guns were fired. They both seemed to pick up the ship bodily and also sort of shake it so that everything from every corner would come tumbling down. In the compartments below deck, you could hardly breathe from the dust after the big guns had fired.

Of course, she was covered all over in paint. This came from generations of painting, which we later learned, to our cost, was inflammable. We were big on damage control, very meticulous about air testing all the compartments. It was amazing how many times you'd find a compartment that wasn't really watertight. You'd put air pressure on it and see if it held the pressure. That will search out the smallest leaks. We were really good on damage control. That was one area where the Navy was ready for war, in spite of the Pearl Harbor experience.[*]

Paul Stillwell: Did you go through the usual rotation through various departments that's considered part of junior officer development?

Admiral Gayler: Yes, I certainly did. As I mentioned last time, I started out as an assistant communicator, and my job was the coding board. I went from there to the 16-inch guns and started out as a junior officer in the third division, which had the third turret, the after high turret. Then, most fortunately, my division officer got ordered somewhere else, so I got to be a big, fat division officer. I was the proprietor of two 16-inch guns.

Then I went to the antiaircraft division, which then had 5-inch/25-caliber guns. They were on a high pedestal mount and fired fixed ammunition. Each projectile weighed about 90 pounds, so the job of loading the ammunition required a very powerful, tall man, sort of like a pro football tackle. He had to be able to reach out for this big weight, lift it over his head, slap it in the tray, and get his hands out of the way before the power rammer rammed it.

I've described to you the personnel stability in the ship. The result, over the years, was that there had been sort of a Darwinian selection of people going to the sixth division. They were all gigantic. Every morning I would have to go out and tell these enormous and skeptical guys about the coming day's operations. All of them were older

---

[*] On Sunday, 7 December 1941, Japanese carrier planes attacked and heavily damaged American warships at the naval base at Pearl Harbor, Hawaii. The U.S. Congress declared war on Japan the following day.

than I was, because I was then only 21. I think that training in public speaking has lasted me the rest of my life—the best training I could possibly have had.

Paul Stillwell: Did you feel any awkwardness in being thrust into a situation in which your subordinates were older and knew more on their particular specialty than you did?

Admiral Gayler: I'll give you an honest answer. No, I didn't.

Paul Stillwell: Why not? Did you acquire some sort of poise through the Naval Academy or elsewhere?

Admiral Gayler: I don't know. I think it's one's attitude toward those things, mostly. I don't know where it comes from.

Paul Stillwell: What else in the gunnery department do you recall?

Admiral Gayler: Oh, it was a very interesting sort of phase. There was a lot of seamanship, a lot of marlinspike seamanship, a lot of gunnery, very advanced stuff in the antiaircraft business. We had the forerunner of the modern computers, actually, in the antiaircraft computers. We had these huge mechanical computers that were linked to the stereoscopic spotters. You could see the shells going out in space in depth, and you would try to estimate whether the burst was on this side of the sleeve or that side of the sleeve. We didn't hit much, but it was fun.

Paul Stillwell: You didn't have the benefit of radar then, which was a big disadvantage.

Admiral Gayler: No, there was no radar then, so the range finding was all optical. The *Maryland* had the largest main battery range finder in the fleet, and it had been captured or liberated from the German cruiser *Magdeburg*.[*]

---

[*] The light cruiser *Magdeburg* was launched in November 1917, then stricken from the German Navy in November 1919, nine months before planned completion. She was scrapped in 1922.

Paul Stillwell: I didn't know that.

Admiral Gayler: You know how great the Germans were in optics. It was a stereoscopic range finder at the time when all of ours were coincidence range finders. The effect of that was it could do a much better job than the American type, and we were the only battleship that had it. And do you know, some characters from the Bureau of Construction and Repair came along and said we had to get rid of that range finder, because it was unauthorized topside weight. This was in a battleship, for God's sake. The thing couldn't have weighed more than a couple of tons on the outside.

Captain Davis was really fussed about that, so he told me to see what I could do in the way of putting together a reply to the bureau, asking for permission to keep the range finder. I thought for a while and decided to investigate how much sand we carried to holystone the deck. It turned out that we carried 120 tons of sand pretty high up on the ship. So we wrote that up again and sent it in. We never heard about it from the "Bureau of Destruction and Despair" again.

Paul Stillwell: So you got to keep your range finder?

Admiral Gayler: We got to keep our range finder. Isn't that dumb?

Paul Stillwell: It seems so typical of that period to emphasize form over substance.

Admiral Gayler: I wish I felt as confident as you do that that period is over.

Paul Stillwell: Well, I'm speaking specifically of that. There was great emphasis in ship handling—turning exactly in the wake of the ship ahead, whether that had any combat value or not.

Admiral Gayler: Oh yes, we had to do it very precisely. Certainly the ability to steam in formation and to maneuver on signal to do what the admiral wanted to do had combat value. Whether the extreme precision to five or ten yards had or not, I don't know. I rather doubt it. But that was a big thing, yes. You stood up there with a so-called stadimeter, which was a special kind of coincidence range finder, taking sights all the time. You had to make sure you weren't 20 yards ahead or 20 yards astern of your assigned station.

Many years later, when I was captain of the *Ranger*, I was able to use that sort of technique to get in there and operate with the destroyers. We had maneuvers as if I were one more destroyer. To the astonishment of the destroyer skippers, why, we were right in there all the time.

Paul Stillwell: Was the *Ranger* maneuverable enough?

Admiral Gayler: Oh, yes, the *Ranger* is a very high-powered ship. You had to compensate a little bit for her mass. You had to give a little extra horsepower on acceleration to take off a little sooner, but give or take that, she could turn with the destroyers. She could outrun the destroyers we had.

Paul Stillwell: Did the German range finder you had enable you to shoot better than your counterparts in other battleships?

Admiral Gayler: We had what was considered then the way to do it. We plotted the range line, and we had the coincidence range finders too, but the stereo range finder line was always far more consistent. The coincidence ranges were jumping all over the place. The stereo was clearly better. I don't know why we never built any, except possibly for the timing. Radar first came into the fleet in about 1940, as I recall, and this was '36. I guess there really wasn't time to get into that before radar superseded it.

Paul Stillwell: Was aerial spotting the primary means of knowing how well you did?

Admiral Gayler: Yes, yes. And, of course, we flew floatplanes, SOC-1s and SOC-3s, as I recall, which were biplanes on single floats.* We'd bat them off the catapult on top of number-three turret, my turret, with a gunpowder charge. It was violent as hell. The first flight I ever had off the ship was in the back seat of one of those with Lieutenant Bill Gentner at the controls.† We non-flying ensigns who wanted to go up as observers signed up on a list. My turn came up in the middle of the night. So there I was, climbing up into this vibrating thing in the dark and being violently batted off the catapult behind this guy that I hoped knew what he was doing.

Of course, you know how we recovered those floatplanes. The battleships would make a turn, each creating a slick, which lasted I don't think more than about a minute. The slick didn't take care of the swells, but at least it took care of the smaller waves. Then each one of the floatplanes would land in the slick, taxi up, and be hooked on like a lifeboat. It was a pretty sporty business, but it worked all right. They were called Cast recoveries.‡

Paul Stillwell: One account was by Jimmy Thach, who said he blacked out temporarily as he went off the catapult.§ Did you experience that?

Admiral Gayler: No.

Paul Stillwell: Apparently the force was so overwhelming and so sudden that Thach did.

Admiral Gayler: I don't really remember those catapults very well, except they were very violent and very short compared to the ones on the carriers, the steam cats, where

---

* The Curtiss-built SOC Seagull was a biplane that first entered fleet squadrons in 1935, primarily in a floatplane version to perform observation and scouting missions for battleships and cruisers. It served through World War II. The SOC-1 version was 31 feet long, had a wingspan of 36 feet, gross weight of 5,437 pounds, and maximum speed of 165 miles an hour. It was armed with two .30-caliber machine guns.
† Lieutenant William E. Gentner, Jr., USN. Later, as a vice admiral, Gentner commanded the Sixth Fleet, 1963-64.
‡ "Cast" was the word used for the letter C in the phonetic alphabet of the period.
§ This is in the Naval Institute oral history of Admiral John S. Thach, USN (Ret.), about his time as a floatplane pilot in the light cruiser *Cincinnati* (CL-6) in the late 1930s.

you were just plastered back into your seat. You can't do anything until the end of the ride, and then you take charge and fly off with the airplane.

Paul Stillwell: Did you stand bridge watches in the *Maryland*?

Admiral Gayler: Oh, yes.

Paul Stillwell: What do you recall from those?

Admiral Gayler: It gets a little blurry now between the bridge watches I stood on midshipman cruises and as a junior ensign as officer of the deck, and then as a jaygee, when I was officer of the deck in destroyers.* But you know the scene, responsibility for the navigation and the inner working of the ship, and all the rest of it.

Paul Stillwell: Having been in ships that did have radar as a matter of course, how was it to operate in those ships with no radar in low visibility?

Admiral Gayler: Of course, we didn't know what we were missing. We used to keep formation with fog buoys. Each ship would trail a buoy astern, and you were close enough so that you could usually see it, and you'd take position on the buoy instead of on the ship ahead, which you couldn't see. That was a useful thing to do.

Paul Stillwell: Did you have a sense then of tactical development, or were you still too much from the worm's-eye view?

Admiral Gayler: No, I thought of tactics all the time. In fact, most of us did. We'd sit around the JO mess and talk about how to do this and how to do that—always an improvement on how we were actually doing it, of course. I think we were all tacticians at heart in those days.

---

* Jaygee—lieutenant (junior grade).

Paul Stillwell: Well, there were no really startling developments during that period. It was pretty much keeping on with what had been. Radar introduced the need for different things.

Admiral Gayler: The rate of change was not high. No, I think it'd be fair to say there were no startling developments. The naval theory of the day was that of the fleet in being. The decisive encounter was to be between the battle lines. The destroyers were ancillary to that. The aircraft were very much ancillary to that. Even the very terminology—Aircraft Scouting Force—relegated aircraft to scouting function.

Paul Stillwell: In your junior officer mess discussions, how much did current affairs and the international political situation get involved?

Admiral Gayler: Quite a bit. We were interested in politics. I thought, with some hubris, that our particular junior officers' mess was full of some pretty exceptional people. Yes, we were interested. And I think we knew, to a man, that war with Japan was coming.

Paul Stillwell: Who were some of these exceptional individuals that might be worthy of note?

Admiral Gayler: Well, Jesse Gay is one of them. Roscoe Dillen, Arthur Purdy, Tom Brown.[*]

Paul Stillwell: One junior officer from the class of '36 who was there later became a Japanese language specialist—Gilven Slonim.[†]

Admiral Gayler: Oh yes, Gil. He was a little apart. This is not a criticism. You know how cliquish young people are. He was a little apart from the rest of us. He was subject

---

[*] Ensign Roscoe F. Dillen, Jr., USN; Ensign Arthur M. Purdy, USN; Ensign Thomas A. Brown, USN.
[†] Ensign Gilven M. Slonim, USN.

to seasickness, poor guy, and we used to kid him about it: "Up anchor, down Slonim." After retirement he got a doctorate and writes extensively on politico-military affairs; we correspond. He is very sea power-oriented. I have a somewhat more unified perception.

Paul Stillwell: Another Japanese language officer who was in the ship at that time was Lieutenant Redfield Mason. Do you recall him?

Admiral Gayler: "Rosie." Yes, I do. He was a little tough on us JOs, as I recall. From the worm's-eye point of view, he was a little hard to get along with. I don't really remember him very well.

Paul Stillwell: Do you have any memories of Roscoe Hillenkoetter from that time in the *Maryland*?

Admiral Gayler: Yes, I remember him as a very likable officer, always easy to get along with. I also knew his family quite well, mostly through my sister.

Paul Stillwell: How much of a social life off the ship did junior officers have with officers at his level?

Admiral Gayler: Well, they were very good about it. They used to have sort of soirees. Captain and Mrs. Davis would have parties and invite us all. Then various of the senior officers would have you in for a family dinner occasionally, that sort of thing. I remember a few that were aloof, but not many. It was a pretty happy ship.

Paul Stillwell: Did the annual fleet problems contribute usefully to preparation for war, in your estimation?

Admiral Gayler: Well, they were certainly a great improvement over not having them. Looked at in retrospect, they were a little stilted, a little artificial. They were not what hindsight says in all respects we should have been practicing at. But yes, I think they were useful.

Paul Stillwell: Did submarines have much role in the fleet thinking of that period?

Admiral Gayler: I can't tell you. I never had anything to do with them until I got into the destroyer Navy. Then, of course, we were very much concerned with them. I think the attitude in the battleships was that they would zigzag; other than that, let the destroyers take care of the problem. We weren't too much worried about submarines. I can't recall any exercises in which the battleships paid any attention to anything except other battleships—not to air and not to submarines.

Paul Stillwell: Did you give to any thought to becoming a submariner yourself?

Admiral Gayler: No, not really. I think I might well have if I had not gone into aviation. I went in aviation for lots of reasons, not all of which had to do with flying, but had to do with responsibility at an early age and that sort of thing—plus pay!

Paul Stillwell: Did you find that you didn't get enough of a challenge in the battleship Navy as far as responsibility?

Admiral Gayler: I think I was ready to move on. Pretty static society, actually.

Paul Stillwell: Is there anything to say about the ports you visited, other ships you worked with?

Admiral Gayler: Well, we used to go up and down the West Coast. It's almost impossible to reconstruct the social atmosphere. Every time we went into a port, the entire city would turn out, even big cities like San Francisco. We'd be guests of the city, and the debs would send invitations to the officers, and the men would be entertained, and they'd declare Fleet Week and celebrations, and visitors all over the place. It was pretty nice.

Paul Stillwell: The armed forces were placed much more on a pedestal then in society.

Admiral Gayler: I think they were, yes. For one thing, we weren't anything like so big as we are now. I don't have the statistics at hand, but I think the peacetime armed services couldn't have aggregated more than a couple of hundred thousand at the outside. There just weren't that many of us, which made a difference, and then there was a social cachet about being a naval officer that was not inconsiderable. You were automatically of a social elite wherever you went. Not like it is now.

Paul Stillwell: Wasn't there more of a perception that a naval officer, let's say, was a completely honorable person, and his word was his bond, and that sort of thing?

Admiral Gayler: I think that's true, yes. I think that's true. And there was a good deal of discipline about that too. I recall one officer who was behind on his rent bill or something. The skipper really laid it into him on that. He took an interest in the reputation of his officers.

Paul Stillwell: Perhaps it's a disadvantage that the outside world was so unquestioning, that this status quo just kept perpetuating itself to the point of being unprepared when the war came.

Admiral Gayler: I don't know that I buy either one of your theses. I don't think it had an awful lot to do with military preparedness one way or the other. Spit and polish has some disadvantages, perhaps, but it also has some military advantages—I mean some real ones. When you talk of real leaders like Napoleon, Rommel, or Nelson, nobody would accuse them of not being combat-oriented.* They understood the value of it and insisted on it. So I don't think I buy that premise, that it had a lot to do, adversely, with readiness.

Paul Stillwell: I was thinking more in terms of the idea that the battleship was going to continue to be the ultimate arbiter. That seemed to go unquestioned.

Admiral Gayler: That's a different thing from this business of prestige and whatnot that we were talking about. I think that was just a failure of imagination. Also, when an officer has spent his career mastering one technology and then becomes a very senior person, he'd have to be a little bit more than human if he didn't have some reluctance to give away that and enter another technology that people vastly junior to him were the masters of. That was the problem with the battleships and the aviation. We're seeing other examples of that now. One is the difficulty that many senior people have entering into the world of information processing, which is going to be dominant. It is already, except we don't fully realize it.

Paul Stillwell: Well, that is inevitably going to be a problem always—that the senior officers have grown up in a less developed situation.

Admiral Gayler: Yes, by definition. I think, however, that it can be taken care of by a conscious effort of will. The way that I like to express it is that you should not identify yourself too much with a particular hardware. You may be expert in it, but you shouldn't be sentimental about it. It's very easy to be sentimental about destroyers, but I don't think we should build destroyers.

Paul Stillwell: While we're on that topic, why not?

---

* Napoleon Bonaparte, also known was Napoleon I, was a military leader who served as Emperor of France from 1804 to 1815. Erwin Rommel, known as "The Desert Fox" was a German field marshal in World War II, forced by Hitler to commit suicide in 1944. Lord Horatio Viscount Nelson (1758-1805), British naval hero of the Battle of Cape St. Vincent, 1797, Battle of the Nile, 1798, Trafalgar, 1805.

Admiral Gayler: Because they are thin-skinned, because they are not capable of sea keeping in heavy weather. Because they are inherently noisy, and inherently at a disadvantage with respect to submarines. Because of the fact that a submarine can choose his acoustic environment, and a destroyer cannot. Because at least the way we now design them, they are primarily dependent on high-power radar emanations, and the radar is always a better beacon than it is a detection device, by the laws of physics. Because they are becoming enormously expensive in a way that is not at all consistent with their vulnerability. All these reasons.

Paul Stillwell: How would you alternatively fulfill the missions that destroyers do?

Admiral Gayler: With submarines, long-range, high-performance air, and space surveillance. Space surveillance is going to be better than anybody imagines.

Paul Stillwell: Do you rule out the value of naval gunfire?

Admiral Gayler: Except in a very limited role of the smaller caliber weapons in fire support for amphibious landings. I think amphibious landings won't occupy the dominant position. They will still be important but won't occupy as significant a role as vertical envelopment will. Other than that, yes, I think they're superseded. After all, the range is limited, the accuracy is limited. We have missiles that will fly very much farther and very much more accurately. We are very reluctantly, very conservatively moving into the missile age in the Navy. We have not yet appreciated the fact that it's better to have weapons that hit than weapons that miss.

Paul Stillwell: You mentioned the value of spit and polish. Could you articulate that?

Admiral Gayler: It's a part of a pride of outfit, and the pride of outfit is a morale matter that has extraordinary military value. It generates that camaraderie which makes people do things for their outfit, and for the people to the right and left of them, which they might not otherwise do by themselves or for themselves. It generates a spirit of getting the job done—perfection, if you will. If you teach true perfection in nonessentials like ensuring square corners when making a bunk, that carries over to a habit of mind which says, "I won't get 99% of those things, I'll get 100% of them." It's also a matter of self-respect and the drive of people, particularly young people, to be part of an elite. It's a very powerful drive. That's really the reason I went into naval aviation. I heard it was very tough, and that's why I wanted to do it. Other examples are the Marines, Seabees, paratroopers, and attack submarines.

Paul Stillwell: Would you concede that such an approach has disadvantages if carried to ridiculous extremes?

Admiral Gayler: The way you phrase the question answers itself. If something is ridiculous, you have to concede that it isn't a good idea. I don't think I had any experience all the long time that I spent in the Navy with what I would call spit and polish to ridiculous extremes. I thought Bud Zumwalt made a mistake in relaxing as much and as fast as he did.* I'm a supporter of his. I supported him then, in public, but I didn't see much advantage to letting sailors have sloppy-looking hair and beards and all that kind of stuff, putting everybody in a chief's cap.† I'm glad we've got them back in sailors' hats now.

Paul Stillwell: Anything else to wrap up your days in the *Maryland*?

Admiral Gayler: Well, I was an engineer for a while. I had forgotten about that. That was an electric-drive ship, of course. I was fascinated by the then still fairly new technology of handling the heavy currents and the big switching operators and whatnot. It would all look very antediluvian now, but it was very impressive in those days.

---

* Admiral Elmo R. Zumwalt, Jr., USN, was Chief of Naval Operations, 1970-74. His office issued a series of policy directives that attempted to deal with such issues as enlisted rights and privileges, equal opportunity, and Navy families. Junior personnel viewed them much more favorably than did their seniors. See *U.S. Naval Institute Proceedings*, May 1971, pages 291-298.
† On 14 June 1971 Admiral Zumwalt announced that enlisted men in the pay grades of E-6 and below would be converting over a period of time to a more officer-like blue uniform. Included would be jacket, tie, white shirt, creased trousers, and a combination cap with a visor, similar to that worn by chief petty officers.

ADM Noel A. M. Gayler, Interview #2 (11/4/83) – Page 54

Thought to have enormous advantages. Actually, I don't think it did. It was very heavy, of course, for the most part. It was good for maneuvering, but that's about it.

Paul Stillwell: Fuel economy was a great concern at that time. Did you get involved in that?

Admiral Gayler: No, I don't think so. I don't remember.

Paul Stillwell: Did you have a flag officer on board during that time?

Admiral Gayler: Rather rarely. We were the relief flagship. I don't remember any of the flag officers. I mentioned before that when I was a communicator, I used to use the vacant admiral's cabin and his safes to stow away all my codes and go lock myself up in there and study the codes.

Paul Stillwell: Was that considered a misfortune to have a flag officer embarked?

Admiral Gayler: It didn't make much difference to me, but I'm sure the captain didn't like it much. Maybe I'm generalizing from my own experiences, although I had one flag officer embarked with me when I was captain of the *Ranger* who was just marvelous, Francis Foley.[*] He lives down in Annapolis there.[†] But I had a couple of others who were "nervous Nellies," and that was just really dreadful to live with.

Paul Stillwell: Well, in 1938, then, you moved on the USS *Maury*.

Admiral Gayler: She was a brand-new ship of a brand-new class.[‡] There were only four

---
[*] Rear Admiral Francis D. Foley, USN, was Commander Carrier Division One, 1960-61. Admiral Foley's oral history is in the Naval Institute collection.
[†] Admiral Foley died in 1999.
[‡] USS *Maury* (DD-401) was commissioned 5 August 1938. She had a standard displacement of 1,500 tons, was 341 feet long, and 36 feet in the beam. Her design speed was 38.5 knots. She was armed with four 5-inch guns and 16 torpedo tubes.

of them built.* They were a nominal 1,500 tons, and they were the first in the fleet with what was then the very high-pressure steam.† The propulsion plant was a marvelous job of engineering. I went to her as assistant engineer when she was fitting out in San Francisco, and so I was involved in the final buttoning-up and all the sea trials. The trials were held off San Francisco in cold, still water. Of course, cold water makes a difference, because you've got a better vacuum on the turbines and the still water helps for obvious reasons. Under those ideal conditions, she made 42 knots. We haven't built ships like that since then.‡

I remember that one part of the trials was to back on the backing turbines for four hours straight. She made 24 knots backing. It was spectacular. The *Maury* had a sort of a square stern, and it produced this wall of water way up above you. It stayed there like a sort of permanent waterfall as she backed, with the rudder slamming from one side to the other. It really put her through the paces, marvelous ship in engineering. I'd say she had a fleet speed of 38 easily. She had 16 torpedo tubes and four 5-inch guns. I don't know why the hell we have so much trouble putting any armament on 9,000-ton ships like we do now. But they were some ships. There were only four of them built; *McCall* was our buddy ship.

Paul Stillwell: What were your duties then as engineer? Was this a step up in responsibility?

Admiral Gayler: On the trials I was the fellow who had to work up the developed horsepower. We had an elaborate system of strain gauges on the shafts. She had a nominal 50,000 horsepower, as I recall. We figured out we were making 62,000 or something like that on the trials. I hadn't had so much fun until they got the *Ranger* up to full power one night.

---

* The sister ships in the *Gridley* class were the *Gridley* (DD-380), *Craven* (DD-382), *McCall* (DD-400), and *Maury* (DD-401). All were built at the Bethlehem Steel shipyard in San Francisco.
† The steam pressure in the plant was 565 pounds per square inch and the temperature 700 degrees Fahrenheit.
‡ Other conditions that contributed to the high speed were the ship's clean bottom and light load. Under normal service conditions, the speed was reduced a few knots.

Paul Stillwell: That's a considerable horsepower-to-displacement ratio, which explains the speed.

Admiral Gayler: Yes, and she had a clean bottom too. A beautifully built ship, beautifully built ship. A wonderful job of construction.

Paul Stillwell: The captain of the *Maury* was Lieutenant Commander E. M. Thompson.[*] What do you remember of him?

Admiral Gayler: I thought he was a terrific ship handler and a very good skipper. He was, unfortunately, very overweight. He was known as "Fats." But apart from that and the fact that he liked the bottle when he was ashore, why, he was great. He was a good captain. I liked him.

Paul Stillwell: He was the executive officer of the USS *Massachusetts* at the Battle of Casablanca in '42, and said the captain let him do the ship handling because he was so good at it.[†]

Admiral Gayler: Yes, he was very good at it. He was a good officer to learn the destroyer maneuvers under.

Paul Stillwell: Were you a good ship handler in destroyers?

Admiral Gayler: Yes, partly because I'd had boats all my life.

Paul Stillwell: Do you think that was useful for you later when you came into carrier experience?

---

[*] Lieutenant Commander Edward M. Thompson, USN.
[†] Allied forces invaded Casablanca in French Morocco in November 1942. The French forces in the port resisted, so American ships bombarded the port.

Admiral Gayler: Oh, yes. Of course, I had a small diesel ship before I had a carrier, which also was useful in getting a hand back in. But I did a lot of study, too, about ship handling. I was determined I was going to handle the ship myself and not be a prisoner of tugs and pilots and all that kind of stuff. Later on, after my first couple of months on the *Ranger*, I never had any tugs or pilots, which was not solely a vanity. It was really a matter of war-readiness. I didn't want to be in a position where I would be handicapped if I couldn't find a tug, and all of a sudden we had to sortie and that kind of stuff.

Paul Stillwell: This is one disadvantage of the current system, where officers go directly from commissioning to flight school and don't get to serve junior officer experience in surface ships that you had.

Admiral Gayler: I think that's true. On the other hand, they get longer useful careers as aviators, so it probably balances out.

Paul Stillwell: And not everybody is going to become a carrier skipper either.

Admiral Gayler: That's right.

Paul Stillwell: How was Thompson in terms of leadership qualities?

Admiral Gayler: I thought he was fine. He used to be on my neck all the time, but I probably had it coming to me.

Paul Stillwell: You said one of the reasons was that you didn't get your logs written soon enough.

Admiral Gayler: Exactly.

Paul Stillwell: What kind of adjustment did you have to make to go from a ship with dozens of officers in the wardroom to fewer than a dozen?

Admiral Gayler: Not very much, because, you see, I went from the JO mess to there. I don't know precisely what you mean by adjustment, but no sweat.

Paul Stillwell: Well, sometimes there's a safety-in-numbers concept that doesn't apply in the destroyer Navy. Each man certainly has to pull his own weight.

Admiral Gayler: I see what you mean. No, I didn't have any problem with that. It's much easier to be responsible for something than not to be. It's much easier to be in charge than to be an assistant. It's much easier to be an executive than to be an adviser. So anytime you've got a chance, why, you move that way.

Paul Stillwell: In terms of spit and polish, how would you compare the destroyers with the battleships?

Admiral Gayler: Not much different. We were not the grungy Navy; we were not the oil-smeared, dirty-dungaree Navy by a long shot. We kept a pretty smart ship.

Paul Stillwell: Was there any tendency to sort of look down on the four-pipers at that point?

Admiral Gayler: We didn't have any contact with them. There weren't any four-pipers around. Maybe there were with some of the old-timers.

Paul Stillwell: Was there curiosity about these new gold-platers as a considerable technological advance on the part of old-timers?[*]

Admiral Gayler: I simply don't remember being in contact with any veterans of the four-piper Navy. I'm sure there were some, but didn't get on that much. We were very proud of the ship. She was good.

---

[*] The first of the "gold-platers," the modern destroyers designed in the 1930s, was the USS *Farragut* (DD-348), commissioned 18 June 1934. They replaced the old four-pipers as the front-line destroyers in the U.S. Fleet.

Paul Stillwell: In what ways was she good? You've mentioned gunnery.

Admiral Gayler: Well, she was a marvelous sea boat, very maneuverable, very high-powered, as you pointed out, very fast, well arranged, good living accommodations for men and officers. It was a damn good design, that ship—better than the subsequent ones, I thought.

Paul Stillwell: The *Sims* class had a little problem with top-heaviness. Did you encounter any stability problems?

Admiral Gayler: No, she was okay in stability. She was not stiff, but she was not a roller either. She was just about right the way we had her. I suppose they got her loaded down later on. Ships grow in weight, you know, especially topside weight.

Paul Stillwell: What do you remember about the ship's operations once the engineering trials were completed?

Admiral Gayler: I was a watch-stander when we took a shakedown cruise to Samoa and then to Tahiti. I can remember I was the junior officer on the ship, so I always got the midwatch, every night. As I recall, we were 12 days on the passage from Hawaii to Samoa, steaming along at 15 knots. There was nothing around, nothing going on, the ship just rolling: roll, roll, roll, roll. I got so goddamned tired of hanging on. There was nothing to do about it.

Then we got to Samoa, and I found it extraordinarily interesting, because 40 years before that, almost to the day, my father had been out there building a coaling station. One day the ship went over to an outlying group of islands called the Manua group. The old chief, Tanumafili I, had died the year before, and he had just been succeeded by a new one, who was Tanumafili II.* Tanumafili I had been a friend of my father's. Since I

---

* The Samoan head of state, known as the Malietoa, was Tanumafili I from 1898 until his death in 1939. He was then succeeded by Tanumafili II, who reigned until he died in 2007 at the age of 94.

was the junior officer in the ship, I was always the boarding officer. When I went ashore, I saw my dad's picture under the palm in the chief's *fale*, his round hut.

Tanumafili the younger was an extraordinary figure. Samoans are very big, and this guy was gigantic. I suppose he was 6-8 and 290, something like that. He was big, with legs like coconut palms. He greeted me in a checked sports jacket, not entirely unlike the one you're wearing, a lava-lava made of the same material, and bare feet that were elephantine, and a little garland of flowers around one ankle. But this guy had graduated from the University of California, so we had a great time talking.

Later on I was sent over to pick up a fugitive. He was an American, a long-term expatriate, and the *Maury* was handy for taking him. He was on a tiny little atoll called Swains Island. You know how the atolls are formed at the peak of a subterranean volcano, and the coral makes a ring around them. This was a classic one, absolutely circular, with a lagoon in the middle. I remember the ship stood off the atoll, because there was no place to anchor. It was 1,200 fathoms deep about a mile away from the beach. I went ashore in one of their outrigger canoes to pick up this fugitive who had knifed a man in a brawl in Pago Pago, Samoa. Not only did he come forward willingly, but the local people greeted me. They laid out the braided mats, and we had a ceremony of greeting with kava. Kava is the most horrible stuff—sort of milky and slightly narcotic. When you swallow it, you can feel it sort of paralyzing the back of your throat as it goes down. They use that for ceremonial purposes.

From the reception I received, you'd have thought that I was a long-lost brother instead of someone coming in there to take this guy back to justice. I had gone in with trading material, including a self-sharpening razor they called a Rolls Razor. I thought that and a few other gewgaws would be very attractive to some native. Just as an afterthought, I threw in three or four skivvy shirts. The natives weren't the least interested in anything else, but the skivvy shirts were real prizes. So I traded them off for the lahala mat, coral "jewelry," and stuff like that while I was in there. It was a very pleasant little visit.

There were about 150 people on that little atoll—men, women, and children. They were all half-British, because the place had been settled originally by an English sailor named Swain and three or four Samoan women.

Paul Stillwell: How would you explain the warmth of the reception you received?

Admiral Gayler: It was cultural with them. And the place was unspoiled. I don't know what Samoa is like now, but the tradition of friendliness to strangers was very pronounced, and they liked Americans. They'd had very good treatment from us.

During that shakedown we also went to New Zealand, which was very interesting. This was in the years immediately before World War II. The New Zealanders were extremely anxious about their position, their vulnerability with respect to Japan. So we were there as a single American ship. They sent a Cabinet officer down to the dock to greet us when we came in, and they provided a car and driver for each officer in the wardroom, all six of us. Can you imagine? When you went ashore, people would stop you and want you to come home and meet their daughters.

In those days the New Zealanders were much more English than the English, the county English. They went in for marvelous tea parties, with the ladies in great, big round hats. I remember them celebrating Guy Fawkes Day, which, of course, they celebrate with fireworks like we celebrate the Fourth of July. This was one of those decorous parties with the ladies in white hats and chiffon dresses. Somebody dropped a match into the box of fireworks, and these things started going off in all directions. People were going into the hedges. It made for a very lively party after that.

I remember being taken around to Rotorua. That was the first time we had seen Rotorua and the Maoris there. Of course, the Maoris are precisely the same race as the Hawaiians, so they were not unfamiliar to me, but they were much less modernized.

Paul Stillwell: I've heard Australia, during about that period, characterized as very friendly and outgoing, whereas New Zealand had more of the reserve that one associates with the British. Did you observe that?

Admiral Gayler: I didn't think they were very reserved, other than very British, much more than the Australians. Aussies don't really like Britishers much; they call them Pommies. But the New Zealanders couldn't have been more hospitable.

Paul Stillwell: Do you remember any other trips or operations, other than the one to the South Pacific? What was the routine?

Admiral Gayler: Well, I remember the battle practices very well. With that one exception, the routine was pretty much either stateside or to Hawaii, annual exercises. That one shakedown cruise was before we joined the fleet, actually.

During the rest of my time on the *Maury*, I remember that I got kind of tired of being the junior guy in the wardroom all the time. All the "George" jobs fell to me, but it was all right.*

Paul Stillwell: What sort of "George" jobs?

Admiral Gayler: Oh, shore patrol and a bunch of housekeeping jobs that traditionally devolved to the junior guy. So I was assistant engineer for a while, then I was assistant gunnery.

Then in 1939 they had a problem over on the *Craven*, one of our sister ships.† She needed a gunnery officer, so there I went to take the job. I was very full of myself, because I was a jaygee in what was normally a lieutenant's billet. The *Craven* was at bottom in fleet gunnery, and in one year we brought her up to runner up. We almost took it. The guy who beat us out was Arleigh Burke, skipper of the *Mugford*.‡ He was rough competition.

We would have taken them, except for one night battle practice. I had a marvelous fire controlman by the name of Wade, just a terrific guy. He was the technician, really, but he was so good at everything that I also made him my director operator. And he was very good. We went swimming through all of these practices, getting high scores. In one night battle practice, however, Wade picked up the wrong

---

* "George" is the standard nickname for the junior officer in a Navy ship.
† USS *Craven* (DD-382), a *Gridley*-class destroyer, was commissioned 2 September 1937. She had a displacement of 1,850 tons, was 341 feet long, and 35 feet in the beam. Her design speed was 38.5 knots. She was armed with four 5-inch guns and sixteen 21-inch torpedo tubes. She served throughout World War II and was eventually decommissioned on 19 April 1946.
‡ Lieutenant Commander Arleigh A. Burke, USN, was a top-notch destroyer officer both before and during World War II. From 1955 to 1961 he served as Chief of Naval Operations, the longest tenure for anyone in that office. The guided missile destroyer *Arleigh Burke* (DDG-51) is named in his honor.

target, and the ten seconds that it took us to get him back on the right target was enough to make the difference. He could have killed himself, he was so despondent about it. It was amazing how seriously we took those things.

That night battle practice was something else, because that was also a searchlight operation. You'd come tearing in and pick up the target by searchlight. Of course, time was of the essence. You'd start firing right away, see the splashes, and try to spot him. There was always the subliminal worry that you were going to shoot the tug instead of the target.

The diciest thing in that period before radar came when we were making night torpedo-firing approaches. We'd tear in at 28 or even 30 knots, with the battleships coming the other way at 15. We would be looking and looking. When we made visual contact with the loom of the battleship, we'd light it up with the searchlights, fire off our torpedoes, and wheel and get out of the way. That was a very sporty thing to do.

Sometimes you got pretty damn close when you were closing at a combined speed of more than 40 knots. I don't think, to the best of my knowledge, anybody ever got banged doing it, but sometimes it looked awful close to me. Of course, we carried great big searchlights before the radar days, and all of a sudden from straining your eyes, trying to see the first little loom, to the bright illumination. It was very dramatic.

Paul Stillwell: In the same division with the *Mugford* was the USS Helm, commanded by Lieutenant Commander P. E. McDowell, whom I talked to.[*] He said that even in a line abreast or anything, Burke would always be putting on an extra knot or so, always seeking the advantage.

Admiral Gayler: Yes. I saw Admiral Burke just yesterday at a Golden Eagles lunch. He's an honorary naval aviator, you know, so he was there.

Paul Stillwell: Marvelous fellow.

---

[*] Lieutenant Commander Percival E. McDowell, USN.

Admiral Gayler: Marvelous. Admiral Pride was there too, Frank O'Beirne, and Dutch Duerfeldt.[*] I guess those were the only real old-timers.

Paul Stillwell: I think Admiral Pride is probably senior among all that group.[†]

Admiral Gayler: Yes. He looks fine. He had that same penetrating look. I used to work for him when he was chief of bureau, and I was a fairly young officer, so I remembered that look very well.[‡] [Laughter]

Paul Stillwell: Do you think the annual competition for the battle efficiency "E" was a useful stimulus in the fleet in those years?[§]

Admiral Gayler: Oh yes, I really do. Those exercises did focus attention. Because of the necessity of a fair competition, they were a little stereotyped in the tactical situations, but I thought they were very good. We had this little bound book, the orders for gunnery exercises, known as OGE, which was sort of your bible as to how to do it. When I was on the *Craven*, I found one set of rules that made it possible for you to get an infinite score, because there was a way in which you could get a zero in the denominator. [Laughter]

Paul Stillwell: Unbeatable.

Admiral Gayler: I worked very hard to try to do that. I didn't quite make it but came close. But that was not serious gunnery, of course. It was just fiddling within the rules.

Paul Stillwell: The war in Europe started during this time you were serving in the

---

[*] Admiral Alfred M. Pride, USN (Ret.), whose oral history is in the Naval Institute collection; Vice Admiral Frank O'Beirne, USN (Ret.); Rear Admiral Clifford H. Duerfeldt, USN (Ret.).
[†] Pride was commissioned in 1918, O'Beirne and Duerfeldt in 1926.
[‡] As a rear admiral, Pride served as Chief of the Bureau of Aeronautics from 1 May 1947 to 1 May 1951.
[§] An "E," for excellence, is generally awarded to a ship or component of a ship as a result of top performance in competition with other ships during a given time period.

Craven.* Did this have an effect on the U.S. Navy's operations, to your observation?

Admiral Gayler: All of us junior types were worried to death that Franklin Roosevelt would send everything to the Atlantic and neglect the Pacific, as we were throughout the war.†

Paul Stillwell: Did it heighten an interest in battle readiness, or was there any need to heighten it?

Admiral Gayler: No, I think we were pretty realistic about it, pretty readiness-conscious. We were remarkably up on damage control. There had been a big push by someone; it must have been one of the Chiefs of Naval Operations. It was about the time I first went to battleships, and damage control was the name of the game. There was a tremendous flurry about fixing all the defects in all the compartments. That went on, to my knowledge, until the war started. We received a lot of payoffs, too, although we missed a few things. Losing ships to fire was the one that we missed, like the *Lexington*.‡ She was hit with five torpedoes and three heavy bombs, and still operating aircraft. We lost her in the fire, not because she was sunk. We sank her ourselves.

Paul Stillwell: There was a useful change in doctrine during the war. Instead of sinking heavily damaged ships with your own forces, later an effort was made to save them. Partly that involved control of the seas also. But that was an improvement as the war proceeded.

Admiral Gayler: I wouldn't have called it doctrine; I would have thought it was just a tactical judgment on the spot. I doubt if the *Lexington* could have been saved. I know

---

* World War II began on 1 September 1939, when German ground forces invaded Poland. Two days later Great Britain and France declared war on Germany.
† Franklin D. Roosevelt was President of the United States from 1933 to 1945. He had a great deal of personal interest and was also concerned about the strategic needs involved in a potential two-ocean war.
‡ The carrier *Lexington* (CV-2) was sunk in the Battle of the Coral Sea in May 1942. Gayler was on board as part of Fighting Three, as he discusses in interview number 3.

the story of the *Franklin*.* In fact, I saw her just after she came in, and you wouldn't believe a ship beaten up like that could make it. But the *Lexington* was enormously on fire, just unbelievably. Everything in the ship was burning. I don't think we could have saved her. We tried to, but the whole damn ship became uninhabitable, except for a comparatively small space all the way forward and all the way aft. Gasoline fires were burning furiously, torpedo warheads cooking away.

Paul Stillwell: I'm not suggesting her as the prime example. The *Wasp* maybe would be a better example.†

Admiral Gayler: Yes, maybe so.

Paul Stillwell: How did your interest develop in becoming an aviator?

Admiral Gayler: I remember the *Craven* being anchored in San Diego harbor one day, and of all things I was watching the patrol planes come in and make landings and take off again. I was just idly thinking, "You know, there's no real reason why I can't do that." I was rather a late starter. I had been five years in the fleet before I went to Pensacola—three years in battleships and two years in destroyers—but I went down and wrote the letter of application. The skipper was nice enough to try to talk me out of flying, but then he did approve my application.

Paul Stillwell: I think that was an obligation on the part of the gun clubbers, wasn't it?

Admiral Gayler: Maybe so. Well, I think frankly he knew he had a good gunnery officer and didn't know what the next guy would be like. I was pretty proud of being gunnery officer on that ship. We did very well, really.

---

* The carrier *Franklin* (CV-13) was hit by bombs near Japan in March 1945, resulting in great damage and loss of life. After her fires were extinguished, she was able to return to the United States under her own power, though she never did go back into active service.
† USS *Wasp* (CV-7) was damaged by Japanese submarine torpedoes while operating near the Solomon Islands in September 1942. She was sunk by torpedoes from a U.S. destroyer to keep her from falling into enemy hands.

Paul Stillwell: Then you took your flight training at Pensacola. Could you describe that?

Admiral Gayler: In those days, the net was full of sea stories about how hard Pensacola was, how very difficult it was to get through there, how the students were hazed by the instructors, and all of that. Really, gossip was full of all that. So I arrived there on a very hot afternoon in March 1940 without any real idea of what in the world was going to go on. I reported in and was assigned a billet in one of the new BOQs.* It turned out that because I had been in the fleet for five years, I was very senior, compared to the rest of the people going through flight training. I think I was next to the senior officer in the place as a student.

While I was unpacking my stuff, in came this funny little figure in a lieutenant commander's khaki uniform. He was not more than 5-4, I guess, nearly bald, big nose, and a waxed mustache with points. He had a marvelous, energetic air. He came in and said, "I'm your new roommate." I've always been glad that I was polite, because I welcomed him, and I thought to myself, "Jesus Christ, who is this guy?" Well, it turned out that it was Luis de Florez, the father of special devices, and one of the men that I have always thought of as one of the real greats. He was a renaissance man in his extraordinary interest and knowledge in science, in culture, psychology, in training, particularly because he had vision. He really had vision.†

He was a reserve lieutenant commander, and he'd been flying since 1912. When he was a young man, he was in England during World War I, and he was so damn good, he was shortly in charge, essentially, of the British toluene production, the chemical process. The significance of toluene won't escape you: TNT—trinitrotoluene. He then spent years as sort of an inventor and really is the man who invented continuous-process oil refining. He put together the idea of continuous-process instruments instead of batch oil refining. He held a lot of patents there. He flew a great deal, was a devoted aviator. He designed and built and patented a lot of aviation instruments, always had an airplane or two that he had of his own.

---

* BOQ—bachelor officers' quarters.
† The Admiral Luis de Florez Flight Safety Award, presented since 1966, recognizes "outstanding individual contributions to aviation safety, through basic design, device or practice."

On this occasion, although he had already been flying for many years, he wanted to become a designated naval aviator. So he wanted to go through the flight-training program, from primary right on through. He put in to the dear old Bureau of Navigation, as it was then, for flight training.* Of course, they gave him the horselaugh. But what they didn't know was that his roommate at MIT, which he graduated from as an engineer, was a man named Charles Edison, who was then Secretary of the Navy.† So pretty soon he showed up in his negative-stagger Beechcraft with his orders to go through flight training.‡ He and I were the two senior officers there, so we bunked together. I have been so grateful for that chance ever since. He really was wonderful.

Paul Stillwell: What was he like?

Admiral Gayler: Oh, he was interesting, he was funny, he was one of the world's best raconteurs, but he also was one of the most interesting people to talk to seriously. I remember sitting on the sand at the beach in Pensacola when we were halfway through the training. He started asking me about what we were going to do when war came for naval aviators, how were we going to get enough. I thought, "Well, we'll have to build more training bases, and do that kind of stuff."

I remember him saying, "No, no, I don't think so. I think we're going to have to do more than that. I think we're going to have to find some new way to train." And that was the beginning of the idea of the special training devices. The Link trainer was in existence, but that was about the only thing.§

He went to England during the war, wrote a report to the Secretary of the Navy on the way the English were training fighter pilots. They had a lot of cobbled-up, rudimentary training machines that they had just built under the flail of war necessity. He

---

* Prior to World War II, assignments of naval officers were made by the Bureau of Navigation. On 13 May 1942, it became the Bureau of Naval Personnel (BuPers), a title that better described its function.
† Massachusetts Institute of Technology. Charles Edison, son of inventor Thomas Edison, served as Secretary of the Navy from 2 January 1940 to 24 June 1940.
‡ Negative stagger was an unusual arrangement for a biplane in that the lower wing was ahead of the upper one.
§ Edwin A. Link, Jr. (1904-1981) was a pioneer in the field of designing flight simulators. He built his first pilot trainer in 1929 to cut down on training costs and improve flight instruction. He served as chairman of the board and president of Link Aviation, Inc., of Binghamton, New York.

put that all together in a report, and he was put in charge of the business. He took over a garage at 610 H Street here in Washington, and made that a special devices center. He built all the training devices, the bombing trainers for the Army Air Forces, and all of the specialized trainers for the Navy.

He finally branched out into portable antiaircraft guns, which he personally took out to the fleet to try to sell. Of course, the Bureau of Ordnance was just furious that he was infringing on them. He had a very smart idea; he was an inventor. It was a barrel-sized thing with twin .50-caliber machine guns, power-controlled with a lead-computing gyroscopic sight, then a very new innovation. The power head was the power head of an outboard motor. So the whole damn thing was self-contained in this tub. You could put it on any old ship—tanker or anyplace where you had a field of fire. For the day, it was a very formidable short-range antiaircraft gun. He almost literally took them out under his arm. He was friends with all the senior people, and they were very enthusiastic about it in the fleet. But, of course, the Bureau of Ordnance dragged their feet, and they never built any. He was a marvelous man. Anyway, he was my roommate.

Paul Stillwell: Most men of vision aren't as practical as you've depicted him.

Admiral Gayler: Very practical and a marvelous talent for making friends. He knew everybody, and he didn't have an awful lot of respect for channels, and he didn't need to.

Paul Stillwell: Well, not when you know the Secretary of the Navy.

Admiral Gayler: Not only that, but he knew a lot of people. He was really very good. And great fun. Later, when I was associated with him in special devices, I would go with him when he went to the Congress to testify on money bills. They always shoved money at him. He always came out with more money than he put in for. He was so effective as a salesman. He always had some interesting attraction, and he would show these fascinated congressmen. He had wonderful stories to tell.

Paul Stillwell: What do you recall about the flight instruction itself?

Admiral Gayler: I had an instructor named George Omer, and he was a reserve captain in the Marine Corps.* From my standpoint, he only had two faults—he didn't like regular officers, and he didn't like naval officers. He used to give me a bad time over the gosport.† He would tell me something, and I could make no retort. I just had to take it. But the situation had a useful indirect effect, because it was so miserable riding with him that whenever I had a check ride, I was very relaxed with other instructor pilots. I did fine on the check rides. I can remember Omer's final valedictory to me when I got through primary flight and got out from under his wing. He said, "I don't know why the hell they let you in," or something like that.

Paul Stillwell: How were you in terms of natural aptitude for flying?

Admiral Gayler: I think it came pretty naturally to me. I don't recall ever having any difficulty. I always rather liked it.

Paul Stillwell: Do you see a correlation there between that and athletic ability?

Admiral Gayler: I was never much of an athlete, so in my own case I don't see much correlation. No, as a matter of fact, come to think of it, there was a very famous and very talented athlete in my class, who was a contemporary of mine in fighters, and he wasn't that good. In fact, he pranged a couple of airplanes.

I'll tell you the kind of guy who's not going to be a good flier. I had another classmate who went to Pensacola the same time I did, and he washed out. He stood very high in my class academically, and he was a good officer. When he didn't do well in the flight training, he was called before a board that would determine whether or not he would get another chance. He was explaining to the board that when he put the stick over, he knew that it moved a lever arm which moved the bell crank, which depressed the aileron, and increased the lift on that side of the airplane, but he said he couldn't run

---

* Captain George D. Omer, USMCR.
† The gosport was a flexible one-way speaking tube for communication between different cockpits in an airplane.

through that fast enough. The rest of us would just move it back without much conscious thought. [Laughter]

Paul Stillwell: I talked to Captain Paul Ryan, who was the class of '36, and he said that in trying to land the Yellow Peril, he'd always try to land when he was still 40 feet in the air.* So there are problems that some people, I guess, just had built in.†

Admiral Gayler: I think the mechanical process of flying has very little to do with thinking mechanical, such things as landing it. I've thought about that a great deal. It is a patterned right-brain operation, much like a total Gestalt impression. You learn what sequence of impressions creates good landings, and you do that without much thinking about it.

Paul Stillwell: Just like trying to hit a baseball. If you had to analyze all those steps that are involved, it's in the catcher's mitt before you have a chance.

Admiral Gayler: Exactly. Exactly.

Paul Stillwell: Was there a fair portion of regular officers in your class? The aviation cadet program was going pretty well.

Admiral Gayler: That's right. They were almost all aviation cadets.‡ There were maybe a half a dozen of us regulars in a class of 40. One of them was my wife-to-be's brother. That's how I met her.

---

* "Yellow Peril" was the nickname for the yellow-painted N3N trainer, a biplane equipped with a centerline pontoon. It was 26 feet long, had a wingspan of 34 feet, gross weight of 2,792 pounds, and a top speed of 126 miles per hour.
† Lieutenant Paul B. Ryan, USN, entered flight training about the same time as Gayler. He washed out and subsequently went into submarines.
‡ In the aviation cadet program, which was instituted in 1935, individuals enlisted in the Naval Reserve, then were trained as aviators and sent to the fleet in cadet status until later being commissioned as officers. In 1939 the program was modified so that individuals were commissioned upon successful completion of flight training.

Paul Stillwell: Well, you could go into a little more detail there.

Admiral Gayler: His name was Alexander Groves.[*] He was of the class of '37. I was in '35, and at the Naval Academy the classes that are two years apart are associated on the cruises and so forth. So, generally speaking, you get to know them better than you do the class immediately before you or behind you. We were in the same platoon in the seventh company, and the same squad. So I got to know Sandy Groves quite well, although he was two years behind me. We went to flight school at the same time, because I was retarded.

I had always liked him, and he mentioned that his sister Caroline was going to graduate from college that year. She was going to come down and keep house for him in a little beach house at Pensacola. So we would have a place to swim and all that kind of stuff. I remember thinking, "Well, I think I'll check out Sandy's sister." So, sure enough, I was driving down the road there, and there he was parked at a little gedunk place where we all went to have a gedunk in his open convertible.[†] I zoomed up alongside of him, and there was his sister. I met her then, and we just had our 42nd wedding anniversary yesterday.

But the story has a tragic ending, because he was killed not very long after that.[‡] It was in the Yellow Peril. We flew a V of V's in those days, and the way you broke them up to land was that the leader would push down, and then the two guys would go like that. Sandy was an extraordinary man, very thoughtful, a wonderful officer, but absent-minded. He had told his sister Kay (my wife) once before that he found himself flying without putting his belt on. On this occasion, he had evidently done the same thing. He was flying the student lead in this formation, and when he pushed down, the acceleration bumped him out of the airplane. The chute nearly opened, but it was 400 feet. It didn't have quite enough time, so they found him under his chute.

Paul Stillwell: That was a very graphic demonstration to you that you were getting into a hazardous business. Was that a concern?

---

[*] Lieutenant (junior grade) Alexander Groves, USN.
[†] "Gedunk" is a Navy slang term for refreshments such as candy, sodas, and ice cream.
[‡] Groves was killed 2 August 1940.

Admiral Gayler: I always knew it was hazardous, but I didn't let it bother me. It was just the personal side was all. Sandy's sister went on back home after that, and I didn't see her for a couple of years. I sort of kept track of her. I grabbed her quick and married her when I next saw her. [Laughter]

Paul Stillwell: Did you take sort of a fatalistic attitude as an aviator?

Admiral Gayler: No, not at all. I don't think fatalism has any place in aviation. No, I think I was pretty meticulous about airplanes and about tactics, and about everything else. I had a very useful streak of cowardice when it comes to that. [Laughter] No, I don't believe in fatalism for aviators. That's totally the wrong way to look at it.

Paul Stillwell: I don't think cowardice is a word one associates with someone who has as many Navy crosses as you do.

Admiral Gayler: They're not really representative, you know. Nobody but God will know what everybody did. I lost a good half of my friends in World War II.

Paul Stillwell: If you don't take a fatalistic attitude, do you take it that the people who didn't make it were not as careful as they should have been?

Admiral Gayler: I wouldn't say they weren't as careful. How can I put it? If you're advancing in a field of fire, you may be as careful as the guy next to you, and you may still be the one that gets hit when he doesn't. Now, is that fatalism? That doesn't say you don't duck. It doesn't say that you don't take precautions. That doesn't say that your death can be attributed to carelessness. There are some that can.

There was one very interesting thing that I saw a little bit of toward the end of the war. This involved people who got shot at too much and were not so much careless as tired. They just got so goddamned tired they couldn't be bothered to go around on the suspicion there might be a sniper here. They'd walk through instead and take their chance. But that's a different phenomenon. That's just psychic weariness. Sometimes you see it in aviators too.

Paul Stillwell: There was another syndrome, and this has been described in some submarine skippers. They did so well in avoiding danger that they'd become a little bolder each time, maybe overconfident, and that's what wound up killing them.[*]

Admiral Gayler: Yes.

Paul Stillwell: Did you see that in aviation?

Admiral Gayler: My two war cruises were curiously different. The first one, we were really up against it, most of the time one carrier by ourselves. I think in the Coral Sea Battle, as I recall, we had seven fighters. Four of them we sent to the Japanese, and three of them we used and left back in combat air patrol. I don't want you to take these numbers too seriously. I have not refreshed myself. I might be wrong, but it was something like that. And the Japanese were all over us.

The second war cruise, there weren't enough Japanese to go around. The most dangerous thing was people diving on the same Japanese, as far as air-to-air combat was concerned. But the thing that was terribly dangerous was the flak, because you can't really do much about whether the antiaircraft fire is going to hit you or whether it's going to miss you. On the other hand, if you're mixing it up with a guy in a dogfight, you've got your half of it, and you can do something about it.

I would like to record that I'm doing all of this from memories more than 40 years old. I have not refreshed myself with documents. I may be full of inaccuracies. I'm just telling it as I remember it.

Paul Stillwell: Telling it very well, I should say.

---

[*] This phenomenon is described in the Naval Institute oral history of Captain Slade D. Cutter, USN (Ret.), a Naval Academy classmate of Gayler.

Admiral Gayler: Thank you.

Paul Stillwell: On the subject of aviators and heroism or whatever, the new movie *The Right Stuff* has come out. Tom Wolfe puts forth the thesis that he gathered from astronauts and test pilots that there's sort of a pyramid that people climb.[*] At the very top are those that have this magical quality. When an aviator dies, this theory suggests that he just didn't have "the right stuff." Was there any thought of that in your flying days?

Admiral Gayler: I would characterize that as bullshit. I don't think much of Tom Wolfe. I think he's got a vulgar view of things. I don't think he understands anything about test pilots. I don't like his book. Anybody who can characterize a trip to the moon in terms of an astronaut having to urinate in his suit is too crummy for me. This is not to say that I don't have great respect for Chuck Yeager and all the astronauts and the rest of those people.[†] I'm talking about the writer.

Paul Stillwell: Back to Pensacola, what was the balance between flight training, per se, and ground training, classroom training?

Admiral Gayler: The classroom training occupied a lot of time. I didn't find it awfully useful. I think it probably was to others. What I'm saying is I came off the Naval Academy and five years in the fleet, and the sorts of things they were teaching, like elementary navigation and whatnot, were pretty familiar to me.

Paul Stillwell: Do you think that that gave you an advantage in going through flight school?

---

[*] Thomas K. Wolfe's book *The Right Stuff* (New York: Farrar, Straus, and Giroux, 1979) described the early U.S. astronauts and their origins as military test pilots.
[†] Flying as a military test pilot, Charles E. Yeager became the first man to exceed the speed of sound on 14 October 1947 in X-1 rocket. Because of military security, his feat received no publicity at the time. He didn't become a national celebrity until the publication of Wolfe's book.

Admiral Gayler: As I recall, in flight school, you were evaluated, I would have guessed, about 95% on work in the air. The ground school was just something that was a clear necessity as background and training, but I don't think was used to evaluate people.

Paul Stillwell: Did the regular officers seem to stand out better in the class, as a group, because of their experience?

Admiral Gayler: No, we assimilated remarkably fast. There was something about the atmosphere of being students that knocked off rank and rates effectively. In fact, I can't now remember whether some individuals were regular officers or cadets, as I knew them later on.

Paul Stillwell: What was the social atmosphere during the off-duty periods of that training?

Admiral Gayler: Oh, it was terrific. Lots of attractive young ladies, lots of dances, lots of swims, lots of dates, Florida beaches, high-powered cars, the whole shooting match. A young fellow's dream.

Paul Stillwell: A stereotype is that aviators are more boisterous than other types of naval officers.

Admiral Gayler: Yes, I think it's definitely true.

Paul Stillwell: How would you explain that?

Admiral Gayler: Boisterous isn't quite the right word. I think that aviators tend to be somewhat less pedestrian and somewhat more live-it-up types, like activity, tend more to extroversion, perhaps.

Paul Stillwell: Going back to the kind of Darwinian selection you saw on the antiaircraft gun crews in the *Maryland*, do you think the same thing might apply here—that a certain type of individual goes into aviation?

Admiral Gayler: As far as character traits, yes, I think so. I don't want to overdraw it, but I think so. I don't want to suggest that there aren't a lot of people in the surface Navy that aren't gung-ho too, but yes.

Paul Stillwell: Is a greater willingness to take risks part of that, would you say?

Admiral Gayler: Oh, I think you'd have to say that—objectively, in those days at least. And I think carrier aviation is still a more risky enterprise than being a destroyer sailor.

Paul Stillwell: I think that's pretty commonly accepted.

Admiral Gayler: I wouldn't make too much of it, but I think there's a concatenation of character types.

Paul Stillwell: Were there some wild parties during your Pensacola time?

Admiral Gayler: Not wild in the sense that most people would say wild now, but actually in the dating business and whatnot, we were a pretty straitlaced outfit. At least if there were such parties, I wasn't in on them. There were no orgies; there were none of those kinds of things. Just a straight boy-and-girl sort of thing of the time. This was 1940 college prom-type stuff. The later days when the girls and boys all shacked up together were undreamed of then. We'd have been ostracized.

Paul Stillwell: What was the sequence of planes you went through in learning to fly?

Admiral Gayler: I started out with the Yellow Peril, N3Ns. We were envious of those that had the Stearmans, the N2Ss. The N3Ns were built at the Naval Aircraft Factory.

We felt there were tremendous differences. It was a little heavier and a little bit less maneuverable. Then from that to instrument training in the North American SNJ, a monoplane that the Army called the AT-6.*

From that I went to fighters. I had a hell of a time getting on the fighter list. I was originally on the VP list, in spite of the fact that I had originally gone to flight school because I had been watching the patrol planes.† By the time I was at Pensacola, I decided I wanted fighters. But they were very arbitrary about it. They didn't ask you what you wanted. You just showed up and were assigned. So I went around trying to find a swap, and I couldn't find anybody who wanted to swap with me. I finally offered my car to somebody who would swap. It never really happened, though, because about that time a vacancy did open up. I got on the fighter list.

Paul Stillwell: I don't think too many people would have wanted to go into patrol planes then, would they?

Admiral Gayler: Oh, a lot of people did. A lot of people didn't want fighters. I don't know why, exactly.

Paul Stillwell: Generally, my understanding was that patrol plane duty went to more experienced aviators who had already had single-engine experience. So it was probably unusual to go right into fighters.

Admiral Gayler: You're right. That's the way it had been before. But my particular time was right at that moment of great expansion, because we all knew the war was coming and were starting to shove people through the training programs very fast. So some of those traditional practices went by the board. The main idea that went by the board is that a naval aviator should be totally well rounded in all of these things. That was the beginning of specialization.

---

* The SNJ Texan was a land plane that was a standard trainer through World War II. It had dual seats so the instructor and student could sit in tandem. The plane was 27 feet long, had a wingspan of 42 feet, gross weight of 4,440 pounds, and a top speed of 167 miles per hour.
† The VP or patrol plane community was then represented primarily by the two-engine PBY flying boat.

Paul Stillwell: What do you remember about your fighter training?

Admiral Gayler: The next airplane was what we called the F4B-4, which was a Boeing biplane, stick-and-canvas fighter, a little tiny thing that you practically strapped on your back.* It was extraordinarily lively and maneuverable. The Army Air Corps P-12 was the same airplane. That was my fighter training.

Paul Stillwell: Did you experience a sense of exhilaration from flying a fighter?

Admiral Gayler: Yes, I liked fighters. I liked the whole works. Each one of them was a little different. I may have the sequence wrong. We had some training in TBDs, the old Douglas Devastator, which flew like a nice old carriage.† I think that was it. I never got any formal training in flying boats. We were accelerating, of course. In the old days, of course, you got everything, but I missed that. And I didn't really fly big flying boats until I was a test pilot at Patuxent. I put the R3Y through tests. I now marvel at my temerity, because I didn't know enough about flying big boats to put in your eye, but I did it anyway. [Laughter]

Paul Stillwell: Were you getting tactical training along with flying the airplanes itself?

Admiral Gayler: Not much tactical but lots and lots of gunnery. We were shooting at towed sleeves to develop our marksmanship.

Paul Stillwell: I'm curious how early lessons learned were being incorporated from the war in Europe and the Sino-Japanese War.

---

* Boeing F4B-4 fighters first entered fleet squadrons in 1932, then were replaced by Grumman biplanes in 1938. The F4B-4 was 20 feet long, wingspan of 30 feet, gross weight of 2,750 pounds, and top speed of 176 miles per hour.
† The Douglas TBD Devastator torpedo plane first entered fleet squadrons in 1937. It was 35 feet long, wingspan of 50 feet, gross weight of 10,194 pounds, and top speed of 206 miles per hour. After TBDs were essentially annihilated in the Battle of Midway in June 1942 they were withdrawn from operational service.

Admiral Gayler: I guess it would be fair to say practically none. My impression was that this was the routine in which they'd trained naval aviators since time immemorial and that the incorporation of the lessons learned, if they came at all, must have come much later. My first introduction to real tactics as such was under Jimmy Thach in Fighting Three.*

Paul Stillwell: I was going to mention his name next, because he was certainly on the leading edge of that. He said in his oral history that an intelligence report out of China led him to develop the Thach Weave.†

Admiral Gayler: You see, Jimmy was a very thoughtful guy, a marvelous, marvelous skipper, but he thought about things. That was entirely in character. The rest of us were fat, dumb, and happy compared to him. We were great on gunnery. We got so we could shoot, but tactics was an unknown thing to me until I joined Jimmy Thach's squadron.

Paul Stillwell: Before we put you into VF-3, is there anything else on flight training to cover?

Admiral Gayler: I've probably forgotten something, but I do recall how miserable and unstable the Link trainer was, trying to learn to fly on instruments. The details are of no consequence, but we moved from Pensacola to some other field, and I've even forgotten the name of it, for instrument training. All of that was under the hood in SNJs, as we did in those days. I think that was about it.

Paul Stillwell: Could you describe your first encounter with a carrier and landing on the deck?

---

* Lieutenant John S. Thach, USN, was commanding officer of VF-3. He eventually retired as a four-star admiral; his oral history is in the Naval Institute collection.
† The Thach Weave was a back-and-forth flying maneuver developed shortly before World War II by then-Lieutenant Commander Thach while in command of Fighting Three. It was a means of enabling the F4F Wildcat to counter the better-performing Japanese Zero fighter. Thach's oral history contains an interesting description of how he devised the tactic.

Admiral Gayler: Oh, yes. I reported in to Fighting Three, which was in two tiny little hangars right down by the waterfront in San Diego. They're still there. The squadron was just transitioning from Grumman F3Fs, biplanes, to Brewsters, which were monoplanes.* The Brewster was thought to be a real hot machine. In fact, there was considerable debate in those days whether it was really possible to fly monoplanes off a carrier because of their purportedly adverse stall characteristics. So without further ado, I was in the cockpit of one of these things and learning my trade under Thach in Fighting Three, operating first out of San Diego.

Paul Stillwell: Had you not landed on a carrier before you got to that squadron?

Admiral Gayler: I had not landed on a carrier before I got to the squadron. My first landing was on the *Lexington* in a Brewster. I was a little rough. I got a cut a little bit right of the centerline, picked up the wire, and ended up looking in the muzzle of an 8-inch gun about as far away from me as you are. [Laughter]

Paul Stillwell: For the record, I'd say that's about three feet. [Laughter]

Admiral Gayler: But from then on it went a little better.

Paul Stillwell: It was bound to get better.

Admiral Gayler: Well, in those days they used to say, "There's only two kinds of naval aviators; those that had been in the fence [the barrier], and those who were going to be." I got better. Toward the end there, I was quite comfortable coming aboard, even before

---

* The Grumman F3F fighter, which first entered fleet squadrons in 1937, was 23 feet long, wingspan of 32 feet, gross weight of 4,795 pounds, top speed of 264 miles per hour, armed with two .30 calibers. The Brewster F2A Buffalo entered the fleet in 1940. It was 26 feet long, wingspan of 35 feet, gross weight 7,159 pounds, top speed of 321 miles per hour, and armed with four .50 calibers.

we left San Diego. I don't know why I qualified on the *Lexington* because we were attached to the *Saratoga*.* That must have been an available deck or something like that.

We had a comparatively short period in the San Diego area. We had trouble with the Brewsters because the landing gear would bend out of shape if it came up underneath. It would get knocked back by landing, so it wouldn't fully retract. There were a few other troubles, but I liked the airplane. In fact, I made a cross-country flight in a Brewster, taking it from the factory on Long Island out to California. I recall that, because I found it convenient to land for fuel in Des Moines, Iowa. The fact that my wife-to-be came from Iowa, and was living in a town called Webster City, a little north of Des Moines, obviously had nothing to do with it.

Paul Stillwell: Utter coincidence.

Admiral Gayler: Utter coincidence. So we had a very pleasant reunion there, and the next morning I got out to start this damn thing and go on my way. The Brewster had cartridge starters. You know, sort of a shotgun shell you put in the ring, and you fire it up. It was a hot day, and those damn 1820 engines were miserable to start on a hot day.† To make a long story short, I shot off my whole box of cartridges, and there I was. So I scrounged around, and there was some kind of a reserve outfit that had a little bungee starter for starting their little airplanes. And I got these guys over there on this thing. Of course, they gave it a mighty tug, and the bungee snapped, and everybody went on their butt. Then we had to fabricate a bungee with a leather cuff that would fit. Do you know about bungee starters?

Paul Stillwell: Not in detail, no. It's a cord that you pull.

Admiral Gayler: It was an elastic cord with leather cuff on the end of it that fit over the propeller tip. You get the propeller in the right position, and then you get all the energy

---

* USS *Saratoga* (CV-3) was commissioned 16 November 1927. She had a standard displacement of 37,700 tons, was 888 feet long, 106 feet in the beam, an extreme width of 130 feet on the flight deck, and had a draft of 24 feet. She had a top speed of 33.5 knots and could accommodate about 60-70 aircraft.
† The F2A had a 1,200-horsepower Wright R-1820-40 engine.

into the elastic, and then as you eased it over by hand, the elastic would give it a throw. I don't know, we finally got the damn thing started and got it out to the West Coast.

Paul Stillwell: The sequel would be that you had to stay overnight near your wife-to-be.

Admiral Gayler: I'd already done that. It was time for me to go. [Laughter]

Paul Stillwell: I'm curious. Where did the plane stop on a transcontinental hop then? There weren't naval air stations there.

Admiral Gayler: You stopped where you could get gas. You needed 100 octane. Only a few areas had 100 octane, and they obviously had to be military people. So there were a few of those.

Paul Stillwell: Did you just give them a chit for the gas, or how did that work?

Admiral Gayler: I don't remember now. I think so. Don't really remember.

Paul Stillwell: Did you have a specific desire to get into Fighting Three, or were you seeking any fighter squadron?

Admiral Gayler: Any fighter squadron. I knew Fighting Three was one of the traditional old squadrons, and I was pleased to go there, particularly because I'd heard of Jimmy Thach's reputation.

Paul Stillwell: What can you say about your relationship with him?

Admiral Gayler: Well, Jimmy was such a remarkable man, a remarkable officer, and a remarkable leader in so many ways, it's hard to know where to start. But he was farsighted beyond most people, a really thoughtful and analytic guy, and yet the sort of fellow who could be almost a father figure even to some hardened old man of the world of five years' fleet experience, as I was. So he was something else. I learned a great deal from him and will always be in his debt.

Paul Stillwell: What can you say about his leadership in relation to junior officers and enlisted men in the squadron?

Admiral Gayler: Oh, I think it was all that you would want. He led by leading. He was the first guy off the deck. He led by precept. He clearly understood what he was doing and why, and yet at the same time, he invited participation, invited ideas. He gave encouragement at the right time, occasionally the stick as well as the carrot, but he was very good. You had the feeling that he knew what he was doing.

Paul Stillwell: Can you provide examples of both the stick and the carrot with Thach?

Admiral Gayler: His method was both sort of gentle and effective. He would reward by handing out responsibility, and he would use a stick by withdrawing it gently, until you learned the business better.

After my initial landing experience, we took a cruise to Hawaii on the *Saratoga* and did intensive training in the Hawaiian area in gunnery and tactics. Don Lovelace was the squadron exec.[*] Since I was third in seniority, I was the flight officer. In a way, that was slightly unfortunate, because I was a very inexperienced pilot compared to some of the other guys. But Jimmy was very helpful in bringing me along. I did the best I could with it and picked things up along the way.

Paul Stillwell: Did you have any sense of awkwardness in that as flight officer you were supposed to be training things that you were only learning yourself?

Admiral Gayler: You bet I did. That's why I was humping it. And we had a couple of guys in the squadron who were quite experienced pilots. I remember flying with Rolla

---

[*] Lieutenant Donald A. Lovelace, USN, became executive officer later. In early 1941 Gayler's classmate, Lieutenant (junior grade) Robert W. Jackson, USN, was exec. Though Gayler was senior on the lineal list, he had less aviation experience than Jackson.

Lemmon and John Lackey.* They were the old-timers, ex-aviation cadets who had been flying a long time. I flew on Rolla's wing most of the time when I was learning. There was a little flap about that, and I said, "Hell, if I don't belong leading this, I'll learn the trade."

Rolla had an interesting habit. Before we really got into the Thach tactics, we still flew in three-plane sections. When we were still operating out of San Diego, Rolla would come in screaming over Point Loma, coming around to land.† Then he would roll over on his back at 800 feet. Of course, we would dutifully roll over on our backs with him. We would scream around the field on our backs, then roll out and land. I got on him once, and I said, "Rolla, what the hell are you doing?"

He said, "I dropped my pencil on the bottom of the cockpit." I knew he was lying like a rug. What he was really doing was hazing me a little bit, as some of the old-timers did.

Paul Stillwell: When did you make the transition from the three-plane section to the twos that were used for the Thach weave?

Admiral Gayler: Somewhere about that time. We weren't in a three-plane section very long.

Paul Stillwell: Was there some experimentation at that point to see what tactics would work? Do you remember being involved in that?

Admiral Gayler: Jimmy worked out the idea of the Thach Weave and diagrammed it like a football coach. And we would go up and practice it with practice attackers. The idea was very contingent on timing. You had to make the break at just the right time. But if you did it at just the right time, you'd always end up on the tail of anybody who was on the tail of your buddy, and it also was a very good lookout position, because you could each watch 6:00 o'clock of the other fellow. When an attack run started, you were far

---

* Ensign Rolla S. Lemmon, USN; Ensign John H. Lackey, USNR.
† Point Loma is a strip of land that juts southward at the western edge of the entrance to San Diego Harbor. It is near the North Island Naval Air Station in Coronado, where the squadron was based.

enough out so you and your wingman had room to turn toward each other. Then, after you passed close by, nose to nose, you covered his tail and he yours. Then you turned back and repeated it, so no matter where the enemy fighter came from, one of the two of you would be in a position to take a shot at him.

Paul Stillwell: As I understand it, it didn't require any verbal communication. The very fact of turning toward would be the signal.

Admiral Gayler: Yes, sometimes. In real combat, it's very difficult not to say, "Hey, skipper, here they come."

Paul Stillwell: As he explained in his oral history, the good guys in this exercise ran their airplanes at half-power to simulate the relative disadvantage they would have against the Zero. Do you remember that?

Admiral Gayler: No. All I remember is conserving gas, which came out the same way.

Paul Stillwell: What do you recall of those operations around Hawaii in 1941?

Admiral Gayler: The reason I remember flying the Brewsters there was that we began to have a lot of engine trouble with the master rod bearings failing. That, of course, would stop the engine. I think Jimmy Thach had a forced landing, as I recall, and a couple of other guys also.

One day, when I was out over the water about 30 miles south of Oahu, my engine froze up and quit. So I looked around, and there was a big, fat cruiser. Being eager to make sure that the people on watch noticed me—since I was going to make a water landing—I timed it so that I went by right in front of the bridge as I was settling. But I misjudged it a little bit. The plane settled a little faster than I thought she was going to, so I got a goddamned sight closer to the ship than I meant to. I went right over the top of number-two turret, right in front of the captain, and went splash nearby. I got their attention all right. [Laughter]

When I landed, the deceleration knocked me out briefly. The gunsight was right in front, and I knew that that would tear up my face if I hit it, so I had my hands in front of my face. My head hit my hands and it knocked me out for ten seconds, I suppose. Fortunately, one thing that the Brewsters had was that they were watertight. They floated like corks. So there I was with a perfectly floating airplane. The cruiser sent out a whaleboat and got a line on it, towed it over to the ship, pulled it out of the water, dripping away. All I got was a little cut on the cheek.

Curious coincidence. I had a dreadful little dog of a jalopy that I wanted to sell, because I was going someplace. I had been trying to get hold of this lieutenant commander who I had heard was interested in getting a jalopy. And damn if the guy who picked me up out of the water wasn't that guy. [Laughter]

Paul Stillwell: Didn't he think that was an extreme method for advertising your car?

Admiral Gayler: Sure was. Then I guess we went back.

Paul Stillwell: What was your reception on board the cruiser? Were they giving you a hard time about almost hitting the ship?

Admiral Gayler: Oh, no. No, they didn't say anything about it. I think they probably thought I did it on purpose. I didn't disabuse anybody.

Paul Stillwell: Was the plane able to be saved?

Admiral Gayler: Yes, we washed her down with fresh water and flew her after that. The crash broke a Plexiglas out of the belly, but that's about all it did, except saltwater immersion. It was extraordinary. None of the rest of them would do that, but she would. That had been a design requirement, and she was pretty light. She didn't have an awful lot of fuel on board, I don't think. It was the end of the hop. I think we were doing high-altitude flights. Jimmy was great. He had us do very high-altitude tactics, too, and I think it was then that our master rod bearings would give up.

Paul Stillwell: Thach had a fetish about gunnery, I take it. Would that be fair to say?

Admiral Gayler: He had a fetish about war readiness, including gunnery. I got to be a pretty good gunner under him, so I could, generally speaking, fill a sleeve full of holes. The best shot in the squadron was a fellow named O'Hare.[*] You've heard of him.

Paul Stillwell: Yes. In his oral history, Admiral Thach talked about his arrival, and said there was a humiliation team, of which you were one of the members. This team would take up new men up and show them they shouldn't be too cocky about their abilities as fighter pilots. But this didn't apply to O'Hare. He was fully capable as soon as he arrived.

Admiral Gayler: He was a natural. He was not an athlete, by the way. He was a little tubby. But he was a natural shot.

Let's finish it up here; it's a little bit overtime. We can start off next time with some more sea stories about Fighting Three.

---

[*] Lieutenant (junior grade) Edward H. O'Hare, USN, was one of the pilots in VF-3. On 20 February 1942, while the squadron was in the *Lexington* (CV-2), he earned the Medal of Honor for saving the ship by shooting down five Japanese bombers. O'Hare Airport in Chicago is named for him.

Interview Number 3 with Admiral Noel A. M. Gayler, U.S. Navy (Retired)

Place: Admiral Gayler's office at the American Committee on East-West Accord, Washington, D.C.

Date: Thursday, 1 December 1983

Paul Stillwell: Admiral, we finished last time by talking briefly about Butch O'Hare. What so you recall about his service in VF-3?

Admiral Gayler: Butch I didn't know awfully well. I don't think anybody knew him awfully well. He was kind of a loner. As it happened, he and I ferried a couple of the new Wildcats from Bethpage out to North Island.[*] I did two ferry trips during that period before the war—one with Brewsters and one with Wildcats.[†] The one that O'Hare was along was with Wildcats, and we sort of made the trip out together, and I met his family. I remember meeting his sister, who was and is a very pretty lady. But I don't think Butch was particularly close to anybody in the squadron. We soon found out that he was a phenomenal shot. He was a good pilot, and he was always very friendly, but he was not one of any identifiable gang. I never did know him very well in a personal sense, although I knew him very well as a squadron mate.

Paul Stillwell: Was he cocky because of his skill advantage over others?

Admiral Gayler: No, no, he wasn't. He was pretty modest about it. Pretty modest about it.

Paul Stillwell: After he was designated to receive the Medal of Honor, he told Commander Thach that he didn't want to go back and speak on behalf of war bonds, suggesting a sort of shyness. Did you see that?

---

[*] Bethpage, Long Island, was the site of the Grumman factory.
[†] Grumman F4F Wildcat fighters first entered fleet squadrons in late 1940. The F4F-4 was 28 feet, 9 inches long; wingspan of 38 feet; gross weight of 7,952 pounds; and top speed of 318 miles per hour.

Admiral Gayler: Yes, I think that's right. But he was a fine guy. He was all right. He was just a little bit of a loner, as I recall. Not aloof but liked his own company.

Now, let me think. I've forgotten if I've already told about the first time I got the Order of the Rising Sun.

Paul Stillwell: I don't think so.

Admiral Gayler: Well, I have actually received the Order of the Rising Sun twice in my career, once when I was a lieutenant (junior grade), and once when I was a four-star admiral. The first time I got it, I was on the deck of the *Saratoga*, and I'm pretty sure it was during that training cruise to Hawaii in 1941. It was an award for destroying four American airplanes. [Laughter]

Paul Stillwell: How did you accomplish that?

Admiral Gayler: As flight officer of the squadron, I was the one who was responsible for training and readiness in the system we had then. I was always very concerned that we practice intensively our gunnery, which in those days was firing against a sleeve towed by another fighter. It had never been the custom, however, to do that at sea. You always did it when you were ashore in the training phase. And here we were on this long sea cruise and no opportunity to keep our gunnery skills refreshed.

So I lobbied and lobbied and lobbied, with Jimmy Thach's support, to try to do this aboard ship, which had some difficulties. You had to launch with the sleeve and a towline made up in a special container under the wing, which wasn't too bad, because we could make rolling takeoffs; we didn't have to be catapulted. But then you had to recover the thing to see whether anybody had hit it. We painted the bullets, of course, to see who had gotten what hits—if there were any.

The whole idea was a little dicey for the carrier skipper, Captain Douglas.* He didn't much like that idea, because you'd have to drop the thing on deck. It had a big iron ring in the front that could have done some damage. But I lobbied and lobbied, and

---

* Captain Archibald H. Douglas, USN, commanded the USS *Saratoga* (CV-3), 1 June 1940-12 April 1942.

finally personally pledged that I would tow the sleeve, I would bring the damn thing back, and I would put it on deck. So finally the carrier skipper reluctantly consented. We got off and had a successful gunnery shoot, and then I came back to drop the thing on deck. The plan was to fly about 20 feet off the deck and just drop it. I'll never understand, but there was an air burble or something that affected my plane. Just as I came over the deck, I dropped about ten feet and towed that damn sleeve right through the parked airplanes. I didn't destroy four airplanes, but I damaged four. So the next day, they had a ceremony on deck—a great big cardboard rising sun, and presented me with that for destroying four American airplanes. That was the first time.

Paul Stillwell: You said you also won that Order of the Rising Sun award as a flag officer. How did that come about?

Admiral Gayler: Oh, it was just one of those honoraries. When I was CinCPac I made an official visit to Japan.* Curiously enough, I had come to know the Premier reasonably well, Mr. Ohira, because I'd known him when he was Foreign Minister.† He had done a very unusual thing. He had given a party in my honor at a geisha house, and quite absolutely unprecedented, I believe, in Japanese tradition, he invited my wife, because ladies are never invited to these things. She sat next to him at one of the low tables like this, and charmed him. He told us all about his youth as a wrestler, with his stocky, bull neck. He spoke not very good English but intelligible English, and so we had a great time. I had a good personal relationship with him as Foreign Minister, and as Premier he remembered. It was an honorary thing. I didn't do anything for it, but the second time makes for a good story. [Laughter] I have never told the Japanese about the first time.

Paul Stillwell: You mentioned the transition from the Brewster to the Grumman Wildcat.‡ Could you compare the two planes?

---

* Admiral Gayler later served as Commander in Chief Pacific from 1972 to 1976.
† Masayoshi Ohira was Japan's Minister of Foreign Affairs, 1962-64 and 1972-78. The visit Admiral Gayler recalls may have been after his retirement. Ohira served as Japanese Prime Minister, 1978 to 1980.
‡ The Grumman F4F, which entered fleet squadrons in 1940-41, was 29 feet long, wingspan of 38 feet, gross weight of 7,952 pounds, top speed of 318 miles per hour, armed with six .50-caliber machine guns. It was the Navy's primary carrier fighter in the early part of World War II.

Admiral Gayler: I liked the Brewster better. But the decision to go with F4Fs was a good one, because the Brewsters had no protected tanks, and they'd have torched like Zeros.* In fact, as you probably know, there was a hell of a debacle when the Brewsters tried to fight the Zeros in Singapore. They were also out at Wake with the Marines.† We never went to combat with the Brewster, but I liked it as a flying machine.‡

The Buffalo had a couple of features that were vastly superior to the Wildcat. One is that you didn't have to wind up the landing gear with your hood open, and another was that the airflow around the Wildcat was such with the hood open, which was the standard for takeoff and landing, you got this terrible, loud, organ-pipe noise from the airflow. If you got a little bit high in speed, it was just absolutely deafening. It wasn't just annoying. You couldn't hear yourself think. And the F4F didn't have quite the performance of the Brewster in simulated dog-fighting. The Brewster could lick her. But she was a much better airplane to go to war with, because she had protection, and the Brewster did not.

Paul Stillwell: Was the training out of North Island up to the point when the war started?

Admiral Gayler: Yes, except for that very intensive month we had in Hawaii. We really flew then. We didn't have anything else to do. We knew the war was coming, and we had a hell of a lot of flying both day and night. We did an awful lot of night flying, awful lot. Also a lot of day gunnery out of Ford Island.§

Paul Stillwell: Maybe you could describe that night flying in greater detail, because that was very rare at that point.

Admiral Gayler: Yes. Jimmy was a perfectionist about being able to do everything, and so we did do a lot of night tactical work, rendezvouses, intercepts—no radar, of course— but intercepts under visual fighter direction. We gave a lot of attention to enhancing

---

* The Japanese A6M Zero fighter was highly vulnerable when hit in the fuel tanks by machine gun fire.
† Japanese forces invaded and captured Wake Island in December 1941.
‡ Land-based Brewster Buffaloes were in the Battle of Midway in June 1942 and suffered heavy losses.
§ Ford Island is in the middle of Pearl Harbor.

night vision. Absolutely mirror-clean windshields, adaptation, all that stuff. Jimmy was ahead of the times on almost all the technical aspects, and then we would learn how to pick up the target airplane against the night sky or by seeing the barely luminous exhausts, and making an approach on that. That's how Butch eventually got killed, as you know.[*]

And we did some night carrier work, which was the first time for me. I was so goddamned scared that the muscles in my legs were jumping involuntarily while I was making an approach. I don't whether everybody else was as cowardly as I was. I was really scared of those. After a while I got very used to it, did an awful lot of night work. No problem, but in the beginning it got your attention.

Paul Stillwell: Was the deck illuminated at all for that?

Admiral Gayler: Yes, we used dustpan lights, as they were called, which was a sort of metal shield that looked like a dustpan so that the lights were visible only from about 15 degrees on either side of aft as a protection, for tactical reasons. The result of that was that you couldn't see the deck until you were practically in the cut position. But then, in those airplanes you didn't see much anyway. You had to depend on the batman.

Paul Stillwell: The LSO had luminous wands.[†]

Admiral Gayler: Charlie Jett was the LSO's name.[‡] I think it was that early that he had an ultraviolet illumination and a luminescent suit and luminescent paddles. We later on found out that the ultraviolet interfered with the night vision of the LSO because it makes your eyeballs fluoresce. That's why the Navy dropped that and went to the wands.

Paul Stillwell: Was there a great safety consciousness within the squadron?

---

[*] Lieutenant Commander Edward H. O'Hare, USN, was killed the night of 27 November 1943. He was the pilot of an F6F Hellcat while it flying with a radar-equipped TBF. See Eugene Burns, "Butch O'Hare's Last Flight," *The Saturday Evening Post*, 11 March 1944, page 19, and Steve Ewing and John B. Lundstrom, *Fateful Rendezvous: The Life of Butch O'Hare* (Annapolis: Naval Institute Press, 1997).
[†] LSO – landing signal officer.
[‡] Lieutenant Charles M. Jett, USN.

Admiral Gayler: Not to the point of inhibiting operations, but yes. We generally liked to explore all the envelopes. We did a lot of high-performance climbs to altitude, good for training, until we began to lose engines in the Brewster. This was the R-1820 single-row Wright engine. The master rod bearing would fail at high altitude. I mentioned in our last interview the time that happened to me.

Paul Stillwell: I think Thach had the advantage of coming along at a time when the Navy couldn't afford to be as conservative as it had been, because visionaries had had difficulties in previous years.

Admiral Gayler: Oh, yes. That's right. That's right. The war itself and the preparations for it were a real opener in that sense. But, of course, the most liberating thing to us was the Pearl Harbor attack.[*] That settled once and for all the argument about the Gun Club and the airplanes.[†]

Paul Stillwell: Was there an active hostility between brown shoes and black shoes, in your perception?[‡]

Admiral Gayler: I don't think so much hostility as a set of mind. I think that far more than either failures of intelligence or failures of awareness or the ins and outs of whether President Roosevelt did or did not want war with Japan, or any of those things, to me the nearly complete, the 90% explanation of how something like Pearl Harbor could happen devolved from the mind-set of the commanders, all of whom had been brought up in the big-gun Navy, all of whom were identifying with the battleships and believed that they

---

[*] In late November 1941, the Imperial Japanese Navy dispatched from the Kurile Islands in the North Pacific a task force built around six aircraft carriers. A force of some 350 fighters, dive-bombers, and torpedo planes attacked U.S. military installations on the island of Oahu, Hawaii, on Sunday, 7 December 1941. The principal focus of attack was the collection of American warships at the naval base at Pearl Harbor. The U.S. Congress declared war on Japan the following day.

[†] "Gun Club" was a term used to describe the officers who served in battleships, cruisers, and destroyers. They felt that the warships' big guns were—and would remain—the predominant naval weapons. Once aircraft carriers came to prominence early in World War II, the influence of the Gun Club began to wane.

[‡] In the early days of naval aviation, the aviators wore brown shoes with their khaki uniforms and green uniforms. They thus acquired the nickname "brown shoes" to distinguish them from the traditional surface ship officers, who were known as "black shoes."

were the decisive instrument, all of whom believed almost as a matter of faith that battleships were essentially invulnerable to air attack.

So I think that while the senior commanders, and indeed the President, might have believed they could be attacked or could even be attacked in the anchorage or in the moorings at Pearl, I don't think any of them actually imagined that an air attack could be more than a raid. That was the terminology—air raids. The image of "raid" suggests something that may be a nuisance, but that's it. So I think it was that failure of imagination, failure of comprehension of these very fine officers with their limited horizons. Now, the reason I'm dwelling on this at such length is because I see exactly the same thing happening right now in the military posture of this country and specifically the Navy—that failure of imagination with respect to the consequences of nuclear weapons and other modern things.

Paul Stillwell: Projecting yourself back to the mind-set of that period, did you find yourself going along with what was considered the conventional wisdom?

Admiral Gayler: No, in those days, I was then in aviation. I was a gung-ho, young fighter pilot, and for two successive seasons we simulated attacks on Pearl Harbor. We always came in from the south rather than from the northeast, as the Japanese did. But essentially the results were the same. We almost always achieved surprise, even though it was a scheduled exercise. And we almost always had no difficulty penetrating to the ships, in spite of the fact that the Army Air Corps were, first with their Seversky P-35s and then with their Curtiss-Wright P-40s, were always there as a defending force. And, of course, we fighters would tangle with them. We'd go around and around in a Dagwood-type scramble with the Army Air people, but in the meantime, the torpedo planes and the dive bombers would go about their business beating up the ships.

I'm afraid I thought that the higher command would see these things and take appropriate action more or less automatically. It didn't occur to me that what seemed to me to be obvious would not be obvious to people with a different mind-set.

Paul Stillwell: Well, there was thought given to the idea that Pearl Harbor was vulnerable to air attack, or raid, or whatever, but not that it would start the war. I think that was the thing that made so much difference, that at least you'd be in a hostility situation.

Admiral Gayler: That was part of it. That was part of it. But I think most of it was the feeling that nothing like that could really be decisive, major importance.

Paul Stillwell: It certainly was.

Admiral Gayler: Yes, it certainly was. And there were some palliatives too, the notion that you couldn't use torpedoes in Pearl Harbor, because it was too shallow. Of course, you know about that. The torpedoes that we had, and the torpedoes the Japanese had originally, would make a big, deep excursion when they were dropped in the water. But the Japanese foresaw that, and of course fixed up their torpedoes with wooden shrouds, I believe, so they couldn't dive. And the theory was that without torpedoes you couldn't do much damage to battleships anyway. Of course, they sank the *Arizona* and *Nevada* with modified 15-inch AP shells dropped from a high altitude.[*]

Paul Stillwell: Where were you at the time of the Japanese attack, and how did you become aware of it?

Admiral Gayler: Oh, I was in Fighting Three, in the *Saratoga*, and we were in San Diego. That Sunday I was actually on the beach with my wife, and somebody said, "Got to get back to the squadron right away." We got back, and the radio was blaring with the news. We pilots and the squadron wives all sat around on ammunition boxes all afternoon long while we belted up ammunition. We were so unready we didn't even have the ammunition belted up. Then we sailed in *Saratoga* for Hawaii early the following morning.

---

[*] AP—armor piercing.

Paul Stillwell: You refer to her as your wife. In the last discussion we had of her, she was still your fiancée when you made the night stopover in Iowa.

Admiral Gayler: That's right. With marvelous foresight, we were married on the third of November of that year, so we had been married just a tad over a month before the war started.

Paul Stillwell: Were you married in Iowa?

Admiral Gayler: No. We were actually married in Reno, Nevada. I used to annoy my wife by saying that we were married there after she left her first husband. Of course, she never had a first husband before me. She'd get really mad at me.

We went to Reno, because we suddenly decided we ought to get married right away. There was a three-day waiting period in San Francisco, which I didn't have the leave for. So we took off in a car and tore across the mountains to Reno, where they were more liberal. We caught the clerk at the courthouse about five minutes to go before he closed. Then we found a friendly Baptist minister, who enlisted his wife and a couple of friends as witnesses, and we were married.

Paul Stillwell: Had your fiancée by then moved to California?

Admiral Gayler: No, she was out visiting a cousin of hers. I think my presence had something to do with her being out there, but she never admitted it.

Paul Stillwell: What kind of operations were you involved in once the war started?

Admiral Gayler: What happened was that the *Saratoga* was sent out to fly off some airplanes to relieve Wake Island, which was already under attack.* The island fell while we were on the way, so we dropped off the planes at Midway instead. After that we went

---

* After steaming out from the West Coast, the *Saratoga* arrived at Pearl Harbor on 15 December. Two days later she left for Wake, but it fell to the Japanese on 23 December, while she was still en route.

back and operated around Hawaii. In doing that, for reasons that were not obvious to a jaygee, we screwed around at comparatively slow speed. We had gotten a couple of sort of funny radar contacts with the old CXAM radar. In retrospect what the radar saw was probably a Japanese periscope. But, in any case, we chose not to do anything much about it.

If you can believe it, we were still in white service uniforms for dinner. Just at dinner time one evening, all of a sudden, WHOOM, one of those big torpedoes that the Japanese had hit us amidships, and seemed to pick up that carrier about six feet and push it aside.* Of course, we all ran to general quarters, but never had any follow-up on the submarine. It knocked a great big hole in the *Saratoga*, flooded three firerooms, and killed six people, but we didn't have any major casualties.

At that point the *Saratoga* was sent back to Bremerton for repairs, and Fighting Three was divided into two teams and sent to the *Lexington*.† I was in the team sent over to join Fighting Two, commanded by Paul Ramsey.‡

Paul Stillwell: What do you recall about the preparations for combat?

Admiral Gayler: If you can imagine, for years there had been provision for armor plate for our fighter planes, but it wasn't installed. You were supposed to make airplanes lighter in peacetime. And here we were going into combat. So every night they'd take one squadron of airplanes down in the incredibly hot hangar deck of the *Lexington*. Buttoned up, operating off New Guinea, you can imagine how hot it was. The aviation mechs and metalsmiths would labor all night long to get the armor plate installed one airplane at a time. They'd pass out and be pulled out by the heels. Then another guy would crawl in and work. As the flight officer, I used to roll the bones to see who got the armored airplanes. So much for readiness and provision for armor plate.

---

* The carrier was torpedoed on 11 January 1942 while operating 500 miles southwest of Oahu. The oral history of Rear Admiral Ernest M. Eller, USN (Ret.), the *Saratoga*'s gunnery officer, contains another account of the incident.
† The *Lexington* (CV-2) was a sister ship of the *Saratoga* (CV-3). Both of them had been commissioned in late 1927 and had a great deal to do with the development of aircraft carrier doctrine in the 1930s as war approached.
‡ Lieutenant Commander Paul H. Ramsey, USN.

Paul Stillwell: What was the mood of the squadron as you contemplated facing the Japanese—an eagerness to get into action? Apprehension?

Admiral Gayler: Eagerness, I think. We all felt Pearl Harbor very keenly. We all felt that we were about to get a chance to get our own back, and we were ready to go for it.

Another mood, which is almost difficult to explain, is absolute confidence that we were going to win. We might get smoked as individuals, but we believed that America was going to win. It never crossed anybody's mind that the reverse of Pearl Harbor didn't bother anybody at all in a strategic sense. It was just a chance to get back at the bastards for a sneak attack.

Paul Stillwell: Since they had been so successful, not only at Pearl Harbor, but in Southeast Asia and the Philippines and so forth, was there any sense that you were up against a very formidable enemy—perhaps invincible?

Admiral Gayler: No, I don't remember anybody talking like that. We had heard vague rumors about Zeros, but we didn't know what they were. The first good look at a Zero I ever had was not in an intelligence picture but in the air.* We knew that there was a new-type fighter and it was pretty good. You tend to be pretty parochial. You don't necessarily look at the big picture. You want to know what you're going to be up against. But no, I don't think so.

Of course, the enormous Japanese successes in the Far East and Indian Ocean were against almost no opposition. They just cleaned up. The one exception was Singapore, and I always thought that was very interesting, because what the Zero cleaned up on there were the Spitfires, possibly an earlier mark of Spitfire than the one used in the Battle of Britain.† But anyway, the Spitfire—which was so successful against the Germans—was cleaned up by the Japanese first team of Zeros, which is the only cross

---

* The Mitsubishi-built A6M Zero was the best-known fighter plane in the Japanese Navy in World War II. The standard A6M2 had a top speed of 317 miles per hour and was armed with two 7.7-millimeter machine guns and two 20-millimeter cannons.
† In the summer and fall of 1940, during the Battle of Britain, Royal Air Force Spitfire and Hurricane fighter planes defended Great Britain against bombing raids by the German Luftwaffe. The raids were intended to soften up Britain for a planned German amphibious invasion across the English Channel. The invasion never materialized.

comparison between the theaters that I know of. I don't know much about the specific history of that. I don't know what mark Spitfire; I don't know how much training the pilots had. Singapore was sort of a disaster area anyway, apparently from morale and training and readiness standpoint, so maybe that had a lot to do with it.

Paul Stillwell: Can you project back in your mind and think—did you feel a sense of liberation from Pearl Harbor in that now since the carriers were the only thing, that you were freed of that strategy that employed the battleships?

Admiral Gayler: I think it came out rather that we were very conscious of the responsibility that was now ours—solely, totally. Nothing else mattered.

Paul Stillwell: Did you view that as an advantage?

Admiral Gayler: Oh, sure. Of course.

Paul Stillwell: Your first action was on the 20th of February. Can you describe that day?

Admiral Gayler: Well, it started out with Jimmy Thach and his wingman finding a Kawanishi flying boat and smoking it.[*] We were on deck, and I can still remember on the far horizon the big plume of black smoke. That was the first whiff of enemy action that we had seen. Then we were running in toward Rabaul, and we had a CAP up.[†] Red Gill was the fighter director, as I recall.[‡] We had some intimation before we were launched on that CAP that we were going to have business that day. Looking back at it now, I imagine that it must have been some kind of signals intelligence. But we didn't know anything about that. We just had this sort of general word, "Look out, something's going to happen."

---

[*] This was the plane assigned the nickname "Emily" by the Allies for designation purposes.
[†] CAP—combat air patrol, a force of fighter planes deployed in the air to intercept incoming air raids headed toward a naval force.
[‡] Lieutenant Frank F. Gill, USN.

So it was not an entire surprise when Gill vectored us toward these guys. They came in in two waves of nine. The first wave was Bettys, and the second wave was Type 97s.* I believe my wingman for that flight was Peterson.† Somewhat foolishly, I led him to a position so we could make an overhead run. That entailed getting up into here and turning back toward and rolling over like that. We wound up firing almost vertically down finally, as opposed to a high-side run. I say foolishly, because in retrospect I realized that it took me too long to climb into the attack position. What O'Hare later did with all of his crowd was just to barge in there and shoot them.‡ Which is what I should have done, but I didn't.

In any case, we did get into position. We did make an overhead run and a couple of high-side runs. I set one guy on fire, and the other guy started to burn, while a couple of us were shooting at him. We got all but one on that, and the one, I think, was the fellow that got down to the carrier in that famous picture, taken close aboard when he was trying to kamikaze them.

Then I'm a little vague on the sequence of events, but I was still airborne when the other group came but way out of position. That was when O'Hare and Dufilho went up after them.§

Paul Stillwell: Had your doctrine really covered what kind of an approach to make on a bomber?

Admiral Gayler: No, but in the context of all of our training, we had standard approaches, and one of the preferred approaches was the overhead. It was a good way to hit, and it was a hard way to defend against. Because from the standpoint of the bomber, you're coming down on him very rapidly. But what I didn't fully realize is it was a pretty high-performance airplane. We didn't have much speed margin, so it just took a long

---

* The Mitsubishi Type 1 two-engine, land-based torpedo bomber was known by the Japanese as the G4M and by the Allies as the Betty. The Nakajima Type 97 carrier-based torpedo bomber was designated by the Japanese as the B5N and by the Allies as the Kate.
† Ensign Dale W. Peterson, USNR.
‡ O'Hare shot down five Kates from one wave of nine.
§ Lieutenant (junior grade) Marion W. Dufilho, USN, was O'Hare's wingman.

time to get into position. If I had it to do over again, I would not have taken that particular approach.

Paul Stillwell: But you don't know that until you try it, do you?

Admiral Gayler: After all, I wasn't all that experienced. First enemy I'd ever seen. I think I had about maybe 50 hours or something like that.

Paul Stillwell: Whether consciously or unconsciously, how much did the self-preservation instinct enter into a situation like that?

Admiral Gayler: Well, it sure did. Not on that first run, but as we were chasing them on subsequent runs, we ran into the flak from the *Lexington*'s 5-inch guns—big, black shell bursts all around us. I began to think, "This is getting pretty dangerous." I don't think they hit anything, but they were there. Then a couple of the Japanese broke off and started hightailing it for home. I chased one of them for a long, long time. The Betty had the small 7.7-millimeter machine guns in the tail turret. One of those starred my bulletproof windshield, right in front of me. When that hit, I jumped, and I became aware of how you could get shot doing this. I chased him until I was almost out of gas. I think we got a recall from Gill.

Paul Stillwell: How much of what you do in a situation like that is conscious? How much is reflex and instinct?

Admiral Gayler: Almost all the latter, I think. Almost all the latter. It was almost all instinct or habituated training. I would make a lousy quarterback, because I couldn't stand back there in the pocket or scramble or keep my eye on six receivers and flip to one of them. I'm just not that way.

Paul Stillwell: What sort of reception did you get when you got back on board the ship?

Admiral Gayler: Oh, the sailors were always enthusiastic. We used to tape all the gun muzzles with masking tape just to keep them dry and from corroding in that wet, hot climate. So the sailors would rush up and see that you'd shot away the masking tape: "What did you get today, Lieutenant?" The pilots were sort of blasé about it.

The flight leader would always go immediately up to the bridge to report to the captain of the ship, but he was usually pretty preoccupied with what he was doing. In this case, since Captain Sherman had just been dodging bombs, he was not interested—at that instant, I mean—in tales about what we'd been doing.* I'm not throwing off on him; he was just preoccupied. He was still fighting a war after we were back aboard.

Paul Stillwell: Did the crew tend to put the aviators on a pedestal, particularly the fighter pilots?

Admiral Gayler: If they did, I wasn't conscious of it. See, I didn't know the *Lexington* people very well. I was almost a stranger there.

Paul Stillwell: What was your relationship in the wardroom with the non-flying type officers?

Admiral Gayler: Oh, I don't think that we paid an awful lot of attention to them. I wasn't in the wardroom a hell of a lot. There was an awful lot of snacking in the ready room and that kind of stuff—standbys and whatnot.† It was pretty much catch-as-catch-can. The wardroom was more like a fast-food joint than the wardrooms we often think of.

Paul Stillwell: The ready room was really your headquarters.

Admiral Gayler: The ready room was the place.

---

* Captain Frederick C. Sherman, USN, commanded the *Lexington* from June 1940 until she was sunk in the Battle of the Coral Sea in May 1942.
† The ready room of an aircraft carrier is the hangout for squadron personnel on board ship. It is used for pre-flight briefings, post-flight debriefings, and off-duty recreation

Paul Stillwell: How would you describe the atmosphere in the ready room and the things that went on there?

Admiral Gayler: Well, our ready room on the "Lex" was very small and very crowded. Jimmy complained about that and got back a marvelous answer: that we flew the smallest airplanes, and therefore we got the smallest ready room. Actually, we had more pilots than some of the other people. It had always been like that. There were some vestiges of that kind of stuff left—war or no war. And it was a busy place, people getting ready for flights, people sitting there in standby in some readiness condition, people eating, people making cups of coffee, people horsing around. We played a lot of that game where you slap each other's hands. Oh God, your hand was about that big before the day was over. I'm still pretty good at it. That was a good way to spend your time.

Paul Stillwell: Were people seeking release from tension through that, do you think?

Admiral Gayler: I don't know. I think maybe in those days I wasn't awfully aware of things like that. I wasn't particularly tense myself, and I wasn't looking for it in other people.

Paul Stillwell: Was that your center for recreation when you were not flying?

Admiral Gayler: As I recall, the ship was buttoned up all the time. I was pretty goddamned busy because the administrative burdens didn't stop just because the war was on. I don't even remember anything that you would call recreation. Occasional walk on the flight deck at night. Other than horseplay.

Paul Stillwell: What about cards and acey-deucey? Were they indulged in?

Admiral Gayler: No, I don't think so. Maybe acey-deucey. I used to get annoyed at some of the ex-avcads that I thought were kind of lazy, [unclear] them up once in a while.

But still not as much as you would normally, because we all knew there was a war on. Some of them may have been playing acey-deucey; I can't remember.

Paul Stillwell: Who typically briefed before a mission?

Admiral Gayler: Always Jimmy when he was there. If he wasn't, it was Don Lovelace or I, strictly by seniority.

Paul Stillwell: What would be the basis of your briefings? Where did the information come from?

Admiral Gayler: Most of it was just routine CAP and had to do with the assignment of people and patrol sectors and altitudes and communications—much of it repetitive stuff. We didn't really get what you'd call mission briefings until the Coral Sea.

Paul Stillwell: Was there any intelligence input before the action on February 20th?

Admiral Gayler: I infer that there was, but there wasn't anything direct.

Paul Stillwell: You just knew there was an enemy out there.

Admiral Gayler: We knew for some reason that we were going to have business that day.

Paul Stillwell: How did you spend the time between that action and the Coral Sea Battle in early May?

Admiral Gayler: Lots of false alarms, as I recall, high-speed runs to nowhere, and heightened tension. But nothing happened. I had assumed that they were trying to make the contacts that they actually did make later on in the Coral Sea. My inference from what I now know is that a lot of it was informed by intelligence reports, but it wasn't clear when it was going on.

Paul Stillwell: Did you still put up a daily CAP during that time?

Admiral Gayler: Oh yes, daily CAPs were going all the time. So in a sense, it was fortunate that we fighter pilots got most of the flying.

Paul Stillwell: How was logistic support during that period?

Admiral Gayler: Damn if I know. We never ran out of ammunition and never ran out of food.

Paul Stillwell: Or gasoline?

Admiral Gayler: Or gasoline. Usually we had a tanker in there with us, the *Neosho*.

Paul Stillwell: She was sunk during the Battle of the Coral Sea.

Admiral Gayler: She was our task group tanker. I think we had her alongside at least once.

Paul Stillwell: You had practiced the night operations. Were you doing any of those once you were deployed?

Admiral Gayler: Well, on the night of the seventh of May, we had that famous close brush with the Japanese force when they damn near landed some planes on us.[*] And we had some night flying that night. I was up with the last CAP. It got damn dark, and the weather was bad too. We lost a pilot from weather somewhere along the line.

Somewhere along the line, and I think it was that same day, I was shot at in the landing circle of the *Lexington*. They had a whole bunch of .50 calibers, independently operated on the catwalk. Somebody started shooting, and in those days the fire discipline

---

[*] This was the beginning of the Battle of the Coral Sea. It was a standoff tactically but a strategic victory for the United States, because it prevented the Japanese from landing in Port Moresby, New Guinea, which would have been a jumping-off place for invading Australia.

was very good, so everybody started shooting. The landing signal officer—it was either Charlie Jett or Bud Needham—realized what was happening, because he knew who he had in the landing circle.* He turned around and hit the guy across the face with his signal flags and knocked him away from his gun. Gradually the word went up the line and they realized who I was. Christ, I had my wheels down and my flaps down. [Laughter] So I've always been very conscious about identification.

Paul Stillwell: Did you practice any coordinated strikes with the rest of the air wing—the bombers, the torpedo planes?

Admiral Gayler: We certainly did in the Pearl Harbor area. Don't take this too seriously; I don't recall any practice group gropes while we were actually off the New Guinea coast.

Paul Stillwell: That turned out to be a shortcoming in the Battle of Midway, of course, that there wasn't more coordinated action. Torpedo Eight went in unescorted and got slaughtered.†

Admiral Gayler: I won't speak to Midway. I wasn't there. But my understanding is that it was more a fact that the scouts found the Japanese and had limited visibility, limited time, limited fuel, and limited everything else. There wasn't time to get together. Our attack against the Japanese in the Coral Sea wasn't all that well coordinated, although it was better. We did attack at more or less the same time, but not in the nifty precision that we had practiced. The visibility was very bad. You couldn't see much. Big towering columns of rain clouds, sort of like pillars. You'd go around them, and all of a sudden you'd see the carrier. Here he is, and there he's gone.

Paul Stillwell: How was the antiaircraft fire you faced when you got around the Japanese ships?

---

* Lieutenant Ray C. Needham, USN.
† Ensign George H. Gay, USNR was the only crew member to survive from the 15 pilots and 15 air crewmen from Torpedo Squadron Eight (VT-8) who attacked the Japanese fleet during the Battle of Midway in June 1942. He later wrote a memoir about his experiences, *Sole Survivor: the Battle of Midway and its Effect on His Life* (Naples, Florida: Naples Ad/Graphics Services, 1979).

Admiral Gayler: I didn't pay any attention to it at first, because the Zeros were up there, and that was all I was paying any attention to. But then when I broke off and got this guy out of my tail by flying through a cloud, I broke out and was circling one carrier. He started to shoot at me, all by myself, with his 5-inch. But he wasn't coming anywhere near, so it didn't matter too much. I did a complete circle to look at him very carefully to see if he was hurt. I couldn't detect damage. I was running on the smell of gas fumes, so I started heading for home. He was out about 250 miles, which was beyond what we really had fuel for.

Paul Stillwell: Can you compare the quality of American AA fire with the Japanese, since you were the target of both?

Admiral Gayler: Well, I wasn't the target. I may have been around, but I wasn't the target. Well, pretty poor sample. Those were the only two experiences I had. But the Americans were a lot closer than the Japanese. The Japanese were plainly just lagging. It was shoot, shoot, shoot, shoot about a half a mile behind.

Paul Stillwell: What comparisons can you draw between American fighter pilots and Japanese, based on your tangling with them?

Admiral Gayler: Pretty small sample. I think the guy that I tangled with was a much better pilot than I was, much better. He got on my tail pretty promptly, and he was a very good shot. He had his wingmen all the way out here, and they went by on both sides. If he had not been quite such a good shot, he would have nailed me. As soon as I saw them, of course, I took the stick with both hands and pushed it down, violently. Then I came around and found another one and made a big hairy, climbing turn, taking a long shot at him and fell out of it for lack of air speed. Just before I fell out, I saw him starting to burn. That was about it. It was just such an incredibly confusing, mixed-up, screwed-up situation. Poor visibility and people yelling on the radio. Clouds all over the place. I can't give you any coherent description of it.

Paul Stillwell: Then you got back to the ship, and she was not in very good shape.

Admiral Gayler: I didn't even know she'd been hit until I landed. She was making 25 knots, operating airplanes; she looked okay from the air. It was only when I landed that I realized there was a problem. The first thing I noticed was nobody paid any attention to me, contrary to what I told you before. Usually the sailors would come up and say, "Hey, how did you do?" Nobody paid any attention, and I looked around and some of the faces were looking sort of strange. Then I saw flecks of fire-fighting foam all over the deck, and I knew she had been hit.

So I went up to make my report to the captain, who sent me up to make a report to the admiral.[*] Then I went back and talked to Captain Sherman again. He asked me to go down and see over the side where he thought a torpedo had hit. So I got my plane captain to hold onto my heels and leaned way out over the side of the nettings. I counted five great big holes, each one of them about the size of that wall or bigger.

Paul Stillwell: Well, for the benefit of those who don't see the wall, I'd say that's ten feet high.

Admiral Gayler: I don't know. They were great big holes, maybe 20 feet in diameter or so. They looked like to me they were big, water swirling in and out. Because we were on an even keel and making 25 knots, going along fine.

Paul Stillwell: It wasn't the holes that did the ship in.

Admiral Gayler: It wasn't the holes. It was the gasoline fires, of course, and the paint fires, fuel-air ratio explosions and whatnot.

Paul Stillwell: How long did you remain on board the ship?

---

[*] Rear Admiral Aubrey W. Fitch, USN, Commander Task Group 17.5 was on board the *Lexington*.

Admiral Gayler: Oh, it was a busy day. I would think it was at least two and a half or three hours from the time I landed until the time the captain gave the orders to abandon ship. There was a lot of things going on, explosions in the ship. One main plane elevator went up on a column of fire and turned over and landed on the deck with a clang. There was a lot of concern about fighting fires. I was trying—fruitlessly, it turned out—to get another strike organized, because I knew there was at least one undamaged carrier in the Japanese force. At the time, we thought the planes would be able to launch, but we found out we couldn't fuel, so that was the end of that. But I spent a lot of time on that. I was mustering people in the squadron and rushing around taking care of squadron business while all the rest of the fire fighting was going on.

Finally, we were sort of driven by the fire to the extreme end of the ship, the stern. I know you've heard this story, but the ship's service ice cream plant was in the extreme port quarter, and some clown passed the word that there was free ice cream. So while they were abandoning ship, sailors were lining up for free ice cream. Of course, they puked it up as soon as they had been swimming in salt water a little while. People don't realize how young they were. God, they were only 18 or 19—20 at the most.

Paul Stillwell: Even if you couldn't get a strike off, was there any attempt to save the planes, send them over to the *Yorktown*?

Admiral Gayler: Well, there was a lot of thought about that, but in the end we couldn't do it.

Paul Stillwell: Were you prevented from doing that by the fires themselves?

Admiral Gayler: Yes. We just couldn't get a clear deck with all the activity going on.

Paul Stillwell: One of those saved in the abandon ship was the captain's dog. I guess he was high on the priority list.

Admiral Gayler: That gives the wrong impression, I think. It's literally true. The captain did take Wags with him and went, but Frederick Sherman was a marvelous guy, and he was the last guy to leave the ship. He took his little dog along with him when he left. There was no thought of giving the dog priority over people or anything.

Paul Stillwell: What can you say about his leadership as the ship was on fire?

Admiral Gayler: He was clearly very calm, clearly very much in command. He was very much at ease with Admiral Fitch, who was equally calm.[*] Of course, we were unable to do a hell of a lot, except receive reports and direct fire-fighting efforts to continue. The mortal blow was when the gasoline explosion below deck killed a damage control officer and most of his experienced people.[†] There was really nothing Captain Sherman could do about that. He and the admiral had a little colloquy, and then the admiral said, "Ted, it's time to get the people off."[‡] There was no disagreement, no argument. And it clearly was. The damn ship was burning like a torch, from the extreme bow to the extreme stern.

Paul Stillwell: Was the departure a disciplined one?

Admiral Gayler: Yes. No panic, no screaming, no hollering, going down the lines, most of them. A few people warning, "Now, don't jump." You know, it was 50 feet down. You would drive somebody like a nail if you landed on him. People were going down the lines. It was a pretty orderly operation. The only real problem was the ship was lying broadside to the wind and drifting about nearly as fast as a man could swim, and we were all going off on the lee side, so it was difficult to get away from it. The ship kept drifting.

Paul Stillwell: Were life jackets being issued, or did men have those on for the battle anyway?

---

[*] Rear Admiral Aubrey W. Fitch, USN, Commander Task Group 17.5, embarked in the *Lexington*.
[†] This individual was Commander Howard R. Healy, USN, the ship's first lieutenant and damage control officer. The explosion was at 1247 the afternoon of 8 May.
[‡] This discussion was shortly after 1700 in the afternoon.

Admiral Gayler: Most people had them on anyway. As I recall, I still just had my aviation life jacket. I'm pretty sure I didn't inflate it. That's pretty strange. I felt comfortable; the water was warm. There was no panic, no worry about getting picked up. The destroyers moved in with cargo nets.

Paul Stillwell: Was the water relatively smooth?

Admiral Gayler: Yes, calm.

Paul Stillwell: How long were you in the water?

Admiral Gayler: Oh, maybe an hour and a half.

Paul Stillwell: What ship did you wind up on?

Admiral Gayler: *Chicago*.[*]

Paul Stillwell: Were you picked up directly by her or a destroyer?

Admiral Gayler: I scrambled up the nets, pretty tired.

Paul Stillwell: Where did you go from there?

Admiral Gayler: We went to Tongatabu in the Tonga group.

Paul Stillwell: The Friendly Islands.

Admiral Gayler: The Friendly Islands. And there we transferred to some dreadful old bucket. Took a long, long time by slow boat to get back to San Diego. That was the worst part. That was too damn long. We heard all of the rumors about Midway, you

---

[*] USS *Chicago* (CA-29) was a heavy cruiser.

know, but no real information. Of course, you know the *Yorktown*'s history. She hustled back to Pearl Harbor and got repaired in four days, and made it out there.*

Paul Stillwell: How did you avoid being in the part of the squadron that went to the *Yorktown*? Thach and Lovelace went on her.

Admiral Gayler: I don't know. Literally, I don't know.

Paul Stillwell: How long a period did it take to get back to the West Coast?

Admiral Gayler: I think it was about three weeks.

Paul Stillwell: What does one do to get in a new duty station when his ship has been sunk?

Admiral Gayler: Just after the Battle of the Coral Sea, I received dispatch orders to report to Anacostia for duty as a test pilot.† I didn't do anything about it on my own.

Paul Stillwell: Had you applied for that duty?

Admiral Gayler: There was a place on the annual fitness report form to say what you'd like to have as your next duty station. I'm pretty sure I checked it off on that, not with any real expectations of getting it, but just to see it as a nice thing to go for.

Paul Stillwell: Were you surprised to get that kind of duty when you had been an aviator for such a short time?

Admiral Gayler: No, not very. I felt better about my flying and figured I was up to it.

---

* The *Yorktown* (CV-5) was the only U.S. carrier sunk in the Battle of Midway.
† Anacostia is a section of the District of Columbia. It is across the Anacostia River from Washington. Until 1944, when the function was transferred to Patuxent River, Maryland, the air station at Anacostia was the site of the Navy's service testing of new aircraft.

Paul Stillwell: How do you think you came to be picked? Was that probably on the basis of reports from seniors?

Admiral Gayler: Must have been, I guess. I don't really know. I was a little surprised but certainly pleased.

Paul Stillwell: So then I presume you collected your wife and headed across country.

Admiral Gayler: Yes. We were under instructions not to say what had happened. The fact that the *Lexington* was lost was kept secret. I showed up in a borrowed pair of khaki uniforms that didn't fit me very well and I had no baggage, but I provided no explanation.

Paul Stillwell: "Here I am."

Admiral Gayler: "Here I am, and I've got orders to Anacostia." [Laughter]

Paul Stillwell: What types of things were you testing then? Did you have to go through the school before beginning to do test flights?

Admiral Gayler: There wasn't any school in those days. The school consisted of Commander Fred Trapnell, who was probably one of the best test pilots we ever had.[*] Figuratively speaking, he was on one end of the log, and I was on the other. There were other experienced people there, Tommy Booth for one.[†] But Trap was really the guy, and I think he had a very good idea of what I was up to and what I wasn't up to. He brought me along in more or less routine things like making takeoff measurements and whatnot.

The big breakthrough was when we got together to fly the very first Hellcat and evaluate it, which was the F6F-2.[‡] He flew it, got out of it, and motioned me into it. I

---
[*] Commander Frederick M. Trapnell, USN.
[†] Lieutenant Charles Thomas Booth II, USN.
[‡] Grumman F6F fighters first entered fleet squadrons in early 1943. The most commonly employed version of the airplane was the F6F-5, which was 34 feet long, wingspan of 43 feet, gross weight of 15,413 pounds, and top speed of 380 miles per hour.

came down all full of ideas about it. I can see he was a little bit amused, but not very. And so we went on from there.

It was a fascinating duty. Because of wartime pressures, we just flew everything in sight. Time was at a tremendous premium. For example, there was little chance to put engines on test stands to see whether they were going to come apart at their rated war emergency power settings. So we did the tests in the airplanes themselves. We shut down the regulator, entered the time, saw what came off the engines, put that back on, and tried it again to see whether the fix worked.

But at Anacostia, it was unbelievable. We flew every damn thing out of that field. One runway was 2,200 feet long and ended in an earthen dam at the Anacostia River. The approach was down by St. Elizabeth's hospital, right by the stacks. There was a missing brick in the stack; I used that as a marker. I would fly just below it and below such and such a speed to (a), get over the telephone wires, and (b) slow enough and short enough to get over that slot before I wound up against that dike. We had to use that runway in the wintertime because the prevailing winds here are westerly. It was just the beginning of the tricycle landing gear era, and, of course, the ones with the conventional gears would ground-loop.

Let's see. We flew all the Navy stuff, and all the Air Force stuff, the P-47s, P-51s, P-39s.

Paul Stillwell: Why did Navy pilots fly Army Air Forces planes?

Admiral Gayler: Comparative evaluation, tactical development. We had a P-51, which was really slicked up, that we used as our speed pacer. We had carefully calibrated the speed on it, and then we would use it to fly wing on the plane under test. When the relative motion was zero, you could tell the speed of the test plane from this calibrated P-51. You won't believe how we did it. We used to calibrate the damn thing by flying up the Potomac River about ten feet off the water, going like the hammers of hell between marked points and timing them with a stopwatch that we kept on one knee.

One point for these runs was a pontoon bridge where the Woodrow Wilson Bridge now is, and the other one was the tip of Hains Point. And we would go roaring up the river in the middle of the war. When we got to the point on Hains Point, we'd pull up in a big chandelle, fly around the Washington Monument and the White House, then back down the river in the opposite direction to compensate for the winds. Things were so much different in that era that I can simply imagine what would happen if anyone tried something like those maneuvers today.

Paul Stillwell: It seems an unlikely place to have your flight test operation.

Admiral Gayler: Oh, Anacostia was where it was.

Paul Stillwell: Wasn't it a case that really the capability of the planes had outgrown this old field? You speak of the short runways.

Admiral Gayler: Yes, and, of course, halfway through that tour we went down the Patuxent River, which was interesting, because we put the place in commission.* It was nothing but runways. We used to say the Army Air Forces built the quarters first, then built the runways later. The Navy always builds runways first, and then they get around to building the quarters.

In my time there, we never had any quarters. So I had to go scrounge a place for my wife and family out in the Maryland tobacco country. One day I borrowed a little Widgeon seaplane that belonged to the Canadian liaison officer. His big fat Canadian Government gave him a little amphibious airplane to have for utility purposes. We borrowed that and went scouting up the coast of Chesapeake Bay. We saw this big white house sitting on a hill. When we flew by it real close, we could see that the place was all boarded up, the shades were drawn and whatnot. So I landed in the water, taxied up on the beach, and that attracted most of the population of Dares Beach, Maryland. Included was the agent who had the rental of the house, and I made the deal that day. That was

---

* Patuxent River Naval Air Station, Lexington Park, Maryland, was commissioned on 1 April 1943. By mid-August transfers had been made of flight test, radio test, aircraft armament, and the development squadron. Service test was transferred in 1944. On 16 June 1945 the Naval Air Test Center was established and took over test functions that had been performed by the air station. The station included a 10,000-foot runway, then the longest in the U.S.

fun. We had a little colony. There were four of us there, including Jim Ferguson and Al Boyne.

But we flew every damn thing. One year I had 52 different types in my logbook—not models, types. Everything from great, big flying boats to Focke-Wulf 190, Messerschmitt, Zero. We flew the Zero in simulated combat against all of our own fighters. I've got more time in a Zero than anybody who hasn't got slant eyes. We were in such a damn hurry to evaluate it that we didn't even repaint it. Once I was flying a damn Zero around Washington, with the Japanese meatball on it. The Army had a patrol of P-47s over the capital by then. Guys would head toward me, and I would ease way over Chesapeake Bay. I didn't know what they were going to do if they saw a Japanese airplane.

Later on we did the same thing with a Messerschmitt. Al Boyne picked up an ME-109 at Wright Field and brought it back.* Of course, it was marked in German. So we developed a sort of clock code, saying, for instance, that takeoff of the manifold pressure was at ten minutes to 12:00, throttle back to 10:30, things like that. While Al was flying over the mountains to get here, he noticed that the oil pressure had suddenly going down to zero, whereas the oil temperature climbed up to five minutes to 12.

He knew he had to put it somewhere, so he looked around and found a little emergency field. He damn near made it, but she quit on him. He landed with a great clang about 50 yards short. Fortunately the Germans had shoulder straps that crossed over top, which we didn't. He hit really hard, and the airplane went sliding down the runway, knocking him out. He woke up in this German airplane with a farmer standing over him with a pitchfork saying, "Get out of there, you gol-durned Nazi." [Laughter]

Al was still sort of coming out of it at that point. He said he was pretty sure he wasn't a Nazi, but he wasn't quite sure who he was. So he got his wallet and looked in it to see who he was. [Laughter] Oh, we had some bizarre times.

We had a British steam-cooled airplane, a Westland Whirlwind, to evaluate. This thing worked pretty well in the air, but on the ground, about 30 seconds after you started an engine, the safety valves would lift, and these two big plumes of steam would come out. At that point the tower would hit the fire signal, and the fire trucks would rush out

---

* Wright Field, near Dayton, Ohio, was the Army Air Forces equivalent of the Navy's flight test facility.

and block the runway so you couldn't take off. You'd go around and carefully brief the guy on duty before you got in the thing, but, of course, the watch would have changed.

We had the Skyrocket and the first F5F.[*] I put all the Navy types through test, all the mods of the F4U, all the mods of the F6F, the first airborne flights of the 4360 engine.[†]

Periodically we would come to Washington to give briefings on our progress in these various projects.

Paul Stillwell: Were these briefings for people in BuAer?[‡]

Admiral Gayler: People in BuAer, principally.

Paul Stillwell: Did they seem generally satisfied with the way things were going in the tests? Was there pressure to get the things out faster?

Admiral Gayler: Tremendous pressure to get things out faster. We also faced some pressure to underwrite airplanes that we weren't willing to underwrite, particularly for stability and control reasons. A really interesting one was the F4U-1, which they were extremely anxious to get out right away because it was, at the time, the highest performing standard airplane in the world. And it was a high performer, no question about it: speed, climb, everything else, even turning.

However, it had several drawbacks. The cockpit was too low and there was a lot of gadgetry in it that was unsatisfactory. So even though we were under great pressure to underwrite that for carrier operations, we did not. I didn't think it was suitable for combat, either, because you couldn't see out of it very well, in spite of its high performance. So the compromise was arranged that we would mock up something that you could see out of and Chance-Vought would build it.

---

[*] The D-558-1 Skyrocket was the first jet developed by the Douglas Aircraft Company. The F5F was a Grumman fighter prototype that did not go into production.

[†] The Vought F4U Corsair was in production longer than any other U.S. fighter plane of World War II. It first entered fleet squadrons in 1942. The F4U-1 was 33 feet, 4 inches long; wingspan of 41 feet; gross weight of 14,000 pounds; and top speed of 417 miles per hour.

[‡] BuAer—Bureau of Aeronautics, which was the Navy's agency for the development, testing, and maintenance of aircraft.

I remember that we went down to the little old tin seaplane hangar that still exists over at the Anacostia side, and three of us sat in the airplane. Big John Ferguson represented the big guys; I did so for the middle-sized guys, and Johnny Hyland, who was later CinCPacFlt, did so for the little pilots.* We used stiff welder's wires and masking tape to outline what we needed for visibility. We took pictures of it and induced the bureau to tell the contractor, "That's the way to build it."

Vought's representative objected mightily. He said it would cost ten knots in top speed and to have all this, that, and the other would cause the collapse of the war effort, practically. But we insisted, and that's the way they built it, and that was the precise enclosure shape of the F4U-3s, -4s, and -5s, which were so successful. I've always been amused at that.

Oh, yes, incidentally, when we finally got that airplane to evaluate the speed loss, there wasn't any. But it was marvelous, in a way. That's the way you got things done, and the whole process took only a couple of months.

I was the project pilot on the first jet, the YP-59.† That was so secret it had dummy wooden propellers on it. We had to trundle it out before dawn and take the propellers off before we could fly. She was designed to have five hours between overhauls on the engine, but she never made it that long. She burned through the burner cams before then.

Then I had as a project the first American-built turbine engine, which was built by General Electric. A big, tall, lanky Dutchman named Krone was the engineer who designed it. He came down and practically put it in his lap.

Paul Stillwell: You were one of the very first Navy pilots to fly a jet, weren't you?

Admiral Gayler: Yes.

---

* Lieutenant Commander John J. Hyland, USN, was stationed at Anacostia from 1942 to 1944; during that time he served as a test pilot and also as personal pilot for Admiral Ernest J. King, USN, the Chief of Naval Operations and Commander in Chief U.S. Fleet. As a four-star admiral Hyland commanded the Pacific Fleet from 1967 to 1970. His oral history is in the Naval Institute collection.
† As the designation indicates, this was an Army Air Forces plane. The P-59 Airacomet, manufactured by Bell, was 38 feet long, wingspan of 46 feet, and had a top speed of 410 miles per hour. It did not get into combat.

Paul Stillwell: How did you compare that to a reciprocating engine? Was it easier?

Admiral Gayler: Much easier. The first great thing was that you could see where you were going, which was an unprecedented luxury. It was quiet, and the YP-59 happened to have a very, very low wing loading. It was kind of like a glider. It was a very simple airplane. And that jet wasn't any higher in performance than the prop planes. The main thing was you never knew when the engines were going to burn through the burner cams, so you had to be careful about your temperatures.

Paul Stillwell: I can see some rationale in your assignment to that, because you had had the combat experience, so they could draw on that knowledge for things that would be useful in fighter planes.

Admiral Gayler: I was expected to have a lot more combat experience than I actually had. I guess I was all they had at the time.

Paul Stillwell: Very experienced combat pilots were in short supply in the Navy, so I don't think you had too much competition.

Admiral Gayler: That's probably right.

Paul Stillwell: Since you flew U.S., Japanese, and German planes, can you draw any comparisons in the qualities of each?

Admiral Gayler: There are several time eras. You could list them in sort of this order. The best combat airplane I flew down there was the Bearcat, the Grumman F8F.[*] But it never saw combat. Next to that was a pretty even tie: the F4U-4s and F4U-5s and the P-51Gs. The P-51 was faster in a dive, a little cleaner. About equal in climb. Those were the best. Next I would say the Focke-Wulf, and then one of the late mark Spitfires,

---

[*] The F8F Bearcat was among the finest piston-engine fighters ever in the U.S. Navy. To speed was 421 miles an hour. The plane first reached an operational squadron in May 1945, too late to make an impact on the Pacific war.

the Mark 12, as I recall. The Zero was a sort of different class. It was an extremely good airplane at high altitude, had a light wing loading, very clean airplane, and beautiful maneuvers, beautiful turns. It had a fairly heavy aileron, but you could muscle them around. Very long range. A very economical airplane.

Paul Stillwell: Was the one you flew the same plane that had been recovered in the Aleutians?*

Admiral Gayler: Yes. The poor guy had just got nicked in the oil line, and he put it down on what he thought was grass, and it was muskeg.

Paul Stillwell: Would you put all of those above the F6F that you've mentioned?

Admiral Gayler: Yes. The P-47 would be next, then the F6F. The Hellcat was a lovely, comfortable airplane to fly, but it was pretty slow compared to the others.

Paul Stillwell: What about comparing it with the F4F?

Admiral Gayler: Oh, a hell of a lot better airplane than the F4F. Much better. It was an enormous improvement, and Grumman cranked out 600 a month. After all, numbers count too.

Some of the others, let's see. Focke-Wulf was a nice little airplane. It was sort of like the Bearcat. In fact, the Bearcat was largely modeled after it. Bob Hall quite consciously picked up a lot of features from the Focke-Wulf.† When we got the thing, it was on a barge coming down the Anacostia River. It came with no information, no nothing. Just here the airplane is, test it. I looked in the cockpit, and it had a lot of indirect controls, push buttons that were marked and abbreviated in aeronautical German. I couldn't tell what the hell they did. You know, on most airplanes, you can tell this controls the flaps, this is for something else, and so on. So we put the plane on a chain

---

* For details see Robert L. Underbrink, "The Day the Navy Caught a Zero," *U.S. Naval Institute Proceedings*, February 1968, pages 136-137.
† Robert L. Hall was a versatile employee for Grumman, working as an engineer, designer, and test pilot.

fall and put a hydro-compressor on it. Then I sat in the cockpit and pushed each button to see what would happen. I've always been glad they hadn't invented the ejection seat. I'd have been off the top of that.

Paul Stillwell: Was there any emphasis on planes that would be particularly useful at night, since you had had some experience with night flying before?

Admiral Gayler: Yes, there was a lot of emphasis on that. Of course, we were very vigorously trying to develop night fighters, the F7F-5N, I think it was, was a night fighter we put through tests.* And, of course, the F6F in its various radar versions, a lot of emphasis on that. Even more later on in Air Development Squadron Three, which is another tale coming up later. It was, as I say, a very high-powered thing with Commander, later Captain, Fred Trapnell—"Trap," as everybody in naval aviation knew him, taking the—he was the man who really set the tone of the place, quite remarkable aviator and officer.

We had the Navy's first helicopter there. And we had a plane with a hands-off automatic landing system. This is 1944 I'm talking about. Forty years ago they had hands-off automatic landing, all the way down to touchdown. These airliners don't do it yet. It's amazing how retarded we have been.

Paul Stillwell: At what point would you take your hands off?

Admiral Gayler: You watch it like a hawk and let it take you all the way down. That was the idea.

Paul Stillwell: You had it on automatic pilot then?

Admiral Gayler: Yes, on automatic pilot and automatic landing sequence—40 years ago.

---

* The Grumman F7F Tigercat was a twin-engine plane, built primarily in a night-fighter version. Too late for operational service in World War II, it was displaced by jets soon afterward.

Paul Stillwell: Was this all geared in with the altimeter?

Admiral Gayler: It worked off a special radio. I don't know how reliable it was. I'm not sure I would have done it at night, but in the daytime, when you could watch what was happening, it was all right.

Paul Stillwell: So it was actually from the ground, is that right?

Admiral Gayler: Yes. It was an adaptation of a beam—I've forgotten the name.

Paul Stillwell: Your comment about all those push buttons sort of bears out the observation I've heard that the engineering in German planes was much more sophisticated than Japanese.

Admiral Gayler: It depends on what you mean by sophisticated, of course. If you mean complicated, yes. A lot of people confuse those two ideas. Sophistication can be very simple, elegant. It can be sophisticated too. In fact, that's what you should look for in design—not complication. I thought the Zero was a very well designed airplane. Everything worked, everything was handy. Where the Japanese lost out was they didn't have the high-powered engines we eventually developed. They were trying to do on 1,200 horsepower what we were doing on 2,000, 2,400, even 3,000 later on.

Paul Stillwell: There's a story that the engine was switched in the F6F that made it much more powerful.

Admiral Gayler: That's right. The F6F-2 had an R-2600 engine in it, and the standard 3s and 4s and 5s all had an R-2800.[*] It can make an appreciable difference. Yes, the first model was underpowered.

---

[*] The Wright R-2600 Cyclone engine had rated horsepower of 1,700. The Pratt & Whitney R-2800 initially produced 2,000 horsepower; later versions increased that to 2,100 and then 2,400.

Paul Stillwell: Did you have much chance to get off duty during these two years?

Admiral Gayer: Sure, it was routine shore duty, in a way, except instead of going to an office, you would go down to the runways and do your stuff.

Paul Stillwell: What was your experience initially in flying helicopters?

Admiral Gayler: I didn't get a chance at it until later on, because the skipper, Paul Ramsey, out of interest and whatnot, took the project on for himself. In the course of one of the early investigatory flights, he and—I think it was Ferguson—settled into the water right off what we called the Gold Coast at Patuxent, which is where the officers' quarters were. They were rescued by somebody's boy in a rowboat. Paul always claimed he had carburetor icing, but I'm not so sure. Those things were so underpowered, if you turned down wind, you were likely to settle into the ground. It was an absolute "no-no" to say anything about that, particularly the rescue. [Laughter]

Paul Stillwell: This was the Ramsey who had been the fighter skipper in the *Lexington*.

Admiral Gayler: Yes.

Paul Stillwell: Well, anything else on that tour of duty?

Admiral Gayler: During that year at Patuxent, I had 11 forced landings. I got to be very good at it.

Paul Stillwell: What would be the primary cause of these forced landings?

Admiral Gayler: Oh, something would come off the engine, lose engine oil, usually, a master rod bearing fail. Once I remember I blew out the seals on the oil-driven propeller so you couldn't see anything. Engine failures, generally speaking.

Paul Stillwell: Did you have your operations fairly close to the Patuxent area so that these forced landings would be convenient to the base?

Admiral Gayler: Oh, yes. On these war emergency power trials, I did them right over the field. I suppose I could give you a lot more interesting tales about different kinds of airplanes and all their peculiarities, lots of sea stories about forced landings and whatnot, but I think that's about it for this record.

Interview Number 4 with Admiral Noel A. M. Gayler, U.S. Navy (Retired)

Place: Admiral Gayler's office at the American Committee on East-West Accord, Washington, D.C.

Date: Monday, 30 January 1984

Paul Stillwell: Admiral, you had been in on some of the early carrier combat of the war in 1942, then came back to the States for two years as a test pilot. What was your inclination about getting back out to the war in the Pacific?

Admiral Gayler: I was not eager to get back out to the war. I was eager to have command, but I felt I was doing just exactly what I should have been doing, was well qualified, and when my turn came to go out again, fine. But I wasn't champing at the bit.

Paul Stillwell: You got command of a fighter squadron, which was a highly desired assignment.

Admiral Gayler: Fighting 12, yes.

Paul Stillwell: Had you been having any discussions with BuPers on what was coming up for you?*

Admiral Gayler: I saw them occasionally, and possibly I came to somebody's attention through the briefings I gave at BuAer on our flight-test work. I don't know. I really was too busy to pay any attention to it.

Paul Stillwell: Where was the fighter squadron when you reported to it?

Admiral Gayler: Naval Air Station Melbourne, Florida.

---

* BuPers—the Bureau of Naval Personnel made duty assignments for officers.

Paul Stillwell: How much of a chance did you get to work up in the squadron before you deployed?

Admiral Gayler: Pretty good. We worked a lot in the Florida area, and then we went out to a field which we had to ourselves in Seaside, Oregon, of all places, and put the finishing touches on there. It was an unusual squadron, in that we had 54 aircraft assigned to us and about 105 pilots, which was too damn big. It was an experimental way to organize. So we broke into two parts with my exec and next senior officer as de facto semi-skippers of the two parts to make it manageable, if you will.

Paul Stillwell: Were you flying the F6F?

Admiral Gayler: Flying F6Fs, that's right. And then we got an opportunity to transition to F4Us, which I was all for doing, but we had only a weekend to do it, so we finally decided not to.

Paul Stillwell: Was the choice up to the squadron on what plane you would fly?

Admiral Gayler: It was influential, let's put it that way.

Paul Stillwell: You had a different sort of assignment in that you weren't so much an individual anymore; you were a leader of a group of men, and this was a new assignment for you in the aviation field. How did you take to that?

Admiral Gayler: It wasn't all that new. I had been flight officer of a squadron before, which sure isn't the skipper, but he has a certain amount of leadership responsibility. Well, I was far better off as a fighter pilot the second time around than the first. I was pretty fresh-caught the first time around. The second time I had some little combat experience and quite a lot of test experience under my belt, so I felt much more mature as a fighter pilot.

Paul Stillwell: How soon did you get out to a carrier?

Admiral Gayler: I'm pretty vague on dates. I went out to the *Randolph* in time to make the WestPac deployment.[*]

Paul Stillwell: Where did you pick her up, at Alameda?

Admiral Gayler: Yes, and we went out with her all the way out to WestPac.

Paul Stillwell: How soon did the ship and air wing training get going? Could you describe that period?

Admiral Gayler: Well, in a sense, just as soon as we got to sea. Of course, training from a carrier is very much truncated compared to what you can do from the beach for a lot of reasons, safety reasons and availability of targets, and all sorts of things.

Paul Stillwell: Who was the air group commander?

Admiral Gayler: Charlie Crommelin, one of the five Crommelin brothers, one of the most marvelous guys that ever lived.[†]

Paul Stillwell: Why do you say that of him? What qualities did he have?

Admiral Gayler: Leadership, spirit, courage, the works.

Paul Stillwell: His brother John was a very strong leader against the Green Bowl Society.[‡]

---

[*] USS *Randolph* (CV-15) had gone into commission on 9 October 1944. Initially she had on board Air Group 87, which was replaced in January 1945 by Air Group 12, including Gayler's squadron. The ship sailed from Alameda on 20 January and arrived at Ulithi in early February.
[†] Commander Charles L. Crommelin, USN.
[‡] Captain John G. Crommelin Jr., USN. The Green Bowl Society was a secret organization comprised of Naval Academy graduates who gave preferential treatment in assignments to other members of the group.

Admiral Gayler: So was Charlie, and John Crommelin, of course, was totally right on that issue. We had no business having secret societies and "You scratch my back, I'll scratch your back" business within the Navy. Nor do we have any business having secret cabals run by Hyman Rickover, either.* So I think the Crommelin brothers, and John particularly, were both very courageous and very correct in what they did.

Paul Stillwell: Did you discuss that while you were there, or was that an issue of the day?

Admiral Gayler: It was wardroom talk, yes. I knew John quite well, too, because he was the training officer for Fleet Air West Coast, and he was the officer to whom I was really responsible, although nominally responsible to the admiral. I was really responsible to John Crommelin, through Charlie. Charlie was responsible for the air group itself.

Paul Stillwell: Are there any notable incidents from the crossing?

Admiral Gayler: No, I remember it as lots and lots of flying, and that was about it.

Paul Stillwell: What was the fleet preparing for when you joined up?

Admiral Gayler: We didn't have a lot of advance information about what was going to happen. I remember that the invasion of Iwo came as a complete surprise to me when I was briefed on it.† I think quite rightly they didn't involve the air group too much in that sort of thing.

Paul Stillwell: How much of an outline of the strategic picture did people at your level get?

---

* Hyman G. Rickover was considered the father of the nuclear Navy. He ran the U.S. Navy's nuclear-power program for many years, from 1948 until he eventually left active duty in 1982 with the rank of four-star admiral on the retired list. Rickover Hall at the Naval Academy is named in his honor, as is the nuclear-powered attack submarine *Hyman G. Rickover* (SSN-709), which was commissioned 21 July 1984.
† U.S. Marines, supported by the Navy, invaded Iwo Jima in the Bonin Islands on 19 February 1945.

Admiral Gayler: Oh, we had a pretty good idea of what the strategic picture was. I was just talking about specifics. Iwo Jima was not so far in the future, but it was a surprise when we learned of it. It would not have occurred to me to try to take the Bonin Islands, but then I wasn't clued into the B-29 problem and P-51 problem as I was later on.[*]

Paul Stillwell: You'd been away from the fleet for more than two and a half years. Was there any sense of rustiness when you got back into combat again?

Admiral Gayler: I didn't get back into combat again. I never saw another Japanese airplane in the air. The first cruise, there were Japanese all over us, and the second one, I don't want to be too flippant about it, but there weren't enough Japanese to go around. The most dangerous thing was people diving on the same fellow. Then I didn't stay with the squadron very long after we got out there. I went to the staff of the Second Carrier Task Force. That was commanded by Admiral Slew McCain.[†]

Paul Stillwell: What characteristics do you particularly recall about Admiral McCain?

Admiral Gayler: Well, he was a very colorful man. Colorful means he was a character. I think he had great shrewdness in appraising people and knew how to get people to work for him. He was just sort of a delightful figure. He made no pretense of being a great technician of any kind, but he was a fighter and a good leader, and I thought very much like his son, my friend Jack McCain, whom I knew for so very many years.[‡]

Paul Stillwell: Was Admiral McCain the sort to leave the details to his staff?

---

[*] Iwo Jima was captured to supply an alternate landing field for damaged Army Air Forces planes flying long bombing runs from the Marianas to the Japanese home islands. It also served as a base for the fighter planes so they could escort the bombing missions.

[†] Vice Admiral John S. McCain, USN, Commander Task Force 38. McCain's son, John S., Jr., later became a four-star admiral and Gayler's predecessor as CinCPac. His grandson, once a Navy pilot, is now a U.S. Senator from Arizona.

[‡] Admiral John S. McCain Jr., USN, served as Commander in Chief Pacific from 31 July 1968 to 1 September 1972. He was relieved in that billet by Admiral Gayler. McCain's brief oral history is in the Naval Institute collection.

Admiral Gayler: Oh, yes. Yes, the staff was essentially run by Jimmy Thach.*

Paul Stillwell: It might be fair to assume that Thach had something to do with your assignment to McCain's staff.

Admiral Gayler: I think that's a pretty good presumption.

Paul Stillwell: What was your specific billet within the staff?

Admiral Gayler: I was the air operations officer, and that was in the period of the late strikes against Japan. It was essentially my job to divide up the empire of Japan into five parts and see what we were going to clobber next. We hit them for about two days running, and just about the time they would start reacting to that by shifting forces, we'd go somewhere else and hit them. That was during the time of the Okinawa campaign, during which the carriers provided a lot of support.† Later on, when the empire was collapsing, we went after the Japanese fleet.

We had one famous time when Admiral Halsey decided that it was time for the battleships to get into the act.‡ So he told Admiral McCain to look around for a target that we could hit with the battleships. So we on the Second Carrier Task Force Staff looked and looked, and we finally found a secondary coke and iron plant at a place called Muroran, if memory serves.§ Admiral Halsey decided the battleships were going to go bombard it.

Well, it turned out that the air cover required to cover the battleships while they ran in toward the coast and bombarded this joint required more sorties than it would have required to knock it down in the first place. So we presented that to Admiral Halsey, and

---

* Thach, who had been Gayler's skipper in VF-3 when the United States entered World War II, was by 1945 a captain.
† U.S. forces invaded the island of Okinawa, only 340 miles from the closest point in the Japanese home islands, on 1 April 1945.
‡ Admiral William F. Halsey Jr., USN, Commander Third Fleet.
§ On 15 July 1945, a Third Fleet force comprised of three battleships, two cruisers, and eight destroyers bombarded iron and steel plants at Muroran, Hokkaido. The previous day a force of three battleships, two heavy cruisers, and nine destroyers bombarded iron works at Kamaishi, Honshu, the first major surface bombardment of the home islands.

he sent us away with a flea in our ear. He said he was going to get the battleships in there bombarding. So they did, and they went in there and fired away, but unfortunately, the plant was on flat land, and the bombardment was at pretty short range, so the trajectory was very flat. As I recall, possibly erroneously, all the rounds went whistling by and landed in the boonies about a mile behind the plant.[*] Being intolerant as young officers are likely to be, I thought it was a terrible fiasco, but at least the battleships had their day in the sun.

Paul Stillwell: Well, he had grown up in that Navy, so that's understandable.

Admiral Gayler: That's right.

Paul Stillwell: How was Admiral Halsey perceived by the carrier task force commander? Was he perceived as a competent commander?

Admiral Gayler: I think Admiral Halsey was very much liked as a person and as a commander. With the intolerance of youth, we relatively junior members of the staff didn't think that the fleet staff was with us, and perhaps we didn't think that even Admiral McCain quite understood what was going on. But I wouldn't take that as a measured judgment.

Paul Stillwell: Well, it's your perception, and that's the point of this whole thing.

Admiral Gayler: During the terrible losses to kamikazes in the Okinawa campaign, you know, we were losing destroyers up there in the northern station.[†] I think their average life expectancy was a day and a half or something, because the kamikazes coming down the chain would be the first ships they'd see, so they'd dive into them. We tried to persuade Halsey to take the *Missouri* and *New Jersey* and some of the others up there and

---

[*] Other accounts indicate that the bombardment did substantial damage to a steel plant at Muroran.
[†] Kamikazes were Japanese suicide aircraft that began showing up in the Philippines campaign in the autumn of 1944. The pilots attempted to crash their bomb-armed aircraft directly into American warships. Hundreds of them successfully hit their targets and inflicted great damage.

put them on that station.* We figured if a kamikaze hit the *Missouri*, all they'd have to do would be pipe sweepers and go on from there, but he wouldn't do it.† I don't know how seriously this was advanced to him.

Paul Stillwell: Were you involved in trying to devise tactics to combat the kamikazes?

Admiral Gayler: Oh, yes. So was everybody else. The most effective thing, of course, was to get fighters on them early. The fighters slaughtered them, but they still kept on coming. As I say, they would just dive into the first thing they saw. What is remarkable is that so many missed. When you think about it, to drive an airplane into a ship is the simplest thing in the world. There's no reason why you should miss, nor is it a question of flinching at the last moment, because you're just as dead if you dive in the water as if you dive into a ship.

After the war was over, I had some extremely interesting experiences right away in Japan, which I'll tell you about at the appropriate time, but one of them was talking to a bunch of kamikaze pilots who were damn glad the war was over.

Paul Stillwell: You talked about dividing up the empire of Japan and picking your targets. What would that be based on? Where would you get the intelligence?

Admiral Gayler: Mostly air reconnaissance. We were just systematically mopping up all the targets, and it was based on targets to be struck and the defenses to be expected. As I say, we were able to move from area to area faster than they were able to concentrate their defenses. The five only reflected the fact that we had five task groups in those days, four American and one British. They were all together under Task Force 38 or 58, as the case may be.

---

* The battleship *Missouri* (BB-63) was Halsey's flagship at the time.
† The idea was that sweepers with brooms could get rid of the debris from the kamikaze because there would be no damage to the ship herself. The *Missouri* actually was hit by a kamikaze on 11 April 1945 and suffered minor damage.

Paul Stillwell: How much contact did you or the admiral have with the various task group commanders? Did they come aboard?

Admiral Gayler: Yes. We saw them frequently. We were very, very close to them all, easy terms, even informal terms on the radio. I would say it was very close.

Paul Stillwell: What do you recall about your chief of staff?

Admiral Gayler: That was Wilder Baker.* Of course, he was a fine officer and a good chief of staff, but not being an aviator, he was not really in the central event. Jimmy Thach and the admiral really ran it between them. I was one of Thach's assistants, as was Bill Leonard.†

Paul Stillwell: Was Baker pushing for more play for the surface ships?

Admiral Gayler: Not that I recall. I think most of that came from Halsey.

Paul Stillwell: What about Admiral Willis Lee, who was the battleship commander?‡

Admiral Gayler: I know he was, but I don't personally know of his specific requests. I'm sure he wanted a piece of the action, but just how that worked, I don't know. I only recall being one of the delegation that went to call on Halsey and went back with the flea in our ear on that subject. [Laughter]

Paul Stillwell: What would be the basis for your deciding which targets to strike? Were you going for industrial areas or military installations?

---

* Rear Admiral Wilder D. Baker, USN. Aviation flag officers had surface officers as chiefs of staff and vice versa.
† Lieutenant Commander William N. Leonard, USN, later a flag officer.
‡ Vice Admiral Willis A. Lee, Jr. USN, Commander Battleship Squadron Two.

Admiral Gayler: Military installations solely. We in the carrier task force didn't go after populations of cities per se. Of course, some of the military targets were embedded in populated areas, but we didn't go for population. Essentially, we didn't take part in the city-busting strikes against Tokyo or Yokohama or any of those places.

Paul Stillwell: Did you have any contact with the Army Air Forces and General LeMay's group?[*]

Admiral Gayler: Well, I did as an individual, but the force didn't. I got to know General Blackie Moore, who was running the P-51 strikes up from Iwo pretty well as a fighter pilot.[†] I was sent in there on a special mission to talk to him about a range extension because I had done a lot of that work before, and that was their major problem. Because Iwo was some 715 miles within the empire, which is a hell of a long way to send fighters, even P-51s.

Paul Stillwell: How did you avoid mutual interference with Army planes on targets?

Admiral Gayler: Just timing. We never hit them at the same time.

Paul Stillwell: Did you know what the Army aircraft were going to do?

Admiral Gayler: The P-51s were essentially escorting, anyway, so yes. There was an overall coordination, and I remember particularly well when we suddenly got a message telling us not to go within 50 miles of three designated cities. That, of course, was to make room for the atom bomb drops. I don't know whether the third city has ever become public knowledge. Maybe it never should. But there was a third, which was an alternative to Hiroshima and Nagasaki.[‡]

---

[*] Major General Curtis E. LeMay, USAAF, was commanding general of the 21st Bomber Command, which was running B-29 strikes against the Japanese Empire from bases in the Marianas.
[†] Brigadier General Ernest C. Moore, USAAF.
[‡] In the first combat use of atomic bombs, U.S. B-29 bombers hit Hiroshima, on the island of Honshu, on 6 August 1945 and Nagasaki, on Kyushu, on 9 August. See the Naval Institute oral history of Vice Admiral Frederick L. Ashworth, USN (Ret.), who was the weaponeer on the Nagasaki mission.

Paul Stillwell: Did you know why you were being warned off?

Admiral Gayler: It's possible that the admiral did, but I didn't.

Paul Stillwell: What was the reaction in the ship and the staff when the news came?

Admiral Gayler: Well, it was rather curious. On the one hand, we recognized that something new had come along. On the other hand, there was a sort of tendency to extrapolate it and worry whether radioactivity was going to creep all over the islands and all sorts of nonsensical stuff. We didn't have much information on it. We were out aboard ship; there were no newspapers. We got the bare formal announcements and that was about it. A lot of speculation about it.

Paul Stillwell: How much interaction did Admiral McCain have with Admiral Mitscher?[*]

Admiral Gayler: Well, the formal interaction didn't amount to much. The change of watch took place in a couple of days, and my surmise is that they really had little that they had to exchange. The thing had gotten to be pretty much in a routine. They'd done this drill before.

Paul Stillwell: Do you recall anything specific about hitting the Japanese fleet at the end of the war?

Admiral Gayler: Well, it provided a lesson to me and to all officers about not counting your chickens before they hatched. I remember we got a supply of bombs with fuzes that were supposed to make them go off with they hit something hard but not go off when they hit water. I guess it was I who thought up the bright idea of using them if we went after the battleship *Nagato*. She was in one of the almost fjord-like bays where the

---

[*] Vice Admiral Marc A. Mitscher, USN, served as Commander Task Force 58, the fast carrier task force, in 1944-45. He and McCain alternated in command of the fast carriers.

Japanese were squirreling away their remaining ships. There wasn't room enough to use torpedoes, but I thought that bombs with water-discriminating fuzes would have the effect of torpedoes: a close miss would mine the ship and sink it.

In the end, we briefed the carrier air groups on that. What we had figured on was that we'd get some close misses out of their trying to hit it, but when the pilots knew that the misses were going to do the job, why, subconsciously, I'm sure, what we got was one hell of a lot of misses, most of which weren't even very close. I suppose the lesson there is to take into account the psychology of the thing a little bit more than I did at the time. I hadn't thought of that one. In the event, the *Nagato* was hit by a few bombs, but, as you know, she survived until the Bikini atom test.[*]

Paul Stillwell: Did you have information on the whereabouts of U.S. submarines so you wouldn't hit them?

Admiral Gayler: Well, we wouldn't have ordinarily hit them anyway. Practically all the submarines were our own by that time in the war. Of course, we had the rescue submarines up there. We knew their positions very well because we briefed them to all the pilots. I guess the answer is yes, we did.

Paul Stillwell: Did you have any inputs of "ultra" information in the carriers?[†]

Admiral Gayler: Probably did, but while I guessed where it was coming from, it was never briefed to me as ultra. I know that Thach and the admiral had sort of understood that we wouldn't discuss what the sources were, but it was not too hard to figure out where it was coming from when we saw the nature of it.

Paul Stillwell: What kinds of information would that be?

---

[*] In July 1946 Joint Task Force One of the Army and Navy conducted atomic bomb tests against ships in Bikini Atoll in the Marshall Islands.
[†] Ultra—short for ultra secret—was a special security classification given by the British to information gained from breaking the code of the German radio enciphering machine. It has come to be used more broadly to encompass other information obtained from interception and decryption of German and Japanese radio communications.

Admiral Gayler: Having to do with Japanese movements, for one, and also very interesting messages having to do with supply difficulties and frantic requests for this, that, and the other thing. We received some remarkably revealing disclosures of how close to being on the uppers the Japanese were. For instance, we saw proposals to make aviation fuel out of pine root oil and sort of desperate measures like that. We picked up a lot of that.

Paul Stillwell: What do you recall about the end of the war?

Admiral Gayler: I recall it vividly. When the war ended, the first thing that happened was that the first Japanese envoy came out, and he actually came out to our flagship. He was a brother of Akihito, the crown prince. My memory may be tricky on this one. Anyway, he was a relatively young member of the royal family. Of course, we didn't know what he was going to talk about, but he was the object of a hell of a lot of curiosity just to look at him.

Then the surrender settlement was arrived at in principle. Let me get the sequence of this quite correct. Then it was that we arranged for the entrance into Tokyo Bay and the Yokosuka area, which was done by Admiral Badger's task group.* It was thought that the Japanese surrender might not be genuine, or at least that there might be fanatical resistance groups. The course of Badger's force came right by the ports at close range. They were old-fashioned but still had good-size artillery in them, so the ships could easily have been sunk had there been treachery. So it was decided to mount an enormous air demonstration over Tokyo. If my memory serves me right, we put 1,200 aircraft over Tokyo on that day. Some of my friends said it was the most dangerous mission of the war. [Laughter] They all were supposed to fly over at 500 feet and just keep it going—1,200 airplanes from the fleet.

I was detailed to go in with Badger's force. My job was to stand by with a mike in my hand, and if there was any problem, I would call in the air strikes. So I was temporarily detached from Second Carrier Task Force staff and sent over to Badger. As

---

* Rear Admiral Oscar C. Bader, USN. His flagship was the light cruiser *San Diego* (CL-53), which on 27 August 1945 became the first major Allied warship to enter Tokyo Bay since the beginning of the war.

everybody knows, we went in without incident. After that I didn't have anything to do and nobody to report to, so I asked for permission to go ashore and take a look around. Two of us went ashore together. The other man was a reserve officer—a smart, redheaded Chicago lawyer named Charlie Martin. To the best of my knowledge, we were the first Americans to set foot in the Yokosuka area. We went in with our .38s in our hands, looking around for somebody to take a shot at us.

We walked through these enormous, empty, echoing industrial halls. The Japanese had been told to leave everything exactly like it was and go, and they took that literally. We saw an individual draftsman's instruments still on his drafting table, clothes in the lockers, half-eaten lunch on one table. The place was absolutely empty. It was the most eerie thing I ever saw, like the mystery of *Mary Celeste*.[*] I remember walking into a foundry, and there on the hard-pack cinder floor were six long cylindrical objects. I was able to recognize them only because I had done most of the initial jet work at Patuxent. They were [unclear] 006 jet engines that had been carried around by submarine from Germany. Why the hell they were sitting on the floor of a foundry, I don't know, but that's where they were. Then we went over to the naval air station at Atsugi and looked around.

Paul Stillwell: What transportation did you have?

Admiral Gayler: We got a boat. I'm damned if I can think of how we got that boat. I think we just talked some Japanese into taking us over. Anyway, over there we went, and there was a hangar, a seaplane hangar, just full of Japanese copies of the Me-163, a German rocket airplane with no tail.[†] It did a lot of execution against B-17s in the European theater. I've seen some terrible films of B-17s just being shot out of the sky by these rocket airplanes. The Germans operated them quasi-successfully. I think they shot

---

[*] The *Mary Celeste* was a 19th century brigantine. In early November 1872 the sailing ship departed New York with Captain Benjamin Briggs, his wife, young daughter and a crew of eight. The ship carried a cargo of 1,700 barrels of raw American alcohol bound for Genoa, Italy. On 4 December the *Mary Celeste* was discovered, completely abandoned, about 600 miles off the coast of Portugal. The captain, his family and crew were never seen again, nor was there any real explanation for their disappearance.

[†] The Messerschmitt ME 163, also known as the Komet, was the only interceptor-fighter powered solely by a rocket motor to be used in combat in World War II. The first operational use was in July 1944 against American B-17 bombers.

down more airplanes than they lost. I remember the handbook on it, which I guess I had seen at Patuxent before I went out. The rocket ran on red fuming nitric acid and aniline, two liquids coming together. There were instructions that said that if you hadn't gotten to a certain speed, at what we would call now V-0, by such and such a distance down the runway, step out on the wing and pull the chute, because it was about to blow up. [Laughter] Some airplane.

Another hangar was full of baka bombs with that Caproni semi-jet propulsion.[*] Then we went to another building and on the upper floor a mock-up had been in progress. Of course, I recognized what that was, having sat on many a mock-up board. It was partly hardware and partly plywood, just like we do it, painted appropriately. But the thing they were mocking up was to be a jet-powered suicide airplane with a 5,000-pound warhead. It was to be fired from catapults in caves against our fleet when we assaulted the empire. I remember my thinking from the time. I could understand somebody diving an airplane into a ship, but I could not believe that someone would start an entire development program like this. It was essentially a guided missile whose guidance system was going to be a human being. That's what they were doing.

After that, Martin and I didn't have much on our minds, so we went out and hopped on a dinky little electric trolley that was the only vehicle still running. It was just absolutely loaded with Japanese. It's difficult to reproduce the atmosphere. Except from the police, we never got so much as a dirty look. And here we were, the conquerors: big and evil-smelling. Americans don't smell very good to the Japanese under the best of circumstances, and neither one of us had washed for a couple of days. After all of the propaganda about our character and what we were going to do to the women, what we were going to do to everybody else, this is so bizarre you won't believe it. We climbed on this thing just clustered with human beings and inched our way down inside the trolley. A little old gentleman in a Western suit pulled out his calling card and gave it to us.

---

[*] The Okha (nicknamed Baka by the Allies) was essentially a Japanese flying bomb powered by either a jet engine or rocket engine. It was intended as a coast defense weapon flown by a suicide pilot. It was intended primarily as a coast-defense weapon.

Then we went up some little distance to Wahakone, a resort over on the shores of Mount Fuji.* There was a big, good-looking building off in the distance, so we walked over there to investigate. It turned out to be a school for little kids of privileged people in the Japanese society. When we got there, they invited the two evil-smelling, enormous conquerors to sit down on tatami mats, gave us tea, and had the little kids do their song and dance for us. Unbelievable.

More seriously, when I saw the fortitude and the dignity with which the Japanese people went about their life, I had a very drastic change in feeling about them. You know, we had thought of them as being sort of subhuman all the time we were fighting. And they had done some very outrageous things I don't have to recount. But it made a considerable impression.

Later on, as I was trying to make my way back to the ship, I just happened to run across Admiral John Ballentine as he was on his way out to the surrender ceremony on the *Missouri*.† So he said, "Come on, Noel," and totally uninvited I got a place on the quarterdeck, where I saw the famous surrender. I remember how MacArthur had his three strands of hair carefully flemished down on his bald head so it would look like he had a head of hair.‡

I think it was a Canadian who signed in the wrong place, and there was a great flap about that. But I tell you, the thing that made the most impression on me was the Japanese, particularly the foreign minister, whose name was Shigemitsu.§ He had lost a leg in some previous war, and he was dressed in the frock coat and top hat, diplomatic uniform, and had to climb up the ladder. It was not a gangway, just a damned ladder. Nobody gave him any assistance. He did this with the utmost difficulty and the utmost dignity. With him were in signing the articles were three rather crummy-looking Army generals.**

---

* Mount Fuji, also known as Fujiyama, is the highest mountain in Japan at 12,388 feet. It is considered sacred in Japanese culture. It is on the main island of Honshu, about 70 miles from Tokyo.
† The surrender ceremony on board the battleship *Missouri* was on 2 September 1945 in Tokyo Bay. Rear Admiral John J. Ballentine, USN, was Commander Task Group 38.2 when he was detailed to command part of the naval landing force in Japan. His oral history is in the Columbia University collection.
‡ General of the Army Douglas MacArthur, Supreme Commander Allied Powers.
§ Mamoru Shigemitsu signed the surrender document on behalf of the Japanese government. He had lost a leg in an unsuccessful assassination attempt.
** For a detailed account of the surrender ceremony, see Paul Stillwell, *Battleship Missouri: An Illustrated History* (Annapolis: Naval Institute Press, 1996).

ADM Noel A. M. Gayler, Interview #4 (1/30/84) – Page 142

Paul Stillwell: What was the mood at that point—just great relief that the war was over?

Admiral Gayler: I think we knew it was going so well and so tremendously that we didn't have quite that feeling of relief. I think most of it was a case of, "Glad to wrap this up and get on home." A curious thing, I don't think any of us—in the Pacific, at least—ever entertained the thought that we could be defeated in the war with Japan, even when we were down to one carrier. We knew damn well we were going to win. So it wasn't relief in that sense. We knew it was coming.

Paul Stillwell: What enabled you to just go ashore like that? Was there no concern for personal safety?

Admiral Gayler: As I recall, I asked Admiral Badger, who was pretty busy, and he said, "Fine." Off I went. I didn't really belong to him anyway. He had known me. I think he remembered me slightly, because he was the executive officer when I was a midshipman at the Naval Academy.

Paul Stillwell: But did you have sufficient evidence that the Japanese weren't likely to do something treacherous?

Admiral Gayler: Just curiosity. I was tremendously interested, tremendously interested in what the conditions were with these people. A little bit of it was that American idea of being the first on the scene.

I remember one funny thing that happened while we were celebrating in a Japanese officers' club at Yokosuka. This was within three or four days of the surrender, as I recall. It was mostly a crowd of destroyer skippers and a few of us aviators, and we were sitting around in one big room, having some drinks and talking over the war. Evening came along later, and pretty soon these bloody, great, impudent Japanese rats stuck their noses out from holes in the baseboard. We were all armed, you see. Somebody pulled out his .45, and soon we were all shooting at these rats. In a moment, you could hear the whistles shrilling and the pounding footsteps coming up the outside ladder to this room on the second floor. The door burst open and there was a sergeant Marine with his machine gun. He had thought the Japanese were assassinating us all. He had a little trouble sorting that one out.

Paul Stillwell: What was available for drinking? Did you have Japanese drinks?

Admiral Gayler: Yes, the Japanese had left a lot of liquor there.

Paul Stillwell: Did you return to Admiral McCain's flagship after this temporary assignment with Admiral Badger?

Admiral Gayler: Yes, and we just sort of wound things down. It was all pretty anticlimactic after that.

Paul Stillwell: Did you do any touring of Japan during that occupation period?

Admiral Gayler: I did get up to Kyoto but no great amount of touring.

Paul Stillwell: What was there for the fleet to do at that point?

Admiral Gayler: Well, I don't recall anything much. We all began to get orders to here and there, and ships were sent back and so forth. I don't recall that we kept an organized presence there, if you will. I'm sure there was a fleet organization in being. It wasn't a mob scene like Europe, but it was pretty much of a demobilization scene. People were more interested in what they were going to do next.

Paul Stillwell: Were you losing a lot of people then through the demobilization?

Admiral Gayler: Yes.

Paul Stillwell: How long did you stick around?

Admiral Gayler: I personally didn't stay more than a month, as I recall. Like everybody else, I had ideas about what I wanted to do postwar. I asked to be assigned to something connected with research and development. As a result, I got a berth with the Office of Naval Research, Special Devices Center, which was interesting shore duty.

Paul Stillwell: Before that, you had an assignment with Carrier Air Group 61 in the Atlantic Fleet. What did that involve?

Admiral Gayler: That didn't happen. I had orders to Air Group 61 as air group commander. This was to be the first air group that was totally night-oriented, but it never happened. The war ended, and those orders were superseded.

Paul Stillwell: Then in January of '46, you reported to the Special Devices Center.

Admiral Gayler: Well, that was an outgrowth of my previous close friendship and admiration for Luis de Florez. This was his operation, which had been moved, just about the time I went there. Up to then it had been in a garage at 610 H Street here in town, a place that had been commandeered during the war. When I reported, the command went to permanent quarters up on an estate on Long Island near Fort Washington. So I went up there essentially in one of the commissioning details. I was the exec of the place. It wasn't precisely what I had in mind, and yet in another way it was. It was very interesting.

Paul Stillwell: What projects did you work on?

Admiral Gayler: Well, we had a mix of development of optical and electronic devices related primarily to training. They also spilled over into some of the precursors of the high-accuracy electronics that we now see. Not many people now remember that the first earth satellite project was in 1946. This was Project Mouse, a minimum unmanned orbital satellite of earth. The Navy spent about $1 million on preliminary planning and development until somebody came along and said, "Oh, hell, knock off this nonsense.

We've got more important things to do." That cut the program off. The crystal ball was cloudy on that one.

Paul Stillwell: Did you think it was a feasible thing at that point?

Admiral Gayler: Oh, sure. I won't claim that I had the vision to see what is was going to be now, but sure, we thought it was feasible. It was a matter of elementary physics, really, that you put something in orbit if you give it enough impulse.

Paul Stillwell: Were there rocket engines at that point with enough thrust?

Admiral Gayler: Yes, it was a practical proposition. It wasn't much of a satellite compared with the things we put up now. It was a demonstration project, sort of like Sputnik, only smaller.*

Paul Stillwell: What did you pursue that came more to fruition than that?

Admiral Gayler: Well, a lot of electronic work, including the commissioning of either the first or second—it's in dispute—really large-scale general digital computer in this country. It has never received an awful lot of attention because for some reason which now escapes me, it was kept pretty highly classified. It was a whirlwind computer. It was an inspiration of Luis de Florez, again, really, and the scientists that he hung out with, notably Jay Forrester at the servo mechanisms lab at MIT. That was commissioned by our outfit. And we did some intelligence work that I won't go into now.

Then I had an interesting personal experience. It turned out that we were bringing back German scientists immediately after the war. We were afraid they'd get killed as they went through New York because they weren't very popular. So we kind of smuggled them in in an Army transport. Every Friday I would go down with my sailor driver and station wagon and my trusty old survival .38, and pick up these guys through a cargo hatch in the side of the ship and take them out. We segregated them for a month or

---

* The first artificial earth satellite to go into orbit was the Soviet Sputnik, launched in the fall of 1957.

six weeks, sorted them out, figured out who they were and what their skills were and what their attitudes were and what would be an appropriate assignment for them. Almost all of the German scientists went through that place. Wernher von Braun went through, but I'm sorry to say that I don't remember ever talking to him.* He was one of the mob.

Paul Stillwell: What was the general attitude of these scientists?

Admiral Gayler: I think they were, in general, relieved that the war was over, that they were alive, that they were out of Germany. Some of them, like von Braun, obviously were interested in pursuing their trade or their interest, almost independent of whom they did it for. Others were resigned to their fate, perhaps would be a good way to put it.

Paul Stillwell: Was there any specific Navy projects that you worked on then?

Admiral Gayler: A lot of the training projects were Navy-oriented, yes, and there were some submarine detection projects. Some of the stuff we had to keep pretty quiet because the cognizant bureaus didn't like our messing around with them. In a sense, the Office of Naval Research in general, and this outfit in particular, had been set up to do a job which, much like the job that DARPA now does, with the same potential for bureaucratic friction.† In addition, in the hiatus between the end of the wartime NDRC and later on support by other services, the Navy, through the Office of Naval Research supported most of the fundamental science in the country for a period of nearly ten years, through de Florez's vision and that of some other people.‡

Paul Stillwell: Was most of this practical work as opposed to theoretical?

Admiral Gayler: Both. Both.

---

* Wernher von Braun was a German-born rocket scientist who helped develop rockets for his country in World War II, then immigrated to the United States in 1945 and began working with the Army. He subsequently played a considerable role in the U.S. space program.
† DARPA – Defense Advanced Research Projects Agency.
‡ NDRC – National Defense Research Council.

Paul Stillwell: Can you cite some theoretical things that later had applications?

Admiral Gayler: Well, I told you about the satellite one. We did a lot of stuff in the electronic field, the big general-purpose digital computer, a lot of work in optics, simulation. Yes, I would say there were a lot of things that had practical application.

After the Office of Naval Research lost support, largely because of competition from the other services and so forth, it withered a little bit. There was sort of a hiatus in our scientific effort from, say, about 1952 or '53 until Sputnik fired things up again.

Paul Stillwell: Were you working on guided missiles while you were in that office?

Admiral Gayler: Not directly, no.

Paul Stillwell: Any aviation projects that you haven't mentioned?

Admiral Gayler: No, I can't think of any except training devices. We were, among other things, the training device center, and we brought to maturity a lot of excellent training device ideas that would have been very useful in the war, but the war was over.

Paul Stillwell: Were there simulators among those?

Admiral Gayler: Oh, yes, yes. We were Mr. Simulator, I guess.

Paul Stillwell: How long did de Florez stay with this, the whole time you were there?

Admiral Gayler: He was a sort of general overseer. Deak Hibber, who was an extraordinary reserve officer, was the skipper. He was a captain in the reserve. He kept that job for about a year, and then it sort of went back into the regular Navy. Oh, yes, we did a lot of early work in television too. We had a big television that was about that big, great big cabinet and a picture about that big. I remember particularly a man named Art

Hungerford, who was a civilian engineer on it and enormously enthralled by the future of television. The rest of us thought he was pretty much of a visionary, but I guess he was talking to about 10% of what we've seen already.

Paul Stillwell: How was TV used in the Navy?

Admiral Gayler: We thought of it with a special orientation for information exchange and display and conferencing and so forth. I don't think any of us, except maybe Hungerford, foresaw the immense popular and commercial orientation it would have. In fact, television was so new that we were using it for training programs on a trial basis. In lieu of a transmitter of our own, I think there were only two stations in New York at the time that would give us free time to run our training programs. Unbelievable. The screen was small, only about that big, and the image was green, like in the laboratory oscilloscope.

Paul Stillwell: Where did your family live during that period?

Admiral Gayler: That is an interesting story. I went up there, and there was no housing at all to be had. I had three little children at the time. The place where we did our work was an immense, old baronial estate built by Jay Gould and then acquired by the Guggenheim family.[*] Gould built it in an incredible old robber-baron style. The place we used as offices had actually been his stables. They were built out of granite and intended to last for the centuries, so they made good offices. There was also a gatehouse where presumably somebody tipped his hat as the carriages went through or something like that. It was a funny-looking little building and hadn't been lived in for years and years and years and years. I looked at it and I thought, "We can't do anything with that." But my wife Kay was undaunted, and she came up to have a look at it and said, "Oh, well, we can fix this," and we did. We fixed the darn place so it was a pretty comfortable place to live, all with our own hands. There was no Navy money involved.

---

[*] Jay Gould (1836-1892) was a noted 19th century financier and stock market manipulator. He had considerable railroad holdings.

Paul Stillwell: That was pretty convenient to your work.

Admiral Gayler: Yes, it was a lovely location in the old grounds with rhododendrons and whatnot. I walked about a half mile up a winding path to get to work.

Paul Stillwell: The armed services were unifying during that period. Did that have an effect on your activities?

Admiral Gayler: I was pretty detached from that sort of stuff. No. We had a little liaison with the Air Force and the Army, but I don't recall getting into that very much.

Paul Stillwell: You were there until 1948, then went back to sea again in the *Bairoko*.*

Admiral Gayler: Yes, I was operations officer with *Bairoko*, and I guess the most interesting thing now is that we were the carrier for the choppers supporting the Sandstone series of bomb tests.† This was the second test series in the Pacific, following the earlier ones at Bikini. This series was at Eniwetok atoll. You never forget the experience of seeing one of those atomic weapons go off. Not many people are around that have seen them, but it does make an impression on you, 110 kilotons from 19 miles away. It looks like the end of the world. Unbelievable. There's nothing you can read about it, nothing you can say about it, no pictures you can show can quite convey it. So that was a pretty good learning experience for me.

It had its lighter moments, of course. We religiously drilled the sailors aboard ship in the use of Geiger counters and the detection of radiation and the wearing of protective suits and water wash-down and all that stuff. When the explosions took place, they were all atmospheric. We were carefully stationed upwind, so we didn't get any nuclear contamination. We suddenly realized this was a source of great disappointment to the sailors, because here they'd been drilling for the effects of this damn stuff and they

---

* USS *Bairoko* (CVE-115), an escort carrier, was commissioned 16 July 1945. She was 557 feet long, 105 feet in the beam, had a draft of 32 feet, and a top speed of 19 knots.
† Operation Sandstone comprised a series of atmospheric tests of nuclear weapons at Eniwetok in the Marshall Islands in 1948. The series included tests X-Ray on 15 April, Yoke on 1 May, and Zebra on 15 May.

never did get any. Finally one day somebody took a Geiger counter and passed it over the top of the captain's gig, and a passing seagull had made a deposit there and by God, that was radioactive. [Laughter] That was cause for rejoicing.

Paul Stillwell: What was that carrier's role in the overall tests?

Admiral Gayler: Simply support. It was one of the major uses of helicopters, and we supported the helicopter group. We carried the scientists around and did all the "George" jobs and whatnot. But we also were a part of the tests in the sense that we tested the water wash-down for big ships, radiation detection, and drills of this kind and the other kind. We were rather naive about nuclear weapons in those days, and we thought that if you took care to run away from the ground surge and the base surge and do all sorts of things, why, maybe you'd survive a nuclear attack. We know better now.

Paul Stillwell: How is it that you kept getting in these experimental type of jobs? You had asked for the one before. Was this just coincidence?

Admiral Gayler: It may not have been; I don't know.

Paul Stillwell: Well, that didn't occupy your entire time in the ship. What else were you doing?

Admiral Gayler: Regular carrier work. She was one of the tanker conversions. She was not a full-sized carrier, but she was not a jeep either. She was sort of halfway between. She had excellent endurance and pretty good speed and could operate airplanes pretty well. We did regular carrier missions, mostly operating out of San Diego.

Paul Stillwell: She was smaller, so she couldn't have the full capability.

Admiral Gayler: She didn't have the full complement, but she handled the airplanes of the day. I think we had F6Fs primarily.

Paul Stillwell: So this was just a training period, then?

Admiral Gayler: Well, I don't know what you mean by just a training period. We weren't at war.

Paul Stillwell: I mean you weren't doing any other kind of testing.

Admiral Gayler: Other than that one special job, that's right. Other than the support of the Eniwetok tests.

Paul Stillwell: Any other operations that you recall in that ship? Any ASW work?

Admiral Gayler: Usual screening, that's about all. It was an uneventful cruise, outside of the trip out to Eniwetok.

Paul Stillwell: Then you went from there to shore duty at Bureau of Aeronautics in the fighter design branch.

Admiral Gayler: That was a very interesting tour, very interesting, because we were moving rapidly from props to jets and to the advanced jets. We had a lot more control over the programs than people do nowadays, and we were able to come up with some pretty good stuff. I still had my hand in flying, so I did a lot of evaluation of various contractors' plans for new stuff. I've got some time in the F7U, for example, and all the new jets.* So it was pretty fruitful from that standpoint, and we were able to translate that pretty directly into contracts.

One other thing from that time that I recall is that I think we managed to get the first numerical statements about reliability and the requirements. Curiously, they'd never been stated before. Reliability was an adjective, whereas top speed and climb and load carrying and whatnot were numbers. In the design process, when there was a competition

---

* The Vought F7U Cutlass was a swept-wing jet fighter of an experimental design. It had two vertical stabilizers but no tail per se. It first entered the fleet in 1952.

between an adjective and a number, the adjective always lost. So I remember spending a lot of time trying to figure out how we could specify reliability in numerical terms so it could get in there and compete with the others. That was a very interesting tour. Syd Sherby was my principal assistant.* Mel Pride was chief of the bureau in those days. I saw him the other day. He looked fine.

Paul Stillwell: I interviewed him a couple of weeks ago.

Admiral Gayler: Did you?

Paul Stillwell: He fondly remembers that as an era when there were not as many layers of bureaucracy.

Admiral Gayler: That's what I was trying to convey. You had the feeling that you could really get things done. Back then you went up to the contractor's plant and said, "This we want and that we want." They came back with a proposal, you'd get it settled around the table, and that was it. We got some pretty good products out of it. In fact, it's been my experience that the less programs are "managed," the more likely they are to be successful. And when you're able to do things in a hell of a hurry or in great secrecy because it's an intelligence program, you can get some pretty good machines like the U-2.† But that comes to a later time.

Paul Stillwell: You were not an aeronautical engineer, per se. How did you fit in without that background?

Admiral Gayler: I think it's like the story about the beautiful young girl in the whorehouse. One of her customers said, "What's a nice young girl like you doing in a place like this?"

And she said, "Just lucky, I guess." [Laughter]

---

* Commander Sydney S. Sherby, USN.
† The U-2 is a high-altitude reconnaissance plane best known for an incident in 1960 when one was shot down by the Soviet Union.

You've heard that story. It's an old story.

Paul Stillwell: Was that a handicap to you at all, not having that kind of education?

Admiral Gayler: I think it's for somebody else to judge. In my opinion, no. Of course, I had the support, as I say, of Syd Sherby and other well qualified engineers. I'm sort of an engineering buff myself. I understand these things pretty well in principle. I hung out with scientists and engineers all my life.

Paul Stillwell: Well, certainly there would be a need for an operational input, and that is where your background had been so strong.

Admiral Gayler: That's right, but they don't believe in categorizing people quite as tightly as that. It was a very excellent working relationship between the technicians and me.

Interview Number 5 with Admiral Noel A. M. Gayler, U.S. Navy (Retired)

Place: Admiral Gayler's office at the American Committee on East-West Accord, Washington, D.C.

Date: Tuesday, 7 February 1984

Paul Stillwell: Admiral, how did you come to serve as commanding officer of Air Development Squadron Three?

Admiral Gayler: I was then in the Bureau of Aeronautics, working for Admiral Mel Pride. For some reason, which I don't now remember, I was out on a carrier, watching the operations. I saw these people doing what looked like very interesting work with brand-new jets, Banshees, as I recall, so I thought, "This is for me."[*] I reached around to see whether that was possible, and indeed it was. I succeeded Howard Avery as skipper.[†]

One of the remarkable things about that command was the caliber of the officers. As I recall the numbers, out of 13 regular Navy pilots that we had in VX-3 later on, some eight became flag officers: two four-star, two three-star, and four two-star. That's a little unusual, and I realize now, when looking at it, that that's because they selected themselves. The word gets around about the outfits that are doing interesting things. The hotshots—and these men were hotshots—figure out how to get where they want to be. In that way, they sort of self-select. I learned that a reputation like that is probably the best recruiting device in the world. You don't have to go beat the byways. If your outfit is good enough, the good ones will come to you.

Paul Stillwell: There has to be a ratification process, though, deciding which of the applicants to take. How does that work?

---

[*] McDonnell's F2H Banshee was a jet-powered fighter-bomber that first entered the fleet with squadron VF-171 in March 1949. The F2H-2 version was 40 feet long, wingspan of 45 feet, gross weight of 22,312 pounds, and top speed of 532 miles per hour. It had four fixed forward-firing 20-millimeter guns and provision to carry two 500-pound bombs.
[†] Commander Howard M. Avery, USN.

Admiral Gayler: Well, the problem didn't really arise. They were all pretty darn good.

Paul Stillwell: What names do you remember from that period?

Admiral Gayler: Mike Michaelis, Whitey Feightner, Pete Charbonnet, and Fox Charlie Turner—to name a few.[*]

Paul Stillwell: What kind of interaction was there among all these future stars at that point?

Admiral Gayler: We all had a lot of fun. That was a marvelous outfit with a marvelous charter. In those days, the experimental squadrons were VX-1, VX-2, VX-3, VX-4, and VX-5, but only VX-3 and VX-5 really had developmental activity. The others were sort of specialized, more material-oriented outfits. We belonged nominally to the Operational Development Force, which was black shoe-oriented and had a black shoe admiral, so we were reasonably free to do our own thing. In addition, I found it possible to suggest to the appropriate officers in OpNav what we should be tasked to do. So those orders would come down from the CNO to the Operational Development Force and be transmitted to us, and lo and behold, we'd be doing what we needed to do.

Paul Stillwell: What were the most significant projects that you covered during that time?

Admiral Gayler: I suppose the most significant was all of the early work on the development of tactics for the delivery of nuclear weapons by carrier aircraft. You recall that the first weapons were carried on the big multi-engine airplane, the AJ.[†] But then the

---

[*] Lieutenant Commander Frederick H. Michaelis, USN, later a four-star admiral; Lieutenant Commander Edward L. Feightner, USN, later a two-star admiral; Lieutenant Commander Pierre N. Charbonnet, USN, later a three-star admiral; Lieutenant Frederick C. Turner, USN, later a three-star admiral. The oral histories of Michaelis and Feightner are in the Naval Institute's collection.

[†] The AJ Savage was a propeller-driven carrier-based nuclear strike aircraft built by North American Aviation, Inc. It first entered the fleet in squadron VC-5 in September 1949. It was reclassified A-2 in 1962. The AJ-1 version was 63 feet long; wingspan of 75 feet; gross weight of 52,862 pounds; and top speed of 471 miles per hour. It had a maximum bomb capacity of 12,000 pounds.

tactical work for the single-seaters and the attack planes was all ours. We developed the long-range, low-level flights in order to solve the problem of penetration of air defenses and also the problem of reaching targets that were far enough away for the carrier to be safe. We flew all over the United States. In point of fact, they were all very successful. We demonstrated the feasibility of long-range flights at extremely low altitudes for purposes of radar evasion.

Then we first developed a way of very rapidly climbing to altitude for a drop and then the idiot loop.

Paul Stillwell: What was involved in that?

Admiral Gayler: The idea was to get away from the blast of the bomb, and you did not wish to climb up slowly to altitude because you were liable to get shot if you did. So you would fly in near the surface and as you approached the target at as much speed as you could put on, you'd pull up. About here you let the bomb go. It travels over like that. You continue over like that in an Immelmann maneuver, then beat it out the way you came in so you could get a maximum distance away from the bomb.[*]

The long flights were also part of the long-range program. It turned out that you could fly an airplane much farther than most people believe, if you were willing to develop the techniques to do it right. One technique we had with the Banshee airplane, which carried a lot of fuel anyway, of course, was to shut down one engine. Just fly on one engine for the whole flight except for a few moments before you take off on two, shut down one. At low altitude, she had plenty of power on one engine.

We stretched them farther and farther and farther, and one day made, as I recall, 715 nautical miles in and out in the Banshee of the day. Later on, we decided we could do the same thing with the dear old AD, the Skyraider.[†] On the longest one we launched from a carrier east of Jacksonville and went to a target in the Dallas area and back. It was

---

[*] An Immelmann turn is one in which an airplane in flight first makes half a loop and then rolls over to make the second half.
[†] The Douglas AD Skyraider propeller-driven attack planes first entered fleet squadrons in late 1946. The AD-2 version was 38 feet long, wingspan of 50 feet, gross weight of 18,263 pounds, and top speed of 321 miles per hour. In September 1962 Skyraiders still in service were redesignated A-1s.

12½ hours in a single-seater—all below 200 feet. I never saw so many astonished mules and cattle in my life. A very interesting flight.

Paul Stillwell: Please tell me about it.

Admiral Gayler: Well, it was one of many, many such flights. I had never asked permission to make them in this project, other than under the general cover of development tactics, because I was well aware that if I proposed them, I might be turned down. So we just did them, with some confidence that if anybody complained, they complained to the Air Force. So over a period of a couple of years, I guess, we made many, many flights developing the navigation technique and the other techniques of going very long distances, delivering the bomb, and coming out of fighter problems. One time we had the Eastern Air Defense Command looking for us, and they could never see us. You know, it's amazing. You can't see airplanes at a low altitude if they're really down on the deck. And the radars don't see them, of course. Now we have clever determination radars, but in those days we didn't. So we did all of that development work.

It was interesting enough, so we were asked to demonstrate to the Joint Chiefs of Staff and the Joint Staff at Quantico.[*] You remember how they used to have their annual meetings in Quantico once a year, and they would have demonstrations and so forth from the various services? One year we were picked to do the demonstration for the Navy, and we demonstrated the idiot bombing type digs and the low-altitude flying. That was the occasion that I very nearly bombed the JCS. We had an early radar in the F3D, and we practiced and practiced on radar targets which we set up in front of the stands.[†] They did the idiot loops and that looked pretty good.

Then the time came for the radar bombing aircraft, and you know, you look at a bomb, if it elongates, you're all right, but if it stays circular, it's going to hit you or come

---

[*] Quantico, Virginia, which is on the Potomac River south of Washington, D.C., is the site of a Marine Corps base.
[†] The Douglas F3D Skyknight was an all-weather jet fighter used by the Marines as a night fighter and for electronic countermeasures. It was first delivered to VC-3 in 1951. The plane's two-man crew of pilot and radar operator sat side by side. The F3D-2 version was 46 feet long, wingspan of 50 feet, gross weight of 26,850 pounds, and top speed of 600 miles per hour. It had four fixed forward-firing 20-millimeter guns.

pretty damn close. And as this big dummy shape came off the airplane, it stayed circular, and it stayed circular. I was out in front narrating. This was with all the Joint Staff and the Joint Chiefs in the wooden bleachers. And the damn thing didn't elongate, and I could tell it was going to be close. I could hear some scurrying and people trying to get under the stands. And boom! She landed inert but in a great geyser of mud about 75 yards, I guess, in front of the stands. All I could think of to say was that this illustrates the limitations of radar bombing. Well, it turned out that they'd come out that day in buses and parked the buses behind the stand. The buses made more radar reflection than the radar target did, so my guys picked up the wrong target. I had a safety plane flying on the F3D, and he just didn't do his job.

Paul Stillwell: How did you avoid terrain features when you were making those flights so close to the ground?

Admiral Gayler: You did it by very, very careful advance map work, and actually dog-barking navigation, flying from one point to another, from another point to another point, and knowing what the terrain was all the time. It was not too damn difficult in the daytime, but it was very dicey at night. In fact, it was so dicey at night that I finally called it off. I thought we would lose somebody pretty soon. We didn't. But in the daytime it was all right. You had to be particularly careful not so much about terrain, but the biggest hazard, of course, was the transmission lines because you couldn't see them.

Paul Stillwell: Were any particular development efforts tied in with the Korean War, which was then in progress?[*]

Admiral Gayler: Yes, we did a lot of theoretical work about how to suppress and evade antiaircraft fire. At one time I had a proposal to send a team out there to try them out in actual combat, but it was never approved. I think we made some contributions to the

---

[*] The Korean War began on 25 June 1950, when six North Korean infantry division and three border constabulary brigades invaded South Korea. The troops were supported by approximately 100 Russian-made T-34 tanks. In New York that same day the United Nations Security Council adopted a resolution condemning the invasion.

Korean War, but it's a little hard to tell. It was pretty theoretical in Atlantic City, New Jersey, in the peace of the East Coast, and in the flat terrain around there compared to the actual work in Korea. So I guess it was not all that useful.

Paul Stillwell: In what ways did your work differ from that at the Air Test Center at Patuxent River?

Admiral Gayler: Theirs was essentially single airplanes, concerned principally with the mechanical appraisal of the airplane as an airplane. Ours was the development of tactics, a lot of [unclear] work. We did all the original mirror-landing work.* We had some other landing systems we evaluated. We did the first work in how to use the high-frequency radio aids. We did an awful lot of blind landing work, that sort of stuff. A lot of tactical work.

Paul Stillwell: What about the angled-deck carrier?† Did you work on development of that?

Admiral Gayler: Well, we borrowed that from the British, as you know. I remember going to England once, and it must have been when I was in VX-3. The idea was to evaluate the British mirror-landing system. They gave me a Vampire airplane. I don't know whether you remember the Vampire or not, but it was one of the early British jets. It had about 40 minutes of fuel in it. The carrier was not very far out. So I thought, "Well, hell, go out and give it a go." When I got out there, there was about 500 and maybe a mile and a half drizzle, you know, typical crummy British weather. But she was in the wind ready to receive aircraft, so I made a pass and couldn't see much. Then I came back and made another pass and decided to land. That was when I found out they'd had trouble with the mirror; they'd never turned it on. So I didn't get much of an

---

* By keeping in a certain path relative to the image reflected by a mirror on the carrier's stern, a pilot could maintain the proper glide slope approaching to land on deck.
† The U.S. Navy began adding angled decks to its aircraft carriers in the 1950s to prevent landing aircraft that missed arresting wires from crashing into planes farther forward on the deck.

evaluation, but I was glad to be on deck. The Vampire didn't have enough fuel, and I wasn't familiar enough with it to be very comfortable about going back to shore.

Paul Stillwell: What were some of the other projects you had in VX-3?

Admiral Gayler: We did a lot of electronic-related and electronic warfare-related work; much of it was pioneering. We did the evaluation of the air-traffic-control system that is now standard. It was first developed by the Navy. Not many people know that.

We did a lot of work on carrier landing aids, including various different things before we finally settled down on the mirror landing system.

We practiced a good deal of bombing tactics. In one case, we went down to Fort Bragg and evaluated different kinds of armament against radio-controlled tanks, with some rather unexpected results.* All sorts of projects like that.

I discovered when I got there that the squadron did very little foul-weather flying, and I thought that was incomplete, so we instituted a very, very intensive instrument flight rating training program. In the course of about three months, every active pilot in the squadron was a green-card pilot. That took a little doing. We flew all night long to do that.

Paul Stillwell: Was this essentially pioneering work? Was the Navy really not acclimated to night flying at that point?

Admiral Gayler: That would be an overstatement. Night flying was regarded, however, as a sort of specialized activity, particularly night fighting and night bombing. It seemed to me to be obvious that it should be routine and, therefore, that much more of the tactical development work should be oriented toward night and bad weather, which it had not been previously. In order to do that safely, it was necessary to get everybody in the squadron to green card standards, in addition to which it was a practical matter. We did a lot of flying out of other people's air bases, and without a green card, you had a lot of trouble getting clearances.

---

* Fort Bragg is an Army post in North Carolina.

Paul Stillwell: You mentioned electronic developments. What specific things were you working on?

Admiral Gayler: Spoofing, jamming, tactics for radar evasion, a lot of things that didn't work very well. For instance, I had the bright idea that if you crossed blips, you would create problems for the people tracking. When we tried it, it turned out not to be that much of a problem for those doing the tracking. We also worked on deceptive tactics, all sorts of things like that.

Paul Stillwell: Did you have fairly good intelligence at that time on what the Soviet capabilities were in electronic warfare?

Admiral Gayler: Yes, fairly good. I was pretty close to the relevant outfits in OpNav at that time, so we were able to be pretty well up to date on that subject.[*]

Paul Stillwell: Did you work against U.S. planes that simulated the kind of fighter opposition an atomic strike might face?

Admiral Gayler: We had enough assets of one sort or another so we could do it within the squadron. We usually had at least four different types in the squadron at one time, fairly representative of different kinds of Soviet capabilities.

Paul Stillwell: Were a number of the officers within the squadron former test pilots as you were?

Admiral Gayler: Yes: Feightner, Charbonnet, Turner, and one or two others whose names don't come to mind.

Paul Stillwell: That kind of versatility would be helpful in all the varied work that you described.

---

[*] OpNav—the extended staff of the Chief of Naval Operations.

Admiral Gayler: Yes, yes. Versatility was homegrown too. We had a very careful system. I'm very proud of the fact that in all of the time that I had the squadron, we had only one casualty, and that was not project-related at all. That was an administrative flight.

Paul Stillwell: When you have that many future greats together, are there any problems with egos rubbing against each other?

Admiral Gayler: I don't think so. The only pilot I remember that we ever had any ego problem with was a reserve officer whom I won't name. Everybody called him "Steel Head," because he had an aluminized helmet that he liked to wear. He had a little problem with thinking he was a hotshot, but it didn't amount to anything very serious.

Paul Stillwell: You mentioned the Operational Development Force. The rein was pretty loose on you, I gather.

Admiral Gayler: All except for the chief of staff, whom I won't name, who was an aviator, and pretty senior, but in my cocky judgment, not much of a pilot. He was a little annoyed that we were freewheeling too much, so he tried to rein us in, but as I say, we managed to get the projects done from CNO that we wanted. One time he did try to mousetrap me, because among other things, he objected to the fact that these Banshee airplanes, which were very long-range airplanes for the day, enabled us to fly all over the country for one good reason or another. I was out on a liaison flight with VX-5, commanded by Tom Walker.* We were old friends and were working very closely together on something we wanted to do together. This chief of staff got wind of it and immediately, quick like a fox, scheduled a surprise inspection for the following day.

About 10:00 o'clock that night, when I was in San Francisco, I got a worried call from Pete Charbonnet, who was my exec. He told me about the surprise inspection for the next day. So I went back down to the hangar where VX-5 had my Banshee, cranked it up, and left San Francisco about 11:00 o'clock at night. I refueled in Oklahoma,

---

* Commander Thomas J. Walker, USN.

courtesy of the Air Force, and got back into Atlantic City about 6:00 o'clock in the morning. We put on the best darn inspection you've ever seen. That's not remarkable now when everybody flies cross-country, but in those days, to get back in that length of time was a surprise. I can still remember the face of the chief of staff when he stepped off the airplane and saw me there greeting the admiral.

Paul Stillwell: His disappointment was clear.

Admiral Gayler: His disappointment was clear.

One of the other squadron commanders from that period was Pete Aurand.[*] Pete had gotten hold of a movie called "The 86s Are Coming," which had been made by North American to celebrate the arrival of the F-86 into the Air Force inventory.[†] It was a very funny, little amateur movie having to do with ridiculous things. The plane had a big intake opening in the front, and I remember the opening scene when the airplane taxied up. A guy was waving it on, and the next time you saw him, he was down inside that opening—as if the airplane were swallowing him. It was really sort of hilarious, even though it was a slapstick and amateur.

At one point in the brief, I began to show this thing, and the chief of staff I alluded to was glowering because he thought that was pretty facetious for a formal inspection. But the admiral broke up, and everybody else laughed too. [Laughter] It said something like, "This illustrates the problem of the introduction of new airplanes." It was a funny little strip.

Paul Stillwell: The Navy had a version of that, too, the FJ. Did you fly that?

Admiral Gayler: Yes, I guess I went down and flew the XFJ in Dallas. I did all my flying in the FJ before I went to VX-3, as I recall. We never had it in the squadron, but

---

[*] Commander Evan Peter Aurand, USN.
[†] The F-86 Sabre jet, built by North American, was a swept-wing Air Force fighter that achieved combat success in the Korean War. The Navy counterpart was the FJ-2 Fury.

when I was in OP-551, we used to go down and fly various airplanes, XF7U, down at Patuxent and so forth.*

Paul Stillwell: That F-86 was really a hot plane for the Air Force in Korea. I wonder how you would compare it with the Navy mainstays of the period—the Cougar and the Banshee?†

Admiral Gayler: Well, it was a much better airplane than the Cougar, which was badly underpowered and overweight, a very different airplane from the Banshee. Banshee had marvelous high-altitude performance and marvelous range and a better turning capability than the F-86. The F-86 was a good deal faster. So it was sort of a standoff, comparing apples and oranges, really. I was very fond of the Banshee, but I liked the F-86 too. It was just a different kind of airplane.

Paul Stillwell: Why Atlantic City for the base? Was that convenient to where OpDevFor was working?

Admiral Gayler: It was a handy base out in the boonies, and it was one of those leftovers from the great war, I guess. I don't quite know. It wasn't convenient to anything. [Laughter]

Paul Stillwell: Convenient for weekend entertainment, wasn't it?

Admiral Gayler: It was convenient. There were two operating squadrons there, ourselves and VC-4, which was an all-weather training squadron. Joe Gardiner, the skipper of VC-4, was a captain, the senior fleet officer.‡ We got along well, except he

---

* The Vought F7U Cutlass was a swept-wing jet fighter of an experimental design. It had two vertical stabilizers but no tail per se. It first entered the fleet in 1952. The F7U-3 version was 44 feet long, wingspan of 39 feet, gross weight of 31,642 pounds, and top speed of 680 miles per hour. It had four fixed forward-firing 20-millimeter guns and provision for four Sparrow missiles.
† The Grumman F9F-6 Cougar was first delivered to operational units in November 1952. The F9F-5 model was 42 feet long; wingspan of 36 feet; gross weight of 20,000 pounds; and top speed of 690 miles per hour. It was armed with four 20-millimeter guns.
‡ Captain Josef M. Gardiner, USN.

would steal all our stuff when it came in. That is to say, he would demand to know what was new and interesting coming in on the supply system for us to test or do something with. Then he would commandeer it, and I would go negotiate with him, and if the negotiation was successful, he'd give me half of it back. I said all this to his face more than once, so I'm not talking behind his back. He raises Black Angus cattle and was doing that then. He was a famous character too.

Paul Stillwell: Toward the end of your command tour, you were selected for captain, and then you went back to OpNav. You were in OP-551, which was the Military Requirements Branch of the Air Warfare Division. This was the period when you were involved in the development of the plane that later became the F-4.[*]

Admiral Gayler: Yes. I like to think that I had a piece of the F-4 development, and I believe that I may have been the first to devise effective numerical specifications for reliability. Before that time, reliability had always been an adjective that had to compete with numbers like range and speed and altitude and so forth, and always came off second best. I gather from reading the newspapers that it still does, but anyway, we numerically quantified it in all of our requirements. So that was a good thing to do.

I regard the F-4 as being, in a sense, my baby. She was a successful airplane, and we pushed that program hard. We were in constant working collaboration with the folks at McDonnell in developing the design. It started out as an attack plane. Not many people realize it was originally called the AH-1 in the original proposal.[†] It had a very advanced engine structure, aerodynamics, the works. It was a hell of a good design. I guess somebody noticed that the combination of power and drag and whatnot put it well

---

[*] The McDonnell Douglas F-4 Phantom II first entered fleet squadrons in 1961 as the F4H. It was a two-seat airplane with the pilot in the front and the radar intercept officer (RIO) behind him. The F-4B version had the following characteristics: length, 58 feet; wing span, 38 feet; gross weight, 54,600 pounds; top speed, 1,485 miles per hour. It was armed as a fighter with either Sparrow or Sidewinder missiles and also could carry bombs. It had a maximum external stores capacity of 16,000 pounds.

[†] In the Navy's aircraft designation system of the 1950s, A stood for attack and H for the manufacturer, McDonnell. In 1955 the intended mission for the plane changed to interceptor, and the designation became F4H. In 1962, Navy plane designations were converted to conform to those of the Air Force, and the plane became the F-4.

up in the fighter class, as indeed it was. Then it evolved with fairly small changes to the basic airframe into the successful fighter that it became.

I'm trying to remember whether the original design contained the afterburner engines. I don't think it did. The afterburners were still sort of a shaky idea at that time. There was concern about their blowing up and melting through the airplane and all sorts of stuff, and about the controls, as well they might be. Even in the early afterburner airplanes, the exit nozzle had to open way out in order to permit the increased volume of air to get out of the thing. So it was arranged so it would open up at the same time you turned on the afterburner. But in some of the early designs, she'd open up and the afterburner wouldn't light. So instead of getting a big boost and thrust, you'd have a great loss of thrust, and that made things interesting in a carrier approach, for example.

The F3H, the predecessor of the F4H, was a notorious dog, so much so that when she was good and heavy, you had to use afterburner to make a carrier takeoff, and that's what made it binding. If, instead of getting the extra boost, you got a cut, why, it got pretty interesting. Another reason I remember the F3H was that the afterburner, which was rather inefficient, would throw an enormous tongue of bright yellow flame. None of the others did that; they just burned very hot and complete. But this thing, for some reason, threw a long tongue of yellow flame. Several years later, when I was skipper of the *Ranger*, I was terribly pestered by small craft in the Sea of Japan. They were the size of fishing boats, and they didn't seem to care whether they got killed or not. At night, whenever we turned up the engines on the F3Hs, these big tongues of flame would come out, and all the small craft would scatter. [Laughter] I always tried to make sure I had one or two F3H launches when I was up there.

Paul Stillwell: Would you please describe some of the interaction that went on between BuAer and the contractors?

Admiral Gayler: In those days, the working relationship was pretty evident. You'd spend a couple of days at the contractor's plant, and they'd come see you periodically. Of course, even then they had their man watching, keeping an eye on things. Features of the design would be advanced and discussed, and we'd make judgments about whether they met our requirements and were good ways to go. It was a collaborative effort in which there was, I think, complete trust on both sides.

Paul Stillwell: Did McDonnell have a great deal of leeway in the design, or were you pretty specific?

Admiral Gayler: The design was theirs. Our function was to specify the requirements, but an insight that came to me early—I guess was not original, but I felt very strongly—was that the relationship between requirements and satisfaction was not a static statement that, "I set down requirements, you build something to meet them." Instead, it was a continuous interchange in which I would find out from them what was possible, and they found out from me what was desired. We would match it up and iterate it again and again and again. So I felt it was right, proper, and necessary to be very close to the McDonnell designers during those times to get the best mix.

Paul Stillwell: In the process, did you become something of a quasi-engineer?

Admiral Gayler: I think that would be fair enough, yes, to say that. But then that started a long time ago when I was in flight test, because that has a lot of engineering implications. Then you've got to remember that I was five years in the fleet, largely in engineering duty, too, of a different kind, but I've always had a great interest in technical things. Still have.

Paul Stillwell: Was there any sort of competition leading to the development of the F4H? Up to them, Grumman had been the Navy's real fighter supplier.

Admiral Gayler: Grumman and Chance-Vought. Yes, competition always underlay these things, but the Phantom was pretty plainly a winner from time zero.

Paul Stillwell: So McDonnell had won the competition, then it was a case of trying to polish it, or how did that work?

Admiral Gayler: Chance-Vought had a competitor, a derivation of the F8U-1, which was the F8U-3.* The Grumman entry was not exactly a competitor; it was a different kind of airplane, the F11F Tigercat, which I thought always was an extremely successful airplane.† A number of them ended up with the Blue Angels. It was a beautiful looking plane, too, but it was strictly a day fighter. I can't illuminate it much more than that.

Paul Stillwell: Back during that time, the Navy introduced new planes much more frequently than it does now. Are you surprised that the F-4 has lasted as long as it has?‡

Admiral Gayler: It was a very good design. Well, if you look at it from one standpoint, the administration of our fighter assets had been less than perfect. We had a world-beater airplane in the F-4, and then no more new designs for about 15 years. Then, all of a sudden, four new designs were competing with each other in one very short time period. In retrospect, it doesn't look like a very good way to run a railroad, and it isn't.

Paul Stillwell: Was it part of your job to sell the F4H to Congress?

Admiral Gayler: No, that usually was done at a higher echelon. I think Jim Russell took me over once or twice when he was testifying, but only as sort of a backup.§ Later on, when I was in OP-07, I did a lot of testifying, but that was as a junior rear admiral, not as a junior captain.

Paul Stillwell: What else do you remember about Admiral Russell?

---

* The F8U Crusader was a jet fighter built by Chance Vought. It first entered fleet squadrons in 1957. In 1962 the aircraft was redesignated F-8. For details on the F8U-3's competition with the F4H, see the Naval Institute oral histories of Vice Admiral William P. Lawrence, USN (Ret.), and Vice Admiral Donald D. Engen, USN (Ret.).
† The Grumman F11F Tiger was first delivered to Squadron VA-156 in March 1957. The F11F-1 model was 47 feet long; wingspan of 32 feet; gross weight of 22,160 pounds; and top speed of 750 miles per hour. It was armed with four 20-millimeter guns and four under-wing Sidewinder missiles.
‡ The F-4 served in carriers for more than 30 years, reaching the first fleet squadron in 1960 and remaining in use until the retirement of the carrier *Midway* (CV-41) in 1991.
§ Rear Admiral James S. Russell, USN, served as Chief of the Bureau of Aeronautics from 4 March 1955 to 15 July 1957. The oral history of Russell, who retired as a four-star admiral, is in the Naval Institute collection.

Admiral Gayler: He is a great man. As you know, he lives in Tacoma now.* I see him occasionally. Well, I remember a lot about Jim Russell and his extraordinary common sense, his strength and ability, his very Scottishness.

Paul Stillwell: One word that most people use to describe him is "gentleman." That fits very well.

Admiral Gayler: A gentlemanly man, yes. Yes. But don't get it wrong—plenty of force there too.

Paul Stillwell: In the kind of job you had then, I would imagine there's a lot of satisfaction in always being at the new edge in technology.

Admiral Gayler: That was one of the great attractions. But I can imagine now that it isn't so attractive, because now science and technology make it possible to do some things that you're not sure you want to do. In fact, you're damn sure you don't want to do them if you can induce the other guy not to do it either. And I'm not just talking about nuclear weapons, although I am principally.

Paul Stillwell: Was the F-4 a two-seater at the outset?

Admiral Gayler: Yes, it always was, I believe.

Paul Stillwell: That was a new concept itself, wasn't it?

Admiral Gayler: That was one that I was very strongly in support of because I figured that the job of an all-weather predominantly radar fighter was too much for one guy to handle. As I mentioned, there was a design competition involving the F8U-3, which was also a high-performance airplane but a single-seater. In many ways it was a comparable

---

* Admiral Russell subsequently died on 14 April 1996.

airplane, but I thought that was a deficiency that they wouldn't be able to correct. I still don't think it was good judgment for an all-weather fighter.

Paul Stillwell: John Glenn made a name for himself in that era by flying the F8U across the country.[*] Did you encounter him at that time?

Admiral Gayler: You know, I was trying the other day to think when we first knew each other. We were pretty much in the same business, but I haven't been able to pin it down. It was sometime way, way back. See, my problem is that I missed all that space business by about ten years, after 6,000 years of recorded history. I'm still unhappy about it. I once went around to see the boss of NASA, who was a good friend, and tried to convince him that he ought to have somebody up in the upper end of the age spectrum in order to spot in that end of the curve.[†] I remember he looked at me and said, "Nice try, Noel." But that was it. [Laughter]

Paul Stillwell: Well, that tends to bring up the book you don't like, Tom Wolfe's *The Right Stuff*. Initially, the astronauts were not held in very high esteem by the test pilot community.

Admiral Gayler: That's his idea. In the first place, they were all the same people, Wolfe, to the contrary, notwithstanding. All of the original seven were test pilots, weren't they?

Paul Stillwell: Yes.

Admiral Gayler: So I never could understand what the hell he was talking about.

Paul Stillwell: His point was that the Mercury astronauts just had to sit there, as opposed to flying the craft.

---

[*] Major John H. Glenn, Jr., USMC, broke the transcontinental speed record on 16 July 1957 when he flew an F8U-1P from New York to California in three hours and 23 minutes. As an astronaut in 1962 he was the first American in orbit. He was later a U.S. Senator from Ohio.
[†] NASA—National Aeronautics and Space Administration.

Admiral Gayler: That's not to say they weren't test pilots.

Paul Stillwell: Oh, I agree. But in his view, they were not doing as substantial a job.

Admiral Gayler: I don't think Tom Wolfe's view is worth a powder to blow it to hell. He's a kind of journalist that I very much dislike. He sort of snickers, and I don't like it.

Paul Stillwell: What other planes were you involved with in that billet?

Admiral Gayler: Christ. We had everything you can think of. We had F7U-3s, Banshees, IIs and IIIs, every kind of F8U you can think of, ADs, all of the mods of ADs, F3D, old Flying Whale. I latched onto a couple of T-33s, two-seat trainers, which are very handy. That was about it. Not the variety that I had at flight test, but different context. This was tactical work, as opposed to single-airplane work, which it was in flight test.

Paul Stillwell: You mentioned during one of our previous interviews that you tested a large seaplane.

Admiral Gayler: I told you that my first interest in going into aviation had developed while watching PBYs operate out in San Diego before the war. But I didn't actually fly a big seaplane myself until I worked with the R3Y during this tour in OP-551.[*] It had a bow ramp that came down, and the idea was you'd load it with Marines, land on the water, and run it up on the beach. Then the Marines would deploy right from the plane. It worked all right, but the R3Y had some problems.

This was one of the early turbo-prop airplanes, and the power control was arranged so that what you actually did with the throttle was change the propeller pitch. That would change the turbine speed, which would change the demand on the fuel supply, and regulate that accordingly. The result of all of that was it took about a second,

---

[*] The Convair R3Y Tradewind was a flying boat powered by four Allison turboprop engines. It had a wingspan of 146 feet, length of 140 feet, gross weight of 160,000 pounds, and cruising speed of 300 miles per hour. The R3Y-2, equipped with the nose-loading door, first flew in October 1954.

which is a long time, for something to happen after you did something with the throttle. So you were always sort of chasing the throttles around. You'd be going along in this colossal flying boat with some engines going ahead, and some going back, and yawing all over the place. That's how I learned how to fly in seaplanes.

Paul Stillwell: Did you work with Ed Heinemann at Douglas?[*]

Admiral Gayler: I knew him very well, admired him. Yes, I worked with him.

Paul Stillwell: What do you recall about him specifically?

Admiral Gayler: Well, first, that he was extraordinarily competent and made great, good sense, and second, that he was so well recognized to be competent that he defeated the usual attempt of everybody to load everything but the kitchen sink on the A4D.[†] He got the A4D out in about the way he had originally designed it to be, which was a damn good thing for the Navy. As a person, he was warm, charming, and I liked him, a very good man.

Paul Stillwell: How much relationship did you have with the Grumman Corporation?

Admiral Gayler: Pretty close. I used to be up there all the time. I knew old Jake Swirbul reasonably well, and Bill Schwendler, and all of the pioneers up there.[‡] I met LeRoy Grumman, but he was pretty well out of it by then.

Paul Stillwell: Did you, as a government representative, find yourself playing any favorites or attracted by any individuals in this kind of situation?

---
[*] For more on this remarkable man, see Edward H. Heinemann and Rosario Rausa, *Ed Heinemann: Combat Aircraft Designer* (Annapolis: Naval Institute Press, 1980).
[†] The Douglas A4D Skyhawk attack plane first entered the fleet in October 1956 in squadron VA-72. The A4D was 40 feet, 4 inches long, wingspan of 27 feet, 6 inches, gross weight of 24,500 pounds, and top speed of 670 miles per hour. In 1962 the aircraft was redesignated the A-4.
[‡] Production manager Leon A. "Jake" Swirbul and aeronautical engineer William T. Schwendler were with LeRoy Grumman from the beginning. They had begun working—along with Grumman—for aircraft manufacturer Grover Loening in 1924. The Grumman Aircraft Engineering Company started in 1929.

Admiral Gayler: Oh, the great rivalry in those days was between Grumman and Chance-Vought, and I tried to stay pretty well equidistant from them, friendly but equidistant.

Paul Stillwell: You went from there to command of the *Greenwich Bay*.* Had you applied for a ship command at that point?

Admiral Gayler: No. As a matter of fact, I was distressed, because I had been all but promised command of an A3D wing, with the prospect of developing a lot of the tactics for that then-very new, impressive airplane.† I was kind of distressed about it, and I even went so far as go see a couple of my flag officer friends. One of them turned around on me and said, "Do you want to be an admiral or don't you? If you want to be an admiral, take your ship and be glad of it," so I did. In retrospect, of course, it was an extremely interesting tour and very good experience for me. You can't do everything in this world. I did miss that opportunity.

Paul Stillwell: Why did you prefer to go to the A3D job?

Admiral Gayler: I just felt that I knew more about high-performance airplanes than anybody, and that was the kind of thing I liked to do.

As you probably know, the *Greenwich Bay* was a little old white-painted, diesel-powered, smallest class aircraft tender. She was one of the three that relieved each other, heel on toe, sort of a station ship in the Persian Gulf. So in many ways it was really a very fascinating tour of duty and my first exposure to Arabia. It was an Arabia very different from the oil-rich Arabia today but a fascinating experience.

Paul Stillwell: What do you remember about the Arabia of then?

---

* USS *Greenwich Bay* (AVP-41) was commissioned as a small seaplane tender on 20 May 1945. She was 311 feet long, 41 feet in the beam, displaced 1,766 tons, and had a top speed of 18 knots. In 1949 she first began her duty as one of several ships alternating as Middle East Force flagship.
† The Douglas A3D Skywarrior first entered fleet squadrons in 1956 as a carrier-based heavy bomber, capable of nuclear weapons delivery. It was reclassified as the A-3 in 1962. The A3D-2 version was 76 feet long; wingspan of 72 feet; gross weight of 82,000 pounds; and top speed of 610 miles per hour. It had a maximum bomb capacity of 12,000 pounds.

Admiral Gayler: Well, we saw a way of life so strange, so alien that it's very difficult to explicate, except with sea stories of one sort or another. We were based in the Khor Kaliya, in Bahrain, which is, of course, a little island.* It's a quasi-independent sheikdom in the middle of the Persian Gulf. At one time it was a fairly considerable oil-producer but not anymore. It was principally interesting because—from almost the time history began—it had been the jumping-off place, the port from which the Arabs sailed all the way down the East Coast of Africa to Zanzibar in their dhows. The alternation of the seasons was such that they could sail downwind, do their trade, and sail downwind coming back up—if they did it right. They made tremendous voyages in those teak dhows that they built.

In the mid-1950s Bahrain was a small British naval establishment. The Senior Naval Officer Persian Gulf, as he was called, was a great friend. The British operated a lighting service, which was supposed to take care of the navigation marks in the Persian Gulf with one little lighting tender called the *Relum*. It had an old Scotsman as a skipper, retired Royal Navy officer, O'Shea, who was a diminutive little fellow. He would receive you in front of the most enormous rug I've ever seen belonging to anybody.

Downtown Manama, the principal city, was really a fascinating crossroads of the Middle East. It had bazaars of the old-fashioned kind, but they had goods from all over the world. And then there was a big oil operation there, ARAMCO, which, of course, is a consortium.† They had their main operation at a place called Ahwali, about 15 miles away from Bahrain.

I don't know. Talking about Arabia and the Middle East in those days would take me hours and hours and hours. There's hardly anything you could think of that wasn't different, unusual, strange. One extraordinary thing was the climate. People don't realize what it's like out there. In the summertime, the average temperature is 115 degrees with 90% humidity. People think of it as being dry in the Persian Gulf area, but it isn't dry at all. You just had to get used to it. The ship was air-conditioned, but even so, the water temperature was so high that the air-conditioning didn't work very well.

---

* Khor Kaliya was the site of a small British naval base. The island of Bahrain is about 27 miles from north to south by 10 miles east to west—total 231 square miles.
† ARAMCO—Arabian American Oil Company.

I remember one time alongside the dock at Ras Tanura, which was a big oil port; the water temperature was 103 degrees Fahrenheit.[*] The Bureau of Ships tables stop at 90 degrees. And, of course, the hot salt water just ate up unprotected steel like sugar in a cup of coffee. From there, of course, I made the rounds all through the Persian Gulf ports into terrible little joints like Abu Dhabi, other places like that, and then down into the Indian Ocean, really just showing the flag.[†]

Paul Stillwell: How much guidance came from the State Department on your activities?

Admiral Gayler: None. I used to call on the appropriate ambassadors out there, and the sight of another American face, let alone another American ship, was so welcome that we got along like gangbusters. We'd talk about the local politics there, but generally speaking, we were just in the business of making friends and being friendly and showing presence. It's hard to imagine now, with the confluence of money and military power and the history of wars and everything else that's been going on in that part of the world, to realize that our 5-inch gun was the most important military weapon for about 400 miles around. It's just hard to believe it's changed so very much.

We, of course, did our very best to cultivate the various Arab rulers and their entourages wherever we went. We were always asked to partake of a kuzi, as it was called, which was a big roast lamb embedded in a bowl of rice, eaten with your hand— only one hand, by the way. It was a gross offense to use the other one, which was reserved for sanitary purposes. Then if you were the guest of honor, which I usually was, the host would gouge out one of the eyes and offer it to you. They're not awfully good; they're sort of rubbery. I got awfully tired of lamb.

There were some wonderful horses in some of the places. I'm kind of a horse nut. I remember the sheik of Bahrain gave me two beautiful horses that, of course, I had no way of getting back, so I had to decline the gift, but they're great on horses.

We got up at one time and another as far as the Khyber Pass on one marvelous occasion. I was able to take all the off-duty section of my crew to an exhibition by the

---

[*] Ras Tanura is a Saudi Arabian oil port, about 35 miles northwest of Bahrain.
[†] Abu Dhabi, a sheikdom in the southern Persian Gulf, is a member of the United Arab Emirates.

Pakistani outfit that was formerly the Bengal Lancers, before the British Empire in India was broken up. They put on this terrific horse show and gymkhana, and after that, they had some games for the visitors. There I was in whites and the sailors all in white liberty uniform. The first thing they had in mind was musical chairs on horseback. Of course, you know what young sailors are like; they'll try anything. There were a couple of guys from Texas that had been on a horse before, I think, but most of them never had. The object of the game is, you ride around on horseback and when the music stops, you dismount and lead your horse over to a chair and sit down, one chair too few. I got some of the most hilarious pictures of astonished horses and astonished sailors that you've ever seen in your life.

So there were things like that. It was hard on the crew. One thing is in Arab countries, of course, you just dare not, even if you wanted to—God knows why you'd want to—you dare not have anything to do with any of their women. So there was none of that kind of recreation for them, and it was damn bleak duty, really. We did our very best with fishing trips and tours and sightseeing and baseball and everything else to break the monotony a little bit. It was tough, but they were a wonderful, wonderful crew.

Paul Stillwell: Were these men specially selected because it was more difficult duty than serving with the fleet?

Admiral Gayler: I don't think so.

Paul Stillwell: Did they have a shorter tour than most to compensate?

Admiral Gayler: No, we went out as a ship and came back as a ship, which was, oh, about eight months out of Norfolk, with about five of them on station in the Middle East. There were three ships. The latter part of our tour coincided with the first Suez Canal episode. When the canal was closed, we had to come around Africa, which extended our tour another month.*

A destroyer that came out there briefly, *Compton*, managed to knock off one of her screws on a coral head, so we escorted her around. She couldn't make it all the way back to Norfolk without refueling, and I sure as hell didn't want to go into a West African port instead of a Brazilian port, which was what I had my eye on. So we rigged up a dummy arrangement and refueled her at sea with the aircraft refueling gear, all of which we still had on board, although we had no use for it. We never supported aircraft. I remember the pumping rate was so low that we were alongside about four days across the South Atlantic, day in and day out, but we finally gave her enough fuel to make it into Brazil instead of West Africa, got back a month late.

Paul Stillwell: Why was that type ship used for the flagship?

Admiral Gayler: It was cheap, I think. It was a little diesel ship and the crew was fairly small. It was painted white and been fitted with air-conditioning. It was show more than anything else. We had one 5-inch gun and two 40-millimeter mounts, and that was it.

Paul Stillwell: Why was that kind of ship rather than a larger one considered a suitable place for a future admiral?

Admiral Gayler: I don't know whether anybody regarded me as a future admiral or not.

Paul Stillwell: Well, you said you had been guided to take that duty to help your promotion opportunity.

Admiral Gayler: Oh, that was just a friend of mine talking. What he was saying is, if you want to be sure you're not an admiral, why, turn it down. That was the stepping-stone to a carrier command, of course. Most of the so-called qualifying commands were

---

* On 26 July 1956 President Gamal Nasser of Egypt announced that his country was nationalizing the Suez Canal Company. Israeli forces invaded Egypt's Sinai Peninsula on 29 October 1956. Britain and France then intervened militarily on behalf of Israel in an unsuccessful attempt to secure the Suez Canal, which was damaged and closed to traffic. Rather than support the British and French, the United States asked for a United Nations resolution to end the fighting. A cease-fire took effect on 6 November.

tankers, and while the tanker's a much bigger ship, I thought this was much more interesting duty anyway.

Paul Stillwell: That's the point that I was trying to make, that usually it's considered you have a deep-draft command before the carrier.

Admiral Gayler: That was my deep-draft command, 15 feet draft, but more navigation to do in the Persian Gulf with all those coral heads and whatnot. To go into the Khor Kaliya, you really had to wind through there like a snake, and the marks weren't that good. I remember the night before I went in there, I anchored in the outer harbor. The little British light tender, the *Relum*, was in there, so I went in and made friends with the skipper and went over the charts with him and all of the marks, some of which were just stone beacons, so I had to know the place.

Then as I was going in for the first time, my admiral, who, of course, was not navigating the ship, said to me, "I think you've gone on the other side of that marker." He'd been in there many times, and I knew damn well I didn't, because of the briefing I'd had the night before, so we went on up there. It was a dicey moment.

Paul Stillwell: What did he say afterwards?

Admiral Gayler: He was a very, very interesting man, a very warm man—you might say a lovable man from Texas, wealthy in his own right. And he got more enjoyment out of going ashore and getting presents for people. He gave it a great deal of attention and was extraordinarily generous. He would think up everything he could think of that anybody that he might think of might like, and ship it back to them. John Quinn, one of the nicest gentlemen I've ever known, enormously interested in Arabia.[*]

I remember when I reported in to him, he sat me down and told me all about camels for about 45 minutes. I learned a lot about camels, which, by the way, are very interesting beasts, more than most people realize. At the expiration of all this he said,

---

[*] Rear Admiral John Quinn, USN, served as Commander Middle East Force from 22 January 1956 to 3 August 1956.

"Well, I'm glad you're here." And that was the end of it. [Laughter] As far as I know, that was the only official information that he ever imparted to me. But he was a wonderful guy to have around, as was his successor, Jack Monroe, who was a very different sort of man but equally kindly and equally fun to have.* Commander Middle East Force was the job each one of them had. Of course, the only force we had was our little flagship, so that could have been a little crowded. But in the event, it was delightful with both of them.

Paul Stillwell: Well, wouldn't it be logical that the Navy would probably send good diplomatic type admirals to that post?

Admiral Gayler: I don't know. I've seen some pretty undiplomatic ones sent to other places. And then some pretty interesting things happened. On one occasion when the admiral was not there, I was detailed to have a joint naval exercise with the Iranian Navy. And in those days, the Iranian Navy consisted of two small ships. I guess they were corvettes: the *Babr* and *Palang*, translated as "panther" and "tiger."† There was also a motor torpedo boat. So I went in to see what that situation was.

The first thing I did was to talk to my friend, the British Senior Naval Officer Persian Gulf. The situation was then that we were sort of based on the British base, which supported us. We traded off things. He said, "We can't have an exercise with those [unclear]. Don't get within 1,000 yards of them. They'll sink you, they'll run into you."

I said, "Well, I'm going to do that, and we're going to have gunnery exercises."

"Gunnery exercises? They'll blow themselves up! Blow you up, too, if you're not careful!" That was his reaction to it.

Anyway, I came to find out that the Iranian ships couldn't get under way for training because they didn't have any fuel oil, they didn't have any mooring lines, and they didn't have a lot of other stuff. That, it turned out, was because everybody in the

---

* Rear Admiral Jack P. Monroe, USN, served as Commander Middle East Force from 3 August 1956 to 4 September 1957.
† *Babr*, formerly HMS *Derby Haven*, 1,652 tons; *Palang*, formerly HMS *Fly*, 1,040 tons. Each had two 4-inch guns.

Navy was on the take, including the Iranian CNO himself. The money appropriated in Teheran for fuel oil went in his pocket, in addition to which, the skippers were running a nice little racket where they would let sailors go home to farm and mama without hindrance in return for pocketing their pay and allowances. So they didn't have any fuel, they didn't have any mooring lines, they didn't have any radios, they didn't have any crews.

Then I looked around and looked around and tried to find somebody that was identifiable in the Iranian setup as honest. It was a very corrupt society, unbelievably corrupt. The sort of folk hero was a fellow named Ali Baba Visbahan, who was what we would call a chiseler, but apparently the Iranians thought that was great. His exploits, which all amounted to cheating somebody, were celebrated. Anyway, I finally found a guy who, by reputation, was not dishonest, who was Captain [unclear], whom I knew very well. Mostly he was protected because he was a nephew of the Minister of War, and that way he could afford to be honest.

After a bit, it became apparent that we weren't going to be able to get there from here, and all of a sudden, for a reason that I have never fully understood, the Shah announced that he was going to come down and witness the exercises.[*] Whoosh—fuel oil showed up, mooring lines showed up, crews got aboard, and we had the semblance of a show. We went out and did pretty very well, and the Shah came down and stayed for four days in my little ship with me. There was only one decent accommodation, which was mine, so I gave him that, of course, and I slept on deck. The weather was pretty good.

We had our meals together for four days, the Shah and I, and two senior Iranian generals who sat rigidly upright—honest to Christ, I'm not exaggerating—on the edge of their seats like plebes. They didn't speak unless spoken to by the Shah. He and I sat back and had pleasant, I thought rather extraordinary conversations talking to a foreign naval officer. He had a hell of a lot to say about Iranian policy and whatnot, but I was a little bit surprised at what he said. He was still a comparatively young man then. I can't

---

[*] Mohammad Reza Pahlavi (1919-1980) became Shah of Iran (or Persia, as it was then known) in 1941 and held office until his regime was ousted in 1979 by the Ayatollah Khomeini. He died 27 July 1980.

remember how many years it had been since he'd got back on his throne with the help of the CIA.[*]

Paul Stillwell: Not very many.

Admiral Gayler: Not very long. And I will just have to tell you, whatever his reputation may have been in later years, I liked him. I thought he was genuine, and I thought he was impressive in trying to bring his country into modern life, which, of course, is what got him in trouble with the ayatollahs. So I was very distressed when things grew bad.

Paul Stillwell: Did he seem well informed on naval matters?

Admiral Gayler: Oh, yes. He was a very bright man and very interesting, totally fluent in English. We would sit around and talk like this, those two generals sitting up there like this. A very interesting experience.

Those people were unbelievably poor. I can remember we set up a little gunnery target on Kharg Island, which, of course, is now one of the key islands of the oil distribution system, really nothing much but an oversized sandbar. There may have been two Iranian ships. It was short-range battle practice, not radar-controlled or anything. As we were coming up on the range ready to open fire, I was looking through the binoculars, and I could see some figures moving around the target. I said, "Check fire, check fire." What the hell was going on there? We finally had to send in some people to shoo them off. These people were so poverty-stricken that they were waiting there by those targets just for the timber and the canvas that was in them. We would have probably killed a couple of them if we'd actually gone through with it.

You saw the most extraordinary, almost incredible ways in which people live. The desert Arabs, of course, the Bedou, never washed from one year to another.[†] They rubbed down with sand and occasionally with [unclear] butter. And after a while when that sun comes down, they began to be really noticeable.

---

[*] The Central Intelligence Agency was involved in a coup in 1953 that put the Shah's premier in power.
[†] The Bedouin are part of an Arab ethnic group that lives predominantly in the desert and raises camels or sheep.

I could tell you lots of sea stories about Arabia.

Paul Stillwell: Please do.

Admiral Gayler: I don't think they're germane to what we're talking about.

Paul Stillwell: Well, you said you had the only decent accommodation on the ship. What was the admiral's like?

Admiral Gayler: It wasn't as good as mine, actually. In that class of ship there was no emergency cabin. The entire deck just below the bridge was the captain's cabin, which had huge ports that you could look out on all sides. You could practically conn the ship from there, unlike most. It was both the in-port and emergency cabin, and it was very nice.

I could play all the music I wanted to at whatever volume. I'm very fond of operatic. This was before tape recorders, so I had the problem of playing my good records on the ship when it was rolling, because the needle would skate all over the place. I had a lot of time on my hands, so I actually went back to a little shop in the ship and built me a couple of huge gimbals to handle the thing. It had a 20-pound lead weight on the bottom. So the record player would stay upright while the ship was moving around it.

I have a very strong stomach, and I've never been subject to seasickness, but she rolled like hell and she pitched too. When she was rolling and pitching but good, and this gimbal was holding this upright, when you turned and looked at the thing going around at the same time, with everything moving, I had a problem. [Laughter] My wife can't even stand me to talk about it, because she does have a little tendency to mal de mer, and as soon as I start going like that, she says, "Oh, no." [Laughter]

Paul Stillwell: Who established the operating schedule for your ship?

Admiral Gayler: Commander Middle East Force, I suppose in accordance with CNO directives. Basically it amounted to a lot of port visits, again showing the flag.

Paul Stillwell: Did you have social events for people in these ports to visit the ship?

Admiral Gayler: No. We usually had visitors. We usually had whoever was the senior person I would call on, or the admiral and I would call on, and they would have a reciprocal call. They'd come on out.

I remember once the senior fellow in the eastern province of Saudi Arabia then was a rather well known emir named Ahkin Ben-Jaloui, and he was a fierce old bastard. I remember his coming aboard with his bodyguard of about 18 villainous-looking guys with jevalahs and a submachine gun, early jevalah. And I so remember my anchor watch was a young seaman who couldn't have been 20 years old. I think he came from Iowa; if he wasn't from Iowa, he should have been because he sure looked it. The total armament he had was a billy club, and he was tapping each one of these villainous guys, making them put it down, "Scalawag." Just all the aplomb in the world; he knew he was working for his skipper and for the United States, so he had no problem with these guys. It was very amusing.

Paul Stillwell: Was it exceptional for you to get a visitor like the Shah to spend some time on board?

Admiral Gayler: I was about to say he was the only head of state, but it depends on whether you consider the sheiks and emirs as heads of state. They are independent trucial states, or they were then, but he was certainly the most prominent one.

Paul Stillwell: Did you have any high-ranking dignitaries from Saudi Arabia?

Admiral Gayler: Just the various emirs, pro-consuls for their district. There isn't any good correspondence in the Western world as to what they were. They were not just administrators. They had both hierarchical and Saudi Arabia royal positions of some sort, but they were not independent either. The trucial sheikdoms were nominally independent. Whoever was senior in the port, we always had them on board.

Some of the more interesting ones were up in Iraq. We went up to Basra more than once and had very interesting visits from a gentle and very cultivated old man who was the governor of Basra province at that time; he was also a historian. He told me an awful lot about the history of Mesopotamia and about Genghis Khan and what happened when he came in.* The population went from 25 million to 5 million in one year. Heaps of skulls, that sort of thing.

If you fly over the area, you can still see the faint tracing of the ancient irrigation canals in what looks like a featureless sand desert. He told me the tradition used to be that a person could walk from Basra to Baghdad and never be out from under the shade of a fruit tree, but there's nothing there but sand now. I don't think people realize how many, if not most, of the deserts are man-made. It's a really terrible thing. The people there really never recovered—not to this day—from Genghis Khan.

Paul Stillwell: What did you have for logistic support in that area?

Admiral Gayler: We had comparatively enormous refrigerated supply rooms, and we didn't have any other load to carry. We were loaded to the gills with spare parts and what have you, really well taken care of. Then we had some logistic support from the British at Bahrain, and you could get some things to eat, meat and other things, in the various ports we went to.

Paul Stillwell: I guess oil was no problem.

Admiral Gayler: Oil was no problem. You could fuel anywhere you wanted to. I don't recall that we ever had any serious shortage. We baked our own bread. The meals were pretty good. Fresh vegetables were a little hard to come by sometimes, and we had an awful lot of reefer storage.

I remember visiting Basra for the first time, and the U.S. consul there, a Mr. Stuckey, and his wife were two of the most devoted Americans you've ever seen. There they were, all by themselves, more or less, in this very strange and very Arab city,

---

* Genghis Khan was a 13th century Mongol conqueror.

holding down the prestige and the goodwill of the United States. I remember something occurred to me—that they probably hadn't seen any fresh fruit for a while, so I gave them a case of grapefruit from our reefer. You'd have thought I gave them the pearls of Ophir. I've never seen anything like it. When people start throwing off on the Foreign Service and whatnot, I often think of those people and many others out there that really man the drags under some really tough circumstances, totally devoted people.

Paul Stillwell: Was there any particular advantage in having an aviator as CO of that ship?

Admiral Gayler: The only airplane I ever got anywhere near was a couple of rides in a Tempest fighter they had at the RAF station at Bahrain.[*] They let me fly their fighters once in a while just to keep my hand in. The British are nice and informal about things like that, particularly on a distant station. But no, there was no aviation connected with the mission at all.

Paul Stillwell: How were communications that far away from most things?

Admiral Gayler: We were on the regular circuits, the fox circuit from Norfolk.[†] We were in pretty good shape. The principal communication problem was personal communication for the crew. It was a little difficult, but we could get off important messages of a personal character. There wasn't much chance for people to call up their sweethearts and chatter with them or anything like that.

Paul Stillwell: You must have seen an occasional Navy ship. Admiral Peet talks in his oral history about taking the *Barton* out to that area about then.[‡]

---

[*] RAF—Royal Air Force.
[†] "Fox" was the nickname for the fleet radio broadcast, fox being a letter in the old phonetic alphabet and standing in this case for "fleet."
[‡] See the Naval Institute oral history of Vice Admiral Raymond E. Peet, USN (Ret.).

Admiral Gayler: Actually, there was a change while I was out there, and first one, and then two destroyers were out there about half the time. When I first went out there, there was nobody.

Paul Stillwell: What additional role could they fulfill?

Admiral Gayler: They were much worse off than we because it was so goddamned hot out there, and they were not suitable. They weren't specially rigged for it like we were. It was more showing of the flag.

Paul Stillwell: A symbolic presence?

Admiral Gayler: Symbolic presence. I guess I didn't realize it at the time, but this was just the beginning of the transition from an absolutely empty, more or less unimportant part of the world to a key part of the world, as now regarded in the Persian Gulf.

Paul Stillwell: How much spin-off, if any, did you get from the Middle East War of 1956?

Admiral Gayler: Well, it resulted, as I told you, in our having to go around Africa on the way home. We didn't get any direct spin-off. There was some initial rioting in Bahrain, but it wasn't serious, just half a dozen people running down the streets and yelling. When Eisenhower intervened, we became very popular and very volatile people.[*] At least those Arabs didn't. I can hardly illustrate it without breaking my leg, but they would sit perched on any convenient perch, packing case or a table or anything, sitting characteristically with one foot—I can't even do it—with one foot under them like this and Cairo radio blaring away with somebody haranguing them in Arabic, "[unclear]."

Even then, the Palestinians were regarded as trouble all over. The local sheiks were scared to death of them because they were better educated, and they tended to be agitators of one sort or another. They were all over the place. Palestinians had sort of

---

[*] Dwight D. Eisenhower served as President of the United States from 20 January 1953 to 20 January 1961.

moved in and begun to dispossess the locals in many of the sheikdoms. They were thought to be a very serious problem. They were better-educated people; they tended to become the teachers and the leading businessmen and whatnot, and the sheiks were afraid of them.

Paul Stillwell: Was there any pervading feeling about Israel among the people you encountered?

Admiral Gayler: Pretty remote. The Arab-Israeli thing came to my attention in only one way. Just by the law of averages, I had some Jewish crew members. I remember one of them fell sick, and we wanted to ship him out by air, and we had a hell of a time because we couldn't use the airfield in Saudi Arabia. I can't remember the name of the Air Force base. I finally arranged to ship him back through Bahrain and the British, because the Saudis wouldn't let him.

And, of course, they were miserable to people who had to live there, like the people at the oil port at Ras Tanura. They felt very much put upon. The Saudis are Wahabis.* They're a very strict Islamic sect, among other things, not permitting the use of alcohol, so it was back to prohibition days. These people were making home brew and whatnot and very much resented the way in which the Saudis would inflict their ideas on the foreigners. These were oil people from all over the world—not only Americans but Italians and French and British and whatnot, all working for ARAMCO.

Paul Stillwell: You had prohibition aboard your ship for an entirely different reason.†

Admiral Gayler: Yes, that's right. [Laughter]

Paul Stillwell: How much of an intelligence-gathering role was involved in your mission?

---

* A Wahabi is a member of a Muslim sect founded by Abdul Wahhab (1703-1792).
† On 1 July 1914 a general order from Secretary of the Navy Josephus Daniels went into effect. It abolished the traditional wine messes on board U.S. Navy ships, resulting in a prohibition against drinking alcoholic beverages on board. The ban was relaxed in the 1980s to permit the serving of beer and wine—but not hard liquor—at official receptions on board.

Admiral Gayler: Other than overt reporting, very little. I didn't have any special intercept outfits or anything like that.

Paul Stillwell: You went from the *Greenwich Bay* to the CinCPacFlt staff.[*]

Admiral Gayler: Yes, I went to CinCPacFlt staff as operations officer, which was, of course, a choice job. I was very happy to have it. We were promised one of those nice sets of quarters up at Makalapa, but it had to be reworked and all the termites disconnected from holding hands with each other, all that kind of stuff.[†] All that was originally temporary housing built during World War II, and it's been termite haven ever since, a lovely situation. That was planned to take about six weeks.

In the meantime, my wife and I and our five children were all jammed into little temporary quarters. I remember the children were small, and it was so tight that I think we had two of them sleeping stacked over the top of the washing machine. But we were awfully happy to be out there, because my wife really loved Hawaii, anyway, and we were looking forward to going out there.

I was working into my ops officer job. God, I had big things going. I was rearranging all the ways in which the operations were planned, with this going here and this going here, and this going the other place. Then just about a week before we were due to move into our house, Tom Gates, the Secretary of the Navy, came through and sent for me as an individual.[‡] He said, "I'd like you to come back to Washington and be my aide."

I couldn't figure out what that was about, and I had a struggle, because I was just getting my teeth into my job, loved it out there, and we were about to move into the quarters that had been refurbished for us. But there is something very compelling about that man. I came to literally love him. But even then I finally said, "Well, if you're sure

---

[*] CinCPacFlt—Commander in Chief Pacific Fleet.
[†] Makalapa is the name of the area near Pearl Harbor on the island of Oahu, Hawaii, where Commander in Chief Pacific Fleet maintains his headquarters.
[‡] Thomas S. Gates Jr., was a highly respected individual who had a wealth of experience, both in the government and the business world. During World War II, as a Naval Reservist, he served as air combat intelligence officer and flag lieutenant on board aircraft carriers. He was Under Secretary of the Navy from 1953 to 1957; Secretary of the Navy from 1957 to 1959, and Secretary of Defense from 1959 to 1961. The guided missile cruiser *Thomas S. Gates* (CG-51) is named in his honor.

you want me, fine." So we moved back to the mainland again after about six weeks in Hawaii.

Paul Stillwell: Had you been specifically requested for the job in Hawaii too?

Admiral Gayler: I haven't any idea. I don't know anything about how I got those orders.

Paul Stillwell: Did you form any impressions of the commander in chief during that short time?

Admiral Gayler: Yes.

Paul Stillwell: Would you care to impart them?

Admiral Gayler: No. Actually, I'm not going to name the officer. He was a fine, warm individual who had come up the personnel chain of command, the personnel route, very well liked, a nice man. He didn't know anything about operations, which might not have been too bad had I stayed there. That was a pleasant entree, but as far as business was concerned, it was too specialized. He'd been in the personnel business all his life, or so it seemed to me.

Paul Stillwell: Did you come to find out why Secretary Gates had asked for you in particular?

Admiral Gayler: Yes. His then-aide had put the finger on me, Draper Kauffman.[*]

Paul Stillwell: Where did he know you from?

---

[*] Captain Draper L. Kauffman, USN. The oral history of Kauffman, who retired as a rear admiral, is in the Naval Institute collection.

Admiral Gayler: Oh, Draper and I were old friends, I guess all the way back to the Naval Academy. He was two years ahead of me.

Paul Stillwell: Had you had any contact with Admiral Kauffman in the meantime? Had you kept the association going?

Admiral Gayler: Nothing extended. We'd been friends over the years. I don't know what Draper said, but Tom Gates was the kind of man who had enormous confidence in the people that worked around him and for him, and I'm sure Draper mentioned me to him. The interview must have been satisfactory. At the time, I didn't realize I was being interviewed; I couldn't quite figure out what I was sent for, except I thought maybe he wanted to know something about how the fleet was operating. I talked a lot about that, probably more than I knew at the time. I'd only been there six weeks, but whenever I had a job, I liked to really study it very hard in the beginning weeks and sort of get a handle on it. And I had done that. I had worked very hard to understand what was going on.

Paul Stillwell: What qualities in Secretary Gates caused you to develop this great affection for him?

Admiral Gayler: He was so genuine, so absolutely honest, so warm, so friendly, gave you his confidence. He was terrific.

Paul Stillwell: I've gotten the impression from reading Admiral Kauffman's memoirs and others that he was a very hard worker also.

Admiral Gayler: Well, he was a hard worker, he certainly was, but he didn't make it hard on the people around him. You know, my affection for him was the norm. Everybody around him loved him. Once in a while we'd get into a slight jam because Arleigh Burke, who was a very strong personality of his own, I don't think really appreciated my role as an adviser to the Secretary as much as he might have done.* [Laughter] I would get a little feedback of one sort and another.

Paul Stillwell: Did you cross swords with Admiral Burke?

Admiral Gayler: No, not crossed swords. This is only guesswork. The admiral never gave me a bad time, but I just sensed that he felt that I was giving the Secretary too much advice, as opposed to the appropriate offices of the CNO, which would have been all right with me if they could have gotten off their dime, but they never did—for bureaucratic reasons.

One thing that I early discovered was that Gates had considerable naval experience in his own right. He spent the war in the war zone, knew a lot about it. In his both perceptive and gentlemanly way, he would make inquiries about this and that, intended to stimulate thought or possibly to produce action of some kind. When he did, he'd usually use me as the transmission belt, and then I would have to rush down to the appropriate office and say, "Now, look, your problem is not to answer the Secretary's letter. That's not the problem. The problem is the problem. What he wants you to do is to think very carefully about [whatever it was]. Don't worry about answering the letter; do that."

It just was very necessary. You'd find that they were spending their time thinking, "Gee, how the hell am I going to get this inquiry answered?" instead of "What's the problem here we ought to be looking at?"

Gates was a man of absolute integrity and very warm and fun to work with and for. After a while he developed one thing that really endeared him to me. No matter whom he were seeing, with the single exception of Admiral Burke, who insisted on talking to him alone, Gates would always insist that I be present whenever he was talking to anybody.

I remember when he took a trip to Europe, it was very amusing. We went, among

---

* Admiral Arleigh A. Burke, USN, served as Chief of Naval Operations from 17 August 1955 to 1 August 1961. His oral history is in the Naval Institute collection.

other things, to call on Laurie Norstad when he was SACEur.* I don't know whether you know anything about General Norstad, but he kept great state there. He took himself as seriously as MacArthur did and had this elaborate hierarchical setup in Paris. First the major came in to peel me off, and then Gates said, "Come on, Noel." Then the colonel came in to peel me off, and Gates said, "Come on, Noel." Finally the chief of staff, lieutenant general, came in to peel me off, and it was the same thing. So in the end it was the two of us and Norstad, who didn't like it a damn bit; I could see that.

Anyway, that's the way it was, and it was useful for Gates because it was two minds at work, and a useful check on his memory of what was talked about, which was very good. He could have done it independently. He seemed to value it, and I sure as hell did.

He also used to take me over to see Sherman Adams when he was the President's chief of staff.† You may remember that Adams was given an enormous amount of responsibility under Eisenhower. He was almost an assistant President until he got in trouble over a bribe and had to resign. Crazy story.

Anyway, every year, Gates would have to go over to Adams and negotiate with the assistant President, as it were, how to turn in some Navy ships under construction in order to realize enough money to complete the others. In those days, under the ground rules imposed mainly by the Congress, we were not able to project costs accurately, because we were not permitted to make accurate estimates of one sort or another, such as the inflation rate and whatnot. So as the shipbuilding program proceeded, it was clear that we couldn't finish all the ships. We had to sell some of them back for 25 cents on the dollar in order to finish the others. It was a ridiculous operation. Anyway, that's what he would do, and he would always take me on those. That was kind of an education for me.

---

* General Lauris Norstad, USAF, served as Supreme Allied Commander Europe from November 1956 to January 1963.
† Sherman Adams, who had served in the Marine Corps in World War I, was governor of New Hampshire from January 1949 to January 1953. He served as assistant to President Dwight D. Eisenhower from 21 January 1953 until his resignation on 22 September 1958.

He'd go around, of course, to see Uncle Carl Vinson occasionally, and he would try out some idea on "Uncle."[*] Gates was very astute and very good with the Congress. He understood exactly how important it was, who the important people were, how to approach them, and everything else. I don't know how he got to be so good politically, but he was. He really understood it. Of course, he had been Under Secretary before, so he knew a lot about how the Navy worked. But we'd go over to see "Uncle Carl," and Gates would tell him what he was thinking about doing, and the old gentleman would nod and nod and nod. Then once in a while there would be one, and the old man would say, "I wouldn't do that if I were you, Mr. Secretary." And by God, we wouldn't. He was a very powerful man, Carl Vinson, in those days.

Paul Stillwell: Was the Secretary properly deferential then?

Admiral Gayler: No, he wasn't deferential in the sense of being obsequious at all, but he maintained the same kind of straightforward, friendly relationship. That was another thing about him. He didn't differentiate in his treatment of people, whether they were senior or junior. He gave just as much courtesy to the most junior person around him as he did to people like Vinson or Adams.

The other occasion I really remember was when Gates was summoned over by Lyndon Johnson, who was then majority leader of the Senate; Sam Rayburn, who was then Speaker of the House; and George Mahon, who was chairman of the Appropriations Committee, all from Texas, to explain to them the crime in which the Secretary had moved a parachute-packing operation involving 70 people from Texas to Florida.[†]

---

[*] Carl Vinson of Georgia entered the House of Representatives in 1913 and was appointed to the Naval Affairs Committee in 1917. He became the ranking Democrat in 1923 and chairman in 1931. When the Armed Services committee was formed in 1947 Vinson became chairman and held that position, except for two short periods when Republicans held the House, until his retirement from Congress in 1965. The aircraft carrier *Carl Vinson* (CVN-70) is named for him.

[†] Lyndon B. Johnson, a Democrat from Texas, served in the House of Representatives from 10 April 1937 to 3 January 1949 and in the Senate from 3 January 1949 to 3 January 1961. He was Senate majority leader from 1955 to 1961. He was later Vice President from 1961 to 1963 and President from 1963 to 1969.
George H. Mahon, a Democrat from Texas, served in the House of Representatives from 3 January 1935 to 3 January 1979.
Samuel T. Rayburn, a Democrat from Texas, served in the House of Representatives from 4 March 1913 until his death on 16 November 1961. He was Speaker of the House from 1940 to 1947, 1949 to 1953, and 1955 until he died in 1961.

Johnson had sent Ken BeLieu, who later on became Under Secretary of the Navy, and was a very able lawyer, down to Texas for about a month.[*] He interviewed everybody in sight. Before a considerable delegation of the home folks from Texas BeLieu made a marvelous lawyer's case about why it was so improvident, foolish, wasteful, everything else you could think of, to move this parachute-packing operation to Florida. This presentation, which took quite a while, was a masterly job on BeLieu's part. At the conclusion of it, Johnson turned to Gates and said, "Now, Mr. Secretary, in the light of everything that you've heard, don't you think you should reconsider your decision?"

Gates just smiled his sweet smile and said, "No." And that was the end of it. Going back to the Pentagon in the car, Gates said, "You know, Noel, if I had backed up a quarter of an inch, they'd have had my liver." [Laughter] I've never forgotten that. He was terrific.

Paul Stillwell: Did you sit in, also, on his dealings with Secretary McElroy?[†]

Admiral Gayler: Yes, yes, and I can't remember what the hell the crisis was, but I can remember McElroy padding around in his bathrobe and bare feet in the middle of the night, talking to Gates and to me about something. I can't now recall what it was, but it was one of those crises. And McElroy was such an ineffectual figure, particularly when he was waked up in the middle of the night and couldn't find his slippers. He was a soap salesman from Cincinnati.

Paul Stillwell: Proctor & Gamble.

Admiral Gayler: Yes. He was a gentleman; he was a nice man.

Paul Stillwell: Gates eventually succeeded him.

---

[*] Kenneth E. BeLieu at the time was on the staff of the Senate Armed Services Committee. He later served as Assistant Secretary of the Navy (Installations and Logistics), 1961-65; Under Secretary of the Navy, 1965.
[†] Neil H. McElroy served as Secretary of Defense from 9 October 1957 to 1 December 1959.

Admiral Gayler: Gates succeeded him, and Gates, of course, was very much better.* Gates, as you know, of course, set up the Joint Strategic Target Planning Staff, that I was later ordered to, as a way of settling the otherwise totally scrambled setup by which each service was trying to target their weapons as suited them, without coordination and whatnot.† It was sort of a compromise between doing what the Air Force wanted to do, which was to set it all up under SAC, and what Arleigh Burke wanted to do, which was to keep it entirely the hell in the services.‡

Paul Stillwell: This was involved when Polaris was coming into being.§

Admiral Gayler: That's what I'm talking about. Yes, the carrier planes were in the act, too, but not significantly. No, it was the submarines that really made it an acute problem.

Paul Stillwell: Initially, I think, the Navy had in mind about a six-tier chain of command on giving orders, and Secretary Gates said, "That just won't work. You're going to have to simplify it, or we'll go to the Air Force's method."

Admiral Gayler: Actually, all that was done was that the planning function was unified. The operational function still went through the chain of command. I had the responsibility when I was CinCPac, for example, for that part of the world. So although the plan was done in that planning staff, in accordance with JCS directives, that largely was SAC staff, as a matter of fact, because JSTPS was then at least two-thirds SAC as far as personnel were concerned. Both the director and the number-three man were SAC people with operating SAC jobs with a Navy vice admiral sandwiched in between. Still,

---

* Gates served as Secretary of Defense from 2 December 1959 to 20 January 1961.
† In August 1960, at the instigation of Secretary of Defense Thomas Gates, the Joint Strategic Target Planning Staff was established at Offutt Air Force Base near Omaha, Nebraska. The JSTPS is discussed in the Naval Institute oral histories of several officers who were assigned there: Admiral John J. Hyland, USN (Ret.); Vice Admiral Gerald E. Miller, USN (Ret.); Vice Admiral Kent L. Lee, USN (Ret.); Vice Admiral Edward N. Parker, USN (Ret.).
‡ SAC—Strategic Air Command.
§ Polaris was the name for the U.S. Navy's first submarine-launched ballistic missile, which became operational in the early 1960s. Its more-capable follow-on was the Poseidon missile, which entered the fleet in 1970.

the execution was done through the chain of command—unified and specified commands.

Paul Stillwell: I interviewed Commander Paul Backus, who was working in OpNav on the Polaris developments, and he was impressed by Gates's substantive decision-making on Polaris in going for the submerged launch.* This was different from Admiral Raborn's original idea that the ships would surface before they launched their missiles. Gates had enough detailed understanding of it to make the technical decision.†

Admiral Gayler: Gates wasn't like some of these characters they've got now who wouldn't know a ship if it bit them in the butt. He was an experienced naval officer with a lot of sea time, in addition to which he had the, in those days, possession of the *Sequoia*.‡ He would find out from me and others who the real hotshots were at the commander and captain level, and have them out for a cruise down the Potomac. Whiskey was available and the tongues got loosened after a while, and he was so easy that pretty soon the formalities were forgotten, and he was getting the word as it was. So he was very well informed and perfectly capable of making decisions like that.

Paul Stillwell: What kinds of things would be discussed in those meetings on the *Sequoia*?

Admiral Gayler: Well, you mustn't get the idea that they were meetings. They were parties. Usually he was very tactful and careful about it, and usually whatever the officer wanted to talk about, what was uppermost on his mind was what Gates wanted to hear.

Then there was one episode in which both Bud Zumwalt and I thought our naval careers were at an end, having to do with a promotion plan which had been prepared in the Bureau of Personnel.§ It was introduced to the Secretary in a briefing that I attended,

---

* Commander Paul H. Backus, USN (Ret.), whose oral history is in the Naval Institute collection.
† Rear Admiral William F. Raborn, Jr., USN, was director of the Special Projects Office, which developed the Polaris submarine-launched ballistic missile system. He held the post from 1955 to 1962, being promoted to vice admiral in 1960. His Polaris oral history is in the Naval Institute collection.
‡ The *Sequoia* was the yacht assigned to the Secretary of the Navy.
§ Commander Elmo R. Zumwalt Jr., USN, later Chief of Naval Operations from 1970 to 1974.

and it just had some funny-looking figures in it. I couldn't quite figure out what was wrong, but it didn't look right, and so I looked at it more carefully after the brief. About that time, Bud Zumwalt, who had never met me, came down to see me. He was then a commander; I was a captain. I found out he had the same concern. To make a long story short, it was a plan for promotion opportunity that disadvantaged one class in order to promote another one. I think that's the simplest way to say it. It was not fair in promotion opportunity, and what's more, it had been prepared by people who were directly affected, the more senior class who were the people who were going to get the better shot.

Bud was then working for Jackson, who was assistant secretary for personnel, a nice guy.* Bud and I were agreed that this wasn't right, and we blew the whistle. We became pretty famous people over in the Bureau of Personnel. I haven't any idea whether Admiral Smith, the bureau chief, ever knew anything about it or not, but the people who had presented the figures were interested parties.† They were senior captains, and the figures had advantaged this particular class in ways they should not have been. So we blew the whistle on it, and we became Sinbad the Sailor with the Bureau of Personnel. Little typewritten pieces of paper began to appear on my desk, telling me what was going on in the bureau. On one occasion, I was terribly flattered because at a fairly high level, they had convened a meeting to see how to get that son-of-a-bitch Gayler out of town. It was all duly reported to me on this little slip of paper which showed up. To this day I don't know who put them there, I really don't.

Paul Stillwell: Do you suspect Admiral Zumwalt at all?

Admiral Gayler: No, it was coming from within the bureau. He wouldn't have known either, you see. He was in the Pentagon with me. He also was a target. I remember sitting on the couch in his house, and we were discussing what we were going to do in civil life.

---

* Richard Jackson, Assistant Secretary of the Navy (Personnel and Reserve Forces).
† Vice Admiral Harold Page Smith, USN, served as Chief of Naval Personnel from 31 January 1958 to 12 February 1960.

Paul Stillwell: Weren't you protected, though, by being in the Secretary's office?

Admiral Gayler: As long as I was there. But Secretaries come and go, and the Bureau of Personnel has a long memory, including the then-chief, Admiral Smith, who vetoed me later on for a job, but it didn't matter a hell of a lot.

Paul Stillwell: So how did the situation get resolved on the promotion plan?

Admiral Gayler: We got a good one, we got a fair one. We got a fair one.

Paul Stillwell: Did you recognize then Zumwalt as a comer?

Admiral Gayler: I would not have predicted he was going to be CNO in the next few years, not that I would have predicted that he wouldn't be, but he was way junior to me. I didn't foresee that. We became friends pretty fast and we still are, although I gather we're on different sides of the argument about nuclear weapons nowadays, which I don't understand, because he's got more sense than that. But there we are.

Paul Stillwell: One of the events of that time was Sputnik, which caused a great hullabaloo in America in education and so forth. Did that have an effect in the Secretary's office?

Admiral Gayler: Oh, yes, yes. Like everybody else, we came to attention. In fact, we got a little bit embroiled in the initial press reactions. Rawson Bennett, who was the Chief of Naval Research was at the time, very imprudently said the first reports couldn't possibly be correct; the Soviets couldn't possibly put anything that size up into orbit.[*] He would have done well to have kept his face zipped until he had found out what had happened. He was a good man too. He was sort of a scientist and he was a naval officer. He was out of his depth. So we were in the middle of that.

---

[*] Rear Admiral Rawson Bennett II, USN.

Also, I'm the famous guy who did not invite Rickover to the celebration of the *Skate*'s first trip under the ice, and there was a lot of press attention on that, indignant editorials.* I thought it an operational occasion, and I didn't want to see Rickover monopolizing it. I just left him the hell off, and there was a lot of flap about that.

Paul Stillwell: How much interaction was there between him and the Secretary's office?

Admiral Gayler: Some. He used to come in and talk to the Secretary occasionally. He was not his usual obnoxious self, however; he was very well behaved. Later on, I saw him at his obnoxious best, but I have totally mixed feelings about Rickover—great achievement and terrible flaws, disgraceful, absolutely disgraceful history within the Navy of having end-run around the chain of command and contemptuous treatment of individuals, which, in my judgment, should never have been permitted to happen.

I never actually tangled with him until I was CinCPac, and we tangled but good. I think it was a draw. On the other hand, I have to admire his achievement. When I was skipper of an antisubmarine division, I spent most of my time in the submarines. You walk around the ship with the chief engineer, and, "How are things going, Chief?"

"Well, we've got a squeak in the stern planes, we've got some trouble with the air-conditioning machinery, got a steam gland leak on the port turbine."

"How's the nuclear plant?"

"Oh, that just runs, Admiral." That is an extraordinary achievement for a technique so new, so dangerous. You contrast how well the Navy's done and how terribly civilian industry has done. Tremendous achievement. But that business of having his own Gestapo and his own reporting system and his totally improper use of his atomic energy hat to control personnel assignments, and his deliberate humiliation of people wasn't worth it. It shouldn't have been put up with. I never thought so.

Paul Stillwell: Was there any means of holding him down by the Secretary?

---

* On 3 August 1958 the USS *Skate* (SSN-578), under Commander James F. Calvert, USN, became the first submarine to surface at the North Pole.

Admiral Gayler: I don't know. I don't want to make a judgment on that. Secretary after Secretary, I guess, decided that it wasn't worth it to play with a buzz saw. He was a pretty unscrupulous man, and he, for some reason which has always escaped me, had a great following in the Congress. He seemed to get a lot of credence by denouncing everybody in sight except himself.

Paul Stillwell: He wouldn't denounce his friends in Congress; he'd flatter them.

Admiral Gayler: Oh, yes.

Paul Stillwell: Another event of those years is in the news again in Lebanon. What involvement was there in the Secretary's office there, the landing there in 1958?[*]

Admiral Gayler: Very little, as I recall. I think that was done pretty much in the state and operational channels.

Paul Stillwell: The chain of command was revised with an act of 1958, really taking the CNO out of the operational chain.[†] Was there an effect through your office on that?

Admiral Gayler: Only peripherally, because the Secretary was never in the chain anyway. But we got a little of the backwash out of Arleigh Burke's determination not to be out of the chain, no matter what it said. Gates was sort of half rueful and half admiring.

---

[*] On 15 July 1958, at the request of Lebanese President Camille Chamoun, U.S. amphibious forces landed at Beirut to support Chamoun's government, which was threatened by both civil war and the prospect of foreign invasion. Two of the Sixth Fleet's three battalion landing teams went ashore within 24 hours. For details see the account of the U.S. ambassador to Lebanon, Robert McClintock, "The American Landing in Lebanon," *U.S. Naval Institute Proceedings*, October 1962, pages 64-79.

[†] The Department of Defense Reorganization Act of 1958 contained a number of provisions, including removal of the service secretaries from the chain of command; removal of the service chiefs' command authority over their forces; establishment of the principle that the Joint Chiefs of Staff could act only under the authority of the Secretary of Defense; and transfer of control of the Joint Staff from the JCS as a whole to the Chairman.

Paul Stillwell: What can you say of your relationships with Admiral Burke from that period?

Admiral Gayler: I was and am an enormous admirer of Admiral Burke's. I've known him slightly ever since I was a young officer in a destroyer. When I went to *Craven* as gunnery officer, she was the bottom ship in the flotilla, and by dint of busting our butt, we very nearly got her to the top, but we were beaten out by *Mugford*, Arleigh Burke, skipper, who had been up there for a long time. He was just great. I have great admiration for him. I had great admiration for him when he was chief of staff to Second Carrier Task Force, and only by reputation from his time as "31-knot Burke" with the destroyers.

He was extraordinarily good about things like morale, for example, in our Navy. When I was selected for admiral, he sent me around one of those flags with an engraved thing on it. He was a wonderful officer. I don't want to imply in anything that I've said that I ever had any second thoughts about him in any capacity. I just remark he was a "take-charge" guy, and he didn't particularly like having any young whippersnapper giving his Secretary of the Navy naval advice, which he knew goddamn well I was doing.

Paul Stillwell: Did that apply to such things as flag slating?

Admiral Gayler: No, no. I never got involved in people matters except in that one thing that I just told you about. No, no, nothing of that kind. Operational and technical and public affairs, all the things the Secretary does. But no, Gates was incapable of favoritism, anyway. No, nothing like that.

Paul Stillwell: What were you involved with in the area of public affairs?

Admiral Gayler: Well, in those days, the Secretary of the Navy was a more prominent figure than he is now, although the Secretary of Defense had been set up. There was a lot of residual prestige to the office, which doesn't now exist. So he was a public figure, and he was asked for by reporters. He made speeches occasionally, although he was not all that fond of making speeches, and was highly regarded by what you might call the Eastern Establishment. He was a very close friend of Douglas Dillon, who was Secretary of the Treasury at the time and a prominent figure and so forth and so on.[*] So he had a lot of public affairs things to do, as well as the naval public affairs and go open something or preside over something and so forth. And he was very good at it, but as in all public affairs things, there are a lot of slips that are possible, a lot of things that you have to be careful about, and a lot of ways in which you can put your best foot forward.

Just before I came on board, there was a civilian public affairs fellow hired, whose name I won't give you. He was sort of a bull artist, in my view, and he used to like to come in and bull with the Secretary for about an hour every morning. I could see it was irritating Gates to spend so much time at it because it wasn't very substantive. So I gradually closed him off from access, because I owned the door, so to speak. I thought this guy was sort of lazy and didn't really do a hell of a lot, although he talked a good game. We went along like that for a while, and I suddenly noticed he was getting very busy on something, some project that he had, and I was pleased with that. I didn't bother him. I hoped he would come up with something. Then one morning Gates called me up and he handed me this little, limp, leather-bound booklet and said, "Noel, what do you think of this?"

I opened it up, and I could see what this guy had been working on all this time. It was a very carefully worked-out indictment of me for all sorts of crimes, mostly keeping him out of the office and out of the Secretary's hair, but a lot of other stuff too. I looked at it for a minute and saw what the tenor was, and by that time, I'd gotten to trust Gates completely, so I just said, "Well, it looks accurate," and handed it back to him. He laughed and threw it in the "out" basket. About a week later, this fellow was on his way to California to work for the movie industry.

Paul Stillwell: How good was Secretary Gates at pouring oil on troubled waters and angry constituents or congressmen?

---

[*] C. Douglas Dillon was Under Secretary of State for Economic Affairs, 1958-59; Under Secretary of State, 1959-61; and Secretary of the Treasury, 1961-65.

Admiral Gayler: Very, very, very good. He was totally honest and whatnot. There was one congressman named Boykin from Alabama who was sort of a figure.* He was almost a caricature of a Deep South politician. And I can remember his coming up with some of his constituents, who were clearly plain people and good citizens, and they had some grievance or other. It wasn't parachute packing, but it was a comparable thing. They had lost a few Navy jobs. He made this impassioned speech in front of his constituents, sitting in the Secretary's office, and he turned around and gave the Secretary a wink, just like that, and went on without skipping a beat. I realized for the first time that most of those congressional representations are just show biz anyway. It's for the benefit of the constituent. But Gates was very good. He was honest, he was genuine, he was concerned. Sometimes he could and would do something about it properly, and sometimes he couldn't and wouldn't, but always with deep consideration, and they appreciated that.

Paul Stillwell: Did you get involved at all in writing the precepts for the flag selection boards?

Admiral Gayler: No. That's a very sensitive subject, though, because so much is involved personally for people. It's so very important to the Navy to have not only absolute honesty in selection boards, but also the perception of absolute honesty. We might not get the right guys every year, and we probably won't ever select an eccentric genius, but by God, they're straight, they're fair, and they're honest. I've sat on plenty of them and I've been president of a couple, and I think it's something we can be proud of. For that reason, I was just a little bit skittish about the notion of acknowledging that a junior officer did even the first draft of that precept, because I think it's very important to the system that the Secretary be personally involved, and I don't want to give you the impression that the Secretary wasn't. It was his article even though I did a first draft on it.

Paul Stillwell: Did you write speeches for him as well?

---

* Representative Frank W. Boykin, Democrat from Mobile.

Admiral Gayler: Sometimes. But he liked to do his own. He usually wouldn't take my speeches; he said they were okay but they weren't his style. So he more often than not jotted down his own ideas. He never wrote them out in full anyway. He'd speak from notes. He was very good. His style and mine were quite different, and I never quite caught on to his style. So he thanked me for the effort, but I noticed he didn't use them much.

Paul Stillwell: Anything else about that tour with Secretary Gates?

Admiral Gayler: Lots of stories I could tell about his humanness and kindness, but I guess everybody who knew him would tell you that.

Paul Stillwell: How about an example or two?

Admiral Gayler: Well, my three daughters were then about, I guess, 11 or 12, 9, and 8. They had a tiny little place in the back of our house that they called the Navy Club. As little kids do, they liked to hang out in there. Gates came to dinner one night and heard about it. And darn, if he didn't go to some famous sail maker and commission a Navy Club flag for those children and presented it to them. I remember a goat rampant and four stars for the Secretary, and all sorts of decorations—beautifully done by some famous sail maker. Gates always did things first class. Some famous sail maker like Ted Hood or somebody like that.

Paul Stillwell: He had the money to be able to do things first class.

Admiral Gayler: Yes, that's right, he did.

Paul Stillwell: Of course, he didn't have to do anything.

Admiral Gayler: He didn't have to do anything. With his thoughtfulness, you never got the impression that he was throwing it around or anything like that. And, of course, Mrs.

Gates was and is such a wonderful lady. The one thing that bothered her was any appearance of ostentation or anything like that. She rather disliked public appearances for that reason. She really hated to be in a big, black limousine and have motorcycle cops in front. It just really distressed her. In fact, I remember once in Los Angeles, there was some big parade, and we were tearing across town in a big, black limousine with the motor bike escort. She was so embarrassed, she sat on the floor of the car and wouldn't be seen. A lovely lady, Ann Gates.

Paul Stillwell: Next time we'll talk about the *Ranger*.

Admiral Gayler: Yes, that's a good subject.

Interview Number 6 with Admiral Noel A. M. Gayler, U.S. Navy (Retired)

Place: Admiral Gayler's office at the American Committee on East-West Accord, Washington, D.C.

Date: Tuesday, 10 April 1984

Paul Stillwell: Admiral, last time we were talking about your service with Secretary Gates. You went on from there to command the *Ranger*. How did that assignment come about?

Admiral Gayler: Well, Secretary Gates went down to the occasion of the commissioning of the *Ranger*, which was at Norfolk, and I went down with the party.* It was a wonderful ceremony and a bright day on the huge deck of the then-unprecedentedly big carrier, just terrific. I distinctly remember thinking, "Gee, you know, this would be a great command." When my term of service with Mr. Gates was coming near an end, he called me in one day and asked me where I would like to go, and I said I would like to command a carrier. He said, "Which one?"

Without thinking about it at all, I said, "*Ranger*."

Then he went down to talk to Admiral Burke about several important matters, and he never told me whether he mentioned the matter of my command to Admiral Burke or not, but I did find out later on that my orders to another and smaller carrier had been changed to command of the *Ranger*. Perhaps that wasn't a coincidence; I don't know. [Laughter]

Paul Stillwell: Is the picking of carriers something that the CNO would be involved in personally?

---

* USS *Ranger* (CVA-61), a *Forrestal*-class big-deck aircraft carrier, was commissioned 10 August 1957. She had a standard displacement of 56,300 tons, was 1,046 feet long, 236 feet in the beam, an extreme width of 249 feet on the flight deck, and had a draft of 37 feet. She had a top speed of 34 knots and could accommodate about 80-95 planes. She had a long active career before finally being decommissioned on 10 July 1993.

Admiral Gayler: When it involved the wishes of the Secretary, it would. I don't really know what Admiral Burke's style was on that. Some senior commanders take a great interest in it, and others just let the system work. I remember Admiral Smith when he was CinCLant took a great deal of interest in who his ship commanders and who his carrier division commanders were.* I know that because he vetoed me later on. [Laughter]

Paul Stillwell: You were both the beneficiary and the victim of the system.

Admiral Gayler: Or of the non-system, yes. One might say there was a certain amount of pull in one case and a great deal of un-pull in the other one. [Laughter]

Paul Stillwell: You said in an earlier interview that command was always preferable to a staff job. Was this sort of the fulfillment of that ambition?

Admiral Gayler: I think my ambition was more general than that. I liked almost all the jobs I ever had in the Navy. I don't recall ever actually asking for one except on this occasion. I certainly was far more suited, I think, to command. I'd had a lot of them and wanted more, yes.

Paul Stillwell: Did she live up to your expectations?

Admiral Gayler: She was a wonderful ship, absolutely wonderful ship.† She handled like an overgrown destroyer. She operated airplanes like two of the older carriers. She had great endurance, great sea-keeping capability. We mostly had an absolutely marvelous outfit—both the officers and the men. My exec, Al Lewis, who was a hard-bitten ex-oilfield roustabout, was a dynamic and terrific officer.‡ He was responsible principally for the quite extraordinary personnel record we had.

---

* Admiral Harold Page Smith, USN, served as Supreme Allied Commander Atlantic, Commander in Chief Atlantic, and Commander in Chief Atlantic Fleet from 30 April 1963 to 30 April 1965.
† Captain Gayler commanded the aircraft carrier *Ranger* (CVA-61) from 23 May 1959 to 4 June 1960.
‡ Commander Allen L. Lewis, USN.

We were very, very much determined to make the moral leadership program succeed, and we emphasized it. The principal part of it, in my eyes, was not the somewhat preachy tone, but rather the idea of responsibility at all levels. I can still remember the almost incredulous reaction when I had up at mast not only a fireman who misbehaved ashore but petty officers all the way up the line, and held them all personally responsible.* I used to talk often about life aboard a carrier and how you look around right and left, and you will find your shipmate holding your life in his hands, and his in yours.

With that program and some other things that we did, we accomplished some quite remarkable things. For instance, the *Ranger* lowered the venereal disease rate in Japanese ports and Oriental ports down to 15% of what it had been previously, operating about twice as much as any carrier had on the station. Shore patrol reports went down to about 19% of what they had been. It was good behavior, in other words.

Then we did everything possible to communicate. I used to make it a point to get up on the ship's loudspeaker system, usually at least twice a day, once in the morning and once in the evening, to say precisely what we were doing and why. We had closed-circuit television, about 75 sets, as I recall. I used to go on that almost every night, unless we were operating too heavily, and field questions from the crew, which could be either acknowledged or anonymous. They were pretty good. "Captain, why are we doing this?" and so forth. Sometimes I couldn't tell the crew why we were doing this and so forth, but I would find out.

Paul Stillwell: That must have been one of the very first Navy ships to have that kind of system.

Admiral Gayler: Yes. Well, it's impossible otherwise. You can't get the crew of a carrier together on the hangar deck and talk to them without stopping ship's business. You can't do it while you're under way, in any case. What's more, the numbers are so

---

* Captain's mast is a sort of court in which the commanding officer of a unit listens to requests, awards non-judicial punishment, or issues commendations. Most often captain's mast is used for punishment of lesser offenses than those that merit courts-martial.

big and the hangar deck is so huge, you'd just be a little insect anyway. So what you have to do is use television to be able to talk to the crew like a captain should.

Paul Stillwell: Did you miss the personal touch that you'd had in smaller unit commands?

Admiral Gayler: No, there was a lot of personal touch there. You didn't know every sailor on the ship like I did when I had a little seaplane tender out for months in the Persian Gulf, but you knew the key players, catapult chiefs, and the chief storekeepers. I didn't know the snipes as well as some of the others, but I got to know most of the key players.*

Paul Stillwell: You talked about the unprecedented size of the ship. Was there great curiosity in foreign ports when you visited?

Admiral Gayler: Oh, I should say so. Everywhere we went on that cruise, we were the biggest ship that had ever been there. This was before the big oil tankers. We were not only the biggest warship, but the biggest ship. And yes, enormous curiosity.

I remember in Kobe, we had one afternoon 26,400 Japanese visitors. We got them all on and all off safely, without any incident at all, except after the whole thing was over, we got a message from the beach, from the consul, saying two children were missing. So we searched the ship, and we couldn't find those kids. We finally found them in the tailpipe of one of the airplanes. They'd curled up in there and gone to sleep, and we sent them back. I got a note, which I still have somewhere, in Japanese, with a little translation on it. It was a sort of receipt for the two children in good condition. I've got it somewhere. It amused me to no end.

Yes, we were always the object of curiosity, and there were other things, too, about her unprecedented size. Every time we went into a harbor, of course, we were sort of testing whether the charts were any good. In a couple of them I thought it prudent to go in behind a helicopter with a lead, just to see that the water that was supposed to be

---

* "Snipe" is a Navy nickname for personnel in the engineering department.

there was there. For example, in Kobe, the channel was only supposed to be 40 feet, and we were drawing about 35 or 36. To get some idea of scale, here's a thing over 1,000 feet long and a couple of hundred feet wide, and under her bottom, between her and the ground, is that much. You can imagine the flows that go as this big body displaces the water through the narrow way. You get some very screwy effects from it, important in ship handling, but even more important that you really do have the four feet or so, which is supposed to be under your keel.

Paul Stillwell: Not only that, I'd think you'd have problems when you don't have much way on, just controlling such a huge mass.

Admiral Gayler: Yes, and I picked up something from the harbor pilot in Yokosuka; he was a retired chief boatswain's mate.* He taught me the old merchant trick of dropping your outboard anchor, in the case of the *Ranger*, of 15 fathoms of chain on it, and dragging it along. The effect of that was to create considerable resistance so that you could use a lot more engine power without picking up too much speed, but even more importantly, to get the turning point right up at the bow instead of about a third of the way back. And so you could drive the ship at a considerable angle right up to a dock, knowing as soon as you took the power off, she'd slow down and stop, and then crank her around hard with the engines. It was very powerful. I used to be able to put the *Ranger* alongside the dock at Ford Island when the trade winds were blowing off the dock without tugs or anything, using that trick.† You'd never be able to do it otherwise. Because there wasn't much room there either.

Paul Stillwell: What other things did he teach you?

Admiral Gayler: Oh, just sort of a manual, which confirmed a lot of book study and observation from my smaller command about how the propeller currents affect the ship in shallow waters. I saw how a backing bell would breast you out bodily, because the

---

* Yokosuka is a port city on the Japanese island of Honshu. It is near Tokyo and Yokohama. Atsugi Naval Air Station is nearby.
† Ford Island is in the middle of Pearl Harbor, Hawaii.

stream current comes between you and the dock, particularly if the dock has some kind of a solid face.* Another was how to keep your position oriented by picking up some landmarks so you weren't totally dependent on the navigator to get you cuts and bearings. That was particularly useful to me in Alameda.† Alameda is a fairly tight place. A couple of people have come to grief there with carriers. There is a way to orient yourself with respect to the runways and whatnot, so you know you're exactly where you want to be in the turning basin. And this pilot was sort of bold too. He showed me that you could use plenty of power when you needed to twist her or stop her or whatnot without untoward effects and things like that.

Paul Stillwell: One of the unfortunate aspects of the Navy system or non-system is that once you learn all this from practical experience, it's time to leave the command.

Admiral Gayler: Well, that's right. That's one of those things. I used to be a pretty good fighter pilot. I had no opportunity to do that. I used to be a pretty good ship handler. I've always thought that for a lazy man, the job of being a harbor pilot would be just absolutely wonderful. Because all you've got to do is know what you're doing. The working hours are short, the work isn't hard; it isn't even difficult. All you've got to be is right. It's like aviation in that respect.

Paul Stillwell: When you encountered local pilots in some of these overseas ports, were they in awe of a ship of that size?

Admiral Gayler: I never took a pilot after the first month or so I had the ship, for two reasons. One, honestly, I suppose it was a little bit of an ego trip to handle the ship without one. But, more important, I thought it was a matter of readiness too. I did not wish to be dependent on tug and pilot in case of a war emergency of some kind. I wanted

---

* Each order to the engines is accompanied by a bell sound on the engine order telegraph. Thus, a "bell" is synonymous with an engine order. The fewer the number of bells in a given landing, the better.
† Alameda Naval Air Station, which opened in November 1940, was on the east side of San Francisco Bay, near Oakland, California.

to be able to get out of a place without prior notice and without assistance, and if necessary, I wanted to be able to go in the same way.

Paul Stillwell: What were some of the other places you visited in the Orient?

Admiral Gayler: Well, we used to go into Kobe and Osaka quite a lot. And, of course, when we were out there, we were practically home-ported in Tokyo, Sagami Wan. In my cruise, that's all we did in Japan. We never did go into Sasebo with her. I don't now remember even whether there's enough water there for her or not, but for some reason we didn't go there. And Australian ports—Sydney, that was about it.

Paul Stillwell: It was about that time that President Eisenhower encountered some hostility from the Japanese leftists. Was there any spillover to the Navy in that regard?

Admiral Gayler: No. That was always sort of a put-up thing. That was a special demonstration not really directed against Eisenhower. It didn't have any spillover into Japanese ports that I recall. Our people got along pretty well. In fact, we had remarkably few incidents. The one thing that I wanted to do was keep our young sailors out of the hands of the experienced women on the beach, if that's the right way to put it. So we went to great trouble to organize more constructive things for them to do. We always sent in a pretty good sized party by plane a couple of days before, to organize tours and trips and get them up to Kyoto and all that kind of thing. I'm sure a lot of the men went out with the bar girls, but I don't think there were nearly as many as would have otherwise.

Paul Stillwell: With a new ship such as that, were you working on tactical development with other fleet units?

Admiral Gayler: I'll say. You know, they always haze a new ship that's joining up the Seventh Fleet. Usually it was some reason, and I knew that. So we took great pains to continue operating all the way across the Pacific, which was very difficult, because we had a prescribed speed of advance, 16 knots. And the winds were tailwinds all the way. So in order to operate, we either had to turn into the wind and lose distance or we'd have to run like a son-of-a-bitch downwind, and I did both. I kept a full flight schedule every day, all the way across, for training purposes.

Most of the time I could make enough speed—34, 35 knots—so that even with the tailwinds, I had enough wind for catapulting, five or six knots. And then we used very close timing, miserly. At the lowest possible speed, we'd turn into the wind to recover aircraft. We'd get right back on course again, then run like hell to catch up. As a result, we arrived on station in pretty good shape as far as the air group was concerned.

We had an immediate tactical problem that was cast in the form of the defense of Taiwan or something. It was actually a two-carrier-versus-one-carrier battle. And we suckered them. We started off at 6:00 o'clock one evening with the force of two carriers, a tanker, and some destroyers. The opposing ships were a couple of hundred miles away from us, and, of course, they had our location pretty well.

So I put the tanker in the middle of the destroyers and had them looking like a carrier task group. Then we took the *Ranger*, and we ran at 34 knots all night long to get around the island of Okinawa. Just about dawn we anchored alongside a pinnacle rock off Tori Shima; then we operated for three days at anchor. And you know, they never did find us. It just didn't occur to them that that was what we were doing. We'd send the airplanes over Okinawa at very low altitude, where they couldn't pick them up, make them run at very low altitude 150 miles to the east, and then come up as if they had been launched from that position.

Of course, we were listening to these guys all the time; we could hear them searching, hear them cursing. Finally somebody figured out that I'd been involved in some very long-range experimentation when I was a test pilot and started searching 800 miles from home. It was lovely. In the hot wash-up, why, they claimed they found us the first night, and, of course, they hadn't. They weren't even within an island of us.

Paul Stillwell: Did you have any surveillance by Communists on your operations?

Admiral Gayler: If we did, I didn't know about it. We didn't have any political troubles at all.

Paul Stillwell: Did you have a flag embarked during your time in command?

Admiral Gayler: Sometimes and sometimes not. Most of the time, yes.

Paul Stillwell: Who was the admiral?

Admiral Gayler: Well, Bill Gentner was most of the time I was back in EastPac.[*] Then it was Francis Foley was when I was in WestPac, and he was wonderful, just wonderful.[†]

Paul Stillwell: You had known Gentner before, hadn't you?

Admiral Gayler: Yes.

Paul Stillwell: What can you say about those two individuals?

Admiral Gayler: Francis Foley was an absolutely marvelous guy, and we got along like gangbusters. We used to see which one of us could load the most outrageous pun on the other one in the morning launch. But he was first-class. He knew when to take charge and responsibility and when not to. Incidentally, his ops officer was Mickey Weisner, who was later on first my fleet commander and then my successor at CinCPac.[‡]

Paul Stillwell: Did you get to fly at all when you were skipper of the *Ranger*?

---

[*] Rear Admiral William E. Gentner, Jr., USN, Commander Carrier Division Seven.
[†] Rear Admiral Francis D. Foley, USN, Commander Carrier Division One. Rear Admiral Foley's oral history is in the Naval Institute collection.
[‡] Captain Maurice F. Weisner, USN.

Admiral Gayler: Well, yes, I did. I used to fly with the A-4s, usually, because I was more comfortable in that airplane than with the others.* But on a couple of occasions I flew with the A-3s.† One night we experienced what I have to think was an almost providential, extraordinary coincidence. What happened was that we launched the whole deck in the middle of the night in the Japan Sea, where it was pretty cold. I was always up on land-launch radio frequency when we launched, and about a third of the way through this launch, I just heard someone shout, "We're getting out." That's all.

Now, the problem was, who and where? Since the voice said, "we," of course, that told us that the plane had to be either an A-3 or one of the Guppy airplanes that had a crew in it, because all the rest of them were single-seaters.‡ The Guppies hadn't launched yet, so that narrowed it down to the A-3s. But which one? Because I had been flying with those guys the day before, I recognized the voice, and from that we could tell what plane it was and where it was in the climb-out pattern at that time. So we cranked up the ship's engines and ran 25 miles to the north, and, sure enough, there were the tracer flares. We got those guys out. They had just about had it in that cold water.

Can you imagine? Just because I recognized a voice did we have a handle on who they were and therefore where to look for them in the middle of the night. We ran away from the destroyers on that occasion. The *Ranger* was faster. I called up the chief engineer and told him I wanted every turn, never mind what happened to the engines. We got it too. She was really moving.

Paul Stillwell: I take it they didn't have some sort of beacon on their plane that could serve for search and rescue.

Admiral Gayler: She should have had IFF and a distinctive reply.§ I can only speculate that they got out of it so fast that they didn't get a chance to be interrogated. What

---

* The Douglas A4D Skyhawk attack plane first entered the fleet in October 1956 in squadron VA-72. The A4D was 40 feet, 4 inches long; wingspan of 27 feet, 6 inches; gross weight of 24,500 pounds, and top speed of 670 miles per hour. In 1962 the aircraft was redesignated the A-4.
† The Douglas A3D Skywarrior first entered fleet squadrons in 1956 as a carrier-based heavy bomber. It was reclassified as the A-3 in 1962.
‡ "Guppy" was the nickname for the AD-5W, which was a three-seat airborne-early-warning variant of the Douglas AD Skyraider
§ IFF—identification, friend or foe.

happened, interestingly enough, was that the vertical tail folded on the cat shot, and as he picked up speed in the climb-out, why, the plane became uncontrollable and they decided they had to get out of it.

Paul Stillwell: What does the CO of a ship that large do? How does he spend his days?

Admiral Gayler: Well, if you're under way, you spend your days on the bridge or in the emergency cabin. I never used to see my other cabin from the time I left port until the time I got back in. Almost concurrently, you were doing the normal ship's business, which included setting all the tone of the administration, which, of course, the exec and the department heads are doing primarily, planning for exercises, executing them, operating the ship, keeping a vigilant eye out for sea and weather and safety. I spent quite a lot of time trying to think up smart tactical exercises of one sort and other, develop tactics and train people.

Then you have the normal business of holding mast. Sometimes I'd hold mast up on the bridge while exercises were going on because I couldn't leave the bridge, and there was no other time. I couldn't let it hang. When I took over that ship, the captain has been seeing about 80 people a day at mast. The brig had an average population of 15 to 20. Then one wonderful Christmas Eve, we had the brig empty, and we got the mast cases down to about 10 or 12 a week. So that was a tremendous improvement, for which Al Lewis gets most of the credit. But we worked very hard on that.

We did one thing that saved a hell of a lot of petty cases. It was an interesting experiment that I think everybody else picked up after a while. We had three big mess halls on the ship for the crew, and I was always seeing people about fights in the mess lines. You'd have the senior petty officers standing there in line for the mess at feeding hours, and there would be a moment when the cat crews could go down and eat, and the chief up there would have said, "Now, listen, you sailors get down there and get your chow, and get up here." So here are these big, dirty youngsters and these old-time petty officers in uniform, and the friction in the mess lines and whatnot. So we finally thought, "Why not just keep the mess halls open cafeteria style 24 hours a day? Let anybody who wants to eat go down there and eat whenever he wants to and eat as much as he wants to."

The supply officer was horrified. [Laughter] He said, "Captain, these kids will eat you out of house and home." Of course, he had an allowance.

But I said, "Let's try it," and there was a big bulge for about a week, and then it worked out where you really could go down and eat anytime you wanted to. So the food consumption went back to normal, but we had no more people at mast and no more trouble about fights in the mess line. It was so much more efficient that we were able to close one of the three mess halls and use it as a recreation room.

Paul Stillwell: Amazing how solutions suggest themselves.

Admiral Gayler: Yes, yes.

Paul Stillwell: You talked earlier when you were in the battleship *Maryland* about this sort of Darwinian selection by which the ammunition loaders were all very tall men.

Admiral Gayler: Yes. That was the sixth division.

Paul Stillwell: I wonder if there's a Darwinian selection for carrier COs that they're all men of great stamina. I'd think you'd need it in that job.

Admiral Gayler: I think you do need stamina. I don't know how Darwinian the selection is, but you sure need stamina. I remember laughing about it. One time I got one of these census forms that had a lot of questions on it. One of them called for you to check off whether you worked, as I recall, less than 25 hours a week, 25 to 35, 35 to 45, over 45 or maybe it was over 50 hours a week. I sat down, just for laughs, and counted up the number of hours, and I put down 126. [Laughter] It was literally true, I mean, between being on the bridge and being alert. But then you learn habits to cope with it. You get waked up a lot and I, as I think everybody does, got so I could come awake and figure out what the situation was, take a look at the compass and say something, go back to sleep.

In fact, you almost welcomed it, because going back to sleep was so pleasant. But yes, it does. There are a lot of jobs on that carrier that require long hours: air officer, cat crews, all the rest of those people.

Paul Stillwell: Did you have a talented group of officers on the *Ranger*?

Admiral Gayler: I thought they were first-class, I really did. The department heads and the assistant department heads and division officers particularly. If there was a class of people I was disappointed in, it was the very junior officers who were ROTC graduates or otherwise from the big prestigious schools.[*] They weren't much good. They were smart and capable, but not interested in their people. I had to be sort of merciless about making them do their jobs. I began to think that an eastern university education was the ruination of anybody. I'm not sure I haven't changed my mind either.

Paul Stillwell: Are there any individuals from that wardroom who particularly stand out in your mind?

Admiral Gayler: Well, I talked about Al Lewis. Yes, the chief engineer, Hank Ryder, was a tremendous officer.[†] They were all pretty darn good.

Paul Stillwell: As far as operations, was there anything besides volume of flights that you were able to do better than the smaller carriers because you had a big deck?

Admiral Gayler: Yes, we did an awful lot of foul-weather operation, and we had an advantage in that, too, both in terms of sea state, but particularly in terms of the bigger deck and the more confidence you had in very low visibility approaches. We did a lot more, and we paid a lot more attention to it.

---

[*] ROTC—reserve officer training corps.
[†] Commander Henry S. Ryder, USN.

Paul Stillwell: In Admiral Thach's oral history, he talked about getting command of the *Franklin D. Roosevelt*.[*] He called it almost an unfair advantage over the *Essex* types.

Admiral Gayler: Yes.

Paul Stillwell: And you had an advantage even one more step beyond that.

Admiral Gayler: Yes, that's right.

Paul Stillwell: Did you participate in operations with the smaller carriers?

Admiral Gayler: Only in exercises in which we were opposed to each other. I don't recall we ever put together a carrier task group. I don't recall that we did.

Paul Stillwell: Were you involved in the strategic targeting as a carrier skipper?

Admiral Gayler: No.

Paul Stillwell: Did you carry nuclear weapons?

[No reply on tape; the recorder was turned off temporarily. Admiral Gayler's answer when the recorder wasn't running was essentially the standard Navy reply at that time as to whether or not an aircraft carrier had nuclear weapons on board at the time—neither confirm nor deny.][†]

Paul Stillwell: Did you get involved in protocol-type things, with visiting dignitaries and what have you?

---

[*] Captain John S. Thach, USN, commanded the aircraft carrier *Franklin D. Roosevelt* (CVA-42) from May 1953 to April 1954. His oral history is in the Naval Institute collection.
[†] On 27 September 1991, several years after this interview, President George H. W. Bush announced a unilateral initiative to cease deployment of tactical nuclear weapons on board U.S. Navy surface ships, attack submarines, and land-based aircraft during "normal circumstances."

Admiral Gayler: Oh, yes, we had some very interesting ones. We had the Japanese Emperor's brother and his wife and their family out for a day's cruise. They were really terrific. They were very pleasant people and enormously interested in everything that was going on. I can remember her particularly, because in spite of the fact that she was then not in her first youth, she was a very pretty woman.

Paul Stillwell: Any such activities in the United States?

Admiral Gayler: Well, several times I had the Secretary's guests, people of some distinction, usually. They enjoyed the hell out of it. I met those people. I can't remember any other really big shot, but a lot of interested and prominent people, particularly in the San Francisco area. They used to embark for day cruises as guests. Then we took one group from the West Coast to Hawaii.

Paul Stillwell: Did you have any sort of outreach program for the families of the crew members?

Admiral Gayler: Outreach is one of those fancy words that I eschew, but yes, we had a lot of things going on for the families to attempt to make them feel part of the family. And you had to look out for them too. I remember we were alongside the dock in Alameda, and we had repairs to make to the high-pressure turbines. This was a couple of days before Christmas Eve. We suddenly got a notice that the naval shipyard was sending tugs over so we could move over to Hunters Point and get this job done. In the first place, as I told you before, I wouldn't have needed tugs anyway, but without consultation, without anything, they were going to move the ship. And it's a considerable distance, particularly for sailors without much money to get from one side of that bay to the other. It just disrupted the Christmas plans of the families of all the people there.

So I sent back to the shipyard commander and said I wasn't going to move. He was outraged and promptly got on the phone down to Coronado, where the AirPac command was.* I had called there about 30 seconds earlier talking to the ops officer, so we didn't move. Then I got hold of the masters in that shop at the shipyard. I talked to them a while about what the job was that had to be done. Sure enough, they sent a dozen skilled mechanics over, and they and the ship's force were able to pull the top off the turbines, get the rotors out, take them over to the shop, repair them, and put them back in again. I didn't need to move the damn ship in the first place. But people are so careless about the welfare of sailors when it comes to things like that.

Paul Stillwell: Well, there again, it was a logical solution.

Admiral Gayler: Yes. But it just doesn't occur to them. It may have cost them a few bucks, I don't know, to send the men over there. But they were just in the habit of saying, "Well, the ship's going to come in here for overhaul and come in here for repairs." I had a slight advantage because I grew up in a Navy yard. I knew something about that end of it too.

Paul Stillwell: Did you have much contact with either the First Fleet or the Seventh Fleet commander?

Admiral Gayler: Seventh Fleet commander, yes. I used to go in and report to him informally, but not close contact.

Paul Stillwell: Did you have any contact with ships of foreign navies during operations?

Admiral Gayler: No, I had some later on when I was a cardiv commander but not when I was skipper of the *Ranger*.†

Paul Stillwell: Anything else on that ship before we move to your next assignment?

---

* AirPac—the type commander was Commander Naval Air Force Pacific Fleet.
† Cardiv—carrier division.

Admiral Gayler: Oh, I think that about covers it. She was a marvelous ship. She was ahead of her time everywhere she went. I was privileged.

Paul Stillwell: In the summer of 1960, you moved to London as naval attaché. Did you have an interest in intelligence that led to that?

Admiral Gayler: Actually, I was under orders to the National War College when I was selected for rear admiral. I had actually traveled to Washington, started picking up my mail, and checking in there. I wanted very much to have that year at the National War College, because I figured that it was precisely the right time. After all, the stated purpose of a place like that is to educate people who may have higher command, and here's a guy who's already selected. They were a shoo-in to know that they had the right kind of guy, so I called up my detailer and he laughed and said, "Noel, you're not even on my list anymore."

I didn't ask for the post in London. Frankly, I didn't particularly want it, although I recognized it would be an interesting thing to do. I also knew that there wasn't a hell of a lot substantive to it—at least I thought so at the time. And I was right, but I had a couple of special details when I was over there that were pretty interesting.

I remember calling on one of my predecessors who was quite a senior rear admiral, and he was quite happy to tell me all about it. He spent at least 30 minutes telling me how to pick out a good tailor in London. The more he talked, the more my heart sank, because he began to create this image that I just really didn't want anything to do with.

But it turned out to be a very interesting tour in a lot of ways, first because we had quite good rapport and quite good access with a lot of English society, not only military but civil. And the two ambassadors in my time were Jock Whitney and David Bruce.[*] Bruce was an especially very impressive guy. We got along great. The chief of station was Frank Wisner, who had been so senior in the CIA and who later, unfortunately, ended his own life here in Washington. He was a complex, extremely intelligent, very interesting man. We used to talk a lot about lots of things.

---

[*] John Hay Whitney, publisher of the *New York Herald Tribune*. Bruce was a career diplomat.

That's really when my interest in the intelligence community, other than from the standpoint of operational intelligence, was piqued. But it was a hell of a lot of socializing. We were on the so-called diplomatic list, and that meant that every night we went to two or three receptions and a dinner. I mean, every night. The only thing that saved my liver was that I played squash every noon right around the corner. That was the only counterbalance.

I made friends with George Brown, who was, as they put it, shadow Minister of Defence, Labourite. Quite a famous character. He was a character too. He had a little cubbyhole office in the Houses of Parliament and I'd go down there and talk to him. Watkinson, who was the Defence Minister, was sort of unapproachable, sort of a stuffed shirt, but in the British system, the shadow minister must be kept informed of everything that goes on.[*] So Brown was actually just as good a source as Watkinson would have been and a hell of a lot more approachable.

I'd go in and see him and he'd say, "Have a drop," pull open his drawer, take out a bottle and pour a drink for me and pour a drink for himself. Then he'd start telling stories. He was a marvelous raconteur; he came from a labor union background, but an engaging character. Every now and then he'd put on this great show for me. I think it was a show. He'd purport to be in a rage and call up Watkinson and give him hell over the telephone, almost visibly cocking an ear to see that I was taking this all in.

Not having that much to do, to be truthful, I used to go a lot to the debates in Parliament. I began to have a good understanding of the British Parliamentary system. Also, much less happily, I gained a good understanding of the basic problem that the poor British have. That's the real hatreds that exist between the classes there. It was shocking. I don't mean debating points, not only noise, I mean a venom between some of the left wing Labour and Tories, back and forth, in the way they [unclear] each other on the front page. Churchill came in a couple of times.[†] He was in his old age then, but there would always be a deferential silence when he got up to say a few things. I've always been sorry I never met him. I'd loved to have known him.

---

[*] Harold Watkinson served as Britain's Minister of Defence from 14 October 1959 to 13 July 1962.
[†] Winston L. S. Churchill, born in 1874, had been Great Britain's Prime Minister during World War II, again held the office from 1951 to 1955. Afterward he still remained as a Member of Parliament.

One day, in the summer of 1961, I was minding my own business when I suddenly received peremptory orders from the Navy Department to report to Baghdad on the 14th of July. Presumably this was because I had been in the Middle East before. I don't know whether you know anything about Baghdad in the summer, but in July, the average temperatures are 116 degrees or more. The humidity is also high, curiously enough.

An extraordinary collection of people had been assembled for the third anniversary of the great and glorious revolution, by which the then-dictator had come into power.[*] I still don't know how he did it, but he had formal representatives from both kinds of China, who were then at swords' point, both kinds of Korea, both kinds of Germany, a Russian lieutenant general, poor little guy. He was a little fat guy, and he was there in the frightful heat of the Baghdad summer in one of those thick sort of gray-green felt, practically, uniforms that the Russians have. He was visibly melting like an ice cream cone. Here I was in summer whites, and I was pretty hot, but I was a lot cooler than that. I never thought I'd feel sorry for a Soviet lieutenant general, but I felt sorry for that guy.

This was the revolution in which, you may remember, the King and the Premier, Nuri Said Pasha, were killed and their bodies dragged through the streets.[†] He was Nuri Said Pasha, about whom Lawrence wrote so much in *The Seven Pillars of Wisdom* and was his collaborator in the World War I campaign against the Germans.[‡] So I had been fascinated by the opportunity to meet him when I had the *Greenwich Bay*. He was then an old man and very urbane, very fluent in English. I wasn't awfully happy at the thought of traipsing through the desert after his murder, but it was a very interesting experience.

Kassem was an extraordinarily charismatic character. He had an eye like a crazy horse, and he was tall for an Arab—a fine-looking man. He had this marvelous sort of half-salute and half-wave when the Bedou troops would come charging by on their horses. Then the Centurion tanks and the Russian T-34 tanks came rumbling by. The

---

[*] On 14 July 1958 a military coup took place. The leaders were Brigadier General Abdul Karim al-Kassem and Colonel Abdul Salam Mohammed Arif. Al-Kassem became Premier.
[†] The King was Faisal II; the Prime Minister was Nuri as-Said.
[‡] T. E. Lawrence, better known as "Lawrence of Arabia."

Hercules and the Antonov-22s, I guess, would go rumbling overhead. For the first time, I really began to wonder about the point of all the arms supply abroad. This guy had totally eclectically taken arms from East and West, and where the hell that was getting either one of them, I couldn't figure out and I can't figure out to this day. And that's a serious comment, by the way; it really is.

Then we went following him around in various places where he did ceremonial jobs and made long speeches in Arabic. We had a representative from our embassy there, and he goddamn near died because he understood Arabic and he said it was always the same damn speech, and he was tired of it. And you know their system—they harangue forever; a two-hour speech is nothing. When a speech is in a language you can't understand, it just was awful. But he was an interesting man, and he had sort of a garden reception for us. Believe it or not, they had a garden with some green grass—at the expenditure of a hell of a lot of water. Kassem made a speech in which he said how welcome we all were, and he wanted us to see everything, no holds barred, in the whole country.

When my turn came during the receiving line, I said I would like very much to get down to Basra to see what it was like, since I'd been up there before. I knew full well that he had grounded the attaché's airplane. But he said it would be fine. The Army Chief of Staff, standing right by him, was just glowering at me.

So we got up real early before the order could be countermanded and took off. As soon as we made one circle around the city of Baghdad, we got our first big intelligence question answered. This was the time they were threatening to take over Kuwait. The British had an aircraft carrier up in the Persian Gulf, and the big intelligence question of the day was where was the Iraqi second division. Was it in camp, was it moving south? This was before the days of satellite observation. And the other question was, where were the 12 Soviet motor torpedo boats, which we knew had been supplied to the Iraqis? Were they going to come down some night and attack the British carrier?

Well, one turn around the airport, and you could see the second armored division in camp, so we had the answer to that. I knew damn well they weren't going to go anyway, because those people don't like to go out in the middle of the desert in July. They have more sense than that, particularly in armor. It just gets too hot to touch out there. I knew some of those people, anyway. They were people with fat bellies and liked to hang out around the air-conditioner. Anyway, we confirmed that.

We went down to Basra and were greeted there by the military governor of the province. He had been Kassem's division commander when Kassem was a colonel and took over this coup. Instead of killing his commander, he must have liked him, because he was a likable man, and sent him down to take over Basra province in the name of the revolution. With three staff officers, four of them in a car, we drove the couple of hundred miles from Baghdad down to Basra. He told me all the way down there he didn't know whether they would take the place over or whether they would be dragged out and shot as soon as they got there. Can you imagine the journey? God, those countries are something else.

He was sort of a likable guy and a benign guy, and he took a view of Basra and Basra Province as sort of a combination booster and mayor. He took me down to the waterfront and showed me all of the improvements in the housing and all that stuff. Then nothing would do but we had to go drive up in a Jeep and see a monument outside of town. The Shatt-al-Arab is the big river that runs into the Persian Gulf, put together by the confluence of the Tigris and Euphrates Rivers. Along the bank there are about 100 yards of date palms and then sand on the one side and river on the other. So for a long time we drove along this track in a jeep. I didn't want to go, but the governor was just very insistent.

We got there to see the monument, and it was a crumbling little piece of red sandstone. It memorialized the British campaign in Mesopotamia, as it was then called, 1894. In front of it the Arabs had built a great big almost a sort of billboard-like monument of gray marble with incised Arabic lettering in gold. I asked for a translation of that. It was all about how they had kicked out the foreign invaders and whatnot. I thought to myself, "You son-of-a-bitch, you've taken me all the way out here to look at this vainglorious thing which you've stuck right in front of a monument to people who, whatever they were, were brave men and died for their country."

But then he did a very curious thing. He quite ostentatiously turned his back on me. We had been walking along this path, and then he stood about 20 feet away with his back turned to me. I thought it was very peculiar behavior. I couldn't figure out what was going on. A light finally flashed, and I started to look around. Right down there through the date palms, sort of half-obscured, there was a little jetty, and there were 11 of the 12 Soviet-built torpedo boats we were interested in. He stood there with his back turned to me while I counted them. I looked to see if they had any torpedoes in their tubes and all the rest of that stuff. Then, without a word, we climbed back into the Jeep and went back into Basra.

One of the fellows he had with him was a little fat artillery colonel, and on the way back he had a problem. He had just been made CNO of the Iraqi Navy, and he didn't have any charts. So he asked if I could get him some charts. I said, sure, I'd get him some, and about six months later, why, I sent him some nice HO charts.[*]

That night I was able to report with quite a lot of certainty that the Iraqis weren't going to go down the Shatt-al-Arab and attack the British aircraft carrier, because they never would have found their way. Bizarre, bizarre, crazy, crazy, crazy, bizarre place. Now that I look back on it, of course, it was a time of tremendous transition, and I'm certain it bears no resemblance to the modern Middle East at all.

Paul Stillwell: Why would the governor let you see that pier?

Admiral Gayler: He wanted me to. He wanted me to. He was pro-Western.

Paul Stillwell: But he couldn't do it overtly.

Admiral Gayler: He couldn't do it overtly, so he did it this way.

Paul Stillwell: You said you had had a couple of interesting details while you were in that job. Was there another one beyond this?

Admiral Gayler: Well, yes. I got a little bored over there, to be truthful, and interpreted my charter to Her Majesty as being I had business wherever Her Majesty had her forces.

---

[*] HO—Hydrographic Office.

Paul Stillwell: A pretty broad charter.

Admiral Gayler: Well, as a matter of fact, it got me as far north as the North Cape of Norway, and as far south as Marrakech in Morocco, and as far east as Baghdad, so it wasn't too bad. Among other things, I went up to Linkoping in Sweden to fly the Soviet fighter, just for the hell of it, really, but it was an evaluation mission. That was very interesting. It was a couple of days after Christmas and they were having a cold spell. Boy, I want to tell you, a cold spell in Linkoping, Sweden, is cold. So that was my one and only visit to Sweden. It was very interesting. I think the rest of it is more or less what attachés do.

Paul Stillwell: Well, what do attachés do? How much intelligence duty is involved in the work?

Admiral Gayler: It's a very special relationship with Britain, very different from any other station, as you know. An intelligence relationship with the British is very close, and there are very well-established direct channels. So the attachés don't conduct espionage against each other, never have. It's more representational for them. Because of my background, I got to get into some of the technical aspects, too, saw a lot of development stations.

I flew all over Scotland one rough, goddamned day on a low-altitude mission. They were interested in having me do that because I had been doing that kind of work in VX-3 here at home. But it was much rougher over there because of the Scottish mountains and the bumpy air; it would kind of shake your teeth loose.

Paul Stillwell: Why did we really need an attaché for representation when CinCNELM was there?*

---

* CinCNELM – Commander in Chief U.S. Naval Forces Eastern Atlantic and Mediterranean. At the time it was Admiral Harold Page Smith, USN.

Admiral Gayler: There were obviously institutional problems there. CinCNELM was not on the diplomatic list. The attaché was on the diplomatic list, reporting to the ambassador. Depending on his personality, the four-star admiral really didn't like the two-star admiral to be invited by the Queen when he wasn't and all that crap.

By the way, the Queen is a perfectly marvelous person. That's the first time I ever knew her, and she really is.

Paul Stillwell: Tell me more.

Admiral Gayler: Well, the British were launching their first nuclear submarine at a place called Barrow-in-Furness, and the Queen attended.[*] In British circles, that is a signal honor, makes it an extraordinarily dignified occasion. They invited, among other people, Hyman Rickover.[†] Rick was in one of his moods while he was in the passageway actually right outside the room where the Queen was receiving people. In a loud voice he was saying, "This is a all a bunch of stuff. All it is is an American power plant in there [which is true], and what is all this about . . ." in a very sort of obnoxious way. I'm afraid I actually sort of physically corralled him into a corner and kept an incident from happening.

But, anyway, we did the usual, were introduced to the Queen, including my wife, who was and is a very pretty woman, and five children. So we were immediately on the wavelength of talking about the children. The Queen has a remarkable memory, considering all the people she met, because she used to remember us—remember Kay, really—on every subject and occasion, and say something about the children. Years later when we entertained them for a day in Hawaii, she remembered and picked it right up. Extraordinary, considering the thousands and thousands and thousands of people she has presented to her. She is a very nice person. It was social and it was fun. If you scrambled around, you could find things to do, but as your question implies, it's very hard to see that there would be any grievous injury if we did without it.

---

[*] The first British nuclear-powered submarine was HMS *Dreadnought*; she was launched 21 October 1960.
[†] Vice Admiral Hyman G. Rickover, USN, was then head of the Navy's nuclear power program.

Paul Stillwell: Do you think there was a friction developed between you and Admiral Smith there that had its feedback later? Was that the origin of it?

Admiral Gayler: No, the origin of it was that incident I mentioned about the Bureau of Personnel and the promotion system. That happened when Admiral Smith was the chief of bureau. As a matter of fact, Admiral Smith was very courteous to us when we were in London, and we got along fine. But I think he didn't like that promotion situation at all, and I can see why.

Paul Stillwell: How much in the way of dealings did you have with the Royal Navy officers?

Admiral Gayler: Oh, a lot. I saw a lot of them, Frank Hopkins in particular, who was then their senior carrier fellow, a marvelous guy. And the redheaded fellow who was later on First Sea Lord and then died rather suddenly, also a marvelous guy, Mike Le Fanu.[*] Then one of my guys from VX-3 had been an exchange pilot was over there. He then was a wing commander, so I got to go down and fly with them. Another guy who also had been an exchange pilot there was an RAF type, and I had some connections through him at the pilot level, which is much harder to get.[†] So that was pretty good. I used to go down and fly Buccaneers once in a while.[‡] What a dog. And let's see, what else?

Paul Stillwell: Did your job bring you into contact with Admiral Mountbatten?[§]

Admiral Gayler: Yes. I wouldn't want to overstate it, but I knew him. We had him to dinner a couple of times, as I recall. Quite a marvelous guy. He didn't suffer fools gladly, a little on the austere side. Quite a marvelous guy. I think to murder him and his

---

[*] Admiral Sir Michael Le Fanu, RN, served as First Sea Lord from 1968 to 1970.
[†] RAF—Royal Air Force.
[‡] The Blackburn Buccaneer was a jet-powered attack aircraft with nuclear weapons delivery capability. It first flew in 1958 and was subsequently operated by the Royal Navy and Royal Air Force, 1962 to 1994.
[§] Admiral of the Fleet Lord Louis Mountbatten of Burma, RN, Chief of Defence Staff, 1959-65.

[unclear] in the way those people did was just shocking.* By the way, what he had to say about nuclear weapons was very sensible; he said they're for the birds, as I do. Some people think he was killed for that.

Paul Stillwell: I hadn't heard that explanation.

Admiral Gayler: Some people think that. Some British people think that. There are some very curious things about his assassination which, to a fellow of a very suspicious nature, would suggest that maybe the Irish didn't do it; somebody else did.

Paul Stillwell: I had not heard that supposition at all.

Admiral Gayler: It's all circumstantial. There were some very curious things about the Irish group that took "credit" for it, a splinter group which had never been seen before or since. Well, anyway, that's just real speculation. I don't know anything about it.

Paul Stillwell: Did it make any difference in the attaché operation when President Kennedy took over from President Eisenhower?† We got a new ambassador, for one thing.

Admiral Gayler: Well, I think the whole tone of everything sort of perked up when Kennedy came in. I can't remember anything very specific. He was extremely popular in England and did a lot to defuse the resentment in Tory circles, right-wing circles, over Eisenhower's role in Suez.‡ There was a lot of resentment about that in one segment of that society. That society is, or was then, much more segmented than ours. There was a

---

* Mountbatten was assassinated in 1979 when the Irish Republican Army planted a bomb in his boat.
† John F. Kennedy served as President of the United States from 20 January 1960 until he was assassinated on 22 November 1963.
‡ On 26 July 1956 President Gamal Nasser of Egypt announced that his country was nationalizing the Suez Canal Company. Israeli forces invaded Egypt's Sinai Peninsula on 29 October 1956. Britain and France then intervened militarily on behalf of Israel in an unsuccessful attempt to secure the Suez Canal, which was damaged and closed to traffic. Rather than support the British and French, the United States—led by President Dwight D. Eisenhower, asked for a United Nations resolution to end the fighting. A cease-fire took effect on 6 November.

distinct high Tory outfit that thought they'd been betrayed and were even a little unpleasant socially about that. I remember one denouncing me bitterly for that one. But, yes, I saw a difference in tone.

You remember when Kennedy went over for that meeting with Khrushchev in Vienna and they had that hard meeting.[*] Then he came back through England to talk to Macmillan about what had been going on.[†] The Presidency was so new and the President's party so disorganized, that they actually kept the President waiting about an hour while they rounded up important characters like Jackie's hairdresser and people like that to get the hell on the presidential airplane.[‡]

So Kennedy came over to the little lounge they called the Queen's reception room, which we had for VIPs. He came over by himself—with Secret Service, of course—and chatted with us. He picked me out because I was there in uniform. I'd known him slightly when he was a senator. He saw a familiar face; that was about it. We chatted over our Scotch, and he said, "I'm going to make a speech tomorrow in Annapolis, Admiral. What should I say?"[§]

I thought two or three noble things to say about the naval career and gave them to him, and he said, "That's very good, Admiral, but I don't think I'll do that. I think I'll tell them how to go from reserve lieutenant (j.g.) to commander in chief," and he did. [Laughter] He was marvelous.

I didn't see much of him then, but I saw quite a lot of Dave Powers, who, you know, was a Boston Irish politician who was half political adviser and half just personal friend and kind of crony. Powers is a very interesting man. He told me all sorts of yarns about the campaign and Kennedy up at 6:00 o'clock in the morning on a Wisconsin winter day, and shaking hands at a factory until his own hand was like this, said Powers, bleeding. The things we put these guys through are unbelievable.

---

[*] The Kennedy-Nikita Khrushchev summit meeting was in Vienna, Austria, in May 1961.
[†] Harold Macmillan was the British Prime Minister.
[‡] Jacqueline Kennedy was the President's wife.
[§] This speech in Annapolis is discussed in the Naval Institute's oral history of Rear Admiral John F. Davidson, USN (Ret.), who was then Superintendent of the Naval Academy.

Paul Stillwell: It's going on right now.*

Admiral Gayler: Yes, yes, yes.

---

* The interview took place during the campaign of 1984 that led to the reelection of President Ronald Reagan.

Interview Number 7 with Admiral Noel A. M. Gayler, U.S. Navy (Retired)

Place: Admiral Gayler's office at the American Committee on East-West Accord, Washington, D.C.

Date: Friday, 20 April 1984

Paul Stillwell: Admiral, do you have any more recollections to add to your tour in London that we discussed last time?

Admiral Gayler: I believe I told you about the unexpected trip to the desert in Baghdad and all the curious things that happened there. Other than the opportunity to get around Europe, which I took by virtue of declaring that I was accredited anywhere that the British went, and the extraordinary business of living downtown in a great city and a unique city like London, and of seeing the British governing system at firsthand, marvelous opportunities to meet people, no, I have not much more to add to that.

I was certainly ready for other duty by the time my two years were up. Although this was a pleasant cruise, it was a little bit outside my bailiwick.

Paul Stillwell: Did you express a preference concerning your next tour from there?

Admiral Gayler: Oh, yes. Obviously I wanted sea duty, and at one time, I had some reason to believe that I was going to get a heavy carrier group. But I was not satisfactory to some people, so I ended up with CarDiv 20, an antisubmarine group.[*] Looked at professionally afterwards, I think that was a good tour, because I got into the antisubmarine business and learned a lot. I probably would not have learned as much by repeating the heavy carrier experience, which I already knew quite a lot about.

Paul Stillwell: What was your flagship in that division?

---

[*] CarDiv – Carrier Division

Admiral Gayler: Well, I had three sort of rotating flagships: *Essex*, *Randolph*, and *Lake Champlain*. *Lake Champlain* was interesting because at that time, she was the last straight-deck carrier left in the Navy. I took advantage of that one day to set what I think is a record, and by the nature of things, will not be broken. I day and night carrier-qualified, angled deck and straight deck, in one 24-hour period. Since there are no more straight decks left, I think I've got that one locked up.

Paul Stillwell: What were your primary areas of operation?

Admiral Gayler: It was all East Coast. We were based in Quonset and operated as far south as Guantánamo and Vieques.[*] I actually took over command in the Mediterranean. I was given that marvelous thing—a month's leave—when I left the attaché's office. So my wife Kay and I gave the five children, who were pretty adult by then, our Volkswagen bus and let them tour Europe. The two of us took the little sports car, little Sunbeam Alpine, and toured in leisurely fashion across France and the Alps-Maritime down to Nice, where I took command.

A lot of funny things happened on the way down that don't have much to do with the naval career. I remember distinctly that when the time came for me to take over my command and get in uniform, I had an awful time putting my shoes on because I'd been wearing sandals for a month. [Laughter] We really went native on the way down and had a marvelous time.

Then one very funny thing happened. I had just taken over command, and I was up in the admiral's cabin doing some paperwork. My wife was ashore. I was to meet her that evening at a hotel in Nice, and my Marine orderly came in with this curious look on his face and said, "Sir, there's a girl at the port gangway. She wants to see you."

I said, "What do you mean, there's a girl at the port gangway who wants to see me?"

He said, "Yes, sir, there's a girl in a speedboat at the port gangway, and she says she wants to see you."

---

[*] Quonset Point, Rhode Island, was the site of a naval air station until the mid-1970s.

I was about to say, "Oh, tell her to shove off," and then I thought, "Maybe I'd better find out what this is."

So I went down, and as I was crossing the hangar deck to get over to the port side, I noticed that the ship had a considerable list to port. That was because every sailor in the ship was in the port catwalks looking down at that boat. As I got there, sure enough, there were several girls in bathing suits in this pretty little mahogany speedboat, sort of looking up there. I finally got close enough to recognize that one of them was Kay. She had fallen in with some friends. They were all going to go water skiing, and she thought, well, she'd just stop off at the flagship and let me know where she was. That gave me great prestige in my new command; I'm pretty sure of that.

As I said, I learned a good deal from that cruise as Commander Carrier Division 20. The principal task, of course, was the antisubmarine operations by a designed carrier task group. I think I got the idea pretty early on at a hot wash-up after one of the exercises when we assembled in the wardroom of my flagship. Included were one admiral, one captain chief of staff, one captain operations officer, four or five commanders, destroyer skippers, three or four commanders, squadron skippers, and several other people. In came the opposition—one lieutenant commander and his lieutenant operations officer. I've always thought that really just about epitomized the force ratio between the antisubmarine forces and the submarine—of that kind of that day, in any case. But it was very interesting.

I used to spend the majority of my time in exercises in the submarines themselves, and I got exercises every time I had a chance. I figured that was the way to learn the business, and, indeed, I learned an awful lot. At that time, working against nuclear submarines, we were at a terrible disadvantage. They used to take great delight in beckoning me over to the sound stack and saying, "Admiral, would you like to hear your flagship?"[*] Of course, I could hear her a long way away. The sound operator would say, "You hear that? That's one squeaky propeller you've got." I became very much aware of what tremendous sea weapon the modern nuclear submarine is and what a very tough job we really do have to contain them.

---

[*] The assembled components of sonar gear are referred to as the sonar stack.

In those exercises—and we had plenty of them—the only thing that I was ever able to do was to sandbag the submarine skipper if he got too bold—they used to get pretty cocky—or get inside the six-fathom line. That will slow down a nuclear submarine too. Of course, they love to take pictures, as they have done for many, many years, through the periscope as you're leaving Quonset, in my case, and then send it up with a pleasant little note saying, "Admiral, we thought you'd like to have this picture of your flagship."

Paul Stillwell: With the periscope cross hairs.

Admiral Gayler: With the cross hairs. But as it happened, I was able to retaliate on that one because through the enormous generosity of Luis de Florez, I owned a little flying boat in those days, a Grumman Widgeon. When the submarines came out on the surface, as they must from New London, I would sometimes go down and bounce them with my flying boat and then send them pictures. [Laughter] The great difficulty was to get submarines to work against, because ComSubLant, of course, had better things to do with its submarines than simply provide services.[*] But they did have allotted to them a lot of individual ship exercise time, ISE, and I found out that if you went down to New London and had a couple of drinks in the bar and were noisy enough, that you could get two or three skippers to come on out and meet you for an informal mix-up. So we had a lot of submarine services and a lot of chance to tangle with American submarines.

Paul Stillwell: I would think they would leap at that kind of opportunity.

Admiral Gayler: Well, they did. They did. Let's see what else happened. We set up something very interesting, which was an informal sea exercise with a French antisubmarine task group, which contained no carrier but had some very well-trained destroyers. That came about because I met the French admiral, and we got to talking about antisubmarine warfare, and we agreed privately that we each might be next Thursday, say, 215 miles southeast of Bear Island, and wouldn't that be a coincidence?

---

[*] ComSubLant – Commander Submarine Force Atlantic Fleet.

This was during de Gaulle's time, and the French admiral was not authorized to have any exercises with us, and I had sense enough not to raise the question with anybody else.[*] So we just met out there and had a very pleasant and, I think, effective exercise together.

The French were very hospitable, and on a couple of occasions I went down on the end of a string from a helicopter and had a wonderful French dinner with a little wine.[†] Unfortunately, that was not available for me to reciprocate on my flagship. So that was pretty good. I was much impressed by their capability.

Paul Stillwell: How would you compare it with the U.S. capability in submarines?

Admiral Gayler: Well, I was talking about the destroyers. I didn't see any French submarines there. As far as I know, they didn't have any there. I thought they were very well-trained and very well up. The direct comparison was a little difficult, because the detection means and everything else were quite different from ours, and the tactics were somewhat different. But I was impressed by them, and I was glad that we had done it. I have never known whether he made any report to the French authorities. Frankly, I can't remember whether I reported on it either, except in a technical way.

Paul Stillwell: How much coordination was there with your ship-based aircraft—S-2s, I presume—and the land-based patrol planes?[‡]

Admiral Gayler: I recall a couple of exercises in which we coordinated. It wasn't very difficult; it was just a matter of assigning different areas for air search and sonobuoy dropping. No great sweat. Then I was in port when Kennedy made his famous speech,

---

[*] As President of France, Charles de Gaulle pulled his country out of the military structure of the North Atlantic Treaty Organization.
[†] The helicopter was equipped with a cable that could raise and lower a person at the end of it.
[‡] Grumman S2F Tracker propeller-driven, carrier-based antisubmarine planes first entered fleet squadrons in early 1954. In 1962 the Tracker was redesignated S-2. The S-2E version was 44 feet long, wingspan of 72 feet, gross weight of 26,867 pounds, and top speed of 253 miles per hour.

announcing the discovery of the Soviet missiles in Cuba.*

All I did was go back to the flagship and go to the various states of readiness, but that crisis dragged on long enough so that before it was over, I relieved as the Northern Barrier Force Commander, and that was extremely interesting. The force I relieved already had contact with four Soviet diesel submarines. I attempted to maintain that contact, but they kept moving apart. Pretty soon I was in the position of one foot on the pier and one on the boat, and it was just getting too far away to cover everything. So we had to let go of a couple. There were no real combat incidents.

The amusing thing from our standpoint was afterwards, when you recall that there was a suspicion that instead of the Soviets evacuating, as had been agreed, they were sending in these Soviet ships that were going out full of people, they were actually sending back Cubans to be trained. I got a peremptory inquiry to determine whether the people going out were Soviets or Cubans. I thought about that for a while and couldn't see any very straightforward way to do it. Suddenly I thought, "Well, why not go take a look?" So I got into a helicopter and flew over there and hovered about 50 feet above the deck, and you could see these out-sized people with great beefy types, sort of pink and burned and whatnot, and I was able to say with a lot of confidence these were not Cubans. These were Soviets going back. Curiously enough, nobody made as much as an angry gesture. I sat there looking at them, and they sort of waved at me.

Paul Stillwell: To whom were you reporting in that instance?

Admiral Gayler: Well, let's see. Paul, I hate to confess, but I've sort of forgotten. I guess my immediate boss was Commander Second Fleet.

Paul Stillwell: I'm curious whether the normal chain of command was followed, or were you getting any direct orders from the Pentagon?

---

* The Cuban Missile Crisis was triggered in mid-October 1962, when a U.S. reconnaissance plane photographed a Soviet nuclear missile site in Cuba and the presence of Soviet bombers. On 22 October President John F. Kennedy went on national television to announce a naval quarantine of Cuba, to be implemented on 24 October. On 28 October Premier Nikita Khrushchev of the Soviet Union notified President Kennedy that he was ordering the withdrawal of Soviet bombers and missiles from Cuba.

Admiral Gayler: No, I was not getting any direct orders. I think that phase had long since gone. I was there just at the tail end.

No, the famous Kennedy orders to the coxswain of the whaleboat didn't occur on my watch, although I have a theory of command that includes provision for direct intervention at the highest level in very exceptional circumstances. I always thought that the first touch of the American-Soviet forces at sea in circumstances like that were exactly what did justify it.

Those are about all the sea stories on CarDiv 20 that occur to me. I could tell you all sorts of stories about the funny horse we had when the family was living up in Quonset, but I don't think that that would be germane. [Laughter]

Paul Stillwell: Let's try it anyway.

Admiral Gayler: No, I think it's a little bit off the subject.

Paul Stillwell: How affective was U.S. ASW against the Soviet submarines in that era?

Admiral Gayler: At that time, against those submarines under those circumstances, it was very effective. They were diesel submarines. They, I believe, were deployed in a hell of a hurry. They were a long way away from home and, I think, probably had never operated that far away. In our judgment, they weren't very well handled, and we didn't have any trouble with them. I wouldn't draw any generalities from that at all about the Soviet submarines or submarine handling, or our capability to handle submarines. In fact, if I were to give my professional opinion as I sit right here now, I think the problem about handling Soviet attack submarines is the single most important military problem we have. It's a source of great distress to me that we neglect problems like that while we go around with nuclear weapons.

Paul Stillwell: Were you able to maintain continuous contact on these boats?

Admiral Gayler: I was until they spread out so much that I couldn't keep them under air cover.

Paul Stillwell: Could you put destroyers on the other two?

Admiral Gayler: The distances were too big. They were a couple hundred miles away. You don't do that very handily with destroyers and with the Stoof at the time, you began to have difficulty keeping a decent coverage even with the airplanes.* And the situation was rapidly cooling off. I don't quite remember the chronology now, but we hadn't been in that situation very long before the agreement was announced, and it became a non-operational situation.

Paul Stillwell: Did you have encounters with Soviet submarines at other times during that tour?

Admiral Gayler: No, I didn't. I never had another one.

Paul Stillwell: When you were in the Mediterranean, did you work with American submarines there?

Admiral Gayler: Not very much. The Mediterranean wasn't an awfully good training ground for our purposes because just for that reason—the submarines were not available. In fact, except as an adjunct to a large exercise, I don't recall working against submarines out there. The Mediterranean part was mostly to show the flag.

Paul Stillwell: And let the sailors see that part of the world, I take it.

Admiral Gayler: Yes, let the sailors see that part of the world, that's for sure.

---

* "Stoof" was the nickname of the S2F carrier-based antisubmarine aircraft.

Paul Stillwell: Do you have any interesting recollections of the ports you hit during that cruise?

Admiral Gayler: Well, it's very poignant now. I remember the extraordinary beauty of Lebanon—this is a personal recollection—both as a city and as a landscape, if you will, and country. But all the rest of them were the standard Mediterranean ports. We didn't go anywhere very unusual.

Paul Stillwell: Was Commander Sixth Fleet your direct reporting skipper?

Admiral Gayler: Yes, that was Sixth Fleet then.

Paul Stillwell: Did he keep you on a pretty loose rein, or how did that work?

Admiral Gayler: He happened to be a great personal friend, so to answer your question, fairly—I don't want to say a loose rein. He was very much on top of things—Dave McDonald—but not intrusive.* He was a good commander in that sense. I don't want to say loose rein. That implies lack of control. There is no question about who the boss was.

Paul Stillwell: You say he was a personal friend. Where had you known him from?

Admiral Gayler: I believe the first time I ever met him, I was a test pilot, and I came up to Washington to report on how the Zero flew or one of those things. He was in BuAer someplace; I believe he was then a commander. I believe that was the first time I ever met him. Then I met him later on when I was with Tom Gates, the Secretary of the Navy, and he was, as I recall, Sixth Fleet operations officer. And we had some good conversations about the operations out there. I was very operationally oriented in those days. I still am.

---

* Vice Admiral David L. McDonald, USN, commanded the Sixth Fleet from July 1961 to 18 March 1963. The oral history of McDonald, who retired as a four-star admiral, is in the Naval Institute collection.

Paul Stillwell: Do you have any conclusions on the relative merits of having either a surface officer or an aviator in that Sixth Fleet billet?

Admiral Gayler: I think philosophically I don't have at all. I don't think it's right to categorize people in that way. There are all sorts of aviators, for example. There are people that wear wings who could barely waddle off the water on a flying boat 30 years ago, and there are people who are real hotshots. So that doesn't tell you too much. And then there are surface officers, for example, like one Arleigh Burke, who knew a hell of a lot more about operating a carrier task group than 99 and 44/100% of naval aviators would. So I think I would not wish to do that.

Paul Stillwell: It was a tradition at that time that that was automatically an aviator's command, and typically one who had commanded a carrier division in there as a two-star admiral.

Admiral Gayler: You can make a pretty interesting case that Sixth Fleet commanders should have some previous experience in the area. If it turns out that that's the progression, I would make the case that a carrier division commander should be an aviator, just like a submarine squadron commander should be a submariner. But when you get to the fleet command level, then I think you just look for the best person.

I personally think it would be a very good idea to have an Air Force or Army officer occasionally as CinCPac. We'll talk about CinCPac later, but I made enormous efforts to move in that direction when I was there. At the higher levels I thoroughly believe in real unity of command.

Paul Stillwell: Did you get involved with any of the astronaut recoveries during that tour?

Admiral Gayler: We picked up one gang, and I'm ashamed to say I have now forgotten which mission it was. Yes, we did. It was not one of the moon people; it was one of the orbital ones.

Paul Stillwell: That was in the Mercury series, I believe.

Admiral Gayler: Yes. I remember it as an operation, but I cannot remember who they were. It was a very straightforward operation, just like picking up anybody else out of the water, parachute blossom, zoom them over there, and go get them.

Paul Stillwell: Were there any special communications laid on for that tour?

Admiral Gayler: Oh, yes, yes. We had special communications for the purpose. It worked very well.

Paul Stillwell: Were there contingency plans if a fellow didn't drop where he was supposed to?

Admiral Gayler: You bet there were. We had contingency plans for picking them up from the South Pole, practically. I know enough about orbital mechanics to know that they would not have landed at the South Pole. That's a figure of speech, but we had lots and lots of contingency plans, yes.

Paul Stillwell: Anything else on that tour?

Admiral Gayler: Yes, just one thing. Sort of a personal recollection. It was on that tour, as it happened in the middle of a tremendous storm, that I learned that Luis de Florez was dying.[*] I would normally have just launched in any old thing to be there, but I was not able to at that time, and I lost my great friend while I was at sea. I then learned after his death—I don't know whether I told you this before or not—that for many years, he had in his will a provision that Lieutenant Gayler was to inherit any airplanes that he owned at the time. That's how I came into possession of his flying boat I talked to you about.

---

[*] Rear Admiral Luis de Florez, USNR (Ret.), died in November 1962 at age 73.

Paul Stillwell: You went ashore again after that and reported to OpNav, and with your test pilot background and development tours, it seemed pretty natural.

Admiral Gayler: Yes. That was a long tour in the Pentagon. I guess it's not very fashionable to enjoy tours in the Pentagon, but I enjoyed that one, although in the fourth year, I had had enough of it. The job that I had was first called Assistant Chief of Naval Operations for Development, and then later restyled Deputy Assistant Chief of Naval Operations for Development. It was changed, because somebody found out on the organization chart that I was only an archbishop and shouldn't be up there among the cardinals or one of those things. But as a practical matter, I was then in the forefront of much of the advanced development of naval aviation and many other things.

I took occasion to push as hard as I could the electronic warfare aspect of things, which I thought then and think now will be dominant. We've been very, very slow and still are in coming to that recognition. And in general, I got a very interesting immersion in high technology.

I have always been sort of a science buff, technical buff. It was a wonderful opportunity to be in on those things. It was a long haul, but it was good.

Paul Stillwell: Harold Brown was then Assistant Secretary for RDT&E.[*] Did you work with him?

Admiral Gayler: I worked with him. I had great admiration for his capability and his mind. I have, frankly, somewhat less admiration for his policies as Secretary of Defense with respect to nuclear weapons, but that he's an extremely capable man, there's no doubt.

Paul Stillwell: How much of your work involved him?

---

[*] RDT&E – research, development, test and evaluation. Brown was later Secretary of Defense in the administration of President Jimmy Carter.

Admiral Gayler: Directly rather little, but in the capacity of getting things through, of course, he was always there. I had a very, very good and pleasant association with Bob Frosch, who later became an extremely good Assistant Secretary of the Navy for R&D.*

Paul Stillwell: Admiral Chick Hayward worked in that area some too.†

Admiral Gayler: Yes, I saw a lot of Chick. I've known Chick for many years. He was one of a kind and very good. I believe he was, up until that time, at least, the only PhD in physics that we had as a flag officer. I used to call him "Admiral Doctor." [Laughter] Chick was great.

Paul Stillwell: How much of your work at that time was driven by the requirements of the Vietnam War?

Admiral Gayler: Essentially none.

Paul Stillwell: Well, but this, I think, would be a progression, since you were there four years as we were building up in Vietnam.

Admiral Gayler: No, my business was with technical and advanced developments. I'm sorry if that wasn't the way it should have been, but as it was, Vietnam didn't impinge on it very much.

Paul Stillwell: So yours was more of a long-range program?

Admiral Gayler: As all development programs are. They're getting to be entirely too damn long-ranged, but yes, I was very little concerned with the day-to-day events. I never thought that there were any valid military lessons from the Vietnamese War anyway, except don't screw it up like that. And in the case of that particular war, don't

---

* Robert A. Frosch was Assistant Secretary of the Navy for Research and Development, 1966-73.
† Vice Admiral John T. Hayward, USN.

lead with the infantry, and don't violate all of Clausewitz's principles of war in order to carry out some notion of marginal return.* We screwed that one up every way you can think of, but military was certainly one of them.

Paul Stillwell: What were some of the specific projects that you worked on during that tour?

Admiral Gayler: Well, I guess everything went over the Navy's plate. Electronic war I've mentioned. That was the time when this rather bum idea of building non-military prototypes of "cheap, simple fighters" was in vogue. I'm afraid we spent a lot of time and energy in a rear-guard fight against that, because the airplanes that have resulted from those developments are neither cheap nor simple, nor are they as good as the ones that were designed to do the job in the first place.

I also remember being doomed to go up once a week, on Saturday morning, to the office of the Secretary of Defense, where Mr. McNamara would preside over a progress meeting on the F-111B.† He was determined that the Navy and the Air Force were going to have one airplane. It was going to be a 111. And he was convinced that the only problem was service parochialism. I think I'm about as tough against service parochialism as anybody you will know, but in that case, Mr. McNamara totally mistook the problem.

The problem was that we, the Navy, were trying to build a high-altitude combat air patrol airplane—very much like the eventual F-14—with good loiter time, good high-altitude performance, capability to control advance long-range air-to-air missiles.‡ The Air Force had a quite different requirement for a low-altitude, high-Q, that is, high

---

* Karl von Clausewitz (1780-1831) was a Prussian army officer who was noted for writing *On War*, which is considered to be one of the foremost books on military matters. It is still studied, long after the death of the author.
† Robert S. McNamara served as Secretary of Defense from 21 January 1961 to 29 February 1968. The F-111—originally designated TFX—was a controversial fighter plane that Secretary McNamara tried to develop in the 1960s for use by both the Air Force and the Navy. The Navy was eventually able to thwart its role as a carrier plane and developed the F-14 instead.
‡ Grumman F-14 Tomcat fighters first entered training squadrons in late 1972. The F-14A version was 64 feet long, wingspan of 38 feet, normal takeoff weight of 55,000 pounds, and top speed of Mach 2.34. It was equipped with a 20-millimeter cannon and was designed to carry a variety of types of missiles—Sparrow, Sidewinder, and Phoenix—or could deliver bombs.

velocity on the deck strike bomber. The difference designed every damn thing in the airplane, from the inlet areas to the configuration of the cockpit to you name it. It wasn't the problem that it was an Air Force and a Navy airplane; that was relatively simple, as indeed, the F-4 illustrated. The problem was that we were trying to build two completely different airplanes for two completely different missions. In spite of his very high intelligence, I thought Mr. McNamara just never caught on to that.

One sort of amusing thing I really remember was one occasion when there was argument before the Secretary of Defense as to what lift coefficients and proposed flaps this airplane would have. That, of course, was one of the factors that would or would not make it carrier suitable. And here was the Secretary of the Navy—if I recall correctly, it was Paul Nitze—and the Secretary of the Air Force personally up there with this chart showing wind-tunnel results and arguing about which way you should draw a curve through to represent the lift coefficient.[*] I always thought of the most inappropriate use of the Secretaries of the services that I could think of, that was just about it. But that was a drill that went on, as I recall, for about a year. It was very tedious.

During that period when I was OP-07, Mr. McNamara got a notice out saying, "Take no favors from contractors, not even lunch." And it had been the common practice to take you out to a nice restaurant to have a bon sejour, stand you to a nice lunch, which was business, really, because we talked nothing but business over the lunch. Anyway, the directive came out, and so I got ahold of one of my kids' little tin lunch pails and made a big sign like that saying, "LUNCH," and I got off the airplane at Grumman and held this up, and somebody zapped a picture of it that appeared in the paper. I thought I was going to get my ass in a sling. [Laughter] I thought that took it a little too far.

Paul Stillwell: Can you speak on that subject more in general? Do you think there are small minds that try to see evil where there's no possible case?

Admiral Gayler: Oh, I think there are abuses. There are people who try to feather their nest while they're still on active duty. The relationship should be, of course, friendly but businesslike and at arm's length. There are too many instances in which—in the hands of

---

[*] Paul H. Nitze served as Secretary of the Navy from 29 November 1963 to 30 June 1967.

inexperienced officers—it becomes too close, and it leads to a little bit more of a predilection to take the contractor's view of something rather than the government's view. Sometimes they become more interested in or at least more receptive to the notion of single-source procurement so that the team can stay in being, and that sort of thing.

I think there's a great deal more of that rather subtle problem than there is anything of overt angling for jobs afterward and that sort of thing. I suppose there's a minority there. It's a very difficult problem. It would be senseless for the country to throw away the expertise in a particular area after an officer retired. Just from the standpoint of the officer himself, he is often misled too. He can be and often is taken and squeezed for a couple of years like a lemon and then thrown away by the company.

Paul Stillwell: And then the company can get somebody new for two years.

Admiral Gayler: And then get somebody new for two years. Yes. I haven't any very convenient solution for that one.

Paul Stillwell: Returning to the F-111, Secretary Korth really got caught in the backlash of that issue.* Eventually the unpleasantness overflowed to the point that he resigned his office near the end of 1963. There were a number of hearings after the award went to General Dynamics, as opposed to Boeing, which was contractor the Navy preferred.

Admiral Gayler: I thought Fred Korth left for some other reason, but my recollection is very hazy about that.

Paul Stillwell: Well, there was some digging into his background after so much hostility grew up over TFX. They found some things that could be construed as conflict of interest in his bank dealings.

Admiral Gayler: I see. Mr. Korth called me down once some time during that tour—I had forgotten about that until you mentioned his name—and asked me to serve him as a

---

* Fred H. Korth served as Secretary of the Navy from 4 January 1962 to 1 November 1963.

special assistant to pass for him as a sort of staff function on all of the development and procurement programs which came up before the Navy. He said to me that he wanted somebody who understood about these things to monitor and give him personal advice about whether he should or should not support them. I thought about that for a while and then told him that I didn't think I should do that. That put me as a junior rear admiral in the position of passing on the CNO's programs. I was perfectly willing to take the risks, but I just didn't think it was a good way to run a railroad. I think he was very much disappointed in me.

Paul Stillwell: The man who got that job was Draper Kauffman.[*]

Admiral Gayler: Yes.

Paul Stillwell: He was head of the Office of Program Appraisal, it was called.

Admiral Gayler: Yes. He didn't have a name for the office. In fact, he didn't have anything very specific about it. I guess Draper probably thought up the office. Draper was a great friend of mine, by the way. I was a great admirer of his.

Paul Stillwell: He went reluctantly to the job.

Admiral Gayler: Yes. Well, I turned it down. I just didn't think it was a good way to run the business. If I had been the CNO and I had had my people come up with a program and I had personally reviewed it and sent it up to the Secretary and had somebody go over it again—it's just an anomalous way to run a railroad. Of course, just between the two of us, I used to do that kind of stuff when I was a captain for Tom Gates, but I never did it in any formal way.

---

[*] In 1963 Rear Admiral Draper L. Kauffman, USN, became the first head of the Secretary of the Navy's Office of Program Appraisal. Kauffman's oral history is in the Naval Institute collection.

Paul Stillwell: You knew the way things were run under the previous administration. Did Secretary McNamara make the kind of changes in R&D that he did in, say, the procurement side?

Admiral Gayler: Oh, yes. Yes, he brought in his analytic people, and the whole R&D program was subject as best they could to the same kind of cost/benefit analysis and all the rest of it. Well intentioned and excellent in theory, but in practice it generated so many different cooks that the broth was, if not spoiled, at least inordinately delayed.

I think there is an interesting observation to be made about research and development programs in defense, and that is that if you can do them in great haste and great secrecy, like the U-2 and the SR-71, and a good many of the intelligence programs, you can get very good results because they can't be managed.[*] It's when you get the detailed levels of management, not only in the Pentagon but finally over here in the Congress, that responsibility is eroded. The time extends inordinately and the costs also. The objective is lost sight of; there's nobody in at the finish that had anything to do with the beginning, and all those other ills that we're very familiar with.

I wrote a paper some time ago at the invitation of the RAND Corporation.[†] When I finished, they deemed it too hot to print. They never published it because I think it trod on a lot of toes, but it pointed out *de facto* that the way to run a program is very much more along the lines of the ones I talked about, or for that matter, the initial Polaris program.[‡] Responsibility has to be concentrated in a small, competent group.

The difficulty is that we try to run too many programs at once, and we try to run programs that do not have support. Therefore they don't have guaranteed funding, and we intervene fiscally with lightning strokes, which have got nothing to do with what's going on. That's why it makes me so very unhappy to see the defense doesn't debate it in terms of how much money you spend on it. That's probably the worst single measure

---

[*] The U-2 and SR-71 were high-altitude photo reconnaissance aircraft.
[†] The RAND Corporation is a nonprofit think tank with headquarters in Santa Monica, California, and other offices in Arlington, Virginia, and Pittsburgh, Pennsylvania.
[‡] Polaris was the name for the U.S. Navy's first submarine-launched ballistic missile, which became operational in the early 1960s. For details see Harvey M. Sapolsky, *The Polaris System Development: Bureaucratic and Programmatic Success in Government* (Cambridge, Massachusetts: Harvard University Press, 1972). Also, the Naval Institute's oral history collection contains a specialized volume of interviews with key participants.

you can possibly make in defense. And the second worst is how many people you have. What you ought to do is do what Max Taylor has written, and many others, me included.* That is, you figure out what you need to do, functional requirements, and you figure out how you're going to do it, hence the technical satisfaction of them. Then you put the execution in the hands of a small, competent and responsible group headed by a single person. Sounds very simple-minded but it works.

Paul Stillwell: Were nuclear weapons any part of your charter in that job?

Admiral Gayler: Peripherally. Not the weapons themselves but the methods of delivery, that sort of thing.

Paul Stillwell: Did you encounter the DSARC process, which has become a slowing-down agent?†

Admiral Gayler: I think I was fortunate enough to escape that. I don't want to be misunderstood. It certainly is not possible when you're talking about that kind and that amount of taxpayers' money and that amount of concern to our security that you can let these things go uninspected or unchecked, but, my God, it's ridiculous now, the number of people in every act. There has got to be some more responsible, much truncated review started. We could talk about this all day.

Paul Stillwell: Who were your primary customers when you were in that job?

Admiral Gayler: My customer was the CNO. My actual customers were the various fleet outfits, and I kept very good liaison with them. I had them up all the time to talk to me, and I got around a lot to laboratories and to the fleet, to ships, and air stations and operating crowds. By that time, by virtue of having been around for a while and particularly duties like test pilot in VX-3, I was well acquainted in the aeronautical

---

* General Maxwell D. Taylor, USA, served as Chairman of the Joint Chiefs of Staff from 1 October 1962 to 3 July 1964.
† DSARC – Defense Systems Acquisitions Review Council.

community, and I kept up to speed with Grumman and Chance-Vought and the Navy labs and so forth. I knew most of the figures there. I regarded them collectively as my customers, as you would put it.

The function we had was an integrative function, to put together the foreseeable fleet requirements. Not the present ones, but the foreseeable ones, together with the foreseeable reasonable developments of technology in a way so that there would be a kind of a servo loop between what you needed and what you could get in a reasonable time period with reasonable financing. I guess my customers were the programs themselves more than anything else.

Paul Stillwell: Would somebody in the fleet say, "I need this and so. Can you develop this for me?"

Admiral Gayler: That very seldom happened. It was more a matter of getting out and asking and deducing from what they said what sort of thing they might go for. I don't recall anybody ever writing in or calling me up and saying, "We need a Mach 2 airplane out here." It doesn't happen.

Paul Stillwell: Did you work with the Operational Test and Evaluation Force?

Admiral Gayler: Yes, together with the others. At that period in history, there was sort of an unfortunate thing. You're talking about OpDevFor, aren't you?

Paul Stillwell: Well, its name was changed in the late '50s, I think.[*]

Admiral Gayler: The trouble with you historians is that you remember everything, so we're at a disadvantage. Well, anyway, whether the name was changed or not, I was always rather unhappy with the way that force was used. It seemed to me that they were often—not always—often fobbed on to less important issues rather than the great issues

---

[*] In May 1959 the Operational Development Force was renamed the Operational Test and Evaluation Force

of the day, and also because they tended to be rather late in their appraisal. Their appraisals came too late in the cycle to do anything much about it.

Paul Stillwell: Well, they had to have a piece of hardware to test. Wouldn't it inevitably have to be pretty late?

Admiral Gayler: Not really. There were a lot of unnecessary delays in getting it into their hands and in writing up the projects and so forth. I don't think many people during this time ever tumbled to what I used to do in VX-3, which was to write the project and send a personal letter to the right guy up here and get it back. That was a very short time-fused thing, so you were pretty up to date. I think it got a little bureaucratic. To answer your question directly, I didn't get much from them.

Paul Stillwell: How much of your work was theoretical, as opposed to applied research?

Admiral Gayler: None of it was theoretical. It was all applied, if I understand your question.

Paul Stillwell: Some people are just working on things to see what they can come up with, as opposed to having a direct requirement that they can fulfill.

Admiral Gayler: I don't make that distinction, you see. As I see the requirement of satisfaction ideally operating, it's a sort of a servo-loop arrangement in which you have a general feel for what it is that you would like to be able to do, not even what it is you would like to have, but what it is you would like to be able to do. Then you try to appraise what technology can give you as a means of satisfying that functional requirement, and you go back and begin to zero in on what the actual instrument might be, whether it's an airplane or a chopper, or you name it, and then back here again to see what the technology could do for you reasonably. You race around that track four or five times before you zero in on something.

Paul Stillwell: How much of the initiative came from your organization and how much from the defense contractors?

Admiral Gayler: We were well aware of what the state of the art was and what the contractors might be able to do, and what's more, we were able to suggest, I guess, that we were interested in such and such an area, and what did you think about it? That came back in the form of some kind of informal response or proposal or whatnot. We were very, very careful not to do that on a proprietary basis, never had any private dealings or preordained contracts or anything. Plus, the contracting end was over in the systems command anyway.

Well, it was a long and interesting cruise, and I was ready to go at the end of that. The next thing that happened was that, to my complete surprise, I was nominated to go to the Joint Strategic Target Planning Staff.[*] That had had a curious history with me, because when Gates was Secretary of Defense, long after I had finished working for him, he called me in one day and asked me what I thought of the idea of setting up that staff, and I said I thought it was a very poor idea. It was a very poor idea because while I thought it was an excellent idea to integrate the SIOP in one command, rather than have the Navy and the Air Force, and to a certain extent the Army, competing for it, that to set it up in an Air Force headquarters under an Air Force commander who was double-hatted as Commander Strategic Air Command, was a mistake.[†]

As a minimum, he ought to make a provision for the staff to alternate back and forth between Navy and Air Force leadership, since it was perfectly clear that the preponderance of the strategic capability would go into the submarines anyway.[‡] Maybe it wasn't as clear in those days as I thought it was, but pretty clear to me. Also, I thought they ought to get it out of a single-service headquarters and put it somewhere else so it could be seen as a really joint staff in support of the Joint Chiefs. With his usual courtesy, Mr. Gates took all that in, but he didn't buy it. He told me the reason he didn't

---

[*] In August 1960, at the instigation of Secretary of Defense Thomas Gates, the Joint Strategic Target Planning Staff was established. The JSTPS is discussed in the Naval Institute oral histories of several officers who were assigned there: Admiral John J. Hyland, USN (Ret.); Vice Admiral Gerald E. Miller, USN (Ret.); Vice Admiral Kent L. Lee, USN (Ret.); Vice Admiral Edward N. Parker, USN (Ret.).
[†] SIOP—Single Integrated Operational Plan, which specified the targeting for U.S. nuclear weapons.
[‡] On 1 June 1992, subsequent to this interview, the Air Force's Strategic Air Command was disestablished, and its place was taken by the newly established joint-service U.S. Strategic Command.

buy it was because of the already large investment in computers out at Omaha. Frankly, I think that's the only major mistake that Gates ever made. I thought it was a mistake then, and I didn't mind telling him so.

So I was ordered to it. I don't know whether anybody out there ever knew that, but I had a funny feeling about it. [Laughter]

Paul Stillwell: Did you have any encounter with Vice Admiral Butch Parker?* He was one of the first to go out there.

Admiral Gayler: No, I didn't. I had heard all sorts of rumors about how the Navy was hazed out there by LeMay and particular by Power, who by all accounts—I never knew him—by all accounts was a mean old bastard who loved to haze the Navy.† But I also inherited Jack Ryan when he went out and completely changed that atmosphere; things were very different then.‡ That indeed turned out to be the case. On a personal basis they just could not have been nicer to me and the rest of the Navy people out there. It was just a very pleasant tour of duty on a personal basis, even when we were downwind from the stockyards, which was much of the time.§ [Laughter]

But it was a funny place. It was a funny place. The place was—and as far as I know, still is—hidebound to an extraordinary degree. The best illustration I can make is a very true story. I went in to see my boss, the Director of Strategic Target Planning, who, of course, was CinCSAC, a four-star Air Force general. We were talking about something or other, and I ventured to say, "Well, I think thus and so."

We were good friends. We used to play squash together and all sorts of stuff, but he rounded around on me and he said, "Noel, it's not your business to think out here. It's your business to do what the Joint Chiefs tell us to do." And that was the attitude throughout. There was nothing except concern with the detailed execution of strategic

---

* Vice Admiral Edward N. Parker, USN, became the senior Navy representative when the Joint Strategic Target Planning Staff was established.
† General Curtis E. LeMay, USAF, served as Air Force Chief of Staff from 30 June 1961 to 31 January 1965. General Thomas S. Power, USAF, served as Commander in Chief of the Strategic Air Command from 1 July 1957 to 30 November 1964.
‡ General John D. Ryan, USAF, served as Commander in Chief of the Strategic Air Command from 1 December 1964 to 31 January 1967.
§ SAC was based at Offutt Air Force Base, near Omaha, Nebraska.

ideas generated in Washington and blessed by the JCS. Of course, I found that pretty onerous before I left.

They were also very uptight—not in a personal way, but in an official way—about Navy participation. I remember once when President Nixon was to be briefed, and it had always been the custom for the CinC to take his number-three officer, who was also an Air Force officer, Major General Magnum. The general would brief the President while the CinC looked on approvingly with one of these very stereotyped standard briefs. This time, the Air Force general, who was a great friend of mine, fell ill. He had the flu or something, so the next thing that happened was that it looked as if I was going to brief the President. So I got ready to do that, but in the meantime, unbeknownst to me at the time, although I found out about it later, the CinC had been in agonized conversation with the Chief of Staff of the Air Force to the effect—I don't think it was personal—to the effect that they just couldn't let the President be briefed on the SIOP by the Navy. So they took poor Jim Ead, who was the major general, my good friend, ops officer, and pumped him full of antibiotics and aspirin and whatnot, and almost literally holding him by the elbows, he tottered in to brief the President rather than have the spectacle of the Navy do it. I think it struck home on how very parochial some of these operations are.

It was an amusing place. I really always had two minds about it. My personal associations and admiration for the Air Force officers were unbounded. We were one of the family, and it was a well-run outfit. I lived next door to the inspector general of SAC, and we used to laugh and conspire together about how he could get on a station unnoticed and unannounced and suddenly pull a drill to see if the big bombers could get off the ground in a hurry like they advertised. And, you know, they do all sorts of things. They clear for one place and go sneaking around to some other place and pull the cord. I became aware that when they said they could get so many bombers off in so many minutes, by God, they could. It wasn't just talk. So I had great admiration for them. I went on some of the low-level flights. I had done a whole hell of a lot of low-level flying, but it was in fighters and attack planes, not in those big, lumbering things. And I've got a lot of respect for them, those airmen and professionals. It was reinforced later on in Vietnam.

But it was certainly a place where independent thinking was not encouraged. I don't know whether you've ever seen a Strategic Air Command brief, but it's kind of like a movie. It's a slide show, dog and pony show, and you've got a slide and some words that go with it, all of which have been approved by the CinC. Then you put it in the can like a movie, and that's the brief on that subject. If you ask a question, someone says, "We'll get you the brief on that, Admiral." Then you're treated to this brief, but it's sort of unfair to ask a major with a pointer anything about it, because in the first place, he's not likely to know, and in the second place, he isn't authorized to deviate from what the hell it says on that slide anyway. So it was an interesting, mixed-emotion experience, tour for me, a very valuable insight into an aspect of the Air Force. And I don't mean for a second to generalize from SAC to the Air Force, because I know that they're not the same thing. For all I know, SAC may be very, very different now. This was many years ago. But I was really struck by how rigid, rigid the operation was.

Paul Stillwell: Would there have been a place for creative, imaginative thinking there?

Admiral Gayler: Oh, sure. But the trouble is, if you do creative, imaginative thinking about nuclear weapons, you end up with the conclusion that you don't want to do that. I have never been able to think of a use of nuclear weapons that didn't end in a logical absurdity. So I can see why thinking wasn't encouraged.

Paul Stillwell: Did you encounter hostility as a result of that?

Admiral Gayler: Not overt. Certainly not personal hostility. The only official thing that came close to a dust-up was their inveterate habit of referring to missile silos attacked as "destroyed" on their briefs. I kept saying, "Well, they may or may not be destroyed. If missiles fire out, you can destroy the silos, but you can't destroy the missiles." That objection was sort of dismissed and overwritten and whatnot, until I finally made a point of it. When the thing was set up, there was a provision made for the Navy deputy to go directly to the Joint Chiefs. And in the bad old days, when there was bad blood between the CinC and the Navy representative out there, that was the reason that we kept a Navy airplane there. Because we even thought that they might deny transportation to the admiral if he wanted to go back to Washington. I'm talking about hearsay and I'm talking about a time before mine, so I'm not certain about this, but I think it's right.

So on this occasion, I had to say, "Well, I'm going to appeal this to the Chiefs." After some more quasi-acrimonious discussion, we ended up with a compromise, which was that the charts would all show a great big question mark, meaning yes, maybe you got it, and maybe you didn't, depending on whether we shot it out first.

Paul Stillwell: Was anti-missile defense a concern of yours?

Admiral Gayler: Yes, it was. We had a scientific advisory board with some pretty good scientists on it, including some people that have been in the ABM business.[*] And why they agreed to serve, I don't know, because they must have realized pretty soon that no matter what they said, it was not going to move out of the stereotyped SIOP. We had a lot of quasi-technical discussions about anti-ballistic missiles, and I came to the conclusion then, which I entertain now, that there's no way to get there from here. You really can't make one that's effective. At least you can't make one that's effective beyond preserving a certain percentage of hard targets from attack. As far as defense of populations is concerned, no. There was a lot of discussion about it.

Paul Stillwell: It was very hotly debated in Congress for a while, too, I recall.

Admiral Gayler: Yes. But this was one of those debates like the Star Wars debate that's so orthogonal because there are people who understand these things arguing one, and there's a set of true believers arguing something else without access to either understanding or data.[†] They just never move. This Star Wars business is like the poor cancer sufferers that go to Mexico and get shot full of Laetril in the hopes it will do something for their cancer.

---

[*] ABM—anti-ballistic missile.
[†] "Star Wars" was a nickname the media pinned on President Ronald Reagan's Strategic Defense Initiative.

Paul Stillwell: Did you get congressmen visiting to get briefed on your operation?

Admiral Gayler: Yes, quite a few. We did a lot of formal briefings, and it was not very productive, I don't think. As I say, it was pretty formal.

Paul Stillwell: They saw the dog and pony show?

Admiral Gayler: They saw the dog and pony show, yes. And that's what the Chiefs saw too. I was always a little bit surprised that the Chiefs didn't want something a little bit more real, but, you know, it was very complicated. It was very complex, indeed, and not many people outside that particular planning staff understood or, I believe, nowadays, understand that complexity of the SIOP and the quite subtle operational problems and solutions that are involved in it. It's the curious outcome of doing with great accuracy and care and complexity something that you probably shouldn't do in the first place if you used your common sense. I think it remains that way.

Paul Stillwell: Is it possible that they were preoccupied by Vietnam and thus couldn't give this the attention?

Admiral Gayler: No, I don't think so. No, this was the province of a full staff working at it full time. They were not distracted by Vietnam.

Paul Stillwell: No, I mean the Joint Chiefs.

Admiral Gayler: Oh, that's possible. I think they were always very interested in it, but they just didn't want to immerse themselves in all of the detail that we used to brief. And then sort of a special language is developed, too, which makes it obscure to people not familiar with the language.

Paul Stillwell: Where would the basic planning decisions come from on whether you target a population or military bases or industrial capacity?

Admiral Gayler: This was done in the form of options, and we got rather generalized instructions from the Joint Chiefs of Staff, and then many different options from which to choose. The thought was that at the time the President would open the black book and choose the options he wanted and direct that they be executed. Of course, they were each complicated. I have never been very much interested in the argument about whether 8 minutes' warning time or 18 minutes' warning time is very different. You couldn't figure out those options in 18 hours. There is no way to make them simple; they're just inherently complex.

Paul Stillwell: Was there any inter-service jealousy on how you would divide the pie, who got how much of it as far as targeting?

Admiral Gayler: In my time, no. We had so many weapons that there was no problem. There was always something from each service to put on anything you could think of. In fact, as I have testified before the Congress recently, the problem there then was not adequately covering targets, but trying to find enough targets for the weapons we had. I have no firsthand and current knowledge, but since we have a lot more weapons now than we had then, I imagine that's even more so the problem now. But the service rivalry didn't come up because everybody had plenty of weapons to get in on every act.

Paul Stillwell: Was there any input from your organization into the SALT talks?[*]

Admiral Gayler: No, not to my knowledge. I don't recall that we ever—let me qualify that. I think maybe we got some questions at one time. But they were not policy-type questions; they were sort of factual questions.

Paul Stillwell: Did you need to get any special clearances for this kind of work beyond what you had before?

---

[*] SALT – Strategic Arms Limitation Talks.

Admiral Gayler: Oh, my. I know at one time I held so-called Q clearances, but then I'd held them before. I think that I just maintained the clearances that I had, as I recall. There is an interesting point about that, too, which I have made publicly recently, and that is that the very high—and in my judgment, unnecessarily high—classification in which many nuclear weapons matters are held. The result has been over the years to get specialized staff groups in the nuclear business, both civilian and military, who have held these clearances and stayed in that business and all of the routines are routed to them to handle. And the result has been the establishment over the years of a sort of a nuclear Mafia, interested in the technology of the weapons and the weapon delivery, and really very little bureaucratic or formal opportunity to question the validity of what they were doing, whether it was a good idea in the first place, understand the purported use of the weapons in the larger context. It just didn't happen. It got much less examination in that kind of way than in very routine, conventional operations. I think that still obtains and is one of the reasons we're in so much trouble.

Paul Stillwell: Has your thinking changed since that time dramatically on the use of nuclear weapons?

Admiral Gayler: No, not dramatically. I think I had reservations about them for a long, long time, and I do believe that they have matured. I've learned more and perhaps thought more about the general policy implications, but there was never a day on the road to Damascus when I saw a great light in the sky or anything like that.

Paul Stillwell: I'm just wondering if you had at least a germ of the idea then how that was received at SAC headquarters.

Admiral Gayler: Well, the situation was quite different then. We really did have a large differential advantage over the Soviet Union, and so some of the rather obvious constraints on any potential use now weren't in existence then. The situation was somewhat different. I guess I didn't raise policy issues very much out there, because I pretty well understood that that wasn't where they were addressed anyway. They were addressed back here in Washington if they were addressed at all. And for the reason that I told you about for so many years being confined to the nuclear Mafia, they weren't raised back here much either.

Paul Stillwell: Did you feel comfortable in that kind of a job?

Admiral Gayler: I thought it was a little boring, to be truthful. It was repetitious once you caught on to what was doing, and then you just went through the same drill. But it was not too long a tour. I was content while I was there, but plenty ready to leave.

Paul Stillwell: You then got another job that was quite different from what you had been doing. How did that come about?

Admiral Gayler: Well, one day at JSTPS in Omaha, I was minding my own business. I think I was in conference with the CinC, and somebody came in and said, "Admiral Moorer wants to talk to you on the telephone." He was then CNO, of course.[*]

Sure enough, he said, "Noel, I want you to come back to Washington and compete for a job."

And I said, "Fine, Admiral, what job?"

He said, "I'll tell you when you get here."

"When would you like me?"

"Well, I'd like you to leave as soon as you can." And so I went out and made my excuses to the CinC and said the CNO wanted to see me, at which point he gave me sort of a curious look, because, of course, he didn't know what the hell was going on either.

I went down and got in my dear old prop airplane, and I went winging to Washington. And it appeared that Admiral Moorer was disturbed because the Air Force had wired the appointment of an Air Force lieutenant general to be the director of the National Security Agency. Moorer felt that the Joint Chiefs had been bypassed, and a more proper way to have done it would have been to have a candidate from each of the

---

[*] Admiral Thomas H. Moorer, USN, served as Chief of Naval Operations from 1 August 1967 to 1 July 1970. His oral history is in the Naval Institute collection.

services and have both the intelligence hierarchy and the civilian hierarchy in Defense and the Chiefs to take a look at it before they put him in such a critical job. So he, Moorer, had demanded a recount, if you will, and pulled me back from Omaha to sort of compete.

So I went around to present myself, if you will, to a couple of people in Defense, civilians who were concerned with intelligence. At the time I didn't know how much they were concerned with intelligence. And who else? Oh, a very old friend of mine, I learned later, who was very deep in the business, was also consulted. I didn't see him. He apparently just knew me. And so without further ado, I found myself nominated. I went in to see Mel Laird, and in about two minutes' conversation he passed on me, and there I was.* I gather the Air Force was real bent out of shape, but I certainly had nothing to do with it.

Paul Stillwell: Why did he pick you?

Admiral Gayler: Well, you'd have to ask him. I don't know. He probably thought I had a smart lip and would get along with these civilians. [Laughter] I really don't know. No, I had known Admiral Moorer for many years. I think he thought I was particularly conversant in the electronic warfare area and would be okay in that job. He might have thought that. I don't really know.

Paul Stillwell: Was there some reason for taking a line officer, as opposed to an intelligence specialist?

Admiral Gayler: Beats me. I think a line officer was the better way to go, but I don't know.

Paul Stillwell: To the extent that you can discuss it unclassified, what did you do?

---

* Melvin R. Laird served as Secretary of Defense from 22 January 1969 to 29 January 1973.

Admiral Gayler: I remember very well what I did. I realized that—well, the first thing I did was go call on Pat Carter, General Marshall S. Carter, who was my predecessor, and he looked at me.[*] He said, "I hope you know what you're getting into," [Laughter] and left me pretty much alone. So the next thing I did was go to Louis Tordella, who was the deputy director, the famous "Doctor T."[†] He had been there for a great many years, and was and is an extraordinarily able and capable man, who knew everything there was to know about it. Sort of as I had done before with Trapnell and learning to be a test pilot and with other people on other jobs, I sort of sat at his knee and learned what the business was about. I worked very hard at it.

The first three months I was there, I left my wife behind, and I worked about an 18-hour day. I would start in the morning. I took over the job before I knew anything about it, really. I would start in the morning and do a regular deal of things that are entailed in the director, with a great deal of help and advice and assistance from Tordella. And when the working day was over, I would go for an hour's athletics or something, a light supper, then go back and talk to the various divisions, briefing on their business, usually until midnight every night.

I did this for about three months, at the end of which I didn't really know the business, but I knew a hell of a lot more about it than I had before, and was fortunate that I did that, because I was soon up testifying before Fulbright and his committee on some things that we were doing that he was very dubious about.[‡] If I had not really been loaded, I might have had a great deal of difficulty. I don't think I ever worked quite so hard to learn a job, because I don't think I was ever quite so unfamiliar with it before I went there. Nor have I ever had experience with anything so complex and so intellectually demanding as that. It was a wonderful tour.

I had a lot of decompression when I left there, because the place is just absolutely stuffed with extremely bright people, and after a while you just got out of the habit of explaining anything to anybody. You didn't have to; they got it on the first pass. I had to

---

[*] Lieutenant General Marshall S. Carter, USA, was director of the National Security Agency, 1965-69.
[†] For more on Dr. Louis W. Tordella and many other individuals involved in the working of the National Security Agency, see James Bamford, *The Puzzle Palace: a Report on America's Most Secret Agency* (Boston: Houghton Mifflin, 1982).
[‡] J. William Fulbright, a Democrat from Arkansas, served in the U.S. Senate from 3 1945, until his resignation 31 December 31 1974. He was an outspoken critic of the U.S. role in the Vietnam War.

decompress a little bit when I left there. It was a marvelous tour. That is a tremendous institution, full of the brightest and most dedicated people I've ever had anything to do with. Really terrific.

Paul Stillwell: Do you think that Congress has a legitimate role in a kind of oversight it performs in places like that?

Admiral Gayler: Oh, of course. The Congress, under the Constitution, has a legitimate role in damn near anything you can think of. But I think in the particular case of the National Security Agency in some aspects, not all, by a long shot, and the other intelligence agencies, that rather obviously has to be handled very carefully. And I'm not talking about political embarrassment, and I'm not talking about covert action and dirty tricks and the silliness of mining harbors. I'm talking about real intelligence.

You see, the kind of intelligence you have to safeguard is the kind of intelligence that you will lose if it becomes known. And some of it is quite critical to us. A lot of people know that we get photographs of the Soviet Union from satellites, but that's just the tip of the iceberg, and there's a great big iceberg down there that we don't talk about, that we don't talk about for very good reason. I think if it were possible to tell the public how much we really do know about the Soviet Union, we'd be a lot less worried about Soviet cheating and break-out and verification and all that stuff than they seem to be. It's a bit of a bind because you really can't talk much about it, and we really ought to be quite reassuring people now to notice that we are complaining bitterly about the detailed character of a Soviet radar, [unclear name], which has yet to go into operation for about three years. That ain't too shabby. And we do a lot of that.

Anyway, NSA, of course, was in and of itself a tremendous outfit in the forefront of technology as well as of linguistics and cryptography and many other skills, all of them varieties of electronics. It was and is, I believe, still one of the major computer operations of the world. So it was a pretty fascinating place to be. It also gave me a seat in the intelligence community which was, as it is now, a very fractionated and jealous community, so it was almost long-standing institutional problem between NSA and CIA and DIA and the various service intelligence activities.

We used to sit around the table once a week in what was then called the Board of National Estimates, I believe, to pass, collectively, on the various major intelligence estimates. It was really pretty amusing. When it came to estimates having to do with Soviet military capabilities and weapon systems or anything like that, you could predict with high accuracy what each one of these representatives was going to say, except me, because I was purple, and Dick Helms, who was the director of the CIA, and who was very good at many other things, but was not much interested in technology, and usually were sort of bored to death when we started talking about that sort of thing.*

You could see what these guys were going to say, because they would work the problem backwards. I don't know whether they did it consciously or not, and I don't impute motives to anybody, but it would always come out that the Air Force thought the Soviet missiles could go farther, had they had bigger throw-weight or something, and the Navy felt that the submarines were bigger than the Air Force, all of those things, except once. Once the Air Force had a substitute. I remember the guy's name, but I'm not going to put it on the tape. And this poor guy wasn't too swift. He was inflating—I believe it was a Soviet antiballistic missile capabilities, in his estimate, and halfway through, he suddenly realized that in so doing, he was imperiling some damn missile the Air Force was plugging at the time, and you could see that realization come over his face. I almost burst out laughing out loud. But those were serious sessions and, I thought, important ones.

The system at the time was that any one of the major people that didn't agree with the estimate could footnote it, and that meant that he could put his dissenting opinion in as a footnote. And that was better than what I understand has since superseded it. It made it tougher reading, but it did give the full flavor of the arguments, whereas requiring the board to come—I don't even know what the successor operation is anymore—to come to a consensus, which tends to water everything down to its lowest common denominator. I think the thing particularly to be guarded against, and a very important and, I may say, a very current danger is the tailoring of intelligence estimates to fit the preconceptions of the people who are going to use them. And that is the

---

* "Purple" is a slang term to describe joint-service staffs, purple supposedly being the color that would emerge from blending the uniforms of the various services. Richard M. Helms served as Director of Central Intelligence/Director of the Central Intelligence Agency from 30 June 1966 to 2 February 1973.

primordial sin in the intelligence business, and I hate to say so, but it happens a lot and shouldn't. And it gets us into trouble like crazy, as it did in Vietnam and does in the nuclear business right now.

Paul Stillwell: How much did the President and Henry Kissinger get involved in your work?[*]

Admiral Gayler: I never had any—let me modify that. I did have some direct contact with the President in one special context, and it was Nixon. But Kissinger was in it all the time. He was, as a matter of fact, one of the people who kept attempting to get the intelligence estimates tailored to fit his preconceptions. Of course, he never said that very openly or very clearly, but it was pretty apparent when he was unhappy with intelligence estimates because they didn't fit his policy. The feedback was pretty strong. I don't think in that time we ever trimmed to suit, but he was particularly annoyed with the dissenting opinions in the footnotes: "Why the hell can't I ever get anything straight from you guys?" sort of thing.

Paul Stillwell: How much interaction did you have with SecDef Laird?

Admiral Gayler: Well, a great deal, a very great deal, and it came about in this way. Bob Froehlke, who was appointed assistant secretary for intelligence, was and is an insurance executive.[†] He is now the head, I think, of the Insurance Institute of the U.S. But in those days, he came from Wisconsin. Froehlke is an extraordinarily charming, gregarious, pleasant man, and he conceived the idea that all of us Defense intelligence people, which was NSA, DIA, and the service intelligence people, should have breakfast once a week with him and the Secretary of Defense.

Laird was very faithful; he showed up. I think it was Friday mornings we had it, and so, in effect, skipping a few weeks, I and the rest of us had breakfast with the

---

[*] Henry A. Kissinger was the President's national security adviser, 1969-73 and later served as Secretary of State, 1973-77.
[†] Robert F. Froehlke served as Assistant Secretary of Defense for Administration, 1969-71, and Secretary of the Army, 1973-75.

Secretary every Friday regularly. And they were business breakfasts, and we talked over the whole business and made reports of what we were doing. After a while we got to be very comfortable. We had our arguments right in front of them, and everything like that.

At the beginning, I was really disdainful about this. I thought, "Oh, God, here's this nice insurance guy coming in here, and he thinks the way to run the business is to have breakfast together all the time." But in the end, I began to realize how very powerful this was. And we began to work together as a community, and to understand each other and respect each other, and so forth. I see a lot of Froehlke. We are on the same board together over here. I've often told him, "Bob, you taught me something, that breakfast is mightier than the bulldozer." That was very interesting, very interesting. And I must say I thought Laird was extremely good in that capacity. He was very understanding, took you seriously, acted on so many insights that he got, very supportive. He was good.

Paul Stillwell: Could you draw any comparison between him and McNamara, whom you worked with in another capacity?

Admiral Gayler: Yes, they were very different people. Laird, of course, was a consummate politician in the very best sense of the word. He had been, as you know, a Republican congressman for many years and member of the Armed Services Committee.[*] So he was deeply familiar with the business. He also knew the Congress inside out and back and forth, and therefore knew how to get things done. He had a lot of instinct for people, an intensely loyal man. He really looked out after his people, which is a good quality in a leader.

McNamara was and is extremely bright, hard-working, analytical.[†] I don't know whether he always was this way, but in the later years, deeply infused with philosophical concern for the human side of things. Sort of a curious mix. Not too much on a personal basis but sort of on a theoretical basis. He didn't concern himself personally as Laird did about the people around him, but in a philosophical way, he concerned himself a hell of a

---

[*] Laird, a Republican from Wisconsin, served in the House of Representatives from 3 January 1953 until his resignation 21 January 1969 to become Secretary of Defense.
[†] McNamara died 6 July 2009, years after this interview.

lot with the welfare of people worldwide and so forth and so on, as he still does. It happens that, although I don't see that much of him, we're close associates nowadays, and help each other as much as we can on a much different footing. So they were quite different people.

I think it would have been much better if Laird had been Secretary of Defense earlier in the Vietnam War. I think McNamara was misled by his great analytical talent and great faith in the analytical method in appraising that war. His approach was inappropriately mechanistic, inappropriately economic for a war that was really an ideological war, sort of unprecedented and virulent political type. It was just not what he was cut out for, whereas what was probably deeply unfamiliar to Laird in detail, he had quite a bit of instinct for the politics of human interaction. I don't mean that to be critical of Mr. McNamara. I have come to have great respect and admiration for him in later years, but he did what so many analysts do, so many analytical people do, and that is to take account of the things which can be quantified and leave out the things that can't be quantified, no matter how important they may be.

Paul Stillwell: You mentioned Secretary Laird's sense of loyalty. How did that manifest itself?

Admiral Gayler: Well, for one thing, Bud Zumwalt—it's just an example; it happens to be me. Bud Zumwalt, who was, of course, my old friend and colleague from the days we both thought we were going to be fired, and who, of course, leaped a lot of senior officers to become CNO, wanted me to be Chief of Naval Material with four stars.[*] And I'm sorry to say I sort of did him wrong. I consented. He asked me when I was in London by long-distance telephone. I was on a trip over there. I consented, and then on the way back, I began to agonize internally because I had only been at NSA a little bit more than a year. And I thought, "You know, it really isn't right to put this outfit, this extraordinary outfit, through the agonies of breaking in a new director and then leave like that, even if you do get promoted."

---

[*] Admiral Elmo R. Zumwalt, Jr., USN, served as Chief of Naval Operations, 1 July 1970 to 29 June 1974.

So I went back to Bud. As a matter of fact, I caught him on the way over to see the President. I rode over in his limousine. I confessed to him, I said, "Bud, you've got to let me out. I need to stay with this outfit. They've got too much invested in me." And Laird, for some reason, was greatly taken by that. He thought that was a manifestation of loyalty to something. And he did the same sort of thing with Don Bennett, who was DIA and who was marked by the Army to go some place higher in rank, and did.[*] Eventually he reached four-star rank. But Laird was like that. He always thought about—I'm not sure rewarding is the right thing, but looking out after people who had done a good job. He didn't just use them and let them seek their own fate.

Paul Stillwell: Well, are you saying, then, that he sort of had the idea that you would get a four-star job after that?

Admiral Gayler: Yes, I'm sure he did. He never told me so explicitly, but I'm sure he did. I'm sure he did. My actual going to CinCPac was, I think, Bud's original idea—Zumwalt and enthusiastically supported by Laird. This is hearsay. I don't think I was his candidate, and Laird had trouble with President Nixon—not because Nixon had any problem with me. I don't think he even knew me. I had met him once when he was Vice President, and I doubt if he would have remembered me. But because he had committed himself to Jack McCain, to leave Jack in that job until young Jack came out of captivity.[†] This is, again, hearsay. I think it's accurate. And Laird felt that it was time for a change, but he had to go back to the President again to make it happen. I felt rather badly about it, too. Jack McCain was a very, very old friend of mine, and I had worked for his father, knew young Jack before he started out. I could very well understand how he would like to stay there, but at that time we had no idea when the war was going to end. It might have gone forever. So that's how that came about. Laird was instrumental. Bud started it, and Laird was instrumental.

---

[*] Lieutenant General Donald V. Bennett, USA, was director of the Defense Intelligence Agency, 1969-72.
[†] Admiral John S. McCain, Jr., USN, served as Commander in Chief Pacific from 31 July 1968 to 1 September 1972, when Admiral Gayler relieved him. His son, Commander John S. McCain III, USN, was then a prisoner in Vietnam. He was finally released from captivity in early 1973 when the active U.S. participation in the Vietnam War came to an end.

Paul Stillwell: You had this series of tours sort of outside of the mainstream of the Navy. Did you have any concern about that?

Admiral Gayler: I didn't have any concern. I think a lot of other people had some concern about whether I could hack it or not, but I didn't. No, I really didn't. In the first place, I hadn't been outside the Navy, for Christ's sake. I had been skipper of a carrier and a skipper of a carrier division, and I hadn't done too badly with those. I was very operationally minded and was up to speed on technology and on seagoing and whatnot. I even had had a tour with the Air Force and a diplomatic tour, so what the hell do you want? And I started out my career as a dogface in the Army, so what the hell do you want for a joint commander? I had no problem.

Paul Stillwell: One ticket that usually gets punched is the numbered fleet command, and you didn't have that.

Admiral Gayler: No, I didn't have that. But I didn't feel at any disadvantage. Actually, the cardiv command and command of a carrier is a hell of a lot closer to real fleet operations than a fleet command is or a numbered command.

Paul Stillwell: In the intelligence business, what can you say about the amount of duplication among all these various agencies that you've mentioned?

Admiral Gayler: Well, the particular area in which I was engaged, there was not so much duplication at the time as great difficulty in making an integrated operation out of it. There was and is for each service a considerable outfit in the business of sigint.[*] There was a determination on the part of each service to maintain that capability for themselves, and a great deal of reluctance to putting it all together into one system, a reluctance which was very strongly supported by the senior operational officers of each service on the usual grounds that if you didn't own it, you couldn't count on it.

---

[*] Sigint—signals intelligence, which is the information derived from intercepted communications.

So there was a tendency on the operational side, which is, of course, not the only side of the National Security Agency, which is, after all, a National Security Agency, and it does report to the Secretary of Defense but not to the Defense department. Of course, he has a second hat for that purpose. So there was—and as far as I know, still is—some concern about being so dependent for this very vital source of intelligence on an agency which is largely civilian, not even totally in Defense, let alone under the control of either the service commander or a unified commander.

Of course, I had these arguments day in and day out, because from my vantage point, I could see very well how much more efficient and effective a unified operation was than a fragmented operation. And it was during my time that a proper management setup was established, the Central Security Service, the military assets that combine into a security service which attains to the state so that the director of NSA is also the commander of the Central Security Service. That has worked reasonably well. I'm not awfully familiar with how it is currently, but it worked reasonably well. I think this is perhaps the place where Admiral Moorer began to be quite dissatisfied with me professionally, because the views I took were not those of the Joint Chiefs on this issue. And later on it boiled up again out in CinCPac.

Paul Stillwell: How did they differ?

Admiral Gayler: He believed, with what I think was and still is the main, current opinion, that these assets were extraordinarily important in the military sense and should be under more direct military control and more directly responsive and more clearly responsive to the military commanders. Well, I argued, and to me it was correct that this lost sight of not only the powerful synergism of the assets, whether operated by this service or that service or the other service, and the very large efficiencies there. But even more importantly, lost track of the fact that there's simply some capabilities that cannot be accomplished except in a place like Fort Meade, with access to linguists and enormous computer capabilities and other things of that kind.[*]

---

[*] The headquarters of the National Security Agency is at Fort Meade, Maryland.

So the operating system that I always advocated was one in which you had a short shunt from the asset to the commander, where the commander could, in fact, use raw what the asset could give him. I have to talk a little bit circuitously here, but there was an enormous amount—in fact, the great bulk of it actually had to be chewed up and digested a little bit before it was, in fact, useful to the commander, and you could not reasonably carry around in ships or up in a division headquarters or some place, the numbers of specialized linguists—some of whom were little old ladies—and computer specialists and other assets that were really necessary to make some sense out of what all of our vacuum cleaners got. But I had my innings. I had my time. Time was available to me. I had the ear. I made the arguments. They were not accepted by the Chiefs, but they were by the Secretary of Defense.

Paul Stillwell: Was any part of the concern that you would be told what answers to find—that is, what conclusions to draw in your work?

Admiral Gayler: No. It was not my concern, at any rate. That was the problem I alluded to previously, but that was a problem having to do with operations of the Director of Central Intelligence and his assessment board. They were not problems for NSA. We just told it like it was, and we never had any problem with that.

Paul Stillwell: Well, I'm fascinated by all of this, but I'm also out of tape, so let's resume this the next time.

Admiral Gayler: Okay. All right.

Interview Number 8 with Admiral Noel A. M. Gayler, U.S. Navy (Retired)

Place: Admiral Gayler's office at the American Committee on East-West Accord, Washington, D.C.

Date: Monday, 7 May 1984

Paul Stillwell: Admiral, last time we were talking about your tenure as director of the National Security Agency, and you alluded briefly to the ships that had been used in the intelligence-gathering aspect. In 1967, the *Liberty* had been attacked.[*] In '68, the *Pueblo* was captured.[†] In '69, an EC-121 was shot down by the Koreans.[‡] What was your reaction when you came in as director?

Admiral Gayler: Well, I think I reacted to those events perhaps more as a naval officer than as a director. One thing that struck me immediately was that our communications were so much better than other communications, than the standard operational communications, in each of those instances, that it should have really galvanized what is called the communication establishment of Defense to pull up their socks and do at least as well as the intelligence community did.

Without going into it too much, I think it's well known that in each case, the intelligence community's communications promptly and quite accurately reported the course of events during those things, whereas the operational communications either never got through or got through very late and somewhat garbled. And that seemed to

---

[*] On 8 June 1967, during the Six-Day War between Israel and Egypt, Israeli aircraft and torpedo boats made a number of attacks on the U.S. communications intelligence ship *Liberty* (AGTR-5). Of the ship's crew of 297, 34 were killed and 171 wounded. Israel claimed that the attack on the *Liberty* was a case of mistaken identity. Many in the ship's crew were skeptical of the claim.

[†] USS *Pueblo* (AGER-2), an electronic intelligence ship, was seized on 23 January 1968 in the Sea of Japan by North Korean naval forces. The ship's crew members were held as prisoners until 23 December of that year. Of the 83 officers and men on board, 28 were intelligence specialists.

[‡] On 15 April 1969 North Korean aircraft shot down a U.S. Navy EC-131 propeller-driven electronic intelligence aircraft about 90 miles southeast of Chongjin, North Korea. All crew members, including 30 Navy men and one Marine, were killed in the incident. The Navy subsequently mounted a strong contingent of warships off North Korea as a show of force, but no hostilities ensued.

me to be a very important military lesson, which I attempted to interest a number of people in the operational community in without too much success.

Paul Stillwell: Were you involved in any way with the Navy investigations or courts of inquiry into these events?

Admiral Gayler: No, they took place before my time in the intelligence community. I thought that—well, as an individual, I thought that we made much too much out of the skipper of the *Pueblo*, who, after all, surrendered his ship.[*] It's very difficult to criticize people in combat when you weren't there, but it wasn't clear to me then and isn't now that he was in extremis and had to surrender. The 121 mission I thought could be criticized operationally, but, again, that's Sunday morning quarterbacking. The thing that shocked me about the *Liberty* is the deliberate savagery of the attack against a presumed ally. I heard later that there were orders to move her out of harm's way, which never got delivered, but I don't know the incident.

Paul Stillwell: Did you have a hand in shutting down the use of this kind of vehicle for signal intelligence?

Admiral Gayler: No comment. Turn off the tape.

Paul Stillwell: On the relationship between the civilian and military sides of the National Security Agency, originally it had started out as an exclusively or almost exclusively military organization and gradually became more civilianized. Is there a case for having a civilian director?

Admiral Gayler: I think you could make a case that the director should not necessarily exclusively always be military. I wouldn't say it the way you have. I wouldn't say

---

[*] Commander Lloyd M. Bucher, USN, was commanding officer of the *Pueblo* at the time of her seizure. A court of inquiry in 1969 recommended that he be court-martialed for loss of the ship, but Secretary of the Navy John Chafee decided not to carry out the recommendation, saying that Bucher had suffered enough during his time as a POW.

there's a case to have a civilian director; I think there's a case to have the best qualified director you can get. And that may or may not be a civilian. I was extremely happy in NSA all the time I was there in the very excellent way in which the civilian and military worked together—toward the same objectives, with the same spirit and loyalty.

The only problems that we had were institutional problems between NSA as an institution and the various service intelligence agencies and capabilities as institutions, not as people. I think the distinction is an extremely important one. There were institutional rivalries. There was never any personal reflection or any instance to my knowledge ever of military and civilian within the agency or within the later set-up Central Security Service operations.

Paul Stillwell: Do you have a problem with all these different organizations getting in the way of each other?

Admiral Gayler: Yes, I do. I think the outfit—by the outfit, I mean comprehensively the intelligence community—is over-organized and has too many specialized turrets for the efficient, comprehensive addressal of the problem. As director of NSA, I was always mildly on the outs with the JCS over this issue. JCS supported the existing, somewhat separate intelligence organizations of the services. I thought then and think now there should have been a great deal more consolidation.

Intelligence is not very service oriented. There is some, of course, the submarine tactics, obviously, in the Navy. And it's hard to pick other exclusive problems that really ought to be addressed by only one service. That was sort of an exception. The collection means overlap, the analysis overlaps, and worse than that, tends to be derived from a service viewpoint, which, however patriotic, from the standpoint of the Navy or the Army or the Air Force, is not the right way to arrive at ground truth.

There are dangers in total consolidation, and I don't advocate that. But somehow we have to find the middle ground, which makes intelligence on the one hand responsive to operational commanders as well as policymakers, and on the other hand, doesn't duplicate and find institutional reasons for differing. I found in the National Security Agency, as I did previously in the old Bureau of Aeronautics, and before that when I was a test pilot and had a couple of civilian assistants, a very powerful synergism that comes from qualified civilian and qualified military but with different qualifications of sitting together at the same desk and working the same problem for the same boss.

It's a model that I think we ought to emulate in the Department of Defense. I've advocated that for many years. It almost completely gets you out of these time-consuming, wasting institutional conflicts, and there's a process of mutual education going on between, for example, the operational naval officer, which I was when I went to the National Security Agency, and the senior and experienced intelligence officers who were there, not all of whom were civilians, but most of them were, but there were exceptions, there were military and they, too. It's very effective mutual education, this symbiosis that is so very powerful, and I would like to see that used as a model in Defense.

For example, I have proposed that the Joint Chiefs—this is a real anathema, by the way—that the Joint Chiefs and the Secretary be supported by the same staff instead of having an exclusively military Joint Staff supporting the Chiefs and the predominantly civilian staff supporting the Secretary of Defense, which creates institutional conflicts and has in the past years led to indifference to the advice of the JCS because people more closely placed to the throne, the assistant secretaries of Defense, are more influential. And it need not be that way.

Paul Stillwell: Now, in coming in as an operationally experienced officer, did this give you a user's viewpoint that was valuable in that job?

Admiral Gayler: I thought so, yes. I did have the user's viewpoint, and I also learned a hell of a lot. I spent my first months there in almost total immersion, as if trying to learn a new language, because I realized at once that the complexities of the job required it.

Paul Stillwell: Is that a disadvantage in not having an intelligence specialist in that job?

Admiral Gayler: Yes, I think it is. No doubt an intelligence specialist would have had less new ground to cover. On the other hand, if he had spent his career in intelligence, he might have perhaps less appreciation of the direct needs of the operators and planners. On the whole, I would support what was done in my case, bringing in an operational officer and requiring him to learn at least some of the trade.

Paul Stillwell: Is this an advantage also, of rotating the job among the various services?

Admiral Gayler: Yes, I think it is, although I think it's almost comical, in fact, I say it is comical, the value that each service seems to place on having their man in that job, because if there ever was a job in the military that had no real service orientation, that is it. It really doesn't make any difference to the position of the service whether an Air Force general is there or Navy admiral or Army general. So it's sort of amusing, the way they struggle to get the job.

Paul Stillwell: In 1970, when Admiral Zumwalt became the Chief of Naval Operations, many senior naval officers reacted to his Z-grams and so forth.* Were you enough removed that you didn't react?

Admiral Gayler: I think I told you before I was very close to him personally and also in those days—we're still good personal friends, although I haven't seen anything of him, and we're on opposite sides of the political spectrum now.† But in those days, we were still relatively fresh, he and I, from some of the personnel battles during that time. I was the Secretary's aide, and he was the aide to the assistant secretary for personnel. And I generally supported him, and publicly supported him on most of the Z-gram reforms. I thought he made a couple of unfortunate mistakes having to do with uniform and hair and whatnot, and was glad to see they have been rescinded, but I thought his general drive was in the right direction, and I was glad to support him publicly.

---

* Z-grams were consecutively numbered policy directives from Chief of Naval Operations Zumwalt that attempted to deal with such issues as enlisted rights and privileges, equal opportunity, and Navy families. Junior personnel viewed them much more favorably than did their seniors. See *U.S. Naval Institute Proceedings*, May 1971, pages 291-298.
† Admiral Zumwalt subsequently died on 2 January 2000.

Paul Stillwell: What can you say about the contributions of the deputy director, Dr. Tordella?

Admiral Gayler: Well, "Dr. T." of course was the power behind the throne there. He'd been there for many years, and he is a highly intelligent, very thoughtful man who was really totally au courant with everything that went on there. He was very generous in educating me, and perhaps it was reciprocal to a certain extent. We got along beautifully. I still see something of him. I am a great admirer of Louis Tordella's. He's the kind of guy you want to have on your side, by the way.

Paul Stillwell: Well, I think the organization needs somebody like that as an institutional memory.

Admiral Gayler: As an institutional memory. That's right. And as a professional. I think there should be—obviously must be—a strong core, a continuing core of professional people in this branch of intelligence, which is much underrated, as a matter of fact, because of the necessarily highly secret nature of it. I don't think anybody in the public, and very few people in policymaking positions, understand how much we are dependent on these capabilities, and so it's something nothing much can be done about. I can't say anything more about it publicly.

Paul Stillwell: In buying the equipment that you use to achieve these capabilities, do you have a problem in communicating a requirement to a contractor, since it is so sensitive?

Admiral Gayler: Well, it's handled in two ways. The requirements, of course, are not target-related. They're related to capabilities. For example, we will ask for receivers of a spectrum of so many bandwidths and this capability and that capability. We don't say that we're going to use it to look at this or that. And, of course, the sensitive part of the business is the successes. The more successful you are, the more important it is to be quiet about it, because if you don't, you lose it. So in that sense, although we did have well-cleared contractors, you did not have to go into highly sensitive matters in order to specify again what equipment you wanted.

Paul Stillwell: What about in computer area? Any problems there?

Admiral Gayler: Only the problem of being the frontrunner. I think NSA certainly had then, and I believe has now, perhaps the most comprehensive array of really high-performance computers anywhere in the world. We've always been in the forefront of computer development and remain so.

Paul Stillwell: How do you go about selling a program like that to Congress, or do you have to?

Admiral Gayler: You have to, to a certain extent, although there's a hell of a lot of credence been accumulated over the years, but generally speaking, you just go over and testify in closed session to a select number of people who have high clearances. I remember I used to go over and physically take the stenotype ribbon back to the agency every night to lock up. We were very careful about it. Interestingly enough, to my knowledge, unlike other deals with the Congress, the confidence has not been violated. I think people, when they recognize the sorts of things that are being obtained, that they themselves understand the necessity. And, of course, there have been some instances—the Korean airliner thing, of course, where the Secretary of State, presumably with the approval of the President, has let it be known that we read Soviet fighter pilot transmissions in remote places of the world.[*] That's their responsibility and simply the elected President's fault. It's not a judgment that I would have made, but it's a judgment that he did make, and it's his responsibility and he has a right to make it.

---

[*] On 1 September 1983 a Soviet SU-15 fighter aircraft shot down a Boeing 747 passenger plane over the Sea of Japan. The 269 people in the plane were all killed. The Korean Airlines plane was on flight 007, which was en route from Anchorage, Alaska, to Seoul, South Korea, but strayed off course and violated Soviet airspace over Sakhalin Island.

Paul Stillwell: Another case in which the public got to see more than usual of the inner workings was in the Pentagon Papers case, which came up during your tenure.* What do you recall about that?

Admiral Gayler: Not much. I'm afraid I was disgusted with the whole damn thing. I didn't pay much attention, to be truthful. The prospect of somebody trying to make hay against the government by the unauthorized disclosure of secret papers was just revolting to me, and to hell with it.

Paul Stillwell: Did you make an attempt to stop that?

Admiral Gayler: The answer is no. I'm trying to think if I ever knew anything about them. No, I don't recall. I don't think anybody was aware that Ellsberg was about to do this.†

Paul Stillwell: Well, after the first ones were published, there was a vigorous attempt through the courts to enjoin further publication.

Admiral Gayler: That horse was stolen by then. No, I thought and I think now it was absolutely insupportable to do that sort of thing.

Paul Stillwell: What can you say about the NSA role in domestic surveillance, the Huston plan, for one thing?‡

---

* In 1971 *The New York Times* and *The Washington Post* published what came to be known as the Pentagon Papers, a government study on the U.S. conduct of the Vietnam War. The government tried to prevent publication of the material, but the Supreme Court upheld the actions of the newspapers involved.
† In the late 1960s Daniel Ellsberg, who had served in the U.S. embassy in Saigon, was part of a group that prepared a study under the direction of Secretary of Defense Robert McNamara. It was titled "History of U.S. Decision-Making in Vietnam, 1945-68" and came to be much more widely known as the "Pentagon Papers." In 1971 the study was leaked to the news media and published. Despite the efforts of the Nixon Administration to prevent publication, the Supreme Court approved the media's freedom to publish the material.
‡ The Huston Plan was a 43-page description of proposed security measures assembled by White House aide Tom Charles Huston in 1970. Its existence became public in the 1973 Watergate hearings.

Admiral Gayler: Well, it's interesting you should ask that question. The Church Committee staff brought me over for questioning shortly after those issues were raised, and I gave them a contemporary memorandum that I'd written on the subject, guiding and limiting the activities of the agency.* They were limited to protection of the life of the President, to criminal investigations, with particular emphasis on drug-running and to terrorist activities, and to one other category that slips my mind right now, none having any political implications, and then the considerable admonition to respect the civil rights of the individuals under surveillance. The committee staff took a look at that and with obvious disappointment, said, "Well, guess we won't need you any more, Admiral." That's the last I heard about it.

Paul Stillwell: How does one prevent abuse of a capability in a situation like that?

Admiral Gayler: I think there's no real protection against the character of the President and the people around him. I was never asked to and never called on to do anything improper. The Huston plan was sent out over the signature of—I want to be precise about this—in a book embossed with the name of J. Edgar Hoover.† He had been appointed by the President to chair the group addressing these intelligence questions. And it was in the form of sort of a questionnaire which we were each asked to indicate our choices on. I did that, sent it back, and that's the last I heard of it, because Hoover soon afterward dissociated himself from the whole operation. Presumably he got after the bookbinder who put his name on it. And that's the last we heard of it.

Paul Stillwell: Did you have any other dealings with Hoover, any recollections of him?

Admiral Gayler: No. I did deal with him on a couple of occasions. He never went to the formal meetings of the Intelligence Review Committee. He always sent a deputy,

---

* Frank F. Church, a Democrat from Idaho, served in the U.S. Senate from 3 January 1957 to 3 January 1981. In the 1970s he chaired the Senate's Select Committee on Government Intelligence Activities.
† J. Edgar Hoover was director of the Federal Bureau of Investigation (known until 1935 as the Bureau of Investigation) from 1924 until his death in 1972.

Sullivan. I really had very little contact with him. I saw him sort of informally, nothing substantive, on a couple of occasions.

Paul Stillwell: Did NSA have any role in the attempt to rescue American POWs at Son Tay in 1970?[*]

Admiral Gayler: Yes.

Paul Stillwell: Can you say any more than that?

Admiral Gayler: No. [Laughter] I will say this much. I believe it was Admiral Moorer's decision or at least his decisive recommendation to attempt the rescue. Even though there were intelligence indications that the prisoners had gone, it was the right decision. I think he understood, as I understood, too, at the time, the chance that it was probable they weren't there. But even to go on the possible was, I thought, the right decision, and I think it's quite unfair to criticize him and others from carrying out the Son Tay raid. You know, they bet on the come, and they weren't lucky.

Paul Stillwell: How much contact did you have with Admiral Moorer during your years at NSA?

Admiral Gayler: Quite a bit. I used to, once in a while, come over and sort of formally brief the Chiefs together, and then on some of the more sensitive operations, we talked together. And then most unfortunately, we had a serious policy difference toward the end of my time at NSA, and that made things a little strained between us, having to do with organization. It was my view, as I said earlier, that the signals intelligence community should be operated as a single entity. It was his view that the services should retain a lot of autonomy.

---

[*] On 20 November 1970 a U.S. commando force landed at the Son Tay prison, 23 miles west of Hanoi, North Vietnam, in an attempt to free U.S. prisoners of war reported to be held there. The commandos did not recover any POWs, because they had been moved to another location shortly before.

By the way, I think it would be time right now to put on the record my deep respect for Admiral Moorer, in spite of the fact that we've been on opposite sides of the political spectrum for some time now. By force of his personality and his extraordinary capacity, he was really the kind of Chairman that this country needs in an operational sense. He never had any more formal authority than any other Chairman, but he was able to run the Joint Chiefs, in my judgment, as no Chairman before him or since has ever been able to do, simply by his extraordinary capacity and the force of his personality. So on a personal note, I deeply regret that we've had these problems, but they were institutional problems; they were not personal.

Paul Stillwell: What about the agency's role in the 1971 Indo-Pakistani War?

Admiral Gayler: No comment on it.

Paul Stillwell: Certainly you had involvement in Vietnam during your next tour as CinCPac. Anything you can say about NSA involvement in Vietnam?

Admiral Gayler: Well, as you know, Vietnam was—I was about to say in retrospect, but I don't think it was in retrospect—I think all of us military professionals recognized for a long, long time that the Vietnam War was being very badly run from a professional military standpoint, because of the limitations of the place on decisive military action, which I attributed—did I talk about this before?

Paul Stillwell: No.

Admiral Gayler: Well, I thought that Secretary McNamara and President Johnson, each from a distinctly different background, came to the same disastrously bad strategy for fighting the war.[*] Of course, the first mistake was the mistake that Omar Bradley, among

---

[*] Lyndon B. Johnson served as President of the United States from 22 November 1963 to 20 January 1969.

others, had warned against so earnestly, and that was leading with the infantry, committing ground troops to an Asian war.*

But putting that one aside, it always seemed to me that Mr. McNamara generalized from his background in economics and analysis to a notion of conducting the war as consistent with the economic idea of marginal return, that the costs to the enemy could be progressively raised to a point where he would see that it was not in his interest to continue, and at that point, a compromise solution—an economic solution, if you will—could be realized. It seemed to me that President Johnson—and I don't want to suggest that it was his responsibility alone, because, of course, it wasn't—but he had a great big piece of it, came to the same idea from his political experience. He had been habituated to finding where people's weak points were and exploiting them, and to arm-twisting and to raising the pressure until it became excruciating, at which point they could get a deal.

So they both, through this confluence of economic theory and political experience, came to the same notion that the thing to do was gradually raise the ante until it became unsupportable to the other side. The problem with that was twofold. One was that they didn't know the nature of the enemy, that he was capable of an almost infinite amount of suffering, and in spite of the fact that they were Communists, that they were not economic men, not by a long shot. They were ideological men. This was a totally different sort of thing. And that further, in this long trumpeted, gradual raising of the ante, that the Communist world, the Chinese and the Russians who were then more or less in concert, were not only enabled, but they were almost compelled to maintain a position before the Communist world to match the raise.

In addition to which we lost surprise, we lost coherence, we lost any idea of the objective, and because of somewhat ill-understood constraints placed on the way the war was fought, we tended to be fighting at a disadvantage not only militarily but also with respect to morale. Not too difficult to fight against an enemy carrier task force when you fully understand the consequences of what you're doing. To fight against flak, surface-to-air missiles in the full knowledge that what you did wouldn't make a damn anyway

---

* General of the Army Omar N. Bradley, USA, served as Chairman of the Joint Chiefs of Staff from 16 August 1949 to 14 August 1953.

because it would either be sustained or negated by political action at home, or to go out on patrol or any of those other war actions where you're liable to get your head shot off. Not that easy; neither our people nor anybody else's are robots of that kind. You have to believe in what you're doing. And that, I think, was the root cause of the morale problems that we all had, the Army in particular.

But toward the end of the war—I'm not picking on the Air Force, but the Thud pilots would go in at 24,000 feet and 480 knots, dropping iron bombs.[*] Christ, you can't do anything that way. They knew it and we knew it. And what hooch down there was worth losing your life over was a very reasonable view that they had. The same thing for [unclear] patrols, same thing for—the destroyers were standing off the coast, they were shooting 5-inch guns at something or other. It was perfectly clear that it wasn't aimed fire at real targets. It was sort of like the Lebanon caper.[†] So it was bad show, and only at the very end did we get effective militarily, and then it was over the hill politically.

Paul Stillwell: What steps do you refer to in the effective militarily—the mining of Haiphong?[‡]

Admiral Gayler: Yes, I think when we went up to Haiphong in December of 1972, which, by the way, has always been miscalled the "Christmas bombing of Hanoi." The facts are we stood down Christmas because it was Christmas, and that we never bombed Hanoi except by accident—one most unfortunate accident when it hit the hospital. But what we did do was totally interdict it by hitting the railroad yards, the railroads themselves, the highways, mining the canals, and knocking down the bridges, and most especially, mining Haiphong Harbor.

---

[*] The Air Force's F-105 Thunderchief fighter was known by the nickname "Thunderthud," which was often shortened to simply "Thud."
[†] In 1982 U.S. Marines were sent to Lebanon as peacekeepers and set up in barracks at the Beirut Airport. On 23 October 1983, a suicide terrorist drove a truck filled with the equivalent of 12,000 pounds of explosives into the Marine barracks. The resulting explosion killed 241 Americans and wounded 70. The Marines withdrew from Lebanon in early 1984.
[‡] In May 1972, confronted by North Vietnamese intransigence at the Paris peace talks and a North Vietnamese spring offensive against South Vietnam, President Nixon ordered the Navy to carry out existing plans for mining the harbors of North Vietnam. On 8 May, A-6 Intruders from U.S. carriers sowed mines at Haiphong, Hon Gai, Cam Pha, Thanh Hoa, Vinh, Quan Khe, and Dong Hoi. The flow of seaborne supplies in North Vietnam ceased immediately.

Now, the mining of Haiphong Harbor, contrary to most of the other military operations, was an extraordinary success because very little effort was required. It was extremely effective, and it had arguably the most effective military operation of the entire war. And it had the singular characteristic that nobody got killed on either side. Now, that's generalship—in this case, admiralship. It's the right way to do business. But we had very little of that in the Vietnam War, and that's one of the reasons for the revulsion against it.

Paul Stillwell: Speaking of those who had a revulsion against the war, what reaction did you have to people like Ramsey Clark and Jane Fonda, Americans who were speaking out publicly against it?*

Admiral Gayler: Extreme anger. I did not understand how, when combat was joined, public figures could actively encourage the enemy. I still feel that way about it. But one of the great things about this country is the way we can heal. We don't fight the Civil War anymore. The Irish have been fighting Cromwell's occupation, which is what now—400 years old? And the Battle of the Boyne. The Asians have their terrible strifes that go back for centuries; so do the Middle Easterners. We don't do that; we heal in this country. So as far as I am concerned, the Vietnam War is in the past emotionally. There are some lessons to be learned. Most of them are not the lessons that most people think should come from the Vietnam War, but there are lessons there.

Paul Stillwell: What lessons would you draw?

Admiral Gayler: I think that the most important lesson, of course, is that we do not embark on military operations where we don't have a clear objective and don't think we're going to win. Just like that. We shouldn't do it. We should not embark on military operations that don't command the clear support of the American public. In this

---

* William Ramsey Clark served as Attorney General of the United States from 1967 to 1969. Later he became an antiwar activist. In 1972 he visited North Vietnam to protest the U.S. bombing of Hanoi. Jane Fonda, an American movie actress, publicly supported the North Vietnamese side in the war and in 1972 visited North Vietnam. In 1988 during a "20/20" with Barbara Walters, Fonda apologized for her judgment in going to North Vietnam and contributing to North Vietnamese propaganda.

democracy, we can't do it. We should not embark on land wars in Asia, where we will always be outnumbered and therefore less likely to be concerned about death than our people are. We should not fight wars of attrition, that wars where generalship can be expected to put our people in winning situations. We should not rely on technology where it's not appropriate to the situation that we're engaged in. We should not fight wars without real unity of command, instead of a patched-up relationship that existed at that time. It wouldn't be too bad to go back to Clausewitz's clearly enunciated principles. I'd say it would be a pretty good idea to observe them in military combat. And, finally, that we should not be so carried away with a certain political view that we risk or lose enormous things over a relatively small potential gain or potential danger.

The damage done to the U.S. military has taken us a long time to recover from, over what was really a quarrel basically over which Vietnamese sect was going to control what had been French Indochina. It was not that much concern to us. Our political misreading was very severe. People confidently asserted that the Vietnamese control of Vietnam would result in their control of Thailand, their control of the SEATO nations, their control of Cambodia and Laos.* Christ, they're still bogged down in Cambodia, for Christ's sake. The poor goddamned Cambodians are giving them a bad time. It just wasn't there in the first place.

The same parallels apply, frankly, to Central America. I cannot believe that the fate of El Salvador will govern the fate of Mexico, observing that Mexico is some 50 times the size of El Salvador, or that indeed the fate of El Salvador will govern the fate of Mexico, which in turn will determine the fate of the United States. That's too much of a leap for me. I think there were leaps of that sort about Vietnam. We should not be at war except for vital reasons.

Now, in the present nuclear area, all of these cautions are magnified by a factor of something between 1,000 and infinity, because what we have to lose is everything. It's difficult to believe that these posturings and propagandas and two-bit reasons for not reaching agreement on reducing the nuclear war threat are justified by any objective that we could reasonably have or that the Soviets could reasonably have. But that's another subject.

---

* SEATO – Southeast Asia Treaty Organization.

Paul Stillwell: In the area of operational communications and intelligence, did Vietnam pose any special requirements for NSA because of the possibility of compromise, interception, etc.?

Admiral Gayler: Run that one by again.

Paul Stillwell: Well, part of NSA's job is to protect our own communications.

Admiral Gayler: Oh, I see. Were there any special penetration security threats?

Paul Stillwell: Right.

Admiral Gayler: I wouldn't say they were special. They're endemic. One of the major threats around this town is that government officials call each other up on the phone and talk about highly classified matters. And they ought to have sense enough to know that that sort of stuff is easily readable by anybody who's interested, and it's more than a presumption to suggest that the Soviets are interested. Those hundreds of pounds of tapes that they ship back in the so-called diplomatic pouch to Moscow are not pop singers. [Laughter] It's just amazing how careless people are and how difficult it is to get some sense of responsibility into highly placed people.

Paul Stillwell: Did you gather evidence of that sort yourself to try to educate these people in the problems?

Admiral Gayler: Yes, I went over myself to brief the senior individuals. Generally speaking, it sort of took like the threat of cancer takes for a smoking addict. Yes, it's difficult, yet people continue to smoke. Usually, to the extent that people gave any reason for it, it was, "Well, you know, it's too urgent; we can't wait for more secure communications," which was usually all.

Paul Stillwell: What about in the war theater itself? Were there measures you took there to protect our communications?

Admiral Gayler: Yes, but we had the same trouble of the fighter pilots and attack pilots get up in the act, the infantry commanders react to each other. We were badly exploited by the Vietnamese. We had the thought, in our Western arrogance, that they weren't up to exploiting us. The hell they weren't.

Paul Stillwell: How good were we at exploiting them?

Admiral Gayler: Pretty good. That's the end of that subject.

Paul Stillwell: Is there anything else on NSA that you want to talk about?

Admiral Gayler: Well, it's an extraordinary place. They are very devoted people; they're highly professional. They tend to be highly intelligent. It takes a sort of decompression when you come out of the place, because you never had to explain anything or tell anybody anything twice. It is really quite a place. In some respects, it's too bad it has to be so secret, but it does. It's a good place.

Paul Stillwell: I would think that's sort of a morale problem, that an individual can scarcely get the public recognition for what he's doing that he probably deserves.

Admiral Gayler: I think that's quite true, that individuals don't get the public recognition that they deserve for quite extraordinary work in all sorts of areas. But I also think that the people there who are professionals understand that and take it as part of the job mostly.

Paul Stillwell: How did you then go about getting the job as Commander in Chief Pacific?

Admiral Gayler: I sat there while Bud Zumwalt nominated me. He was then the CNO. And Melvin Laird enthusiastically supported it, and unknown to me at the time, there was a good deal of opposition from certain individuals in the JCS and around the President. But Laird put his teeth to the bit and made it happen. I had absolutely nothing to do with it. That's just a fact.

Paul Stillwell: What was the basis for the opposition?

Admiral Gayler: I think the JCS people had other candidates and felt omitted from the selection process, and many of them probably regarded me as being a loose cannon, and some of them, as I found to my great surprise later on, did not regard me as being operationally oriented because I'd just had three years at NSA. If they had taken the trouble to read my fitness reports from the *Ranger* and CarDiv 20, they'd find that I was about as tactical a sailor as anybody you could find, but they didn't know that. So for reasons of that kind, I think some people regarded me then and probably do now as a bit of a loose cannon, used to thinking for myself.

Paul Stillwell: Had you expressed any desire on your own for the subsequent billet?

Admiral Gayler: For CinCPac?

Paul Stillwell: No, when you were at NSA. Had you put in a preference card?

Admiral Gayler: No. I don't think you do things at that level by preference cards. I was busy doing my job. Sounds a little naive, doesn't it? It's a fact, though. I've never politicked for any job. In the first place, I don't play games that I don't understand. And I know I don't understand that kind of game.

Paul Stillwell: Would there be any advantage in rotating the CinCPac job among the various services?

Admiral Gayler: Oh, you're just determined to get me in trouble. I think it would be very healthy. I don't think I would have a mechanical rotation, and I think that the Pacific theater is dominantly a theater of naval control and naval warfare. And for that reason, it makes sense that the CinCPac should usually be in that role, I think. But I think that occasionally to have an Air Force officer have the job or to have an Army officer have the job would be a very healthy thing, because it would really call attention to the importance of the joint command system.

When I arrived at CinCPac, I found that the CinC's aide had always been a naval officer and still was, and that he was even on the party line, if you will, of the CNO's communications with the senior flag officers of the Navy. And it was with Zumwalt's understanding and consent that I terminated that and put in an Army officer as my military assistant and terminated the special—I went to Navy communications. I went to very great lengths to try to emphasize the impartiality and unified character of the staff. Whether I was successful, other people will have to judge. I know I worked at it very hard.

I know that the idea would be anathema to any CNO that I ever talked to, but you see, I don't think that control of the sea can be exclusively a Navy problem anymore, any more than control of the air can be exclusively an Air Force problem, or space, for that matter, and certainly not control of the ground an Army matter. I think the Army is more forthcoming in recognizing their total dependence on the other services for support than the Air Force and the Navy. But I think it's time to knock off the ambiguity of the command system, to make the joint command system really work. Some day, some time. The Secretary of Defense, and I think it will take the Secretary of Defense with some cojones to make the change which really makes the unified defense. Hasn't gotten there yet.[*]

Paul Stillwell: What kind of changes would that person have to make?

---

[*] The Goldwater-Nichols Defense Reorganization Act of 1986 went into effect on 1 October of that year. For details, see "DoD Reorganization," *U.S. Naval Institute Proceedings*, May 1987, pages 136-145. It did a great deal to mandate jointness among the various military services. As a result, a good many changes in the overall command structure have been implemented since the time of this 1984 interview.

Admiral Gayler: Well, there would be a number of them. I wrote a paper on that subject at the invitation of RAND some years ago, and it was too hot for them to publish. They have to watch out what their Air Force lines. But I suggested, among other things, that we should support the JCS and the Secretary in his office by the same staff. That we should have a single military officer in command rather than the chairman of the committee, which is what he formally is now, although as I said, if he has enough force and enough capability, he can operate like Admiral Moorer did, but it's not easy.* That we should procure in common almost for all military equipment, and as a consequence, do away with the unsupportable duplication of military R&D efforts, weapons systems, development expenditures, laboratories and you name it.† The list is nine yards long. And that we should, in effect, do away with the service-oriented chains of command, some minor, comparatively minor important supporting measures like the officers who had joint duty evaluated by joint selection boards instead of single-service selection boards.‡

See, the first thing an officer has happen to him when he goes to a Joint staff, is that he gets in trouble with his own service. It's just inevitable. I got in trouble with my own service when I went to NSA, when I went to CinCPac, immediately, because they expect to say, "Jump," and have you respond, "How high?" And you're not in that position; you're looking out for the other people too.

And my wonderful Air Force lieutenant general chief of staff was always in trouble with his service for the same reason. The Army two-star was always in trouble with his service for the same reason, and perhaps not too important at that level, but for the hot shots, the lieutenant colonels and the commanders, it's a very important thing to be evaluated, for example, by an Army officer doesn't cut much ice on your next Navy selection board. It may depend on the character of the selection board, but it tends not to have as much horsepower as the evaluation by—oh, boy, Eddie O'Rourke says this guy is a hotshot, Eddie O'Rourke being somebody that you'd served with. It's quite a different thing. And some other reforms, quite sweeping reforms of that kind. Of course, you'd

---

* The Goldwater-Nichols Act strengthened the power of the Chairman of the Joint Chiefs.
† R&D – research and development.
‡ Goldwater-Nichols mandates joint-service assignments as a requirement for promotion to flag or general rank.

have to get the backing of the President, you'd have to carry the Congress with you, but I think it can be done. In fact, I'd like to have a crack at it, but I don't think I will.

Paul Stillwell: Did you all take a sort of perverse pride in that independence you established?

Admiral Gayler: I think many of us did. Yes. When I said I wasn't sure whether I was able to get it across with the other services, I should except the staff. The staff was really convinced that we were purple and we were not showing favorites, we were going to work together as a unified team. But the setup was poor because of a very senior Air Force general out there, at four-star level, a senior Navy admiral out there, at the four-star level. That's too much. And there was a very senior Army officer, at the four-star level, in spite of the fact that we had a four-star in Korea and a four-star in Vietnam. And just too much room for institutional jealousies there. If you're going to make a unified command out of it, make a unified command out of it. That's a hell of a lot better than CinCLant, where the commander only has the other forces for exercises or war.

Paul Stillwell: There is a different situation there in that the same individual is both CinCLant and CinCLantFlt.* I think you had an advantage in not having that double load.

Admiral Gayler: That's not an advantage. That's a disadvantage. I think Churchill said it best, something to the effect that the executive responsibility is always preferable to disinterested brooding over the affairs of others. And this is when he was offered a job early in the Chamberlain Administration, in the War Cabinet, which was supposed to be a small, select group of people to run the war for the British without executive

---

* The situation changed in 1985, after which the Atlantic Fleet and Atlantic Command were no longer commanded by the same admiral.

responsibility.* And Churchill says he would much rather have had the Admiralty and have something to do. In the end, of course, he got both. That was before he was Prime Minister. And it really is much better. I have learned what I always knew anyway, since I retired. I have learned how much easier and better to have executive responsibility than to be an adviser.

Paul Stillwell: Did you consider yourself an adviser as CinCPac?

Admiral Gayler: No. I'm talking about now. I am an adviser on the outside now, outside the house hollering at the people inside. I think our present nuclear weapon force is just disastrous, but I'm very much on the outside on those issues nowadays. Interestingly enough, though, I'm going down to talk to the Air War College at their invitation. I have talked at the National War College, and I think that speaks quite a lot for the system. I have yet to get an invitation from the Naval War College. I have been speaking at Naval War College since I was a lieutenant. They're not interested in me now. [Laughter]

Paul Stillwell: Before the end of the Vietnam War in 1973, the U.S. part of it, how big a piece of your attention did that consume, as opposed to your other theater responsibilities.

Admiral Gayler: Of course, as you know, I went there in September '72, so I really was only responsible there about less than six months of active fighting. I attended a meeting, that is to say, within about 24 hours, to take charge of the war effort from CinCPac and soon found out that realities were otherwise and put that on the back burner. But no, I was preoccupied essentially until the armistice after December '72. From then on, by political decision back home, although we still had a considerable logistic responsibility to the South Vietnamese and the Cambodians—and I made many visits both to Saigon

---

* Neville Chamberlain served as Britain's Prime Minister from 1937 to 1940. He is best known for signing the Munich agreement with Germany's Adolf Hitler in late September 1938. He agreed to the partition of Czechoslovakia in return for a non-aggression pledge from Hitler. Chamberlain hailed the agreement as a guarantee of "peace in our time." Germany violated the pledge, and Britain declared war on Germany in September 1939. In May 1940 Churchill succeeded Chamberlain as Prime Minister.

and Phnom Penh, up into the hills and everywhere else--to see what was going on. Still, we had *de facto* conceded the war by then.

Paul Stillwell: You say you weren't able to take charge. Was that because charge was in Washington?

Admiral Gayler: That was part of it, and also because it was furiously resisted by some of the—not the combat seniors, some of the other seniors around. I really think the combat seniors would have welcomed it. They were tired of conflicting directives. And actually, much of what I did as CinCPac in those times and later on, too, was to act as a filter and a consolidator of all sorts of conflicting directives that came from Washington—not intentionally conflicting, but it was just that all sorts of voices were talking at the same time. One service in particular was rather outrageous in attempting to sort of run the war apart, not only from me but from JCS.

And Admiral Moorer supported me very strongly, going to the mat on that one, getting that one squared away. But the Secretary of Defense, though he was a fine man, was a politician by nature and thought nothing of calling up the commander in Korea or working through the Chairman or calling up me and not cutting the Chairman in. It was a very conflicting situation.

Then there were some areas where nobody would want you and was prepared to give a decision. When it became evident that the evacuation of Saigon was going to have to take place—you could just see the 25 divisions coming down the peninsula there, all this horse manure about political war had come to an end.[*] It was combat. I tried repeatedly to get some estimate of the number of people and who they were to be that were to be evacuated. We had sort of a practice run in the evacuation of Cambodia, in which the cooperation with the Ambassador Tom Enders and me was excellent.[†] And it

---

[*] On 29-30 April 1975, as Saigon, the capital of South Vietnam, was being overrun by the North Vietnamese, U.S. Navy and Marine Corps helicopters evacuated almost 9,000 people. Included were 1,373 Americans, 6,422 of other nationalities, plus 989 Marines inserted to cover the operation. Graham Martin, U.S. ambassador to South Vietnam, was among the last to leave from the rooftop of the American embassy.
[†] Emory C. Swank, a Foreign Service officer, was U.S. ambassador to Cambodia from 1970 to 1973. Thomas O. Enders, also a Foreign Service officer, was deputy chief of mission in Phnom Penh during those same years.

was a carefully and realistically planned operation, but, of course, it was a very much smaller operation, and a very much better defined one.

To make a long story short, it just never did get anything that you could call a planning figure for either how many or who was to be lifted out. And in the end, people just played out the drama as it happened, still with no directives. And again, with the case of Saigon, there was a very considerable conflict between the ambassador and me on making preparations. We actually had a couple of ships up in the [unclear] of Saigon ready to take on thousands and thousands of people, the merchant captains almost literally at pistol point to keep them up there. We had to let them go finally.

Paul Stillwell: What was the ambassador's reluctance to evacuate?

Admiral Gayler: He was not an easy man to communicate with, but apparently he felt two things. One, that any sign of readiness to evacuate would topple and precipitate a rout, disastrous collapse, maybe even assaults by the disgruntled South Vietnamese against our people. And who am I to say it was an unreasonable fear? I don't know. And then the other, he had a curious idea that somehow or other there was a political fix coming, and he even told me so a couple of times, and told me, as I recall, on one occasion that an armistice had been arranged. Well, I knew from other sources that that was not correct.

As I recall, I had two or three telephone conversations with him over a secure telephone in which we sort of argued this issue. And in my visits with him, there was an institutional question about who the hell was in charge. He relied heavily on the Kennedy directive which said that, in effect, that an ambassador is in charge of all effort in a country. I took the position when we started an evacuation, I was going to run it, and we never did agree to that. So it was not a good thing, although very fortunately, the excellent efforts primarily of our helicopter pilots got us out. It was a close-run thing; it could have turned to worms any time, especially during the night of the last evacuation. Some of the chopper people had been in their choppers for 20 hours. There were suggestions made that they would just have to hold up flying and let them rest, and I rejected those. I was fortunate in having enough personal experience in aircraft to know when you had to, you could fly some more. And if we had ever stopped the operation, we'd have never gotten it going again. That was a bad time. Nobody likes to preside over a defeat and an evacuation, especially a self-inflicted one.

Paul Stillwell: How much autonomy did the naval commanders on the scene have in that situation?

Admiral Gayler: They had a lot in terms of execution. Planning was, I think, well done, primarily from my headquarters and General [Unclear] and his people. But very properly, the detail of the execution was left to the commanders on the scene with one exception: when the recommendation came to me that we cease flying and resume in the morning. I turned that down.

Paul Stillwell: Had there been any attempt to seek a military solution prior to '72 election? This is when Kissinger—

Admiral Gayler: Well, attempts—there were lots of proposals to that end. In my time-- you've got to remember I was only in the job from the first of September of '72—you know what a whispering gallery this place is. There were lots and lots of attempts by the Chiefs, by the Air Force, by others to do something decisive. I think we could all see, all of us professionals could see the futility of fighting it the way we were. I recall that I myself made a speech at the Naval War College. I've sort of forgotten now in what capacity. I was a rear admiral, saying, in effect, you ought to get in or get out. It attracted quite a bit of attention at the time. But attempts in the sense of organized military operations, not to my knowledge. It was all in this crazy context of can we increase the bombing and can we go 20 miles farther north than we used to go, can we bomb at night, does the President have to approve the targets before we can hit them? Johnson was very bad about that. In his elegant language, he is reported to have said, "They can't bomb any shit house out there without my approval," and that's not the right role for a President.

There was a hell of a lot—I think the major impression I have there was that we had no coherent control of the operation at all. People were trying to look at it from the political standpoint. People were trying to run it from a military standpoint. People had very different appreciations of what was going on. There was a sort of a mechanistic school, and I can remember seeing a map prepared regularly of South Vietnam, in which little circles were drawn, ovals, and marked 80% pacified, and 60% pacified, and whatnot. That was such obvious baloney. What the hell does 60% pacified mean?

And it was also the era of the body count and the war of attrition. I think there is absolutely no excuse for a war of attrition. If the damn general isn't smart enough to figure out something better than that, we ought to fire him and get one who can. What we ought to look for is the Stonewall Jacksons, not the attrition types.* You can probably detect I'm a little bitter about all that, and I am. It seems to me that in the Vietnam War, neither the politicians nor others were quite up to their responsibilities. But there are clear lessons. One is that there's no amount of military expertise or capability that will compensate for poorly understood policy and clearly enunciated objectives.

Paul Stillwell: Did you sense, as Watergate progressed, that the President was distracted from paying attention to your area of the world?†

Admiral Gayler: Not particularly. I felt that Melvin Laird had a pretty good sense and the President's backing in the so-called Vietnamization of the war, which was a good thing, and in my judgment, might even have prevailed had the Congress not pulled the plug on what we had clearly committed ourselves to supply.‡ That's not to say that the South Vietnamese weren't pretty inept. They had some good generals. I think General Tran up in I Corps was pretty good. But we'd gotten to a point where we were deceiving ourselves in our military [unclear]. I cited the destroyers firing at nothing in particular. I went in to see Tran, the Vietnamese commander in I Corps, and asked him about the

---

* Thomas "Stonewall" Jackson was a general in the Confederate Army during the American Civil War.
† In June 1972 operatives working indirectly for the Committee to Re-elect the President broke into the headquarters of the Democratic National Committee in the Watergate complex in Washington, D.C. The resulting coverup led to the August 1974 resignation of President Richard Nixon.
‡ "Vietnamization" was a term used to describe the process by which U.S. material assets and combat responsibilities were transferred to the armed forces of South Vietnam.

naval gunfire support. He said, "Oh, absolutely essential. Couldn't do without it." They weren't hitting anything. I used to be in destroyers. I used to be gunnery officer, and I knew damn well they weren't hitting anything, because they had no means to be hitting anything, no targets for them, no way to do it. That was just one sample. I've told you about dropping at 480 knots and 24,000 feet. A lot of it was just show biz.

And one other unfortunate thing is, of course, that we kept upping the ante on military technology in support of the South, and the Soviets kept upping the ante on military technology in support of the North. Over the years, we finally educated and supplied until those people were very formidable in modern weapons themselves, and you couldn't fly over Hanoi without losing a lot of people. It was a bad scene. Hanoi got to be better defended than the Leningrad air defense district. Between the Russians and ourselves, we just raised the ante. Now, war is a relative matter, so you raise the capability of the opponent, you have depreciated your own. And I don't think we have yet learned that lesson from Vietnam. We still seem to insist on pressing high-technology stuff on our adherents around the world in the full knowledge that the Russians will press their high technology stuff on their adherents. Or maybe it's the other way around; it doesn't matter a hell of a lot. And in the end, it gets so goddamned dangerous, we get people shot down flying over Syria, for Christ's sake. It makes you angry, it's so stupid.* But that's aside from the rest.

Paul Stillwell: You discussed the events of '75 when the evacuation took place. What about in early '73 when the Americans were withdrawing and our prisoners of war were coming back?

Admiral Gayler: Well, those are two separate things. The fatal blow that we administered to the South was the cutoff of supply. I was in General Van's presence when the last word was brought to him that the Congress had refused to appropriate the monies for continuing promised military supply, which you recall was a condition of

---

* On 4 December 1983 the aircraft carriers *John F. Kennedy* (CV-67) and *Independence* (CV-62) launched strikes of A-6 and A-7 attack planes against Syrian antiaircraft positions in the Bekaa Valley, east of Beirut, Lebanon, because the AA batteries had fired on U.S. reconnaissance planes the day before. In the raid of 4 December the Syrians shot down two U.S. aircraft.

Vietnamization. You could tell by his face that the play was over. It dragged it out a little bit, but the play was over.

Now, the return of the prisoners—of course, that was a joyous event. I went out there and greeted them all personally, one, because I wanted to, and second, because I thought it would be very important to them coming out. They had been exposed to years of propaganda saying the country had forgotten about them and weren't interested in them and cast them aside and whatnot. And I thought it would be important symbolically to have the senior officer out there on hand, and indeed, a lot of them have told me that it was.

Paul Stillwell: In the events leading up to that, as negotiations went back and forth between—

Admiral Gayler: I had very little to do with the negotiations. I was not consulted. I don't really know who the negotiators were, except they were always associated with Kissinger, or what the basis was for the negotiations. The only thing that I know was that we apparently had no intention of making our agreement stick, because the North Vietnamese began to violate the agreements, the armistice agreements almost immediately in lots of ways which we promptly observed and promptly reported. There was no inclination to do anything about it. So I've never known whether the negotiation commitments were made in good faith or not, or whether it was simply too much of a political burden once more to gear ourselves to stop it.

Paul Stillwell: Was there any attempt to get as favorable a military advantage as possible leading up to the armistice?

Admiral Gayler: We had them by the short hair, and after we shut down Hanoi eight and a half days in atrocious weather, we did it. We very promptly, in effect, sued for armistice and we reached an agreement, and then promptly let them violate it. Bad show.

Paul Stillwell: Anything else on Vietnam before we talk about the other aspects of your job?

Admiral Gayler: No. I could philosophize on Vietnam for a long time, but maybe this isn't the place to do it. The other aspects of the job, CinCPac, were absolutely delightful. Best job in the armed services. I'm not talking about the protocols and the parades and whatnot. I've had enough of the parades to last me the rest of my life. Other than the excellent staff support, we did have a tussle about organizing intelligence properly in the theater. We had, in the theater, a reflection of the fractionated intelligence that I've talked about before. And after a very long, hard-fought bureaucratic battle, we finally got CinCPac intelligence center set up. That was not supported by the Chiefs, but we did it.

And other than that, the ties with all of the leaders of the ASEAN countries were, I thought, extremely interesting and perhaps quite significant.[*] I made all the rounds, talked always to heads of state, and to their principal advisers, both military and political. I was well received in every country, and I made every country out there that wasn't behind the bamboo curtain not once, but many times. I found them very rewarding in improving, among other things, my understanding of the nature of Asian politics and indeed, the politics of many a small and threatened country.

I can remember one thing in particular that the Prime Minister of—I think it was Malaysia, impressed on me, and it was that he couldn't take a certain political step because if he did, he would probably lose his job. And not only that, if he lost his job, he'd probably lose his life. And that reminded me in those places, they play politics for keeps. It was quite a different press to things of that kind.

I also came to know Ali Bhutto in Pakistan, I wouldn't say well, but we were in good rapport. And so I have never been very sympathetic to our cozying up to the present fellow, the fellow who murdered him.[†]

---

[*] ASEAN – Association of Southeast Asian Nations.
[†] In 1973 Pakistan adopted a new constitution, and Zulfikar Ali Bhutto became Prime Minister. His party was in elections in 1977, but many people accused the party of fraud. In July of that year army officers removed him from office and seized control of the government. General Mohammed Zia ul-Haq became administrator of martial law and the following year declared himself President. Bhutto was tried and convicted of murdering a political opponent in 1974. He was executed 4 April 1979.

Paul Stillwell: Zia.

Admiral Gayler: Zia, the fellow who murdered him. I think we ought to have a little more ethical content than that to our foreign policy. In fact, I think we should have a hell of a lot more ethical content than we do with our foreign policy. Ali Bhutto, by the way, was a very impressive man. He was a learned man. I saw his library in Karachi, which he took me to, which he had inherited from his father and built on. And I'm not talking about the building now, although it was a house, really, but quite a well-designed and attractive one. But the marvelous collection of books that he had in the central library, a beautiful paneled room with shelves extending to the ceiling on all sides. In the center there was sort of a—I don't know what you'd call it—almost a crypt about the size of this table that we're sitting at, roughly its shape, and in it were bound limp leather and black limp leather volumes, great big ones like this, with a naked scimitar lying on top of them, and I said, "What are those?" And they were the original Napoleonic journals. What was his historian? [Unclear], something like that, that either his father had kept or he had. He was a real scholar and to have him brutally treated the way he was, and then hanged before dawn. I'm no authority on Pakistani politics, but I thought it was pretty brutal.

Paul Stillwell: Well, it was mainly to keep him out of the way, to have him prevented from staging a comeback, I think.

Admiral Gayler: I expect so. I expect so. I don't know whether he was guilty or not guilty of the charges. Something was trumped up. Anyway, it was a particularly brutal thing to do. So I think that's another one of those people. I remember the Malaysian chief of staff, a colorful old bandit that he was, looked for all the world like a Malaysian pirate, which I expect he was. [Laughter] He was very wealthy. Sukarno had gone, and Suharto was in Indonesia.*

I do have to tell one funny story about having dinner at our embassy, I guess, with the Indonesian chief of staff, who was a Sumatran, General [Unclear]. And you know,

---

* Sukarno was President of Indonesia from 1945 to 1967. General Haji Mohammad Suharto was the second President of Indonesia, holding office from 1967 to 1998.

the Japanese were in Indonesia, so it was rather remarkable that a Sumatran should be the chief of staff. Possibly he was a token, I don't know. But I thought he was a delightful man, able. He had a very attractive wife and daughter. And we were halfway through dinner, and he said quite casually, "You know, my grandparents were cannibals."

I was a little taken aback and said, "Oh?"

He said, "Yes, and the last people he ate was a missionary couple from Boston." Well, I had known that there was cannibalism in Sumatra in the old days. So I took that one in. But the thing that was funny was that his wife leaned over, and in this wifely manner said, "No, no, they weren't from Boston. They were from Philadelphia." [Laughter] To this day, I don't know whether he was pulling my leg or not. I think maybe he was. It made an interesting meal of it.

And then in Hawaii, I was privileged—there's no senior State representation or any official representation out there, so sort of *de facto* that CinCPac is the host and greeter for all of the people coming through, which was quite frequently the prime minister of a country or almost always a defense minister, and a foreign minister would stop in and we would show them hospitality. The president of Mexico at that time was President Echeverria, and his wife was an avowed member of the Communist Party, but I took them around Pearl Harbor in my barge, as I did with many visitors and showed them the sights.*

Mr. Echeverria had just returned from a visit both to China and Russia. He was captivated by the Chinese and very unhappy with the Russians, which I thought was kind of interesting, particularly in the light of something that happened last week. Anyway, he and his wife were so charmed with my wife that we got a special invitation to come to the great [unclear] ceremony next year in Mexico City, which we took. At the time, I didn't realize it, but I stepped into a land mine of some kind, because there was a great fuss about the official representation from the United States to the [unclear]. And Echeverria insisted on giving my wife and me the number-one protocol position, and it created a lot of fuss. It's amazing how little that affects you if you're totally unconscious of it, which has always been my style. But that sort of thing was interesting.

---

* Luis Echeverria served as President of Mexico from 1 December 1970 to 30 November 1976.

Then the Queen of England came through unexpectedly in the royal yacht, and the proposition was that she would be billeted, put up at a downtown hotel on Waikiki. Kay and I knew that would be a disaster, that she wouldn't be able to move without paparazzi and photographers and all that junk. So the Navy had a pleasant beach up Barbers Point, as you know, you've probably been there, which could be made secure.* So I got hold of the British consul in San Francisco, who was trying to manage this thing by remote control, and suggested that we take care of the royal couple for the day at the beach and that would be a lot better. And so we did. Kay and I had a very pleasant day just two on two with the Queen and Philip. We had known them slightly before.

Paul Stillwell: She remembered you had children.

Admiral Gayler: Yes. I told you about this, didn't I? I can't remember how many of these things have already gone on tapes. With opportunities like that, I particularly remember the then-Prime Minister of New Zealand, a man named Norman Kirk.† Have I told you about this?

Paul Stillwell: No.

Admiral Gayler: He was, of course, a socialist, but one of the most interesting men I've ever known in my life. He came up the union ranks and had left school at the age of 12 to be a stationary engine driver, and had never been to school since. But it was apparent that he was a very well read, very literate man, and I asked him, I said, "What about that?"

He said, "I read about a book a day and I have for many years." And boy, it sure showed. So we got along like gangbusters. In fact, an embarrassing incident, when we were up at the bar having a beer together and talking, and apparently there were a lot of people lined up, unbeknownst to me, to meet the two of us. An incident about that. I

---

* Barbers Point, at the southwest "corner" of the island of Oahu, Hawaii, was the site of a naval air station.
† Norman E. Kirk served as Prime Minister of New Zealand from 8 December 1972 until his death on 31 August 1974.

later came to know his opponent, the present Prime Minister, Mr. Muldoon, almost as well.* He was a very different sort of person. So you had opportunities like that.

All in all, the job was at least half political and diplomatic, after the Vietnam War was over. When the Vietnam War was on, almost total preoccupation with that.

Paul Stillwell: What about your relationships with the Filipinos?

Admiral Gayler: Well, I got along like gangbusters with Mr. Marcos and even with Imelda Marcos.† I recall that they, too, had visited China, and when they came back, they came through Hawaii and we had dinner together. It wasn't our dinner. It was somebody else's dinner, but we were there. Anyway, Imelda was my dinner partner, and she was full of Jiang Quing. She is a feminist anyway, Imelda is, and she was sure that Jiang Quing was going to succeed when Mao died.‡ It was obvious he was going. And she recalled that Jiang Quing, Mao's wife, had said after he dies, will have about ten days, meaning about have ten days to organize things. But of course, she deceived herself badly, but Imelda thought so too.

Ferdinand Marcos. He certainly has a bad reputation nowadays. Whether he has changed since the days I knew him or not, I thought he was very sensible, very useful, very literate. I liked him. Imelda was one of a kind, and you realized you were dealing with a personality, but she, too, could be delightful when she felt like it. I was also aware that she was a terrible tyrant and all of those things, but it's interesting.

I knew the Shah of Iran slightly, too, when he was a young guy. I was quite taken with him. He was not the person that he was reputed to be in other days. I seem to have hung out with a lot of dictators. [Laughter] I think Lord Acton's aphorism is absolutely correct: power corrupts, and absolute power corrupts absolutely. I think that's really

---

* Sir Robert David Muldoon was Prime Minister of New Zealand from 12 December 1975 to 26 July 1984.
† Imelda Marcos was the wife of Ferdinand Marcos, who served as President of the Philippine Islands from 30 December 1965 until 25 February 1986.
‡ Mao Tse-tung was head of the Communist Party in the People's Republic of China from the time the Communists seized power in 1949 until his death in 1976.

what happened to them all. Even Mussolini, as a young man, was a very attractive fellow.*

Paul Stillwell: You had that job after the U.S. downplayed its relationship with Taiwan and opened the door with China. Did that have an effect on your job?

Admiral Gayler: No. Of course, among other things, there was a formal abrogation of our responsibility for the military protection of Taiwan, which was a job, of course, essentially assigned to the Seventh Fleet. So it was an end to our military planning, but I was still a military adviser. And Ching-kuo and I met several times as well as the foreign minister, Henry Yu--maybe I have the name wrong, and others. I visited Taiwan several times, consulted with them on their defense.

I soon learned that the defense of Taiwan was not primarily a military matter but primarily a political matter, obviously for the Taiwan Government to protect themselves were ways that they did not wish to take for political reasons. I always advocated that they dig in their airplanes so they wouldn't be subject to surprise attack. That they get had themselves in modest over-water air attack capability and modest antisubmarine capability in order to be able to be keep submarines honest, submerged. Beyond that, that they did not need or had no use for a large standing army, but that was not politically palatable because, of course, a large standing army was one way they, A, maintained themselves in power and, B, kept young men off the streets so they wouldn't get in trouble.

I believe the Soviets keep a large standing army in some part for the same reason. They don't know what the hell to do with all those cadres of young men they have. And I think that's certainly true of many other countries. Not this country. But those rather obvious military precautions and the rather obvious inability of the mainland Chinese to mount any kind of invasion without years of obvious preparation, cut no ice. It was face from beginning to end, as it still is.

---

* Benito Mussolini organized the Fascists in Italy in the 1920s and ruled as dictator in that country until he was executed in 1945.

The other shoe I've been waiting to see drop in the case of Taiwan was the inevitable day when the Taiwanese will take over from mainland Chinese, from the nationalist Chinese. It can't be put off much longer; they're the majority now. They may have ideas of real independence, which the Chinese really never did. They regarded themselves as a part of China just as much as mainland Chinese did. But the Taiwanese may have ideas of independence, and then the fat will be in the fire.

I talked with a few of them, and it was difficult to arrange because of my official position in the government, but I managed to quietly see some of the Taiwan independence people. They made it perfectly clear they're going to prevail sooner or later. I don't know if they have any contingency plan, but they may or may not, I don't know. But it will be a very dicey situation, because the convenient formula with mainland China will no longer apply.

Paul Stillwell: What do you recall of your relationships with the Japanese?

Admiral Gayler: Well, I recall a lot about that very complex society. Much of the time with the Japanese was spent in negotiations about the degree of freedom which our support activities in Japan could be accorded. Generally speaking, the Japanese public was not sympathetic to our efforts in Vietnam. And in the inimitable Japanese way, they were able to figure out all sorts of reasons why they would like to help us but weren't able to. That was a very characteristic Japanese negotiating position. "We really understand why you have to move tanks out of the repair depot, but you know the bridges are too weak to carry them." They are unbelievably fertile in thinking about reasons why something that they don't want to do can't be done. On the other hand, when they want to do it, all of the purported technical and operational difficulties vanish like smoke.

Later on, I got a marvelous chuckle out of their doing the same things to the Russians when that guy defected with the MiG-25 and the Russians wanted it back, and I almost felt for the Russians.[*] I could just envision these Japanese driving him up the wall

---

[*] On 6 September 1976 Soviet pilot Viktor Belenko defected to the United States via Hakodote, Japan, in a MiG-25 "Foxbat" fighter jet.

with all the reasons why they couldn't get the airplane back. [Laughter] So there was a lot of that.

Japan is such a complex society. You're always gaijin there, no matter what you do. And it's very, very difficult for an outsider to understand what it is that's driving them. Even the right way to deal with them—too much openness tends to be regarded as crude, and you don't want to get devious with them because they can get a damn sight more devious than you can. So it's sort of complex.

I had seen Japan every ten years or so since the end of World War II. I was tremendously impressed by their achievements, although I thought you could see them making some of the same mistakes as we have made. I was deeply concerned with what I thought was the bad unbalance—and still do—of the Japanese armed forces. They're very Army-heavy, and it's perfectly clear that their military requirements have to do with the defense of their sea and air approaches. So trying to discuss that just got lots and lots of evasion and phony reasons like amphibious descents on Hokkaido. Shoot, their intelligence was as good as ours, and they knew damn well the Soviets didn't have any amphibious lift that amounted to anything. So it was sort of impossible.

And lots of arm-waving about requirements to shuttle tanks around or something or other. The fact remains that the dominant arm of the Japanese military is Army, and it has a very unfortunate political consequence to it. The Army is, of course, what is remembered so bitterly by the other Asian countries, and it is, in fact, the only offensive capability that the Japanese have. It was my thought then and is now that we should do everything we can—of course they're very sovereign, very independent and very powerful. But to the extent we can influence them, I don't think you can influence them toward taking on responsibility for their air defense and for their sea defense up to some distance. I myself picked 1,000 miles, which I'm amused to see it now become sort of a standard figure. I got it like, this because it's a nice round number and sort of like what the patrol planes of the day could do from base. And we give that lip service, but as in so many Japanese things, it doesn't quite happen that way.

Paul Stillwell: Did you feel a frustration in dealing with them?

Admiral Gayler: No, I think I was sort of prepared for it. I regarded it as kind of par for the course. I was annoyed with them that they wouldn't cooperate more carefully and more systematically and more effectively with the Koreans, with respect to things like air defense. Political animosities got in the way of that. But no, I don't think it got to me in that way. It's just about what I expected, to be truthful. I still think it's a poor show.

I'm not sure if the Japanese really understand what's involved in defense. We have a lot of responsibility for it with this nuclear umbrella stuff we sold them on, just as we've sold the Europeans. Whatever nuclear weapons are, they're not an umbrella. They may be a spear in your own hand with which you dissuade the other guy, but it's sure as hell not an umbrella and there is no protection of Japan, of course. They tend to get parochially alarmed about Russian missiles deployed in Asia. Hell, it doesn't matter very much where a missile starts from; it only matters where it lands. That's something that neither the Japanese nor the Europeans seem to be able to understand.

In fact, I got to have some good friendships among the Japanese. The man that I dealt with that I liked best of all was Ohira, who was the Foreign Minister.[*] When I first knew him, the first thing he said was to thank me for the presence of the Seventh Fleet." And later on he became Prime Minister. Ohira had been a wrestler in his youth, and he was pretty fond of telling me about his youth and his time as a wrestler. He was a still powerful man. And one time, he gave me what was really a signal honor because in a very unprecedented and un-Japanese way, they invited my wife Kay to attend a geisha party which they put on for us. As far as I know, that just isn't done. But she went, had a great time, sat next to Ohira, talked about his youth. It was a successful occasion. That was a very valuable thing.

I got to know Mr. Okawara, who is now the ambassador.[†] He was then in charge of the American desk of the Japanese Foreign Ministry, a very tall man, attractive. I got to know some of the Japanese military. I thought they were thoroughly professional people. And, of course, Japan is a fascinating civilization. We got the usual out of that, including—I guess this was earlier, at NSA, a couple of trips up to Hokkaido, which, of course, is a very different place, very different place from Honshu.

---

[*] Masayoshi Ohira was Japan's Minister of Foreign Affairs, 1962-64 and 1972-78. He later served as Japanese Prime Minister, 1978 to 1980.
[†] Yoshio Okawara was Japanese Ambassador to the United States from 1980 to 1985.

Paul Stillwell: What can you say about the value of a senior U.S. military commander establishing these personal relationships?

Admiral Gayler: I think it's very important and very useful, very important and very useful. It's not easy, and he has to be as sure-footed as he can possibly be, because it's entirely possible in a strange society to really screw it up, give offense where none is meant, and align yourself with what turns out to be the wrong crowd and all sorts of things. It's one of the very many reasons why it's quite important to have such an excellent intelligence center as CinCPac has. No, but I think that a senior American figure who can give full time to the Pacific and Asia is very necessary; these contacts are indeed very valuable.

Paul Stillwell: Is that why you say the job with CinCPac is the best one available?

Admiral Gayler: Oh, it's one of the reasons.

Paul Stillwell: What are other reasons?

Admiral Gayler: Well, I think you have a lot more independence out there than the other unified and specified commanders have, not independence in the sense of going your own way, but I don't think you get the micro-management that the other commanders get. It is the only command—let's see if I'm right about this; I believe I am—it's the only U.S. command in which you have the components under you full time, so that you don't have this divisive business of have got to go on to somebody else. So it's intrinsically a very, very interesting tour, and, of course, it's enormous.

Paul Stillwell: How much interaction did you have with the State Department in that role?

Admiral Gayler: Quite a bit. I was privileged to have an extremely good political adviser, Mort Abramowitz, who is now our negotiator for MBFR in Vienna, an extraordinarily able younger professional.* It had been the custom to negotiate, to assign to CinCPac a senior old veteran of the Foreign Service on his last tour. That had been going on since the year one. I didn't want that. Very fortuitously, Abramowitz had been sort of headhunter for Elliot Richardson during the brief time he was at Defense. And then all of a sudden, Richardson was yanked out of Defense to become Attorney General, and that left Abramowitz sort of hanging in midair like the cat in the cartoon, you know, he suddenly realizes he's in midair.†

And I had never known him, but from a friend I heard about this situation and how able he was, so I recall vividly that whole event, one evening in the Pentagon we talked for about two hours to try to get him to take this job. I think really the prospect of Hawaii was what sold him. He is a very able man. We got along like gangbusters. He knew where everything was at State and how it worked. He was very, very good. So I think we were able, perhaps, to do more along those lines than had been possible before.

Paul Stillwell: Did he provide briefings and coaching for you before you would visit the various foreign countries?

Admiral Gayler: No, it wasn't that so much as sort of consultative. We would sit around a table and talk about—I almost always took him along, anyway, but we'd sit around a table with intelligence people and other people and sometimes ask—Hawaii was a great place, anyway, from that standpoint, because there were lots and lots of Asian scholars and Asian contacts of one sort of another. Occasionally we'd ask civilians out, professors from the university and so forth, who were had a special expertise in a particular area. It wasn't so much a briefing the commander as just sort of a round table.

Paul Stillwell: What about your relationships with Australia during that period?

Admiral Gayler: Oh, they were great. I made several trips to Australia and enjoyed them thoroughly. I saw so many people I even learned to talk Australian. And I played hooky

---

* MBFR – Mutual and Balanced Force Reductions, a series of negotiations between NATO and Warsaw Pact countries in the years from 1973 to 1989.
† Elliot L. Richardson served as Secretary of Defense from 30 January 1973 to 24 May 1973.

a couple of times and went diving off the Great Barrier Reef, which was fun. I didn't hesitate to do a little sightseeing and a little recreation on these trips. I figured it was a long pull and I was there, again, it was good for my mental and physical health to do that sort of thing, and the opportunities were, of course, terrific, in all the Asian countries and Australia, New Zealand alike.

I remember one time, it was so funny, I used to jog every morning. I hated it, but I figured I needed to. Anyhow, I was jogging outside of Alice Springs, which is in the center of the Australian desert, down a dirt road. Alice is a funny town. The boundary stops; there just nothing. I mean nothing. I was jogging away in the early morning before the heat, and all of a sudden, three kangaroos came along running. I knew I was in Australia. I got up to northern Australia, which is, of course, not settled much, and down the Great Barrier Reef, Townsville, of course, Sydney and Melbourne and the rest. Very, very good. Very interesting. I saw a lot of the senior political figures. I even made kind of a friend out of Gough Whitlam, then Prime Minister, and who is almost professionally anti-American.* But I think he made an exception for me, at least on a social basis.

Paul Stillwell: Everyone, I think, needs and benefits from that kind of recreation, but were you ever self-conscious about taking it because of possible criticism in the media?

Admiral Gayler: I was a little careful. I didn't do really dumb things if I could help it. And I had a marvelous public affairs and political adviser by the name of Al Lynn, a colonel in the Air Force, a kind of character, terrific. He's the kind of fellow, if he thought you were saying something indiscreet, he is just perfectly capable of going over in front of the audience and unplugging the tape recorder. He's the man I sent up to Hanoi to negotiate with the Communists about the release of our prisoners, and he headed off several—they were going to try to give them little bags of toilet articles, necessities. As they left the prison camp, can you imagine after the years they'd been in there tortured and ill-treated, the obvious propaganda ploy to try to get the international press the impression that they were treating these people well. He was tough as hell when he had to be.

---

* Edward Gough Whitlam was Prime Minister of Australia from 5 December 1972 to 11 November 1975.

The only time he permitted me to make a real gaffe and stick my foot in my mouth was when he wasn't with me. And that was at a supposedly private briefing in New York, sort of a tour of the horizon of the Pacific theater, and I said quite casually in discussing all our countries there and the Philippines, I said, "Of course, Imelda Marcos wants to succeed her husband." One of the first things you learn is you don't say things in this country in the belief that they won't be noticed in Bangkok because the Thai have got people that are very interested in anything that's said about Bangkok. Same thing for the Iraqis and same thing for anybody. That's something the President hasn't learned yet. Anyway, I said that, and unbeknownst to me, there was a reporter from *Women's Wear Daily*, and he published that little crack, and, of course, it instantly got back to the Philippines and made a hell of a hurrah there, although, of course, it was public knowledge. Indignant denials from Imelda and everybody else. Didn't really create any problems. But he kept me out of trouble.

I had a very, very good staff, and they wouldn't let me do dumb things. I always used to tell my staff, and much more in connection with official things than personal things, the best thing they could possibly do for the admiral is to tell him when he was making a mistake. That's hard to get across, hard to believe, hard to understand that it's preceded—very, very difficult. Much, much easier to tell the old man what you think he wants to hear. But if you get a staff to tell you that, it's great. I had a marvelous Air Force colonel named Bruce Brown, who was very good at that, a hard-nosed character. He was perfectly capable of telling me, "You don't want to do that."

And I would say, "Come on, Bruce. Why the hell can't I go do thus and so?"

I did get into a considerable embarrassment once in Pakistan, because I had ridden horses all my life, but I never had a chance to play polo. And it turned out that in Hawaii, there's a sort of Mr. Polo there, a marvelous man by the name of Fred Daley, and he was kind enough to let me go out and sort of fiddle around playing polo and play scrub games. I never got to be very good at it, but I had a lot of fun. Polo, by the way, is the most underrated game in the world. I think it's the best game ever, just really wonderful.

Paul Stillwell: Why do you say that?

Admiral Gayler: Well, it has four things. In the first place, you have to learn the swings and the hitting, which is like learning six different golf strokes because you've got two strokes on the fore side and two strokes on the other side, one head stroke, and one over the tail. And that in itself is like learning six different kinds of golf. And then you've got the tactics of it, which are like hockey or basketball, at least, and they're as essential. And then you've got the horsemanship, which is an art in itself. The polo ponies don't play the game. A lot of people think they do. Well-trained polo ponies, but the people play the game. And finally, like a couple of other sports, like skiing, there's a little thrill of terror that keeps your interest up. [Laughter]

Anyway, as is usual when people in Pakistan wanted to know what the admiral liked to do, the staff said, "Well, he likes to play tennis and [with a little poetic license] he likes to play polo too." Of course, you know, Pakistan is the headquarters of polo. That is where polo originated, and horsemanship in general. And so I got word that I could go out and have some practice if I wanted to. I figured Pakistani horses, why not? I arranged for that.

I never went anywhere in that country without a motor bike escort, soldiers posted, stopping the odd camel from crossing a road, all that stuff. So I didn't think anything of it when we started off for the polo grounds. And then I began to notice that the cavalcade of cars was slowing down, and suddenly it occurred to me what the hell was happening. They were meeting an arrival time. I had been an aide myself. I could see what was going on, and then I began to have this sinking feeling. Sure enough, when we got there, it wasn't just a scrub game, a little pickup game. The head of the Polo Association was out there, who also was Chief of Staff of the Army, and the marquees, you know, the old British colonial style striped tents and rugs laid out and all that stuff, with a large audience, for a special polo, special match. Christ, I can't play polo for sour apples, and all these people are here. It's like saying, "Well, let's go out and play a little one-a-cat," and all of a sudden finding yourself in Yankee Stadium, on the mound.

At first, I was afraid that I was going to get killed, and then I was afraid I wasn't. [Laughter] To make things worse, I didn't have my glasses with me. Somehow or other, I had mislaid them, and I couldn't see enough to see the damn polo ball very far away, so I spent all afternoon riding people out of the plays, and I don't know what the Pakistanis thought of it, but it was a bad afternoon. We could get into that kind of trouble; people are always ambitious to put you in one of those situations.

Paul Stillwell: Kind of fun to watch, I suppose.

Admiral Gayler: I really sweated on that. It's one thing to get killed, but another to be disgraced. [Laughter] I guess that's enough for today, Paul.

Interview Number 9 with Admiral Noel A. M. Gayler, U.S. Navy (Retired)

Place: Admiral Gayler's office at the American Committee on East-West Accord, Washington, D.C.

Date: Friday, 6 July 1984

Paul Stillwell: Admiral, We were talking last time about your tour as Commander in Chief Pacific and sort of made a ring around the nations and around the Pacific and touched on most of them except Korea. Could you discuss your relationships with that country?

Admiral Gayler: Well, I think they were very close. In those days, of course, as we still are, we were jointly responsible with the South Korean Government for the defense of South Korea against a presumptive attack from the north. So I was very close indeed to not only our own people but the South Korean military commanders of the day, and as a matter of fact, personally with Park Chung Hee, whom I came to know quite well and who I thought talked to me with extraordinary frankness when we were by ourselves, considering he was talking to a foreign officer, even an ally.[*] And then in company with the generals on the scene, I walked all over their DMZ defenses and not only from briefing but from my own eyes got an appreciation of what the defense situation was, which I thought then and think now is really quite good.[†]

Paul Stillwell: What do you feel about the continuing stationing of U.S. troops and other forces in that area?

Admiral Gayler: I think it can and should continue until something happens in the nature of the North Korean regime. I don't think that Kim Il-sung is going to be effectively able

---

[*] Park Chung Hee was President of South Korea from 24 March 1962 until his assassination on 26 October 1979.
[†] DMZ—the demilitarized zone between North Korea and South Korea.

to pass control to his son.* He may be able to nominally, but history shows that that sort of arrangement doesn't usually last very long. If we were to reach a better understanding with the Soviet Union, I think that a lot of the steam would come out of that confrontation. As a matter of long-term geopolitics, I think it's absolutely inevitable that the two Koreas will be reunited some day in the very Korean-most countries in the same way that I think it's inevitable that the two Germanys will be reunited some day.† The trick is going to be able to do it peacefully without creating a war-generating situation somewhere along the line.

Paul Stillwell: Did you have a hand at all in the continuing Korean so-called peace negotiations that have gone on now for some 30 years?

Admiral Gayler: Only peripherally. Nominally I was an adviser, but it was so cut and dried, I remember once my neighbor out at Omaha, when I was in JSTPS was a—his name slips my mind right now, but he was the chief of staff at SAC, and he went out there as a chief negotiator and he outlasted the North Koreans in the famous time when they finally had to go to the bathroom, and he was congratulated on his bladder. I adopted that technique myself later on. But I didn't have anything very substantive to do with those negotiations.

Paul Stillwell: In your relationships with the fleet commanders, I wonder if there was any awkwardness when you came in as CinCPac, suddenly a four-star officer and the man reporting to you was Admiral Clarey, who had already been four-star.‡

Admiral Gayler: Chick and I were good friends personally. If there was any awkwardness, it certainly wasn't on my part, and I think not on his. The first thing he did

---

* Kim Il-sung was Prime Minister of North Korea from 1948 to 1972 and President from 1972 until his death in 1994. He was succeeded by his son Kim Jong-Il.
† On 9 November 1989 East Germany announced a relaxation of restrictions on travel and immigration to the west, essentially opening the country's borders. In October 1990 the German Democratic Republic—East Germany—was abolished, and in 1991 the Warsaw Pact was disbanded.
‡ Admiral Bernard A. Clarey, USN, served as Commander in Chief Pacific Fleet, 5 December 1970 to 30 September 1973.

was to make us, my wife and me, personally very welcome with personal attentions and a welcoming party.

I think that he had some concern as indeed did his successor, Mickey Weisner, even more so, that I would attempt to take over his proper functions as fleet commander.* You remember the history. It used to be a dual job, and then it was separated out, and it is natural to believe that the naval officer would attempt to run the Navy in more detail than he would attempt to run the Air Force or the Army, particularly since there was quite a senior Air Force commander out there and quite a senior Army commander.

I think both of them were sensitized to that concern, maybe having something to do with me personally, because I suppose I'm known as a take-charge guy. But I was quite careful to lean over backwards on that and to try to establish two things, one, the all-service or purple character of the joint job, which I thought then and think now very important. And the other, that my personal staff should reflect that, as I mentioned last time. I thought that very important to do.

To get back precisely to Chick Clarey, I think only one time, to my knowledge, we had a problem with racially motivated riots in Okinawa between Marines and Air Force personnel. Some black Marines beat up some white Air Forcers, a turf problem about who got to hang out in what bar with what Japanese women, a typical thing. I was very tough about that, and I think Clarey believed that I was infringing on his responsibility because I would not take soothing assurances, but that's about the only time, I think, to my knowledge. Maybe you better ask him. Possibly you already have.

Paul Stillwell: No. Did you ever feel any sense of frustration in not being able to do more in the traditional Navy officer role?

Admiral Gayler: Not because traditional Navy, but because the joint command system then and now is not as solid, in my view, as it should be. There are the joint command channels, but there are also too many traditional channels and too many channels of convenience and influence between the various service component commanders and their

---

* Admiral Maurice F. Weisner, USN, served as Commander in Chief Pacific Fleet, 30 September 1973 to 12 August 1976.

parent services. And it leads to a certain parallelism of control and a certain pulling and hauling that's not a good idea. CinCPac is a unique command anyway in that the only peacetime joint command that includes all the services. CinCLant, of course, does not, except during exercises or during war. At least the demarcation between them and CinCLant is not all that clear. And that made a difference. I thought the high rank of the component commanders out there was redundant. Interestingly enough, the Army command, the U.S. Army Pacific, on his own initiative, thought so and got his own four-star job downgraded to two stars. He was a very remarkable fellow.

Paul Stillwell: Who was that?

Admiral Gayler: Don Bennett.*

Paul Stillwell: What else do you recall of him?

Admiral Gayler: Don Bennett was a director of DIA when I was director of NSA, and we had institutional problems which we didn't think of, which we inherited, and which we never settled as to respective roles of those two operations and our roles with respect to CIA and the Director of Central Intelligence.† And that's a can of worms that we really don't have to get into, but the point of it all is that I had and have enormous respect for Don Bennett, and we got along very well.

Paul Stillwell: What can you say about your recollections of the two Navy fleet commanders, Admiral Clarey and Admiral Weisner?

Admiral Gayler: Well, Chick, as I say, was an old friend, much senior to me, and had been Vice Chief at a time when I was a relatively junior flag officer.‡ But I don't think that disturbed our relation. I wasn't with him awfully long. I think I heard a little

---

* General Donald V. Bennett, USA, was Commander in Chief U.S. Army Pacific from August 1973 until his retirement in August 1974. Commanding General Army Pacific is now a three-star officer.
† As a lieutenant general, Bennett as Director of the Defense Intelligence Agency from September 1969 to August 1972.
‡ Admiral Clarey served as Vice Chief of Naval Operations from 17 January 1968 to 30 October 1970.

feedback that he was surprised that I was operationally minded or so operationally minded because I'd just come from NSA. Of course, I'd been a carrier division commander, I'd been the skipper of the *Ranger*, I'd been a squadron commander for a number of tours. I don't know how the hell you could get more operationally minded than that, so I don't know quite how he came about that misconception.

Paul Stillwell: Did he become convinced that he was wrong?

Admiral Gayler: Oh, we never discussed it. This was feedback that came back from other people. I think he probably did, yes. Then, of course, I wanted immediately to go out to see the fleet, as well as Army components in Vietnam, which I did immediately, as I recall, within about three days of being installed. And I used to go down on a string from my helicopter to all ships, including the destroyers, and I think maybe I'm just guessing, I think maybe they thought that was a little unusual. But I wanted to have firsthand knowledge of what they were doing, and I found some very surprising things, too, as you always do.

Paul Stillwell: Such as?

Admiral Gayler: Well, I talked to General Tran, who was a commander up in I Corps, and by the way, I hear he's in California, made it out. But, anyway, he was a pretty good little fighter, I thought, that was his reputation. I asked him about the naval gunfire support, and he said, "Oh, wonderful, couldn't live without it." And then in a couple of days I was out on the destroyer firing, and as an old destroyer officer, I got sort of interested in how they were doing their fire control, because I couldn't figure out how targeting could be transmitted to the ship in timely fashion, and as a matter of fact, how using the fire control available on the ship ever hit anything. Well, I found out, to be entirely frank about it, that they weren't hitting anything. And so, like so many other things in that war, 5-inch fire control was a matter of show rather than actually doing something. They had no way of getting target information and no way of spotting, as a matter of fact, no way of fixing their position very accurately.

Paul Stillwell: Is that the kind of idea you follow up on with the fleet commander and find out what the problem is, how can it be corrected, or maybe if you don't want to do that kind of activity?

Admiral Gayler: I don't really recall what I did about that. I found some other instances in which I asked the cognizant commander to move out fast and remedy, but I don't remember that I did much about that. I think there were so many things wrong with the way we fought that war that this was minor. We had spotting airplanes up there, up there spotting at night, and I was fascinated by that because I spent a lot of time looking for targets in airplanes, how in the world they did this. This was an Air Force outfit. I went around and sat around in the ready room while they were briefing for the mission, and found out that they didn't. I said, "I don't really understand how you do this."

"Well," said their skipper, "we see the hits as they go off; they make little flashes that we can see."

I said, "Yeah, but how about the target?"

He looked a little baffled and said, "Well, that's true, Admiral, we can't see the target." And so he could hardly spot that way. They were presumably spotting for naval gunfire. There was so much make-believe in that war.

Paul Stillwell: You said that when you went to NSA you had a crash course at the outset to get yourself up to speed. Did you find that necessary to become familiar with Air Force and Army operations in the Pacific?

Admiral Gayler: I didn't feel that need too much. Air Force, of course, isn't that all different from the naval air service, and I'd spent so many years in particularly the tactical end, which is essentially identical, except for the fact that we did it better. [Laughter]

Paul Stillwell: Could you elaborate on that, please?

Admiral Gayler: Oh, you know. I've been doing Dagwood sandwiches with Army Air Corps fighter pilots since two years before Pearl Harbor. We've been going around and around. And that's a rather parochial statement, but it's a fact. You know, the Navy's been in the forefront of technical development in aircraft, new weapons, and everything else, including the best airplane the Air Force ever had, the F-4.

Paul Stillwell: The great rivalry between the Navy and the Air Force that was so evident in the late '40s. Had that pretty well cooled off by the time you got to Hawaii?

Admiral Gayler: Some, not entirely. The excellent cooperation between Seventh Air Force and Seventh Fleet, I think, did a lot to cool it off, and some very sensible ground rules, making areas of each outfit responsible for a particular area rather than trying to coordinate on ways which complicate it. I think we did very well together. We gained a lot of mutual respect. The rivalry was always 50% like an athletic rivalry, anyway, between the fighter pilots, I think.

Paul Stillwell: On an institutional level, there were some serious hostilities.

Admiral Gayler: That's right, but that tended to be a lot more in Washington than out in the field, the squadrons, and whatnot. Yes, the fights for money and influence around here are of a different character. By the way, I think a strong Secretary of Defense can and should put an end to that stuff.

Paul Stillwell: You never did say anything specific about Admiral Weisner. What memories do you have of working with him?

Admiral Gayler: Well, Mickey was a very old friend. Before he came out, we had served together when he was operations officer for Admiral Francis Foley.* They rode the *Ranger*, but I had known him three years before that. Frankly, I think Mickey was a

---

* Rear Admiral Francis D. Foley, USN, served as Commander Carrier Division One from February 1960 to March 1961. See his Naval Institute oral history.

little suspicious of me, felt very strongly his prerogatives as fleet commander and had been briefed by somebody in Washington to look out for me; I would try to take over his fleet from him. And I worked very hard to dispel that, and toward the end, I think, we were working together pretty well. It never got to any important level, just sort of touchy.

Paul Stillwell: Did you have a hand in getting him selected to be CinCPac?

Admiral Gayler: No.

Paul Stillwell: That says a lot.

Admiral Gayler: No, I would not have opposed it. I didn't have a hand in getting anybody selected.

Paul Stillwell: Were you consulted?

Admiral Gayler: I take that back. I had a hand in getting my wonderful Air Force chief of staff, Bill Moore, selected to be Commander Military Airlift Command, which I was very proud of.[*] He was a marvelous officer, long since retired, of course. And I say I had a hand; I certainly lobbied with the Air Force. See, one of the major problems in those joint commands is that no sooner does an officer of any service get in them than he's in trouble with his own service almost automatically, because they expect him, when they say jump, to say, "How high?" And if he takes his job seriously, of course, he's going to take the all-service point of view. So it always happens. And in the case of more junior officers, it's very unfair because they have to face selection boards in their own service. Of course, at three- or four-star level, it doesn't make a hell of a lot of difference.

---

[*] General William G. Moore Jr., USAF, served as Commander in Chief Military Airlift Command from 1977 until his retirement in 1979.

Paul Stillwell: It's certainly unfair because people have to be assigned to those jobs.

Admiral Gayler: Well, that's right, and in addition, they not only have to be assigned, but since in the unified command business they are the senior operators, they not only have to be assigned, but they ought to be good people. And in fact, I think that's why so many of them do survive the fact that they do get in trouble with their own services is because they tend to be good people too.

Paul Stillwell: Were you consulted about who your successor would be?

Admiral Gayler: No. No. I did have a talk with the new Secretary of Defense, Don Rumsfeld, about, oh, placement of senior people in general and about the intelligence community and how it ran, and a lot of things like that, but he quite pointedly omitted any discussion of who my successor was going to be.[*]

Paul Stillwell: What are your recollections of Secretary Rumsfeld? How much dealing did you have with him?

Admiral Gayler: Not that much. He wasn't in there very long, but I thought him very businesslike and very intelligent, pretty political, as you might expect from his background, but political in a good sense.[†]

Paul Stillwell: Were there any changes that manifested themselves at your level when Jerry Ford took over as President from Richard Nixon?[‡]

Admiral Gayler: Sort of a sigh of relief. Nobody likes to have a commander in chief in disgrace; that isn't helpful. Ford was well liked. He came through Pearl Harbor not too long after he was President. Kay and I took care of him socially and that sort of thing. I liked him immensely. Just a feeling that now things would settle down.

---

[*] Donald H. Rumsfeld served as Secretary of Defense from 20 November 1975 to 20 January 1977.
[†] Rumsfeld had been a member of the House of Representatives.
[‡] Gerald R. Ford served as President of the United States from 9 August 1974 to 20 January 1977.

Paul Stillwell: Were you involved at all in the Vladivostok discussions on nuclear weapons?*

Admiral Gayler: No, never consulted.

Paul Stillwell: Do you think that a person in that position should be?

Admiral Gayler: Oh, yes. Well, yes. I think that in general the senior military people ought to be more consulted in more views on these major things than they are, not to exclude either the professorial types or the political types, but a more balanced appraisal of what the policy should be.

Paul Stillwell: You have characterized your close relationship and long-standing with Admiral Zumwalt. How would you characterize your relationship with Admiral Holloway after he became Chief of Naval Operations?†

Admiral Gayler: Well, friendly, but I had no real occasion to be much closer. Again, he was not in the joint command chain. I was very much concerned then, and still am, of this curious paradox that while the operational commanders are responsible for fighting, they had then no formal input at all to the statement of weapons requirements or any other requirements.‡ They have some slight formal input now. I used to try to input informally as to what we needed. A lot of resentment from the Navy, not very much from the Air Force [unclear]. I think the absurdities like inability to get together on a heavy-lift helicopter, which clearly all services needed, but the problem was that no one of them wanted to foot the bill. I see by the papers we're still having that problem.

---

* As part of ongoing Strategic Arms Limitation Talks (SALT), U.S. President Gerald Ford and Soviet leader Leonid Brezhnev in 1974 reached in informal accord known as the Vladivostok Agreement to limit the numbers of bombers and other nuclear weapons launchers.
† Admiral James L. Holloway III, USN, served as Chief of Naval Operations from 29 June 1974 to 1 July 1978.
‡ The Goldwater-Nichols Act of 1986 gave the unified commanders in chief a much larger role in procurement decisions than they had had previously.

Paul Stillwell: Were there any changes at your level when Admiral Moorer was relieved as chairman by General Brown?*

Admiral Gayler: No. I had known George Brown before very cordially. It was a sort of personal change. I'd always regarded Admiral Moorer as a boss, a senior. He was considerably senior to me. He was the one who called me up at SAC headquarters and said, "Get your tail back to Washington. I want you to compete to be director of NSA." So I always had that sort of relationship with him. And as you probably remember, the very important Linebacker II operation took place in December, and I was installed on the first of September, so I was not as long in the job there as somebody might have thought I should be.† And I don't think Moorer had that much confidence, so he came on out to the headquarters to make sure that things were going right. I didn't like that very much. I thought that was a little unnecessary, but I could understand it. I was not his choice for the job anyway. I had enormous respect for him as an operator, and I always regarded him as boss.

George Brown, quite different. We were casual friends of some years, and he was more a colleague, and he always treated me that way. As a matter of fact, he was considerably junior to me before he got the job.

Paul Stillwell: When I talked to Admiral Hyland, he expressed some frustration over how very little say he had in what would be done about bombing in Vietnam.‡ Did you feel that same sense of helplessness?

Admiral Gayler: Well, it was pretty late in the war, you remember, and before I had a chance to really get hung up on that, although I had been hung up on it precariously through watching the operation very carefully from NSA—what I'm trying to articulate is that the policy had changed. By December we were going up to Haiphong and shutting

---

* General George S. Brown, USAF, served as Chairman of the Joint Chiefs of Staff from 1 July 1974 to 20 June 1978.
† Linebacker II, a heavy aerial bombing campaign directed against North Vietnam in late 1972. More than previous bombing campaigns, this one emphasized the use of Air Force B-52 rather than tactical aircraft.
‡ Admiral John J. Hyland, USN, served as Commander in Chief Pacific Fleet from 30 November 1967 to 5 December 1970. His oral history is in the Naval Institute collection.

them down, and so I was not dissatisfied with that at all. I was very much for it and in on it.

Paul Stillwell: Well, was it still a case, though, where Washington was having a very large say in the target selection?

Admiral Gayler: Not in that particular operation. Linebacker, we had a well-oiled targeting operation. The Washington interference that bothered me came later in Cambodia when President Nixon rather arbitrarily ordered more B-52s out there. Then he sent Al Haig out on a fact-finding mission.* I talked to Haig for quite a while, and pointed out that we could only sensibly target about five targets a day for our Arc Light strikes because of the difficulties of getting reliable, accurate intelligence on the targets.† Haig's response was that the President wanted more volume. That was not satisfactory to me, and I wasn't ready to bomb until we had something we were pretty sure about. We sort of left that unresolved, as people do in the political world.

    I heard through a channel, which I will not put on tape, afterwards that Haig had represented me to Nixon as being weak. But it wasn't weakness; it was just a sense that I wasn't going to approve any targets that weren't solid. President Nixon had this idea that somehow or other B-52 bombing would scare the daylights out of them or do something, and it did a lot, all right, but you had to be damn sure where it went.

Paul Stillwell: Did you resent that General Haig would be involved and that sort of an anomaly that a White House guy or Kissinger guy would be a military officer and would thus have greater stature than his rank would suggest?

Admiral Gayler: Oh, no. That kind of stuff didn't bother me. It was perfectly natural the guys, the senior staff out there, sent him out to take a look around. The only thing I resented was the report he made. [Laughter]

---

* General Alexander M. Haig Jr., USA, served from 1970 to 1973 as Deputy Assistant to the President for National Security Affairs.
† Arc Light was the code name for the use of Air Force B-52 bombing missions to support ground tactical operations; to interdict enemy supply lines in Vietnam, Laos, and Cambodia; and, later, to strike targets in North Vietnam.

Paul Stillwell: How much did you get to put your oar in the relationship between Washington and the MACV commander?[*]

Admiral Gayler: Not directly. The command situation was, together with many other things in the Vietnam War, screwed up beyond recognition. As you know, Johnson in particular, and Nixon to a certain extent, intervened personally. So there was that channel, and then the Secretary of Defense couldn't refrain from calling up Westmoreland or Abrams, more or less sending directives through him.[†] Admiral Moorer was quite scrupulous about using the joint command channel, but even there he would go directly as well as cutting in CinCPac. And then the component commanders had their unacknowledged but very real links back to their headquarters. It was not a good setup.

Paul Stillwell: How much control did you have over the ground war as CinCPac?

Admiral Gayler: Very little. I used to talk it over with Abrams once a day. He was very good. He was quite scrupulous about it, but I had more sense than to intervene in that anyway.

Paul Stillwell: Did you respect his judgment as the commander there?

Admiral Gayler: Yes, I thought he was first-class. I didn't know Westmoreland that well.

Paul Stillwell: No, he had pretty well been gone as far as . . .

---

[*] ComUSMACV—Commander U.S. Military Assistance Command Vietnam.
[†] General William C. Westmoreland, USA, served as Commander U.S. Military Assistance Command Vietnam from 1964 to 1968. General Creighton W. Abrams, Jr., USA, served as Commander U.S. Military Assistance Command Vietnam from 1968 to 1972.

Admiral Gayler: I know, but he came back to NSA a couple of times when I was there, each time amazed at the information that was available that he had never heard of. I kept saying, "Well, General, it goes out to your headquarters," and we left it at that.

Paul Stillwell: Well, the big squabble with CBS is over what he was sending to Washington, so you're saying there was confusion about what was going from Washington to him.* Do you think it was getting misrouted somewhere? Well, I guess it had to be.

Admiral Gayler: No. I don't know. I can only speculate. What a commander knows about his own headquarters is a task that we all handle in our own way and with our own style. I was always very, very much interested in intelligence, where it came from, what the source was, and how good it was. I didn't just go to briefings and listen; I questioned. Once in a while I would show up in the early morning when the briefers were preparing the brief to see how it was put together and what was briefed and what was omitted, because information comes in through a fire hose, and you can't swallow that all. There's an awful lot of judgment involved there. It only takes a commander to be disinterested a couple of times before he gets cut off.

Paul Stillwell: How do you communicate to people that your antennas are up and you want to hear?

Admiral Gayler: Presence, interest, pertinent questions, demand for performance, usual things.

---

* In September 1982 General William C. Westmoreland, USA (Ret.), filed a $120 million libel suit against the CBS network in response to a program telecast in January of that year. Titled "The Uncounted Enemy: A Vietnam Deception," the documentary implied that General Westmoreland had participated in a conspiracy to underestimate enemy troop strength in Vietnam and thus to deceive the American public. In February 1985 General Westmoreland dropped his suit as part of an out-of-court settlement in which the network paid him no money. Afterward both sides claimed victory.

Paul Stillwell: On the next question, I can guess your answer, but I will ask anyway. How much involvement did you have in the *Hughes Glomar Explorer* operation with regard to the Soviet submarine?*

Admiral Gayler: Quite a bit.

Paul Stillwell: Can you say any more on that subject?

Admiral Gayler: No. [Laughter]

Paul Stillwell: My guess was correct. Anything else on the CinCPac tour that is worthy of including in this record?

Admiral Gayler: Well, let's see. Just an opinion. I think it's quite the best job in the armed services, bar none. But I also think that, as I said a few moments ago, we've got to do quite a lot to reinforce the unified command system to be better at joint operations, to fix responsibility more clearly for operations, to sort out the channels of command, to make intelligence more accessible and more valid. It's a difficult problem of relative role of the ambassador and the area commander for a job like that. With some ambassadors it was a piece of cake, like Whitehead. With others it was extremely difficult, like Graham Martin. We have not achieved the coherence that we should have in operations, in my judgment.

One more thing about the planning. The planning was, I thought, the least satisfactory of all the responsibilities that CinCPac had, and that's not a reflection on any of the officers who were there, who were first-class without exception, but the system is not good. The system really consists of having a whole library or stacks of war plans carefully worked out in advance, almost all of which are impractical from a logistic

---

* The *Glomar Explorer*, a ship with a large concealed opening in the bottom, was built for operation by the Central Intelligence Agency for the purpose of recovering a Soviet submarine. The Golf-class diesel-powered ballistic missile submarine sank 750 miles northwest of Oahu, Hawaii, in 1968. In August 1974 CIA technicians raised the submarine about halfway to the surface from a depth of three miles. The submarine then broke apart and fell back to the ocean floor. Word of the operation became public in February and March 1975 as a result of news media reports. The cover story for the *Glomar Explorer* was that she was recovering manganese nodules from the seabed.

standpoint or incomprehensible from a political standpoint, and what's needed—and none of which, of course, ever fits the actual situation.

So if you actually are going to do something, it is always an impromptu plan, usually on short notice and usually without enough information. So the planning process, I think, needs fundamental reform, and instead of having a library of plans with imagined contingencies, we should instead have a very good database accessible to very experienced planners who, by drilling and drilling and drilling, just like we do everything else, are able to put together and formulate plans for a specific situation on short notice.

I proposed that to the JCS a year or so before I left, as I recall, and got essentially zero support, but I'm sure that's the right way to do it. I'm talking about operational planning.

Paul Stillwell: And example that might be used in that case is the recovery of the crew of the *Mayaguez*.[*] Can you comment on that?

Admiral Gayler: Yes, I sure can. It's perceived in the after light as having been a fiasco because we lost so many people, and perhaps that's right, but it was a perfect example of impromptu planning. Nobody foresaw the container vessel's going to get hijacked out there. And the planning was not only impromptu, but very much hampered by the fact that we didn't have a great deal of information about Koh Tang Island or who the hell these people were or what they were likely to be armed with or any of those things. And we made some bad judgments, for which I certainly bear some of the responsibility. The worst judgment was the final assault on the beach there by helicopter. We didn't think there was anything much there in the way of firepower, and it turned out there was quite a lot. The misconception as to where the people were, I'm not going to go into detail on, but essentially we knew where the bad guys intended to take them, but they changed their minds. Just as simple as that.

---

[*] On 12 May 1975 a gunboat of the Cambodian Communist regime, the Khmer Rouge, fired upon and seized the American containership *Mayaguez* while she was en route from Hong Kong to Sattahip, Thailand. On 15 May U.S. military forces executed a crew rescue operation directed at Koh Tang Island, 34 miles off the Cambodian mainland. In the meantime, the Cambodians had released the *Mayaguez* crew and left the ship herself unguarded. In the rescue attack on Koh Tang, a number of U.S. servicemen were killed or wounded. For details, see *U.S. Naval Institute Proceedings*, November 1976, pages 93-111.

Paul Stillwell: Which, again, points out the value of intelligence.

Admiral Gayler: Yes, yes.

Paul Stillwell: Would there have been a better way of handling a situation like that?

Admiral Gayler: More time. The President personally insisted on doing it immediately. Another day could have probably enabled us to take a good second thought—look at where the assault point was going to be, very likely given us better information on what the opposition was going to be, quite possibly tipped us that our people weren't there anyway, and put the carrier a bit closer.

In an operational sense, it was a hell of a good operation. We got the Air Force choppers out aboard ship, operated them fine, but they were up against that—well, the two big things were the unexpected resistance, which as soon as you say unexpected, of course, you indict your planning, so it shouldn't be unexpected. But the sort of feverish hurry. I never could quite understand why another day made that much difference, and that led to some of the problem.

Paul Stillwell: As you came to the end of your tour in Hawaii, did you feel any sense of regret that it was all ending after all these years?

Admiral Gayler: Oh, you better believe it. I felt that at the age of 62, I was at the absolute height of my powers, if you will, that I knew the area and the people and the assets extremely well, and that it was a mistake to replace me, but I understood the system when I signed up at the age of 16, so—

Paul Stillwell: For the benefit of those who can't see you as you say that, I should say that you winked as you made that remark. [Laughter] Admiral Moorer talked about some of the withdrawal symptoms he felt when he retired, that getting back to the real world, he suddenly had to do things for himself that he hadn't for years, such as shopping, and he was shocked by the price of things. What was your own withdrawal like?

Admiral Gayler: Well, the withdrawal from the kind of support that you have as CinCPac, which is very considerable. You have an able staff, you have a secretary, you have a driver, you have aides that are good, transportation, all of that. That I was prepared for; I knew that was going to happen, and as a matter of fact, it wasn't unprecedented. After all, I'd gone from being skipper of the *Ranger* to second-string dogcatcher in the Pentagon. That's a pretty good comedown. And I'd gone from flag officer at sea to flag officer in the Pentagon, and that's a pretty good comedown too. So I was not unused to that kind of stuff, and I was prepared for it. No, I think the thing that bothered me most, and still does, is being an adviser instead of line responsibility. That's what I miss more than anything else—responsibility for what's done, rather than on the outside jumping up and down and saying, "Hey, you shouldn't do this," or, "You should do this." The role of adviser just doesn't suit me very well. But it's the only role available until you get a job.

Paul Stillwell: Did you have opportunities at that point for jobs in industry, let's say, that had line responsibilities?

Admiral Gayler: I tried out for head of two corporations, rather seriously considered. For reasons of their own, good or bad, they didn't take me. Other than that, no. I didn't get an awful lot of bids saying, "You've simply got to come run our railroad," or anything like that. A lot of people wanted me to help out technically, some of them, I think, with some idea of what influence I might have. You can sort of smell those coming. I didn't do anything with them. And, of course, I had some very interesting associations for a long time with RAND, with Stanford Research, with other sort of think-tank operations, academics, which was very congenial to me. I really wanted to get closer to the academic field and the technical field for many years. A combination of technology and foreign policy is very congenial to me. But the role of outsider when decisions are being made—I still have withdrawal pangs on that.

Paul Stillwell: How did you decide which direction to go, then, finally, after you did retire?

Admiral Gayler: I had in mind that I would occupy myself half my time with things of the mind, of intellect, reading and writing, and about half the time living the outdoor life that I love in Colorado, winter and summer. But it didn't work out.

It turns out that the stimulus of other people interested in the same sorts of things is very important. And then I became increasingly concerned with the dangers of nuclear war, and I felt that because of my experience, which is not unique, I suppose, but maybe more comprehensive than almost anybody else's with the operational aspects of nuclear weapons—I'm not a nuclear physicist, although I do understand something about it, that I had both the capability and perhaps the duty to speak out on the folly of the nuclear war planning that we were doing and the Soviets, and to try to do something about that.

I looked around places to do it, and got nowhere with the administration, so I signed up with the non-profit community, first with the Arms Control Association and then for this outfit, this outfit because they know a hell of a lot about Russia, and they know a hell of a lot about—they've got some very high-powered people, wise people working with and advising us, and because they're activists.[*] They want to do something about it, whereas too many of the outfits just sit back and want to describe it and wring their hands. So it's a very satisfying thing to do, except it's kind of frustrating, too, because so many of the policymakers are deaf.

Paul Stillwell: How much success have you had?

Admiral Gayler: Modest. I don't know how much credit to take, but certainly this administration has moved some from their intransigent nuclear weapons stance. I've

---

[*] "This outfit" refers to the American Committee on East-West Accord, Washington, D.C.

been campaigning for Gary Hart, because I figured he knew more about it than the other candidates.*

Paul Stillwell: There again, that's a frustrating operation at this point.

Admiral Gayler: Yes, yes. Crazy system. You've got a plurality of Democratic votes, but that doesn't make him a candidate.

Paul Stillwell: Have you followed his activities on the military reform movement?

Admiral Gayler: Yes, and I guess I'm in about 80% agreement with the reforms. As almost all civilians, I think almost all civilians, without exception, he doesn't quite understand some of the nuances of the military, but he's pretty good, and he devotes a lot of time and study to it. I would be far more confident in having security matters in his hand than any other senior that I know, senior civilian politician.

Paul Stillwell: For the benefit of this record, could you articulate your position and goals and hopes on nuclear weapons?

Admiral Gayler: Yes, I can certainly do that. I do it all the time.

Basically, I believe that nuclear weapons have no sensible military use, neither the strategic weapons nor the so-called tactical weapons, and no matter what theater you look at, basically because any attempted use inevitably would recoil disastrously on the user, because the danger of escalation of any crossing the nuclear firebreak is extremely high and the consequences of such an escalation are just totally devastating to this country, to our Allies, to civilization in general, and the fact that they would also be totally devastating to Russia doesn't compensate.

Within that, I think that the ideas that we have about the use of tactical nuclear weapons at sea are absolutely insane. The idea of using nuclear depth charges against

---

* Senator Gary Hart, a Democrat from Colorado, was for a time running for President in 1984, but his candidacy was eventually derailed when reporters observed him with Donna Rice, a woman who was not his wife.

submarines in order to get some differential advantage, when by doing so we would open up nuclear war at sea, and we have the big targets, we have the big carriers. One nuclear weapon is one ship, no matter how big and tough it is. Entirely apart from the danger of escalation, entirely apart from the difficulties of getting presidential release, the advantages to the Soviets compared to the advantages to us are overwhelming at sea.

Then I can't think of anything sillier than nuclear antiaircraft weapons, observing that there are friendly fighters in the air with them. I've been shot at by my own carrier in the landing circle. I have no confidence at all in identification, friend or foe. And in addition, of course, the character of the thing essentially blinds anybody that's looking, and if you're up there as a fighter pilot, you're looking all the time, and who the hell wants to be up there in a high-performance airplane and not able to see? So I'm puzzled. I really am genuinely puzzled by the willingness of people to entertain the notion of initiating a tactical nuclear war at sea, even if—and it's a very shaky if—you could guarantee that it wouldn't precipitate a general nuclear war.

Then for the other theater, for Europe, it's clearly not to our advantage to start a nuclear war there. The first consequences would be about one million friendlies killed, mostly women and children, fractionate the alliance. The danger of escalation would be extremely high. Russians don't recognize limited nuclear war. And even if you had a miracle and neither one of these things happened, the relative advantage would still go in the Warsaw Pact because we are far more critically dependent on a much smaller number of important targets, harbors, airfields, depots than the Russians are. So it doesn't make any sense. It's an empty and dangerous bluff.

The other ideas—well, it's expressed in this year's Air Force budget requirements, so-called, for X, prompt hard target kill capability. Well, that is the old impossible idea that the Air Force has, that they had when I was out in JSTPS, which is that somehow or other they can hit Soviet missiles in their silos and Soviet command centers and thus disarm them without getting it back. Well, the obvious thing to do is what the Russians have already declared they will do, and that is to fire out on warning. But there's an even worse alternative, and that is that if we talk like that enough, we may convince them that that is indeed what we have in mind, and then some day when there's a crisis and they're really uptight, they're liable to shoot on the suspicion that we're getting ready to shoot. So I think it's tremendously dangerous and tremendously destabilizing.

And when you look at the aggregate numbers, which are now about 48,000 nuclear weapons between us, it just looks like the height of absurdity. And that's what I think it is, and that's why I'm opposed to further development or deployment or testing of nuclear weapons on a mutual basis with the Soviets, and why I think we should make deep and massive cuts. The way to get rid of nuclear weapons is to get rid of nuclear weapons, and we could quite readily, under Soviet-American supervision, convert nuclear weapons into electric power plant material in a way which would be extremely difficult to reverse, and thus, as a process, begin to get rid of the inordinate numbers of these weapons, and at the same time, improve the political relationship between us, and therefore improve the security of both of us. So that's what I am advocating.

Paul Stillwell: How have you answered the critics who say that the Soviets can't be trusted?

Admiral Gayler: That we don't have to trust them, that we can make agreements with them which we can adequately cover with our own intelligence. I think everybody knows that we get pretty good photographs from satellites. Not everybody outside of the intelligence community knows that that's just the tip of the iceberg, that we know what goes on in the Soviet Union, and many other things that we don't talk about for a damn good reason, because if we did talk about them, we'd lose them. Taken together, and I've testified to Congress to this effect, taken together, I am sure that we have the capability to find any violation of a treaty relating to weapons development, testing, or deployment significant enough to make a difference, remembering that—and I learned this from my targeting experience—that the outcome of a nuclear exchange between the Soviet Union and ourselves is very insensitive to the numbers of weapons.

It makes a great difference whether you target cities or not. It makes a lot of difference whether you fuze on the ground to create fallout. It even makes a difference which way the wind is blowing carrying the fallout. But when you do the necessary calculation of how many millions of people get killed, Russian or American, it turns out that a thousand missiles, more or less, on either side, doesn't make any difference. It's down in the noise. And that's really a very reassuring thought because what it says is that if they're going to squirrel away something, they're going to have to squirrel away one hell of a lot, and we'll find it. So I'm not uptight about that at all. I think we have to carefully craft agreements so that they are verifiable to the degree that they need to be.

The real problem that people get mixed up with is the question of compliance, having found what you think is a violation, what the hell do you do about it? And that, of course, is basically a political question, and in my judgment, the thing to do about it is to do what we have done in the past, and that is to discuss it on a private basis with the Soviets and get them to abate what they're doing, which they do, and they've made some accusations against us, some of which are well-founded, and we have abated doing that.

So when you get agreements with the Soviets which are concrete and specific, which say, "You do this and we'll do that," with time limits and numbers, then the record has been very good. It's when you get into vague things like the second basket of Helsinki human rights and spirit of Camp David and that kind of stuff, the Soviets don't go for that. It doesn't mean anything. We have no choice but to deal with them. Hell, we cannot unilaterally make ourselves secure, and that is the military truth of the day. We have got to deal with them. They're not going to go away, and we can't have security without dealing with them.

Paul Stillwell: Did you have these kinds of thoughts on the non-utility of nuclear weapons when you were on active duty?

Admiral Gayler: Sure. Sure did. I always had a problem because the nuclear business has always been in the hands of the special cadre in staffs, and still is. People stayed with it for years, and it started out because of the extremely high, necessarily high classification, the Q clearances surrounding nuclear weapons. But it's been perpetuated, and the result is that in all the staffs, including the joint staff and elsewhere, generally speaking, nuclear matters are instantly followed over to these people with the right clearances. And so they have not had, at least until recent years—I'm not entirely up to speed now—have not had the sort of overall consideration that they should. I always said

I didn't need any nuclear weapons out in the Pacific, and instantly my guys would come in and say, "This isn't going to be palatable, Admiral." At which point we'd argue for a while and I'd settle for half. That's usually what I—but it's an absurdity. What the hell would you do with nuclear weapons in Asia?

Paul Stillwell: Well, you probably thought about what you would do if ordered to use nuclear weapons. What were those thoughts?

Admiral Gayler: Well, as you probably know, CinCPac is one of the so-called executing commanders in the SIOP. If the SIOP were executed, I would execute it. I can't imagine, so I didn't think very much about the contingency that a commander would be directed to use tactical nuclear weapons, particularly if he said he didn't need them. So I didn't give that one much thought. But in Asia, there's another additional and special problem with any use of nuclear weapons against any Asian people under any circumstances, and that is that in light of history, it would be regarded as a racist act and polarize all of Asia against us.

But you know, Paul, I've thought about nuclear weapons for many, many years, and have worked these trains of thought all the way down to the bottom. And I've never been able to find a use as opposed to a possession, a use of nuclear weapons that didn't end in a logical absurdity. And I really don't understand the thrust. A lot of this is "monkey see, monkey do" between us and the Soviets. Not the least problem from the military standpoint is overweening attention on nuclear weapons is the diversion of command of authority, command attention as well as resources, to things which we can never use sensibly. And we do even now--even at these high budget levels, we neglect some very important things of real military consequence while we screw around with MXes and all that junk.[*] It's a bad scene. I think it's coming along. We're a lot less belligerent in public statements, at least, than we used to be. A long way to go. It hasn't found its expression in the budget requests yet.

---

[*] The Air Force's MX Peacekeeper is a four-stage intercontinental ballistic missile designed to deliver ten re-entry vehicles at ranges of about 6,000 miles. Peacekeeper made its first flight in 1983 and achieved initial operational capability in 1986 when the first ten went on alert. Plans in the late 1970s called for a mobile basing system, but eventually the first Peacekeepers were put into converted Minuteman silos.

Paul Stillwell: You mentioned some fellow activists that are working with you on this cause. What can you say about them?

Admiral Gayler: Well, first, I should tell you that I have bad vibes about activists and causes. I like to think of myself as a senior and experienced military fellow who's making his judgment available. I don't march around with signs; I don't hang out with kooks. I believe very firmly in a strong America, including a very strong military component. I think I know what that is. I think it's the ability to keep the seas and air open and link together the oceanic alliance of ours. I think it has to do with being able to hold the ground at places of our choosing like Europe, Korea, other places. I think it has to do with the ability to project and sustain power at very great distances if necessary. I think nowadays it has to do, together with the civil authority, in dealing with international terrorism. Those are real military requirements, not a goddamn one of them that any nuclear weapon won't handle or has anything to do with.

I don't share the view that the Soviets are out to conquer the world by military force. I don't think even Lenin had that view. What he did was to predict that we would fall of our own contradictions. That's quite different. And Leninism is pretty dead in the Soviet Union anyway; it's mostly lip service. They're behaving like great powers have always behaved. What we need to be with them is pragmatic, not ideological, a very, very wide difference in those two views. What you need as a commander or as an intelligence officer to understand what you're dealing with. Our understanding of the Soviet Union is not very good, and that's a very dangerous situation to be in. By the way, their understanding of ours is probably even worse.

Paul Stillwell: What kind of vibes do you get from your fellow retired naval professionals about your current stance?

Admiral Gayler: Oh, support, of the people who write to me. Nobody who writes to me has done other than support. I get quite a few letters from old fighter jocks, both Air Force and Navy, who say, "Right on." I spoke at the Air War College the other day and laid it all out, more detail than this. I thought I got remarkably little hostile criticism. I don't think they were being polite. On the other hand, I'm well aware that a lot of the retired flags around town are arrayed in the other camp, led by Tom Moorer. I might say quite candidly that I'm very sorry my relationship with Tom has deteriorated over politics, because I have great respect for his abilities. But I think he's dead wrong about the Soviets, about nuclear weapons, the situation.

Paul Stillwell: Well, a common reaction among retired naval professionals is to look with disfavor upon the activities of Admiral La Rocque.[*] Do you get that kind of reaction at all?

Admiral Gayler: No, I don't think I do. I have, as you may or may not know, no association whatever with La Rocque, and that goes back a long way in history, and that's not really appropriate to this. But an incident that happened when I was CinCPac is what triggered that. I make it a hard and fast rule not to criticize the United States or any policy when I'm abroad, and I don't. I also don't take a general critical-of-the-military posture at all; I just focus on nuclear weapons, so I think that differentiates me. But I don't know. I don't want to say that I don't care, because that would not be quite true, but I've gotten to the age now where I think it's my duty to do my duty.

Paul Stillwell: What is your outlook for the years ahead? What are your plans from here on?

Admiral Gayler: Well, right now, in July of 1984, on policies of national interest, you can't do anything but ad hoc it.

Paul Stillwell: What about you personally? How soon do you expect to feel the lure of that cabin in Colorado?

---

[*] Rear Admiral Gene R. La Rocque, USN, retired from active duty in 1972 and became the head of the Center for Defense Information in Washington, D.C. The organization is noted for having views different from those of the Defense Department.

Admiral Gayler: Oh, that. I expect to be in harness until I die. I don't mean I'm not going to take some extended vacations, but I don't expect to quit working. Maybe I'll change my mind. I'm going out next week to help my mother celebrate her 102nd birthday, and she's pretty active. So I'll see.

Paul Stillwell: When this history began, you told me you were born in Alabama because that's where your mother happened to be at the time. Are there any other wrap-up thoughts you want to include on this entire life and career we've been talking about?

Admiral Gayler: It's been a very good one. The Navy has been very good to me. The Navy has been a very exciting life. Not many civilians appreciate the variety. I don't think I've ever had a tour of duty that was very much like any previous tour. I've had a lot more variety in my working life than almost any civilian could expect to have. It's been very satisfying. We have moved from a time when, as a young officer, I could be quite content with the notion that the Navy was the shield of Western civilization. Just as long as I did my job, that I would be attributing to that, to something which in a more complex society makes you think a great deal about, what the country should be doing, the Navy should be doing, what the military force should be doing. So things, I think, are not quite as easy for people nowadays as they used to be. I think I've been very lucky.

Paul Stillwell: How much of a role does luck play in an officer's overall career?

Admiral Gayler: Well, you know what Napoleon said. He didn't care about anything else; he wanted lucky generals. But I don't think it's that. I don't think it plays that much, but there is such a thing as opportunity. Equally fine officers, one may be in an area where he has the chance to demonstrate it, and another in a backwater. A lot depends on the personalities of the people you work for. No point working for Engine Charlie Wilson as Secretary of Defense.* He wouldn't have known whether you did a

---

* Charles E. Wilson served as Secretary of Defense from 28 January 1953 to 8 October 1957. He was nicknamed "Engine Charlie" because he had previously been chairman of the board of General Motors.

good job or not. Mel Laird, very different. But an awfully good life. Ain't over yet, either.

Paul Stillwell: Well, Admiral, on behalf of myself and the people who will be using this record, I'm grateful to you and thank you for the time and effort involved.

Admiral Gayler: Oh, Paul, it's a pleasure, as you know. Nothing is more fascinating than to talk about yourself. I'm sure you've observed that. I'm still interested in what you're going to do with all of this.

Index to the Oral History of
Admiral Noel A. M. Gayler, U.S. Navy (Retired)

AD/A-1 Skyraider
　　In the early 1950s Air Development Squadron Three (VX-3) experimented with long-range flights, 156-157

A3D Skywarrior
　　Heavy attack aircraft that entered the fleet in the mid-1950s, 173
　　Flown from the aircraft carrier *Ranger* (CVA-61) around 1960, 215-216

Abramowitz, Morton I.
　　In the early 1970s served as political advisor to Commander in Chief Pacific, 312-313

Adams, Sherman
　　In the late 1950s, as the President's chief of staff, was involved in Navy budget discussions, 192-193

Air Development Squadron Three (VX-3)
　　Made up of topflight pilots in the early 1950s, 154-155, 161-162
　　Tactics developed in the early 1950s for use in delivering nuclear weapons, 155-156
　　Experimental work in the early 1950s, including work in electronic warfare, 156-164, 254

Air Force, U.S.
　　Movie in the early 1950s about the F-86 Sabre jet, 163
　　Role of the Strategic Air Command in the late 1950s, 195-196
　　Control of the Joint Strategic Target Planning Staff (JSTPS) during the 1960s, 255-257
　　Effectiveness of the Strategic Air Command in the late 1950s-early 1960s, 257-259
　　Bombing of Vietnam in the 1960s-70s, 287, 328-329

Alameda, California, Naval Air Station
　　Homeport for the aircraft carrier *Ranger* (CVA-61) in the late 1950s-early 1960s, 211, 220-221

American Committee on East-West Accord
　　Gayler's role with the organization after he retired from the Navy, 336-337

Anacostia, Naval Air Station, D.C.
　　Site of Navy flight testing, 1942-43, 114-119

Antiair Warfare
　　Development of a lead-computing sight for antiaircraft guns in World War II, 69

Air-to-air gunnery practice in 1941 by Fighting Squadron Three (VF-3), 90-91
Japanese antiaircraft fire in the 1942 Battle of the Coral Sea, 107-108

Antisubmarine Warfare
Role of Carrier Division 20 in the Atlantic and Mediterranean in the early 1960s, 234-242

***Arkansas*, USS (BB-33)**
Naval Academy training cruise to Europe in the summer of 1934, 27-30

Army, U.S.
Gayler attended a West Point prep school at Schofield Barracks in Hawaii 1930-31, 13-17

Army Air Forces, U.S.
The Navy used an Army P-51 fighter in flight tests during World War II, 115-116
Operations against Japan in the closing months of World War II, 135-136

Atlantic City, New Jersey, Naval Air Station
Base for Air Development Squadron Three (VX-3) in the early 1950s, 154-164

Australia
Relationship with the U.S. Pacific Command in the early 1970s, 313-314

Badger, Rear Admiral Oscar C., USN (USNA, 1911)
Commanded a task group that began the occupation of Japan in August 1945, 138-143

Bahrain
Island in the Persian Gulf that served in the late 1950s as the base for the U.S. Middle East Force, 174-180, 185-188

***Bairoko*, USS (CVE-115)**
In 1948 supported nuclear weapons tests at Eniwetok in the Marshall Islands, 149-150
Operations off the U.S. Pacific Coast in the late 1940s, 150-151

Beecher, Lieutenant (junior grade) William G., USN (USNA, 1925)
Served as a Naval Academy company officer in the early 1930s, 23

BeLieu, Kenneth E.
As staff member of the Senate Armed Services Committee in the late 1950s, 193-194

Bennett, General Donald V., USA (USMA, 1940)
Served 1969-72 as director of the Defense Intelligence Agency, 271, 321
Served 1973-74 as Commander in Chief U.S. Army Pacific, 321

Bennett, Rear Admiral Rawson II, USN (USNA, 1927)
In 1957, as Chief of Naval Research, questioned reports of the Soviet satellite Sputnik, 198

Bhutto, Ali
Served as Prime Minister of Pakistan until ousted by a coup in 1977, 303-304

Bombs/Bombing
Atomic bombs dropped on Japan in August 1945 by U.S. Army Air Forces bombers, 135-136
Tactics developed by Air Development Squadron Three (VX-3) in the early 1950s for delivering nuclear weapons, 155-158
Simulated nuclear bombing demonstration for the Joint Chiefs of Staff in the early 1950s, 157-158
Air Force bombing of Vietnam in the 1960s-70s, 287, 328-329

Boykin, Frank W.
Alabama congressman who in the late 1950s contacted the Secretary of the Navy on behalf of his constituents, 203

Brown, George
Labour Party member of British Parliament in the early 1960s, shadow Defence Minister, 223

Brown, Harold
In the mid-1960s served as Assistant Secretary of Defense for research, development, test, and evaluation, 245-246

Bureau of Aeronautics (BuAer), Washington, D.C.
Work of the fighter development branch, 1949-51, 151-154
Relationship with aircraft manufacturers in the mid-1950s, 166-167

Bureau of Naval Personnel (BuPers), Arlington, Virginia
Planning in the late 1950s to deal with the promotion of officers commissioned during World War II, 196-198

Bureau of Ordnance (BuOrd), Washington, D.C.
Opposition to a lead-computer antiaircraft gun sight developed by Luis de Florez in World War II, 69

Burke, Admiral Arleigh A., USN (USNA, 1923)
Aggressive skipper of the destroyer *Mugford* (DD-389) in the late 1930s, 62-63, 201
As CNO in the late 1950s, relationship with the office of the Secretary of the Navy, 190-191, 200-201, 206-207

Cambodia
Seizure of the U.S. merchant ship *Mayaguez* in 1975, 333-334

Carrier Division 20
Antisubmarine mission in the Atlantic and Mediterranean in the early 1960s, 234-239
Role in the Cuban Missile Crisis in 1962, 238-242
Astronaut recovery in the early 1960s, 243-244

Cecil, Lieutenant Commander Charles P., USN (USNA, 1916)
Served as a Naval Academy company officer in the early 1930s, 22-23

Charbonnet, Lieutenant Commander Pierre N., Jr., USN (USNA, 1941)
Served in the early 1950s as executive officer of Air Development Squadron Three (VX-3), 155, 162-163

Churchill, Winston S.
Leadership of Great Britain as Prime Minister in World War II, 295-296

Clarey, Admiral Bernard A. "Chick," USN (USNA, 1934)
Served as Commander in Chief Pacific Fleet, 1970-73, 319-322

Communications
Ciphering of messages on board the battleship *Maryland* (BB-46) in the mid-1930s, 36
Problems in the attack on the *Liberty* (AGTR-5) in 1967 and seizure of the *Pueblo* (AGER-2) in 1968, 275-276

Composite Squadron Four (VC-4)
Navy squadron that operated out of Atlantic City, New Jersey, in the early 1950s, 164-165

Compton, **USS (DD-705)**
Damaged a propeller while serving with the Middle East Force in 1956, 177

Computers
Development of by the Special Devices Center, Fort Washington, New York, shortly after World War II, 145-147

Congress, U.S.
Relations with the office of the Secretary of the Navy in the late 1950s, 192-194, 203
Oversight of the National Security Agency in the late 1960s-early 1970s, 281-283
In 1973 Congress cut off funds for supplying Vietnam militarily, 301-302

Coral Sea, Battle of (May, 1942)
Role of the aircraft carrier *Lexington* (CV-2) and her planes, 65-66, 74, 106-112

***Craven*, USS (DD-382)**
    Operations in the Eastern Pacific, 1939-40, 62-66, 201
    Gunnery practice, 62-63

Crommelin, Captain John G., Jr., USN (USNA, 1923)
    In the mid-1940s exposed the secret Green Bowl Society, 128-129

Cuban Missile Crisis
    Role of Carrier Division 20 in the Atlantic during the operation, 238-241

Cushman, Midshipman Robert E. Jr., USN (USNA, 1935)
    Future Marine Commandant was at the Naval Academy in the early 1930s, 32

Damage Control
    Loss of the aircraft carrier *Lexington* (CV-2) to fire in the Battle of the Coral Sea, 1942, 65-66, 109-112

Davis, Captain Louis P., USN (USNA, 1905)
    Commanded the battleship *Maryland* (BB-46) in 1936-37, 33, 43, 48

de Florez, Commander Luis, USNR
    Received flight training at Pensacola, Florida, in 1940, 67-68
    Inventions, 67-69
    Shortly after World War II, served at the Special Devices Center, Fort Washington, New York, 144-146
    Death of in 1962, 244

Discipline
    Captain's mast cases on board the aircraft carrier *Ranger* (CVA-61) in the late 1950s-early 1960s, 216

Douglas, Captain Archibald H., USN (USNA, 1908)
    Commanded the aircraft carrier *Saratoga* (CV-3), 1940-42, 90-91

Dutton, Captain Benjamin, Jr., USN (USNA, 1905)
    Commanded the training ship *Wyoming* (AG-17) in the early 1930s, 25-26

Echeverria, Luis
    Mexico's President visited the Gaylers in Hawaii in the early 1970s, 305

Electronic Warfare
    In the early 1950s Air Development Squadron Three (VX-3) did experimental work in electronic warfare, 160-161

Elizabeth II, Queen
    Congenial to Gayler and his wife in 1960, 229

Visited the Gaylers in Hawaii in the early 1970s, 306

Eniwetok, Marshall Islands
In 1948 was the site of nuclear weapons tests, 149-150

Enlisted Personnel
On board the battleship *Maryland* (BB-46) in the mid-1930s, 34-36, 41-42
In the crew of the aircraft carrier *Ranger* (CVA-61) around 1960, 208-209, 216-217

F2A Buffalo
In the prewar period of the early 1940s flown by Fighting Squadron Three (VF-3), 81-89, 94

F2H Banshee
Flight characteristics, 164
In the early 1950s Air Development Squadron Three (VX-3) experimented with long-range flights, 156, 162-163

F3D Skyknight
Fighter used in a simulated nuclear weapons attack at Quantico, Virginia, in the early 1950s, 157-158

F3H Demon
Characteristics of the Navy fighter plane flown in the 1950s and 1960s, 166

F4B
Boeing fighter plane used for flight training in 1940, 79

F4F Wildcat
Flown by Fighting Squadron Three (VF-3) in 1941-42, 89, 91-92
Wartime operations in Fighting Squadron Two (VF-2) in early 1942, 98-109
Characteristics, 121

F4H/F-4 Phantom
Development in the mid-1950s of the military requirements for this aircraft, 165-170

F4U Corsair
World War II fighter plane that needed cockpit adjustments because of its long nose, 118-120

F6F Hellcat
Flight testing in 1942, prior to squadron introduction in 1943, 114-115, 121-123
Flown in 1944-45 by Fighter Squadron 12 (VF-12), 126-128

F8U-3 Crusader III
    Competitive flight-testing in the late 1950s against the McDonnell F4H Phantom II, 168-170

F-14 Tomcat
    Evolved from the unsuccessful attempt in the 1960s to create a Navy version of the F-111 fighter, 247-248

F-86 Sabre
    Characteristics of this Air Force jet that flew in the early 1950s, 163-164

F-111
    Attempt in the 1960s to create a multi-service fighter plane, 247-249

FJ Fury
    Navy fighter that flew in the early 1950s, 163-164

Fighter Squadron 12 (VF-12)
    Pre-deployment training and workups in 1944-45, 126-128

Fighting Squadron Three (VF-3)
    Lieutenant Commander John S. Thach as commanding officer in the early 1940s, 80-93, 100, 105
    In the prewar period of the early 1940s flew the Brewster F2A Buffalo, 81-92
    Operations from the aircraft carrier *Saratoga* in 1941-42, 84-98
    In 1941-42 flew the F4F Wildcat, 91-92
    Development of the Thach Weave fighter tactic prior to World War II, 85-86
    In 1940-41 made simulated attacks against Pearl Harbor, 95-96

Fighting Squadron Two (VF-2)
    Wartime operations against the Japanese in early 1942, 98-107
    Battle of the Coral Sea, May 1942, 106-109

Fire Control
    Optical range finders for fire control of the guns on board the battleship *Maryland* (BB-46) in the mid-1930s, 42-43
    Practice with 5-inch guns by the destroyer *Craven* (DD-382) in 1939-40, 62-63
    Development of a lead-computing sight for antiaircraft guns in World War II, 69

Fires
    Loss of the aircraft carrier *Lexington* (CV-2) in the Battle of the Coral Sea, 1942, 65-66, 109-112

Fitch, Rear Admiral Aubrey W., USN (USNA, 1906)
    On board the aircraft carrier *Lexington* (CV-2) during the Battle of the Coral Sea in May 1942, 111

Flight Training
    At Pensacola, Florida, in 1940, 67-80

Focke-Wulf 190 (German Fighter Plane)
    Flight-tested by U.S. pilots during World War II, 117, 121-122

Foley, Rear Admiral Francis D., USN (USNA, 1932)
    Commanded Carrier Division One, 1960-61, 54, 214, 324

Football
    Team in the battleship *Maryland* (BB-46) in the mid-1930s, 34-35

French Navy
    Involved with the U.S. Navy in unofficial antisubmarine exercises in the early 1960s, 237-238

Froehlke, Robert F.
    Served 1969-71 as Assistant Secretary of Defense for Administration, 268-269

G4M "Betty" (Japanese Torpedo Plane)
    Operations in the Pacific in early 1942, 101-102

Gardiner, Captain Joseph M., USN (USNA, 1931)
    Commanded Composite Squadron Four (VC-4) at Atlantic City, New Jersey, in the early 1950s, 164-165

Gates, Thomas S. Jr.
    Served 1957-59 as Secretary of the Navy, 188-206
    In 1960 established the Joint Strategic Target Planning Staff (JSTPS) to control nuclear weapons, 255-256

Gay, Midshipman Jesse B., USN (USNA, 1935)
    Gayler's roommate at the Naval Academy in the early 1930s, 18-20, 33

Gayler, Captain Ernest R., CEC, USN
    Career as a Navy civil engineer in the early part of the 20th century, 2-16, 32, 59
    After having retired, was recalled to active duty in World War II, 12-13

Gayler, Admiral Noel A. M., USN (Ret.) (USNA, 1935)
    Parents, 1-16, 23, 29, 32, 59, 344
    First wife, Caroline, 71-73, 82-83, 91, 96-97, 116, 148, 182, 188, 229, 235-236, 265, 305-306, 320, 326
    Siblings, 6-7, 11-12
    Children of, 6, 31, 188, 204, 235
    Boyhood in the 1910s-30s as a Navy junior, 1-16
    Attended a West Point prep school in Hawaii 1930-31, 13-17

As a Naval Academy midshipman, 1931-35, 17-34
In the crew of the battleship *Maryland* (BB-46), 1935-38, 34-54
Served 1938-39 in the destroyer *Maury* (DD-401), 18, 54-62
Served 1939-40 in the destroyer *Craven* (DD-382), 62-66
Received flight training at Pensacola, Florida, in 1940, 67-80
Served 1940-42 in Fighting Squadron Three (VF-3), 80-98
In early 1942 served in Fighting Squadron Two (VF-2), 98-112
Served 1942-44 as a test pilot at Anacostia and Patuxent River, 113-125
Commanded Fighter Squadron 12 (VF-12) in 1944-45, 126-130
From May to September 1945 was on the staff of Vice Admiral John S. McCain, 130-144
Served 1946-48 as executive officer of the Special Devices Center, Office of Research and Inventions, Fort Washington, New York, 144-145
As operations officer of the escort carrier *Bairoko* (CVE-115), 1948-49, 149-151
From 1949 to 1951 was in the Fighter Design Branch, Bureau of Aeronautics, 151-154
From 1951 to 1954 commanded Air Development Squadron Three (VX-3), 154-165
Served 1954-56 in OP-551, the Air Warfare Division, Military Requirements Branch, of OpNav, 165-173
In 1956-57 commanded the seaplane tender *Greenwich Bay* (AVP-41), 173-188
For a few months in 1957 served on the Pacific Fleet staff, 188-189
From 1957 to 1959 was aide to Secretary of the Navy Thomas S. Gates Jr., 188-206
Commanded the aircraft carrier *Ranger* (CVA-61) in 1959-60, 44, 56-57, 166, 206-222
In 1960-62 was U.S. Naval Attaché in England, 222-234
In 1962-63 commanded Carrier Division 20, 234-244
From 1963 to 1967 served as Assistant DCNO (Development), 245-255
Was Deputy Director of the Joint Strategic Target Planning Staff (JSTPS) from 1967 to 1969, 255-263
From 1969 to 1972 was Director of the National Security Agency, 263-291
Served 1972-76 as Commander in Chief Pacific, 91, 291-334
Post-retirement activities, 335-345

Gentner, Rear Admiral William E., Jr., USN (USNA, 1930)
Flew SOC floatplanes from the battleship *Maryland* (BB-46) in the mid-1930s, 45
Commanded Carrier Division One, 1959-60, 214

German Navy
The incomplete light cruiser *Magdeburg* was scrapped after World War I and contributed her optical range finder to the U.S. battleship *Maryland* (BB-46), 42-43

Germany
After World War II, German scientists were brought to the United States to work at the Special Devices Center, Fort Washington, New York, 145-146

Gill, Lieutenant Frank F., USN
    Served as fighter direction officer in the aircraft carrier *Lexington* (CV-2) in early 1942, 100-102

Great Britain
    Military flight training during World War II, 68-69
    Role of Gayler as U.S. naval attaché in London, 1960-62, 222-234
    Segmentation of society into classes, 231-232

Greenwich Bay, **USS (AVP-41)**
    Former seaplane tender that served in the late 1950s as one of the rotating flagships of Commander Middle East Force, 173-188

Groves, Lieutenant (junior grade) Alexander, USN (USNA, 1937)
    Went through flight training at Pensacola in 1940, 71-72
    Killed in aircraft accident in August 1940, 72
    Sister Caroline married Gayler in 1941, 71-73

Gunnery-Naval
    Practice with 12-inch guns on board the battleship *Arkansas* (BB-33) in 1934, 29-30
    Operation of 16-inch and 5-inch guns of the battleship *Maryland* (BB-46) in the mid-1930s, 36-37, 40-45
    Practice with 5-inch guns by the destroyer *Craven* (DD-382) in 1939-40, 62-63
    Air-to-air gunnery practice in 1941 by Fighting Squadron Three (VF-3), 90-91
    Practice by the seaplane tender *Greenwich Bay* (AVP-41) in the Persian Gulf in the late 1950s, 181
    Gayler's view that gunfire support by U.S. destroyers in Vietnam was ineffective, 300-301, 322-323

Haig, General Alexander M., Jr., USA (USMA, 1947)
    As a member of President Richard Nixon's staff in the early 1970s, made a fact-finding mission concerning bombing in Southeast Asia, 329

Haiti
    Primitive local conditions in the 1910s, 3-6

Halsey, Admiral William F., Jr., USN (USNA, 1904)
    Commanded the Third Fleet during attacks on the Japanese home islands in 1945, 131-135

Hawaii
    Gayler attended a West Point prep school at the Army's Schofield Barracks in 1930-31, 13-17
    In 1940-41 planes from the aircraft carrier *Saratoga* (CV-3) made simulated attacks against Pearl Harbor, 95-96

Heinemann, Edward H.
   Douglas Corporation designer who produced the A4D Skyhawk in the 1950s, 172

Hillenkoetter, Lieutenant Roscoe H., USN (USNA, 1920)
   Served in the battleship *Maryland* (BB-46) in the mid-1930s, 33, 48

Hoover, J. Edgar
   FBI director's name was on the Huston plan for domestic surveillance in the early 1970s, 282-283

Hunters Point Naval Shipyard, San Francisco, California
   Supplied workers to repair the aircraft carrier *Ranger* (CVA-61) at Christmastime in 1959, 220-221

Huston Plan
   Gayler recalled that the National Security Agency was not involved in this plan for domestic surveillance in the early 1970s, 283-283

Hyland, Lieutenant Commander John J., USN (USNA, 1934)
   As a test pilot at Anacostia during World War II, 118-119

Indonesia
   Visited by Gayler in the early 1970s in his role as CinCPac, 304-305

Instrument Flying
   Experimental work by Air Development Squadron Three (VX-3) in the early 1950s, 160

Intelligence
   Used by the U.S. Third Fleet in 1945 in attacking Japanese targets, 137-138
   Role of the National Security Agency in the late 1960s-early 1970s, 265-291
   Problems in the attack on the *Liberty* (AGTR-5) in 1967 and seizure of the *Pueblo* (AGER-2) in 1968, 275-276
   General William Westmoreland's awareness of intelligence while commanding U.S. forces in Vietnam in the 1960s, 330-331

Iranian Navy
   Operations with the U.S. Middle East Force in the late 1950s, 179-181

Iraq
   Visited in the late 1950s by the commander of the U.S. Middle East Force, 184-185
   Visited by Gayler in 1961 on the third anniversary of a military coup in the country, 224-227
   Intelligence about the Iraqi Army and Navy in 1961, 225-227

Italy
    Visited by midshipmen during the Naval Academy training cruise in 1934, 27-28

Jackson, Richard
    In the late 1950s was Assistant Secretary of the Navy (Personnel and Reserve Forces), 196-197

Japan
    U.S. Third Fleet attacks on the home islands in the summer of 1945, 131-137
    U.S. occupation of in the summer of 1945, 138-143
    Surrendered on board the battleship *Missouri* (BB-63) in September 1945 to end World War II, 141
    Around 1960 the aircraft carrier *Ranger* (CVA-61) visited various Japanese ports, 209-212, 220
    Anti-American demonstration around 1960, 212
    Relationship with the U.S. Pacific Command in the early 1970s, 91, 309-311

Japanese Navy
    A Japanese submarine torpedoed the aircraft carrier *Saratoga* (CV-3) in January 1942, 98
    Operations against U.S. carrier planes in February 1942, 100-102
    In the Battle of the Coral Sea in May 1942, 106-110
    Use of kamikazes in the waning months of World War II, 132-133

Johnson, President Lyndon B.
    As a senator in the late 1950s, involved in Navy funding, 193-194
    Strategy concerning the war in Vietnam, 285-287, 299

Joint Strategic Target Planning Staff (JSTPS)
    Role in the late 1960s in the targeting of U.S. nuclear weapons, 195-196, 255-263

Kaigler, Midshipman David Jr., USN (USNA, 1935)
    At the Naval Academy in the early 1930s, 31

Kamikazes
    Japanese use of in the waning months of World War II, 132-133
    Plans for use in the event the home islands were invaded, 140

Kassem, General Abdul Karim
    Became Premier of Iraq through a 1958 coup, hosted Gayler in 1961, 224-227

Kauffman, Rear Admiral Draper L., USN (USNA, 1933)
    In 1957 recommended Gayler to be aide to Secretary of the Navy Thomas Gates, 189-190
    In 1963 became the first head of the Secretary of the Navy's Office of Program Appraisal, 249-250

Kennedy, President John F.
Impact in Europe after he became President in 1961, 231-232
Cuban Missile Crisis in 1962, 238-240

Kirk, Norman E.
Served as Prime Minister of New Zealand from 1972 to 1974, 306-307

Kissinger, Henry A.
Sought to tailor U.S. intelligence estimates in the late 1960s-early 1970s, 268

Korea, North
Gayler's views on the nation's leadership in the 1980s, 318-319

Korea, South
Relationship with U.S. Pacific Command in the early 1970s, 318-319

Korth, Fred S.
Served 1962-63 as Secretary of the Navy, 249-250

Laird, Melvin R.
Served as Secretary of Defense from 1969 to 1973, 264, 268-274, 292, 300

Lake Champlain, **USS (CVS-39)**
Served in the early 1960s as flagship for Commander Carrier Division 20, 235

Leave and Liberty
Off-duty activities for junior officers of the battleship *Maryland* (BB-46) in the mid-1930s in Southern California, 37-39
For crew members of the aircraft carrier *Ranger* (CVA-61) in the Far East around 1960, 212

Lemmon, Ensign Rolla S., USN
In the early 1940s flew as part of Fighting Squadron Three (VF-3), 84-85

Lewis, Commander Allen L, USN
Served around 1960 as executive officer of the aircraft carrier *Ranger* (CVA-61), 207, 216-218

Lexington, **USS (CV-2)**
Platform for Gayler's carrier qualification in 1940, 81-82
Wartime operations in early 1942, 98-106
Sunk during the Battle of the Coral Sea in May 1942, 65, 74, 106-114

Liberty, **USS (AGTR-5)**
Attacked by Israeli aircraft in June 1967, 275-276

ME-109 (German Fighter Plane)
   Flown by U.S. test pilots in World War II, 117

Marcos, Ferdinand
   Relationship of the Filipino President and his wife Imelda with Gayler in the early 1970s, 307, 315

Marshall Islands
   In 1948 Eniwetok was the site of U.S. nuclear weapons tests, 149-150

Martin, Graham A.
   U.S. ambassador to South Vietnam when Saigon was evacuated in the spring of 1975, 298-299, 332

Maryland, **USS (BB-46)**
   Football team in the mid-1930s, 34-35
   Operations off the West Coast in the mid-1930s, 34-54
   Enlisted crewmen, 34-36, 41-42
   Communications ciphering, 36
   Operation of 16-inch and 5-inch guns in the mid-1930s, 36-37, 40-45
   Off-duty activities for junior officers in Southern California, 37-39
   Optical range finders for fire control of the guns, 42-43
   Ship handling in the mid-1930s, 43-44
   Electric-drive propulsion system, 53-54

Maury, **USS (DD-401)**
   Ship characteristics when commissioned in 1938, 54-55, 59-62
   High-pressure steam plant, 55-56
   Operations in the Pacific in the late 1930s, 18, 55-62
   Shakedown cruise to the South Pacific in the late 1930s, 59-61

Mayaguez, **SS (U.S. Merchant Ship)**
   Freighter captured by Cambodia in May 1975, 333-334

McCain, Vice Admiral John S., USN (USNA, 1906)
   Commanded Task Force 38 in the spring and summer of 1945, 130-137, 143

McCain, Admiral John S., Jr., USN (Ret.) (USNA, 1931)
   Served 1968-62 as CinCPac while his son was a POW in Vietnam, 271

McDonald, Vice Admiral David L., USN (USNA, 1928)
   Service in Washington, D.C., during World War II, 242
   Commanded the Sixth Fleet, 1961-63, 242

McDonnell Aircraft Corporation
   Early development, in the mid-1950s, of the F4H Phantom II fighter, 165-169

McElroy, Neil H.
 As Secretary of Defense, 1957-59, 194

McNamara, Robert S.
 As Secretary of Defense in the 1960s, was involved in the F-111 fighter issue, 247-248
 Limited contact between defense contractors and military personnel, 248-249
 Emphasis on systems analysis, 251, 269-270
 Working style, 269-270
 Strategy concerning Vietnam, 285-287

Mexico
 President Luis Echeverria visited the Gaylers in Hawaii in the early 1970s, 305

Middle East Force, U.S.
 Small naval force that operated in and around the Persian Gulf in the late 1950s, 174-188

Mine Warfare
 U.S. mining of Haiphong, North Vietnam, in 1972, 287-288

Missiles
 Concerns in the late 1960s about anti-missile defense, 259

Missouri, **USS (BB-63)**
 Involved in Third Fleet operations against Japan in 1945, 231-133
 The Japanese surrendered on board in September 1945 to end World War II, 141

Moore, General William G. Jr., USAF
 In the 1970s served a chief of staff to CinCPac and as Commander in Chief Military Airlift Command, 325

Moorer, Admiral Thomas H., USN (USNA, 1933)
 In 1969 nominated Gayler as director of the National Security Agency, 263-264, 328
 Professional disagreement with Gayler in the early 1970s on operational intelligence, 273-274
 Served 1970-74 as Chairman of the Joint Chiefs of Staff, 284-285, 294, 297, 328
 Transition to retired life in 1974, 334-335
 Opposed Gayler's views on nuclear weapons, 342-343

Moreell, Admiral Ben, CEC, USN
 During World War II, headed the Bureau of Yards and Docks, 12

Mountbatten, Admiral of the Fleet, Lord Louis, Royal Navy
 Served as Britain's Chief of Defence Staff, 1959-65, 230
 Assassination of in 1979, 230-231

***Mugford*, USS (DD-389)**
    Commanded by aggressive skipper Arleigh Burke in the late 1930s, 62-63, 201

Muller, Midshipman Henry L., USN (USNA, 1935)
    Saluted the Pope when a training cruise in 1934 visited Italy, 27-28

Mussolini, Benito
    Italian dictator who reviewed Naval Academy midshipmen when they visited Italy in 1934, 28

N3N "Yellow Peril"
    Aircraft used for flight training at Pensacola in the early 1940s, 71-72, 77-78

***Nagato* (Japanese Battleship)**
    Attacked by Third Fleet carrier planes in 1945, 136-137

National Security Agency
    Role in the late 1960s-early 1970s, 263-291
    Not involved in the Huston plan for domestic surveillance in the early 1970s, 282-283

Naval Academy, Annapolis, Maryland
    Life for midshipmen in the early 1930s, 17-34
    Academics in the early 1930s, 20-21
    Discipline in the early 1930s, 22-23
    Social life, 24-25
    Summer training cruises in the early 1930s, 25-30

Navigation
    By the aircraft carrier *Ranger* (CVA-61) entering Kobe, Japan, around 1960, 209-210

Newport, Rhode Island
    Home of the Gayler family for a time in the 1920s, 10-11

New Zealand
    Visited in the late 1930s by the destroyer *Maury* (DD-401), 61
    Norman Kirk served as Prime Minister from 1972 to 1974, 306-307

Night Flying
    By Fighting Squadron Three (VF-3) in the aircraft carrier *Saratoga* (CV-3) in 1940-41, 92-93
    By Fighting Squadron Two (VF-2) in the aircraft carrier *Lexington* (CV-2) in early 1942, 106
    Experimental work by Air Development Squadron Three (VX-3) in the early 1950s, 160

Nixon, President Richard M.
   In 1969 received a briefing about the Joint Strategic Target Planning Staff (JSTPS), 257
   In 1972 was hesitant in approving Gayler to become CinCPac, 271
   In 1970 a Nixon staffer proposed the Huston plan for domestic spying, 282-283
   As Commander in Chief during the Vietnam War, 328-329

Norstad, General Lauris, USAF (USMA, 1930)
   As NATO's Supreme Allied Commander Europe in the late 1950s, visited by Secretary of the Navy Thomas Gates, 191-192

Nuclear Weapons
   Dropped on Japan in August 1945 by U.S. Army Air Forces bombers, 135-136
   In 1948 Eniwetok in the Marshall Islands was the site of U.S. nuclear weapons tests, 149-150
   Tactics developed by Air Development Squadron Three in the early 1950s for delivering nuclear weapons, 155-158
   Simulated nuclear bombing demonstration for the Joint Chiefs of Staff in the early 1950s, 157-158
   Roles of the Joint Strategic Target Planning Staff and the Strategic Air Command during the late 1960s, 195-196, 255-263
   Gayler's personal views against the use of nuclear weapons, 262-263, 289, 336-343

O'Hare, Lieutenant (junior grade) Edward H., USN (USNA, 1937)
   In the early 1940s was a member of Fighting Squadron Three (VF-3), 88-89, 101
   Death of in 1943, 93

Ohira, Masayoshi
   Served in the 1970s as Japan's Minister of Foreign Affairs and later as Prime Minister, 311

Omer, Captain George D., USMCR
   Served as a flight instructor at Pensacola in 1940, 70

Operational Development Force
   Relationship in the early 1950s with Air Development Squadron Three (VX-3), 155, 162-163
   Gayler's evaluations of its effectiveness in the 1950s and 1960s, 253-254

P-51 Mustang
   Army fighter plane used in Navy flight tests during World War II, 115-116, 120
   Based on Iwo Jima at the end of World War II, 135

P-59 Airacomet
   During World War II, Gayler flew the YP-59 prototype of this jet fighter, 119-120

Pacific Command, U.S.
Gayler's view on the desirability of emphasizing the joint nature of the command, 293-295, 320-324, 332
Role in 1972-75 in connection with the Vietnam War, 296-303
Relationships in 1972-76 with various nations of the Pacific Rim, 303-319
The command's planning function in the early 1970s, 332-333

Pahlavi, Mohammed Reza
As Shah of Iran, interest in naval matters in the late 1950s, 179-181

Pakistan
Gayler's interaction with the country in his role as CinCPac in the early 1970s, 315-317
Change of government in 1977 as the result of military coup, 303-304

Patuxent River, Maryland, Naval Air Station
Site of Navy flight tests during World War II, 116-125

Pearl Harbor, Hawaii
In 1940-41 planes from the aircraft carrier *Saratoga* (CV-3) made simulated attacks against Pearl, 95-96

Pensacola, Florida, Naval Air Station
Site of flight training in 1940, 67-80

Persian Gulf
Operations in the late 1950s of the small U.S. Middle East Force, 174-188

Personnel
Planning in the late 1950s to deal with the promotion of officers commissioned during World War II, 196-198

Peterson, Ensign Dale W., USNR
Flew in combat in early 1942 as part of Fighting Squadron Two (VF-2), 101-102

Philippine Islands
Gayler's relationship with President and Mrs. Marcos in the early 1970s, 307, 315

Polo
Gayler's connection with the sport, 315-317

Pride, Rear Admiral Alfred M., USN
As chief of the Bureau of Aeronautics, 1947-51, 64, 152

Prisoners of War
Raid on Son Tay, North Vietnam, in 1970 in an attempt to rescue U.S. prisoners, 284

Release of U.S. prisoners of war by North Vietnam in early 1973, 302, 314

Promotion of Officers
Planning in the late 1950s to deal with the promotion of officers commissioned during World War II, 196-198

Propulsion Plants
Electric-drive system in the battleship *Maryland* (BB-46) in the mid-1930s, 53-54
High-pressure steam plant in the destroyer *Maury* (DD-401) in the late 1930s, 54-56

Public Relations
Contacts with the news media and public by Secretary of the Navy Thomas Gates in the late 1950s, 201-204

Pueblo, **USS (AGER-2)**
Seized by North Korea in January 1968, 275-276

Puget Sound Navy Yard, Bremerton, Washington
Service to the fleet in the 1920s, 6-9

Quantico, Virginia
Site of a bombing demonstration for the Joint Chiefs of Staff in the early 1950s, 157-158

Quinn, Rear Admiral John, USN (USNA, 1928)
Served for several months in 1956 as Commander U.S. Middle East Force, 178-179

R3Y Tradewind
Convair-built seaplane tested by the Navy in the mid-1950s, 171-172

Radford, Lieutenant Arthur W., USN (USNA, 1916)
In the 1920s served in Observation Squadron One, based in Seattle, 9

Ramsey, Commander Paul H., USN (USNA, 1927)
Commanded Fighting Squadron Two (VF-2) on board the aircraft carrier *Lexington* (CV-2) in early 1942, 98
Served as a test pilot at Patuxent River, Maryland, during World War II, 124

Randolph, **USS (CV-15)**
Deployed to the Western Pacific in early 1945, 128-129

Ranger, **USS (CVA-61)**
Commissioning of in 1957, 206
Ship handling in 1959-60, 44, 56-57, 210-212
F3H Demons in the air group in 1959-60, 166
Operations in the Pacific, 1959-60, 207-222

Enlisted crew members, 208-210

Was among the early U.S. Navy ships, around 1960, to have closed-circuit television, 208-209, 216-217

Rickover, Vice Admiral Hyman G., USN (USNA, 1922)

Relationship in the late 1950s with the office of the Secretary of the Navy, 199-200

In 1960 attended the launching of the British nuclear submarine *Dreadnought*, 229

Right Stuff, The

Gayler's opinions on this book/movie about test pilots and astronauts, 75, 170-171

Royal Navy

Aircraft carrier experiments in the early 1950s, 159-160

Launching of the nuclear submarine *Dreadnought* in 1960, 229

Relationship with the U.S. naval attaché in the early 1960s, 230

Rumsfeld, Donald H.

As Secretary of Defense, 1975-77, 326

Russell, Rear Admiral James S., USN (USNA, 1926)

Served 1955-57 as Chief of the Bureau of Aeronautics, 168-169

Ryan, General John D., USAF (USMA, 1938)

Served 1964-67 as Commander in Chief of the Strategic Air Command, 256-257

SOC Seagull

Spotted gunnery practice for the battleship *Maryland* (BB-46) in the mid-1930s, 44-46

Saigon, South Vietnam

Evacuation of U.S. personnel in the spring of 1975, 297-299

Samoa

Building of a U.S. Navy coaling station in American Samoa at the beginning of the 20th century, 2-3

Visited in the late 1930s by the destroyer *Maury* (DD-401), 39-40

Sand Point Naval Air Station, Seattle, Washington

Construction of in the 1920s, 9

***Saratoga*, USS (CV-3)**

Operations in the Pacific in 1941-42, 84-98

Torpedoed off Hawaii in January 1942, 98

Saudi Arabia
    Visited in the late 1950s by the flagship of the U.S. Middle East Force, 173-175, 181-183, 187

Selection Boards
    Secretary of the Navy precepts to selection boards in the late 1950s, 203

***Sequoia*, USS (AG-23)**
    Yacht used by Secretary of the Navy Thomas Gates in the late 1950s, 196

Shah of Iran
    See: Pahlavi, Mohammed Reza

Sherby, Commander Sydney S., USN (USNA, 1936)
    Served in the Bureau of Aeronautics in the late 1940s- early 1950s, 152-154

Sherman, Captain Frederick C., USN (USNA, 1910)
    Commanded the aircraft carrier *Lexington* (CV-2), 1940-42, 103, 109-111

Ship Handling
    On board the battleship *Maryland* (BB-46) in the mid-1930s, 43-44
    On board the aircraft carrier *Ranger* (CVA-61), 1959-60, 44, 56-57, 210-212

Simulators
    Used in U.S. aviation training during World War II, 68-69, 80

Single Integrated Operational Plan (SIOP)
    Concern of the Joint Strategic Target Planning Staff (JSTPS) in the late 1960s, 255-263

Sixth Fleet, U.S.
    Role of Carrier Division 20 in the Mediterranean in the early 1960s, 241-243
    Relative merits of the fleet being commanded by aviators or surface officers, 243

Slonim, Ensign Gilven M., USN (USNA, 1936)
    Served in the battleship *Maryland* (BB-46) in the mid-1930s, 47-48

Smith, Admiral Harold Page, USN (USNA, 1924)
    In the late 1950s was Chief of Naval Personnel, 230
    In the mid-1960s, as CinCLantFlt, vetoed Gayler as a carrier division commander, 207

Smoot, Lieutenant Roland N., USN (USNA, 1923)
    Served on board the battleship *Maryland* (BB-46) in the mid-1930s, 35-36, 40

Sonar
On board nuclear submarines in the early 1960s, 236

Son Tay, North Vietnam
Raid on in 1970 in an attempt to rescue U.S. prisoners, 284

Soviet Union
Target of U.S. intelligence gathering in the late 1960s-early 1970s, 266-267
Support of North Vietnam in the Vietnam War, 301

Special Devices Center, Fort Washington, New York
Development work, 1946-48, in training devices and other equipment, 144-148
Used the services of scientists brought in from Germany, 145-146

Spitfire
British fighter plane used against both Japanese and German forces in World War II, 99-100, 120-121

Strategic Air Command
Role in nuclear weapons delivery planning in the late 1950s, 195-196
Effectiveness in the late 1950s-early 1960s, 257-259

Strategy
Gayler's views on the U.S. strategy in Vietnam, 285-289, 299-300

Tactics
Development of the Thach Weave fighter tactic prior to World War II, 85-86
Tactics in Fighting Squadron Two (VF-2) at the outset of World War II, 101-102
Tactics developed by Air Development Squadron Three in the early 1950s for delivering nuclear weapons, 155-158

Tallman, Lieutenant Benjamin Long Edes, USN (USNA, 1935)
Served as a junior officer in the battleship *Maryland* (BB-46 in the 1930s, 33
Clumsiness on board a destroyer in World War II, 33

Taiwan
Changing relationship with the United States in the early 1970s, 308-309

Tanumafili II
Served as Samoan head of state from 1939 until he died in 1007, 59-60

Test Pilots
Navy flight operations at Anacostia, D.C., and Patuxent River, Maryland, 1942-44, 114-121

Thach, Captain John S, USN (1927)
    Commanded Fighting Squadron Three (VF-3) in the early 1940s, 80-93, 100, 105
    In 1945 was operations officer on the staff of Vice Admiral John S. McCain, 131, 134, 137

Thompson, Lieutenant Commander Edward M., USN (USNA, 1921)
    In the late 1930s commanded the destroyer *Maury* (DD-401), 18, 56-57

Tordella, Dr. Louis W.
    Long-time deputy director of the National Security Agency, 265, 280

Training
    Naval Academy summer cruises in the early 1930s, 25-30
    Flight training at Pensacola, Florida, in 1940, 67-80

Trapnell, Commander Frederick M., USN (USNA, 1923)
    Headed the U.S. Navy's test pilot program during World War II, 114-115, 122

VC-4
    See: Composite Squadron Four (VC-4)

VF-2
    See: Fighting Squadron Two (VF-2)

VF-3
    See: Fighting Squadron Three (VF-3)

VF-12
    See: Fighter Squadron 12 (VF-12)

VX-3
    See: Air Development Squadron Three (VX-3)

Vampire (British Fighter Plane)
    Royal Navy aircraft used for carrier tests in the early 1950s, 159-160

Vietnam War
    In the mid-1960s the Navy had no long-range development programs geared to Vietnam, 246-247
    Admiral John S. McCain Jr. served 1968-72 as CinCPac while his son was a POW in Vietnam, 271
    Raid on Son Tay, North Vietnam, in 1970 in an attempt to rescue U.S. prisoners, 284
    Gayler's views on the U.S. strategy in Vietnam, 285-289, 299-300
    U.S. mining of Haiphong, North Vietnam, in 1972, 287-288
    Gayler's view that gunfire support by U.S. destroyers in Vietnam was ineffective, 300-301, 322-323
    U.S. combat operations in late 1972-early 1973, 296-303, 328-330

In 1973 Congress cut off funds for supplying Vietnam militarily, 301-302
Release of U.S. prisoners of war in early 1973, 302, 314
Evacuation from Saigon in the spring of 1975, 297-299

Vinson, Representative Carl, (Democrat-Georgia)
As chairman of the House Armed Services Committee in the late 1950s, involved in Navy budgets, 192-193

Walker, Commander Thomas J. III, USN (USNA, 1939)
In the early 1950s commanded Air Development Squadron Five (VX-5), 162

Watkinson, Harold
Served from 1959 to 1962 at British Minister of Defence, 223

Weisner, Admiral Maurice F., USN (USNA, 1941)
Served as Commander in Chief Pacific Fleet, 1973-76, 320, 324-325

Westmoreland, General William C., USA (USMA, 1936)
Awareness of intelligence while commanding U.S. forces in Vietnam in the 1960s, 330-331

Wisner, Frank G.
Central Intelligence Agency station chief in London in the early 1960s, 222

Wolfe, Thomas
Gayler's opinions on this author's book about test pilots and astronauts, 75, 170-171

Wyoming, USS (AG-17)
Naval Academy summer training cruise in 1932, 25-27

Yokosuka, Japan
Americans celebrated victory at the Japanese naval officers' club in 1945, 142-143
Visited by the aircraft carrier *Ranger* (CVA-61) around 1960, 210

Zero (Japanese Fighter)
In combat against Allied forces in early 1942, 92, 99-100, 108
U.S. test pilots flew a captured Zero in 1943, 117, 121-123

Ziroli, Lieutenant Commander Humbert W., USN (USNA, 1916)
Taught at the Naval Academy in the early 1930s, 28

Zumwalt, Admiral Elmo R., Jr., USN (USNA, 1943)
Involvement in officer promotion planning in the late 1950s, 196-198
Relaxed grooming standards during his tenure as CNO in the early 1970s, 53, 279
In 1970 asked Gayler to serve as Chief of Naval Material; Gayler declined, 270-271
In 1972 nominated Gayler to become Commander in Chief Pacific, 292-293

Launched in 1969, the U.S. Naval Institute's award-winning oral history program is among the oldest in the country. Used in combination with documentary sources, oral histories offer a richer understanding of naval history through candid recollections and explanations rarely entered into contemporary records. In addition, they help depict the atmosphere of a particular event or era in a manner not available in official documents.

The nonprofit Naval Institute accomplishes its history projects solely through contributed funds and gratefully accepts tax-deductible gifts of all sizes for this purpose. This support allows the Institute to preserve the life experiences of today's service men and women so they may enlighten and inspire future generations.

For information about opportunities to underwrite Naval Institute oral history projects, please contact the Naval Institute Foundation at 291 Wood Road, Annapolis, Maryland 21402; by phone at (410) 295-1054; or by e-mail at foundation@usni.org.

www.ingramcontent.com/pod-product-compliance
Lightning Source LLC
Chambersburg PA
CBHW082149070526
44585CB00020B/2148